The Social Psychology of Gullibility

Gullibility, whether we like it or not, is a fundamental characteristic of human beings. In *The Social Psychology of Gullibility*, Forgas and Baumeister explore what we know about the causes, functions, and consequences of gullibility, and the social psychological processes that promote or inhibit it.

With contributions from leading international researchers, the book reveals what social and cognitive psychology contribute to our understanding of how human judgments and decisions can be distorted and undermined. The chapters discuss the nature and functions of gullibility, the role of cognitive processes in gullibility, the influence of emotion and motivation on gullibility, and social and cultural aspects of gullibility. Underpinned by a wealth of empirical research, contributors explore captivating issues such as the psychology of conspiracy theories, the role of political gullibility, gullibility in science, the role of the Internet in fostering gullibility, and the failures of reasoning that contribute to human credulity.

Gullibility has become a dominant topic of interest in public discourse. *The Social Psychology of Gullibility* is essential reading for researchers, social science students, professionals, and practitioners and all those interested in understanding human credulity and the role of gullibility in contemporary public affairs.

Joseph P. Forgas is Scientia Professor at the University of New South Wales. His research focuses on cognitive and affective processes in interpersonal behavior. For his work he received the Order of Australia, and the Distinguished Scientific Contribution Award from the Australian Psychological Society.

Roy F. Baumeister is Professor of Psychology at the University of Queensland. His research deals with self and identity, self-control and self-esteem, finding meaning in life, sexuality, gender, aggression, and emotion. He received the William James Award from the Association for Psychological Science for his lifetime achievements.

The Sydney Symposium of Social Psychology series

This book is Volume 20 in the *Sydney Symposium of Social Psychology* series. The aim of the Sydney Symposia of Social Psychology is to provide new, integrative insights into key areas of contemporary research. Held every year at the University of New South Wales, Sydney, each symposium deals with an important integrative theme in social psychology, and the invited participants are leading researchers in the field from around the world. Each contribution is extensively discussed during the symposium and is subsequently thoroughly revised into book chapters that are published in the volumes in this series. For further details see the website at www.sydneysymposium.unsw.edu.au

Previous Sydney Symposium of Social Psychology volumes:

SSSP 1. FEELING AND THINKING: THE ROLE OF AFFECT IN SOCIAL COGNITION** ISBN 0-521-64223-X (Edited by J.P. Forgas). *Contributors*: Robert Zajonc, Jim Blascovich, Wendy Berry Mendes, Craig Smith, Leslie Kirby, Eric Eich, Dawn Macauley, Len Berkowitz, Sara Jaffee, EunKyung Jo, Bartholomeu Troccoli, Leonard Martin, Daniel Gilbert, Timothy Wilson, Herbert Bless, Klaus Fiedler, Joseph Forgas, Carolin Showers, Anthony Greenwald, Mahzarin Banaji, Laurie Rudman, Shelly Farnham, Brian Nosek, Marshall Rosier, Mark Leary, Paula Niedenthal & Jamin Halberstadt.

SSSP 2. THE SOCIAL MIND: COGNITIVE AND MOTIVATIONAL ASPECTS OF INTERPERSONAL BEHAVIOR** ISBN 0-521-77092-0 (Edited by J.P. Forgas, K.D. Williams & L. Wheeler). *Contributors*: William & Claire McGuire, Susan Andersen, Roy Baumeister, Joel Cooper, Bill Crano, Garth Fletcher, Joseph Forgas, Pascal Huguet, Mike Hogg, Martin Kaplan, Norb Kerr, John Nezlek, Fred Rhodewalt, Astrid Schuetz, Constantine Sedikides, Jeffry Simpson, Richard Sorrentino, Dianne Tice, Kip Williams, and Ladd Wheeler.

SSSP 3. SOCIAL INFLUENCE: DIRECT AND INDIRECT PROCESSES* ISBN 1-84169-038-4 (Edited by J.P. Forgas & K.D. Williams). *Contributors*: Robert Cialdini, Eric Knowles, Shannon Butler, Jay Linn, Bibb Latane, Martin Bourgeois, Mark Schaller, Ap Dijksterhuis, James Tedeschi, Richard Petty, Joseph Forgas, Herbert Bless, Fritz Strack, Eva Walther, Sik Hung Ng,

Thomas Mussweiler, Kipling Williams, Lara Dolnik, Charles Stangor, Gretchen Sechrist, John Jost, Deborah Terry, Michael Hogg, Stephen Harkins, Barbara David, John Turner, Robin Martin, Miles Hewstone, Russell Spears, Tom Postmes, Martin Lea, Susan Watt.

SSSP 4. THE SOCIAL SELF: COGNITIVE, INTERPERSONAL, AND INTERGROUP PERSPECTIVES** ISBN 1-84169-062-7 (Edited by J.P. Forgas & K.D. Williams). *Contributors*: Eliot R. Smith, Thomas Gilovich, Monica Biernat, Joseph P. Forgas, Stephanie J. Moylan, Edward R. Hirt, Sean M. McCrea, Frederick Rhodewalt, Michael Tragakis, Mark Leary, Roy F. Baumeister, Jean M. Twenge, Natalie Ciarocco, Dianne M. Tice, Jean M. Twenge, Brandon J. Schmeichel, Bertram F. Malle, William Ickes, Marianne LaFrance, Yoshihisa Kashima, Emiko Kashima, Anna Clark, Marilynn B. Brewer, Cynthia L. Pickett, Sabine Otten, Christian S. Crandall, Diane M. Mackie, Joel Cooper, Michael Hogg, Stephen C. Wright, Art Aron, Linda R. Tropp, and Constantine Sedikides.

SSSP 5. SOCIAL JUDGMENTS: IMPLICIT AND EXPLICIT PROCESSES** ISBN 0-521-82248-3. (Edited by J.P. Forgas, K.D. Williams & W. Von Hippel). *Contributors*: Herbert Bless, Marilynn Brewer, David Buss, Tanya Chartrand, Klaus Fiedler, Joseph Forgas, David Funder, Adam Galinsky, Martie Haselton, Denis Hilton, Lucy Johnston, Arie Kruglanski, Matthew Lieberman, John McClure, Mario Mikulincer, Norbert Schwarz, Philip Shaver, Diederik Stapel, Jerry Suls, William von Hippel, Michaela Waenke, Ladd Wheeler, Kipling Williams, Michael Zarate.

SSSP 6. SOCIAL MOTIVATION: CONSCIOUS AND UNCONSCIOUS PROCESSES** ISBN 0-521-83254-3 (Edited by J.P. Forgas, K.D. Williams & S.M. Laham). *Contributors*: Henk Aarts, Ran Hassin, Trish Devine, Joseph Forgas, Jens Forster, Nira Liberman, Judy Harackiewicz, Leanne Hing, Mark Zanna, Michael Kernis, Paul Lewicki, Steve Neuberg, Doug Kenrick, Mark Schaller, Tom Pyszczynski, Fred Rhodewalt, Jonathan Schooler, Steve Spencer, Fritz Strack, Roland Deutsch, Howard Weiss, Neal Ashkanasy, Kip Williams, Trevor Case, Wayne Warburton, Wendy Wood, Jeffrey Quinn, Rex Wright and Guido Gendolla.

SSSP 7. THE SOCIAL OUTCAST: OSTRACISM, SOCIAL EXCLUSION, REJECTION, AND BULLYING* ISBN 1-84169-424-X (Edited by K.D. Williams, J.P Forgas & W. Von Hippel). *Contributors*: Kipling D. Williams, Joseph P. Forgas, William von Hippel, Lisa Zadro, Mark R. Leary, Roy F. Baumeister, and C. Nathan DeWall, Geoff MacDonald, Rachell Kingsbury, Stephanie Shaw, John T. Cacioppo, Louise C. Hawkley, Naomi I. Eisenberger Matthew D. Lieberman, Rainer Romero-Canyas, Geraldine Downey, Jaana Juvonen, Elisheva F. Gross, Kristin L. Sommer, Yonata Rubin, Susan T. Fiske, Mariko Yamamoto, Jean M. Twenge, Cynthia L. Pickett, Wendi L. Gardner, Megan Knowles, Michael A. Hogg, Julie Fitness, Jessica L. Lakin, Tanya L. Chartrand, Kathleen R. Catanese and Dianne

M. Tice, Lowell Gaertner, Jonathan Iuzzini, Jaap W. Ouwerkerk, Norbert L. Kerr, Marcello Gallucci, Paul A. M. Van Lange, and Marilynn B. Brewer.

SSSP 8. AFFECT IN SOCIAL THINKING AND BEHAVIOR* ISBN 1-84169-454-2 (Edited by J.P. Forgas). *Contributors*: Joseph P. Forgas, Carrie Wyland, Simon M. Laham, Martie G. Haselton Timothy Ketelaar, Piotr Winkielman, John T. Cacioppo, Herbert Bless, Klaus Fiedler, Craig A. Smith, Bieke David, Leslie D. Kirby, Eric Eich, Dawn Macaulay, Gerald L. Clore, Justin Storbeck, Roy F. Baumeister, Kathleen D. Vohs, Dianne M. Tice, Dacher Keltner, E.J. Horberg, Christopher Oveis, Elizabeth W. Dunn, Simon M. Laham, Constantine Sedikides, Tim Wildschut, Jamie Arndt, Clay Routledge, Yaacov Trope, Eric R. Igou, Chris Burke, Felicia A. Huppert, Ralph Erber, Susan Markunas, Joseph P. Forgas, Joseph Ciarrochi, John T. Blackledge, Janice R. Kelly, Jennifer R. Spoor, John G. Holmes, Danu B. Anthony.

SSSP 9. EVOLUTION AND THE SOCIAL MIND* ISBN 1-84169-458-0 (Edited by J.P. Forgas, M.G. Haselton & W. Von Hippel). *Contributors*: William von Hippel, Martie Haselton, Joseph P. Forgas, R.I.M. Dunbar, Steven W. Gangestad, Randy Thornhill, Douglas T. Kenrick, Andrew W. Delton, Theresa E. Robertson, D. Vaughn Becker, Steven L. Neuberg, Phoebe C. Ellsworth, Ross Buck, Joseph P. Forgas, Paul B.T. Badcock, Nicholas B. Allen, Peter M. Todd, Jeffry A. Simpson, Jonathon LaPaglia, Debra Lieberman, Garth J. O. Fletcher, Nickola C. Overall, Abraham P. Buunk, Karlijn Massar, Pieternel Dijkstra, Mark Van Vugt, Rob Kurzban, Jamin Halberstadt, Oscar Ybarra, Matthew C. Keller, Emily Chan, Andrew S. Baron, Jeffrey Hutsler, Stephen Garcia, Jeffrey Sanchez-Burks, Kimberly Rios Morrison, Jennifer R. Spoor, Kipling D. Williams, Mark Schaller, Lesley A. Duncan.

SSSP 10. SOCIAL RELATIONSHIPS: COGNITIVE, AFFECTIVE, AND MOTIVATIONAL PROCESSES* ISBN 978-1-84169-715-4 (Edited by J.P. Forgas & J. Fitness). *Contributors*: Joseph P. Forgas, Julie Fitness, Elaine Hatfield, Richard L. Rapson, Gian C. Gonzaga, Martie G. Haselton, Phillip R. Shaver, Mario Mikulincer, David P. Schmitt, Garth J.O. Fletcher, Alice D. Boyes, Linda K. Acitelli, Margaret S. Clark, Steven M. Graham, Erin Williams, Edward P. Lemay, Christopher R. Agnew, Ximena B. Arriaga, Juan E. Wilson, Marilynn B. Brewer, Jeffry A. Simpson, W. Andrew Collins, SiSi Tran, Katherine C. Haydon, Shelly L. Gable, Patricia Noller, Susan Conway, Anita Blakeley-Smith, Julie Peterson, Eli J. Finkel, Sandra L. Murray, Lisa Zadro, Kipling D. Williams, Rowland S. Miller.

SSSP 11. PSYCHOLOGY OF SELF-REGULATION: COGNITIVE, AFFECTIVE, AND MOTIVATIONAL PROCESSES* ISBN 978-1-84872-842-4 (Edited by J.P. Forgas, R. Baumeister & D.M. Tice).

Contributors: Joseph P. Forgas, Roy F. Baumeister, Dianne M. Tice, Jessica L. Alquist, Carol Sansone, Malte Friese, Michaela Wänke, Wilhelm Hofmann, Constantine Sedikides, Christian Unkelbach, Henning Plessner, Daniel Memmert, Charles S. Carver, Michael F. Scheier, Gabriele Oettingen, Peter M. Gollwitzer, Jens Förster, Nira Liberman, Ayelet Fishbach, Gráinne M. Fitzsimons, Justin Friesen, Edward Orehek, Arie W. Kruglanski, Sander L. Koole, Thomas F. Denson, Klaus Fiedler, Matthias Bluemke, Christian Unkelbach, Hart Blanton, Deborah L. Hall, Kathleen D. Vohs, Jannine D. Lasaleta, Bob Fennis, William von Hippel, Richard Ronay, Eli J. Finkel, Daniel C. Molden, Sarah E. Johnson, Paul W. Eastwick.

SSSP 12. PSYCHOLOGY OF ATTITUDES AND ATTITUDE CHANGE* ISBN 978-1-84872-908-7 (Edited by J.P. Forgas, J. Cooper & W.D. Crano). *Contributors*: William D. Crano, Joel Cooper, Joseph P. Forgas, Blair T. Johnson, Marcella H. Boynton, Alison Ledgerwood, Yaacov Trope, Eva Walther, Tina Langer, Klaus Fiedler, Steven J. Spencer, Jennifer Peach, Emiko Yoshida, Mark P. Zanna, Allyson L. Holbrook, Jon A. Krosnick, Eddie Harmon-Jones, David M. Amodio, Cindy Harmon-Jones, Michaela Wänke, Leonie Reutner, Kipling D. Williams, Zhansheng Chen, Duane Wegener, Radmila Prislin, Brenda Major, Sarah S. M. Townsend, Frederick Rhodewalt, Benjamin Peterson, Jim Blascovich, Cade McCall.

SSSP 13. PSYCHOLOGY OF SOCIAL CONFLICT AND AGGRESSION* ISBN 978-1-84872-932-2 (Edited by J.P. Forgas, A.W. Kruglanski & K.D Williams). *Contributors*: Daniel Ames, Craig A. Anderson, Joanna E. Anderson, Paul Boxer, Tanya L. Chartrand, John Christner, Matt DeLisi, Thomas F. Denson, Ed Donnerstein, Eric F. Dubow, Chris Eckhardt, Emma C. Fabiansson, Eli J. Finkel, Gráinne M. Fitzsimons, Joseph P. Forgas, Adam D. Galinsky, Debra Gilin, Georgina S. Hammock, L. Rowell Huesmann, Arie W. Kruglanski, Robert Kurzban, N. Pontus Leander, Laura B. Luchies, William W. Maddux, Mario Mikulincer, Edward Orehek, Deborah South Richardson, Phillip R. Shaver, Hui Bing Tan, Mark Van Vugt, Eric D. Wesselmann, Kipling D. Williams, Lisa Zadro.

SSSP 14. SOCIAL THINKING AND INTERPERSONAL BEHAVIOR* ISBN 978-1-84872-990-2 (Edited by J.P. Forgas, K. Fiedler & C. Sekidikes). *Contributors*: Andrea E. Abele, Eusebio M. Alvaro, Mauro Bertolotti, Camiel J. Beukeboom, Susanne Bruckmüller, Patrizia Catellani, Cindy K. Chung, Joel Cooper, William D. Crano, István Csertő, John F. Dovidio, Bea Ehmann, Klaus Fiedler, Joseph P. Forgas, Éva Fülöp, Jessica Gasiorek, Howard Giles, Liz Goldenberg, Barbara Ilg, Yoshihisa Kashima, Mikhail Kissine, Olivier Klein, Alex Koch, János László, Anne Maass, Andre Mata, Elisa M. Merkel, Alessio Nencini, Andrew A. Pearson, James W. Pennebaker, Kim Peters, Tibor Pólya, Ben Slugoski, Caterina Suitner, Zsolt Szabó, Matthew D. Trujillo, Orsolya Vincze.

SSSP 15. SOCIAL COGNITION AND COMMUNICATION* ISBN 978-1-84872-663-5 (Edited by J.P. Forgas, O.Vincze & J. László). *Contributors*: Andrea E. Abele, Eusebio M. Alvaro, Maro Bertolotti, Camiel J. Beukeboom, Susanne Bruckmüller, Patrizia Catellani, István Cserto , Cindy K. Chung, Joel Coooper, William D. Crano, John F. Dovidio, Bea Ehmann, Klaus Fiedler, J. P. Forgas, Éva Fülöp, Jessica Gasiorek, Howard Giles, Liz Goldenberg, Barbara Ilg, Yoshihisa Kahima, Mikhail Kissine, Alex S. Koch, János László, Olivier Klein, Anne Maass, André Mata, Elisa M. Merkel, Alessio Nencini, Adam R. Pearson, James W. Pennebaker, Kim Peters, Tibor Pólya, Ben Slugoski, Caterina Suitner, Zsolt Szabó, Matthew D. Trujillo, Orsolya Vincze.

SSSP 16. MOTIVATION AND ITS REGULATION: THE CONTROL WITHIN* ISBN 978-1-84872-562-1 (Edited by J.P. Forgas & E. Harmon-Jones). *Contributors*: Emily Balcetis, John A. Bargh, Jarik Bouw, Charles S. Carver, Brittany M. Christian, Hannah Faye Chua, Shana Cole, Carsten K. W. De Dreu, Thomas F. Denson, Andrew J. Elliot, Joseph P. Forgas, Alexandra Godwin, Karen Gonsalkorale, Jamin Halberstadt, Cindy Harmon-Jones, Eddie Harmon-Jones, E. Tory Higgins, Julie Y. Huang, Michael Inzlicht, Sheri L. Johnson, Jonathan Jong, Jutta Joormann, Nils B. Jostmann, Shinobu Kitayama, Sander L. Koole, Lisa Legault, Jennifer Leo, C. Neil Macrae, Jon K. Maner, Lynden K. Mile, Steven B. Most, Jaime L. Napier, Tom F. Price, Marieke Roskes, Brandon J. Schmeichel, Iris K. Schneider, Abigail A. Scholer, Julia Schüler, Sarah Strübin, David Tang, Steve Tompson, Mattie Tops, Lisa Zadro

SSSP 17. SOCIAL PSYCHOLOGY AND POLITICS* ISBN 978-1-13882-968-8 (Edited by Joseph P. Forgas, Klaus Fiedler, William D. Crano). *Contributors:* Stephanie M. Anglin, Luisa Batalha, Mauro Bertolotti, Patrizia Catellani, William D. Crano, Jarret T. Crawford, John F. Dovidio, Klaus Fiedler, Joseph P. Forgas, Mark G. Frank, Samuel L. Gaertner, Jeremy Ginges, Joscha Hofferbert, Michael A. Hogg, Hyisung C. Hwang, Yoel Inbar, Lee Jussim, Lucas A. Keefer, Laszlo Kelemen, Alex Koch, Tobias Krüger, Mark J. Landau, Janos Laszlo, Elena Lyrintzis, David Matsumoto, G. Scott Morgan, David A. Pizarro, Felicia Pratto, Katherine J. Reynolds, Tamar Saguy, Daan Scheepers, David O. Sears, Linda J. Skitka, Sean T. Stevens, Emina Subasic, Elze G. Ufkes, Robin R. Vallacher, Paul A. M. Van Lange, Daniel C. Wisneski, Michaela Wänke, Franz Woellert, Fouad Bou Zeineddine

SSSP 18. The Social Psychology of Morality* ISBN 978-1-138-92907-4 (Edited by Joseph P. Forgas, Lee Jussim, and Paul A. M. Van Lange). Contributors: Stephanie M. Anglin, Joel B. Armstrong, Mark J. Brandt, Brock Bastian, Paul Conway, Joel Cooper, Chelsea Corless, Jarret T. Crawford, Daniel Crimston, Molly J. Crockett, Jose L. Duarte, Allison K. Farrell, Klaus Fiedler, Rebecca Friesdorf, Jeremy A. Frimer, Adam D. Galinsky, Bertram Gawronski, William G. Graziano, Nick Haslam, Mandy Hütter, Lee Jussim, Alice Lee,

William W. Maddux, Emma Marshall, Dale T. Miller, Benoît Monin, Tom Pyszczynski, Richard Ronay, David A. Schroeder, Simon M. Laham, Jeffry A. Simpson, Sean T. Stevens, William Von Hippel, Geoffrey Wetherell

SSP 19. The Social Psychology of Living Well* ISBN 978-0-8153-6924-0 (Edited by Joseph P. Forgas and Roy F. Baumeister). Contributors: Yair Amichai- Hamburger, Peter Arslan, Roy F. Baumeister, William D. Crano, Candice D. Donaldson, Elizabeth W. Dunn, Ryan J. Dwyer, Shir Etgar, Allison K. Farrell, Klaus Fiedler, Joseph P. Forgas, Barbara L. Fredrickson, Megan M. Fritz, Shelly L. Gable, Karen Gonsalkorale, Alexa Hubbard, Chloe O. Huelsnitz, Felicia A. Huppert, David Kalkstein, Sonja Lyubomirsky, David G. Myers, Constantine Sedikides, James Shah, Kennon M. Sheldon, Jeffry A. Simpson, Elena Stephan, Yaacov Trope, William Von Hippel, Tom Wildschut

SSP 20. The Social Psychology of Gullibility* ISBN 978-0-3671-8793-4 (Edited by Joseph P. Forgas and Roy F. Baumeister). Contributors: Stephanie M. Anglin, Joseph J. Avery, Roy F. Baumeister, Aleksandra Chicoka, Joel Cooper, Karen Douglas, David Dunning, Anthony M. Evans, Johanna K. Falbén, Klaus Fiedler, Joseph P. Forgas, Nicholas Fox, Marius Golubickis, Nathan Honeycutt, Lee Jussim, Alex Koch, Joachim I. Krueger, Spike W. S. Lee, C. Neil Macrae, Jessica A. Maxwell, Ruth Mayo, David Myers, Juliana L. Olivier, Daphna Oyserman, Jan-Willem van Prooijen, Norbert Schwarz, Sean T. Stevens, Fritz Strack, Robbie M. Sutton, Geoffrey P. Thomas, Christian Unkelbach, Kathleen D. Vohs, Claudia Vogrincic-Haselbacher

* Published by Routledge
** Published by Cambridge University Press

The Social Psychology of Gullibility

Fake News, Conspiracy Theories, and Irrational Beliefs

Edited by Joseph P. Forgas and
Roy F. Baumeister

NEW YORK AND LONDON

First published 2019
by Routledge
2 Park Square, Milton Park, Abingdon, Oxon OX14 4RN

and by Routledge
52 Vanderbilt Avenue, New York, NY 10017

Routledge is an imprint of the Taylor & Francis Group, an informa business

© 2019 selection and editorial matter, Joseph P. Forgas and Roy F.
Baumeister; individual chapters, the contributors

The right of Joseph P. Forgas and Roy F. Baumeister to be identified
as the authors of the editorial material, and of the authors for their
individual chapters, has been asserted in accordance with sections 77
and 78 of the Copyright, Designs and Patents Act 1988.

All rights reserved. No part of this book may be reprinted or
reproduced or utilised in any form or by any electronic, mechanical, or
other means, now known or hereafter invented, including photocopying
and recording, or in any information storage or retrieval system, without
permission in writing from the publishers.

Trademark notice: Product or corporate names may be trademarks
or registered trademarks, and are used only for identification and
explanation without intent to infringe.

British Library Cataloguing-in-Publication Data
A catalogue record for this book is available from the British Library

Library of Congress Cataloging-in-Publication Data
A catalog record has been requested for this book

ISBN: 978-0-367-19014-9 (hbk)
ISBN: 978-0-367-18793-4 (pbk)
ISBN: 978-0-429-20378-7 (ebk)

Typeset in Bembo
by Swales & Willis Ltd, Exeter, Devon, UK

Contents

List of Contributors — xiv

1 *Homo credulus*: **On the Social Psychology of Gullibility** — 1
JOSEPH P. FORGAS (UNIVERSITY OF NEW SOUTH WALES) AND
ROY F. BAUMEISTER (UNIVERSITY OF QUEENSLAND)

PART I
The Nature and Functions of Credulity — 19

2 **The Mask of Love and Sexual Gullibility** — 21
ROY F. BAUMEISTER (UNIVERSITY OF QUEENSLAND), JESSICA A.
MAXWELL (FLORIDA STATE UNIVERSITY), GEOFFREY P. THOMAS
(FLORIDA STATE UNIVERSITY), AND KATHLEEN D. VOHS
(UNIVERSITY OF MINNESOTA)

3 **Gullible but Functional? Information Repetition and the Formation of Beliefs** — 42
CHRISTIAN UNKELBACH AND ALEX KOCH (UNIVERSITY
OF COLOGNE)

4 **Belief in Conspiracy Theories: Looking Beyond Gullibility** — 61
KAREN M. DOUGLAS, ROBBIE M. SUTTON, AND ALEKSANDRA
CICHOCKA (UNIVERSITY OF KENT)

5 **Psychological Science Meets a Gullible Post-Truth World** — 77
DAVID G. MYERS (HOPE COLLEGE)

xii *Contents*

PART II
Cognitive Processes and Gullibility 101

6 **Towards a Credible Theory of Gullibility** 103
JOACHIM I. KRUEGER (BROWN UNIVERSITY), CLAUDIA
VOGRINCIC-HASELBACHER (UNIVERSITY OF GRAZ), AND
ANTHONY M. EVANS (TILBURG UNIVERSITY)

7 **Metacognitive Myopia: Gullibility as a Major Obstacle
in the Way of Rational Behavior** 123
KLAUS FIEDLER (UNIVERSITY OF HEIDELBERG)

8 **The Skeptical (Ungullible) Mindset** 140
RUTH MAYO (THE HEBREW UNIVERSITY OF JERUSALEM)

9 **Comparing Is Believing: Ease of Comparison as a
Means to Induce Gullibility** 159
FRITZ STRACK (UNIVERSITY OF WÜRZBURG)

PART III
Affective and Motivational Processes and Gullibility 177

10 **On the Role of Affect in Gullibility: Can
Positive Mood Increase, and Negative Mood
Reduce Credulity?** 179
JOSEPH P. FORGAS (UNIVERSITY OF NEW SOUTH WALES)

11 **Gullible or Streetwise: How Does the Self
Bias Information Processing?** 198
C. NEIL MACRAE, JULIANA L. OLIVIER, JOHANNA K. FALBÉN,
AND MARIUS GOLUBICKIS (UNIVERSITY OF ABERDEEN)

12 **Gullible to Ourselves** 217
DAVID DUNNING (UNIVERSITY OF MICHIGAN)

13 **The Smell of Suspicion: How the Nose
Curbs Gullibility** 234
NORBERT SCHWARZ (UNIVERSITY OF SOUTHERN CALIFORNIA)
AND SPIKE W. S. LEE (UNIVERSITY OF TORONTO)

Contents xiii

PART IV
Social and Cultural Aspects of Gullibility 253

14 Cultural Fluency, Mindlessness, and Gullibility 255
DAPHNA OYSERMAN (UNIVERSITY OF SOUTHERN CALIFORNIA)

15 Scientific Gullibility 279
LEE JUSSIM (RUTGERS UNIVERSITY), SEAN T. STEVENS (NYU, STERN SCHOOL OF BUSINESS), NATHAN HONEYCUTT (RUTGERS UNIVERSITY), STEPHANIE M. ANGLIN (CARNEGIE MELLON UNIVERSITY), AND NICHOLAS FOX (RUTGERS UNIVERSITY)

16 Gullibility and the Envelope of Legitimacy 304
JOEL COOPER AND JOSEPH J. AVERY (PRINCETON UNIVERSITY)

17 Belief in Conspiracy Theories: Gullibility or Rational Skepticism? 319
JAN-WILLEM VAN PROOIJEN (VU AMSTERDAM)

Index 333

Contributors

Anglin, Stephanie M., Carnegie Mellon University, USA

Avery, Joseph J., Princeton University, USA

Baumeister, Roy F., University of Queensland, Australia

Cichocka, Aleksandra, University of Kent, UK

Cooper, Joel, Princeton University, USA

Douglas, Karen M., University of Kent, UK

Dunning, David, University of Michigan, USA

Evans, Anthony M., Tilburg University, the Netherlands

Falbén, Johanna K., University of Aberdeen, UK

Fiedler, Klaus, University of Heidelberg, Germany

Forgas, Joseph P., University of New South Wales, Australia

Fox, Nicholas, Rutgers University, USA

Golubickis, Marius, University of Aberdeen, UK

Honeycutt, Nathan, Rutgers University, USA

Jussim, Lee, Rutgers University, USA

Koch, Alex, University of Cologne, Germany

Krueger, Joachim I., Brown University, USA

Lee, Spike W. S., University of Toronto, Canada

Macrae, C. Neil, University of Aberdeen, UK.

Maxwell, Jessica A., Florida State University, USA

Mayo, Ruth, The Hebrew University of Jerusalem, Israel

Myers, David G., Hope College, USA

Olivier, Juliana L., University of Aberdeen, UK

Oyserman, Daphna, University of Southern California, USA

Schwarz, Norbert, University of Southern California, USA

Stevens, Sean T., NYU, Stern School of Business, USA

Strack, Fritz, University of Würzburg, Germany

Sutton, Robbie M., University of Kent, UK

Thomas, Geoffrey P., Florida State University, USA

Unkelbach, Christian, University of Cologne, Germany

van Prooijen, Jan-Willem, VU Amsterdam, the Netherlands

Vogrincic-Haselbacher, Claudia, University of Graz, Austria

Vohs, Kathleen D. University of Minnesota, USA

1 *Homo credulus*

On the Social Psychology of Gullibility

Joseph P. Forgas
UNIVERSITY OF NEW SOUTH WALES

Roy F. Baumeister
UNIVERSITY OF QUEENSLAND

Introduction

Gullibility as a scientific concept does not currently feature prominently in social psychology research, and one would search in vain the subject indexes of many social psychology textbooks for entries under "gullibility." So why devote an entire book to this topic, and why do it now? The answer is twofold. First, in the past few years, and especially since Brexit, the election of Trump, and the emergence of crypto-fascist dictators in a number of countries including some inside the European Union such as Hungary (Albright, 2018), the question of human gullibility has become one of the dominant topics of interest in public discourse (see also Cooper & Avery, Chapter 16 this volume; Myers, Chapter 5 this volume). People opposed to these developments often suspect that those who voted for them must be gullible.

Second, even though gullibility is rarely studied directly in social and cognitive psychology, these disciplines do have a great deal to contribute to our understanding of how human judgments and decisions can be distorted and undermined. In consequence, a book dealing with the social psychology of gullibility is highly topical, and as this volume demonstrates, there is a wealth of directly relevant empirical research we can draw upon to understand this phenomenon (Gilbert, 1991; Gilovich, 1991). The objective of this volume is thus to provide an integrative survey of the current state of social psychological research on human gullibility, and so offer an informative contribution towards understanding the role of gullibility in contemporary public affairs.

What Is Gullibility?

Gullible as a term was first recorded in 1793, derived from the earlier word "cullibility" (1728), and possibly connected to "gull," a cant term for "dupe, sucker," which in turn is of uncertain origin. Its etymological roots can be traced perhaps from the bird (sea gull), or to the verb "gull" (to swallow). Some of the synonyms of gullibility, such as credulity, artlessness, ignorance,

2 *Joseph P. Forgas and Roy F. Baumeister*

inexperience, simplicity, also confirm the pejorative character of gullibility. So consensually negative social evaluation, as we shall see later, is an essential component of gullibility.

The standard definition of gullibility, as a failure of social intelligence in which a person is easily tricked or manipulated into an ill-advised course of action, confirms this view. Gullibility is closely related to credulity, which is the "tendency to believe unlikely propositions that are unsupported by evidence" (Wikipedia). Gullibility is thus a factor in social influence processes, as a person's willingness to believe false or misleading information facilitates the influence.

The Criteria for Gullibility

Is there some accepted standard of truth or reality relative to which a person can be judged as gullible? Conceptually, gullibility can be inferred in one of two situations. Either an individual's beliefs are manifestly inconsistent with facts and reality, or an individual's beliefs are at variance with consensual social norms *about* reality. A believer in a flat earth can now be labeled as gullible, since there is ample empirical evidence confirming the true state of affairs. However, the question of criteria for gullibility is far more complex. We often use the term *gullible* to describe persons whose beliefs violate some consensual rather than scientific standard of how reality should be viewed. Serious and largely unresolved philosophical issues about the nature of knowledge within the domains of ontology (the philosophical study of what *is*, the nature of reality), and epistemology (the philosophical study of *how* do we know) also make the unambiguous definition of knowledge, and by implication, gullibility, problematic (see Krueger, Vogrincic-Haselbacher, & Evans, Chapter 6 this volume).

Adopting a Popperian epistemological view, and accepting that all knowledge is imperfect and temporary, offers little help towards defining gullibility. Even on matters amenable to scientific research and potential falsification, such as the iatrogenic climate change theory, there remains ample scope for agnosticism and disagreement (Lewandowsky, Oreskes, Risbey, Newell, & Smithson, 2015). Our knowledge about the world is imperfect, and the more complex the question we address, the more likely that unequivocal answers are difficult to find. We can label those who question the truth of the climate change hypothesis as "gullible," or with a rhetorical flourish, as "deniers," as if there was an absolute and incontrovertible truth here to be denied (see also Jussim, Stevens, Honeycutt, Anglin, & Fox, Chapter 15 this volume). Yet those who remain skeptical or agnostic on this issue can reciprocally label absolute believers in the climate change hypothesis as gullible. Believers in conspiracy theories also often see themselves as careful, motivated skeptics who are motivated by a quest to avoid gullibility, while those who doubt their beliefs are the gullible ones (see Douglas, Sutton, & Cichocka, Chapter 4 this volume;

Unkelbach & Koch, Chapter 3 this volume; van Prooijen, Chapter 17 this volume). As long as knowledge is incomplete and subject to future falsification, identifying gullibility is more a matter of consensual value judgment rather than a statement of incontrovertible fact. Gullibility may thus often be a matter of perspective, residing in the eye of the beholder. It is no wonder, then, that gullibility has been historically an endemic feature of all human societies, as the next section will suggest.

The Social History of Gullibility

Human cultural history is replete with striking examples of human gullibility (Greenspan, 2009; Koestler, 1967; Rath-Vegh, 1963). In an attempt to understand, predict and control the social and physical world, humans have created an amazing range of absurd and often vicious and violent gullible beliefs (Koestler, 1967). Ancient meso-American cultures believed that cutting out the beating hearts of thousands of their captives was essential to preserve the goodwill of their gods and to ensure a good harvest (Koestler, 1967, 1978). Throughout the Middle Ages, witches were tortured and burned to death for allegedly harming others (Pinker, 2012). As recently as at the beginning of the eighteenth century, even a well-educated person might still firmly believe in witches, werewolves, magic cures and magic potions, alchemy, and of course, a flat earth (Wooton, in Pinker, 2018).

Contemporary religious beliefs about virgin birth, walking on water, resurrection, or transubstantiation continue to persist yet they contradict everything we know about the world. Folk tales and literature abound with demonstrations of the pitfalls of gullibility. In the Bible, the serpent's deception, and Adam and Eve's gullibility are the primal source of humanity's eternal fall from grace. Homer's Trojan Horse is a classic tale of deception and gullibility, and Shakespeare's *Othello* is a tragedy brought about by credulity. In tales such as the "Emperor's New Clothes" we learn that the veil of consensual gullibility can sometimes be torn apart by a single voice that reveals the truth. In "Little Red Riding Hood," the heroine is first deceived, but then she learns the art of deception herself to deceive a second wolf. Even more instructive is the character of Pinocchio who had to learn to avoid being duped by others in order to become a full human being (!).

Examples of striking gullibility, self-deception, hubris, and wishful thinking continue to characterize human affairs to this day (Greenspan, 2009), including where one would least expect it, in the halls of academia (Jussim et al., Chapter 15 this volume). Sokal's famous hoax in submitting a text intentionally full of nonsense to a "reputable" post-modernist journal where it was duly accepted is a well-documented recent example of academic gullibility in the humanities. More recently, Pluckrose, Lindsay and Boghossian (2018) perpetuated an even more impressive hoax, successfully publishing seven (!) explicitly nonsensical "academic" papers, including one using text from Hitler' *Mein Kampf* in highly reputable feminist and "grievance studies" journals.

4 Joseph P. Forgas and Roy F. Baumeister

In the economic sphere, irrational gullibility produces recurring investment "bubbles" at least since the famous "tulip bulb" craze in the eighteenth century. Our social rituals associated with April Fool's Day gain their popularity by allowing us to mislead others without adverse consequences, and so practice our skills of deception (Forgas, 2017). These examples, and countless others, suggest that far from being an aberration, gullibility seems a pervasive feature of the human condition. This pattern continues today, with sometimes alarming consequences, an issue we will turn to next.

Truth and Gullibility in Contemporary Public Life

Concern with gullibility in public life has become highly topical in recent years. Gullibility may have played some role in the election of leaders like Trump. His detractors regard his supporters as gullible for supporting a novice politician who claims to be a world expert on almost everything and has a narcissistic view of his own abilities (see also Myers, Chapter 5 this volume). Meanwhile, his supporters view his detractors as gullible for embracing the "politically correct" views and practices and relish Trump's overt, mocking rejection of what they regard as elite hypocrisy. Another recent surprise election outcome was Great Britain's vote to leave the European Union, marked by excesses of credulity on both sides. Voters willingly believed contradictory forecasts of either a smooth exit or impending economic catastrophe. Elsewhere, voters seem blithely willing to elect and re-elect quasi-fascist nationalist leaders who are destroying their hard-won democratic systems (Hungary, Poland, Turkey, Russia, Phillipines, Venezuela), or succumb to misleading messages laced by archaic nationalism and populism (Catalonia, Scotland, etc.).

Gullibility is found across the political spectrum. Fascist leasers from Mussolini and Hitler to Erdogan, Putin, and Orban have exploited voters' gullibility with disastrous consequences. Arguably, the fascism of Mussolini and Hitler was closely linked to the political left. The Nazi party was the "National Socialist German Workers' Party" that admired and copied America's New Deal, while Mussolini was lionized in US progressive circles (Goldberg, 2008). It is especially puzzling how a closed and quasi-religious system of thought such as Marxism could remain the dominant philosophical perspective of many left-leaning Western intellectuals for over a hundred years. This occurred, despite the fact that Marxism's economic predictions have been consistently wrong, its view of history as class struggle has been misconceived, and the social systems it produced turned out to be perhaps the most horrific and genocidal in human history. Part of the answer is that as Karl Popper (1947) showed, totalitarian systems of thought like Marxism are *constructed* to be unfalsifiable, and so their lack of predictive power can always be explained away by "true believers" (Koestler, 1967). Most religions have the very same immunity to disproof.

Over the past few decades, Marxism and Marxist intellectuals have promoted a range of social theories and movements to gullible followers

On the Social Psychology of Gullibility   5

ostensibly to increase social justice and equality, but in reality, relying on the collectivist rhetoric of group rights, identity politics, and collective social class struggle as the sole method of social progress. These quasi-Marxist collectivist movements, like radical feminism and multi-culturalism, are fundamentally incompatible with the Enlightenment emphasis on the rights of the individual (Pinker, 2018). Arguably, some versions of radical feminism even display elements of classical conspiracy theories, suggesting the existence of an entirely fictitious gender-based conspiracy against women. True believers in such ideologies are no less gullible than earlier believers in similarly closed systems of thought.

One important recent influence promoting gullibility is the advent of Internet-based communication. Until recently, it was the privileged class of experts, truth-seekers, and truth-tellers who following the Enlightenment were institutionally established in our social systems and whose job it was to discover and communicate truth. They have now lost their privileged position and information monopoly, and it seems truth in public life is now also at risk. It would indeed be an ironic and paradoxical effect if the immense success of our "scientic age" would be undermined by the very scientific progress and information technology it helped to create. Given the damage that populism, demagoguery, "fake news," and the rising tide of identity politics and nationalism have produced in our public life, a better understanding of the social psychology of gullibility is now recognized as of considerable importance (Albright, 2018; Pinker, 2018; see also Cooper & Avery, Chapter 16 this volume; Myers, Chapter 5 this volume). This is one of the main objectives of this book. First, however, we need to consider *why* gullibility seems to be so prevalent across the ages, the task of the next section.

The Functions of Gullibility

Why is gullibility such a fundamental and universal characteristic of *Homo sapiens*? One of the psychological foundations of gullibility, paradoxically, appears to be the universal human capacity for trust – to accept second-hand information we receive from others as a proxy for reality (Deutsch & Gerard, 1955). Indeed, our evolutionary history (Harari, 2014; Pinker, 2018; von Hippel, 2018) suggests that perhaps the most revolutionary cognitive development of our species occurred when we made the dramatic leap from being creatures who are bound by immediate reality to becoming creatures who can accept and act on consensual symbolic information or "memes" *as if* it was reality (Dawkins, 1976; Dennett, 2017). This ability to accept symbolic information from others and treat it as real is also one major foundation of all human cultural evolution (Harari, 2014). Unlike face-to-face primate groups that can only achieve cohesion and coordination as a result of their daily integrative interactions, large-scale social coordination in complex and impersonal human societies is only possible if individuals consensually accept various shared fictional notions as reality.

In these terms, most of human cultural history is essentially the history of changing fictional beliefs in various symbolic systems of thought (Harari, 2014). For thousands of years, social organization was predicated on shared religious beliefs, legitimizing the divine powers of priests and rulers. In Japan, this fiction was still firmly believed by the majority of the population in the middle of the twentieth century. Similarly, it was consensually believed for most of human history that enslaving others is natural and slavery continued to be a dominant form of economic organization until the recent past. From the current perspective these beliefs could be seen as examples of collective gullibility. Yet modern attitudes toward slavery also indicate gullibility, assuming that it was always morally offensive, when in fact slavery originated as a form of moral progress. It was originally a substitute for being killed in battle, and surrendering soldiers no doubt accepted slavery as an improvement over being tortured to death, which was often the fate of captives in primitive and hunter-gatherer societies. Even today, beliefs in dubious phenomena such as homeopathy, crystals, alternative therapies, anti-vaccination, supernatural interventions in daily life, and even alien abductions, not to mention conspiracies of all kinds, still abound (see also Douglas et al., Chapter 4 this volume; van Prooijen, Chapter 17 this volume).

Gullibility, in the non-pejorative sense of accepting, sharing, and considering *as real* unconfirmed and fictional social information from others can be highly functional and the cognitive foundation of large-scale human social organizations. Our current culture relies no less heavily on shared fictional beliefs than was the case in previous epochs. The idea of the nation state as a fictional symbolic entity is still the basis of much political organization today, yet it was only invented relatively recently (Harari, 2014). Or take the example of paper money: its usefulness is utterly dependent on the shared fictional belief that it has real value. The moment this shared fiction breaks down – in times of war, financial crisis, hyperinflation, etc. – the once valuable banknotes become useless bits of paper.

Our own epoch is based on the dominant cultural and moral values of the Enlightenment: the shared belief that humanism, individual liberty, and equality are universal, desirable, and natural values. Is this not also a fiction? Clearly liberty is neither a natural, nor a universal state for human beings in the real world. Equality is even more nebulous: as long as people are born with hugely different biological, intellectual, and physical characteristics, in what sense can one talk about, or even define equality as a meaningful universal value? As Dahrendorff (1975) showed, the two core values of the Enlightenment, liberty and equality, also happen to be mutually incompatible: any increase in equality reduces liberty, and vice versa. These core beliefs turn out to be just as fictional as the notion of divine royalty. Yet modern "gullibility" in believing these fictions has been extremely useful and allowed modern citizens to design and maintain perhaps the most successful civilization in human history (Pinker, 2018).

On the Social Psychology of Gullibility   7

We could easily imagine some future utopia (or more likely, dystopia) in which our currently shared fictional beliefs about liberty and equality will be considered extremely silly and gullible. Yet this gullibility can be a very useful and adaptive cognitive mechanism that allows large and complex social organizations to function on the basis of such shared fictional beliefs. So today's accepted truth can easily become tomorrow's gullibility as our consensual beliefs change. If gullibility is indeed a universal, and often useful human characteristic, what are the psychological mechanisms that promote it? We shall turn to examining that question next.

Psychological Mechanisms of Gullibility

We have seen that there is good historical and evolutionary evidence indicating that a disposition towards gullibility – seeing the world not as it is, but as it appears and as others explain it – is a deeply ingrained human tendency. In a way, human evolution has left humankind with cognitive predispositions that promoted individual survival in traditional archaic societies, but that are perhaps less well adapted to thriving in a modern one (Pinker, 2018).

Within psychology, human judgments and decisions were traditionally studied using the model of the rational information processor (Piaget, 1950) or "naïve scientist" (Heider, 1958; Kelley, 1967) as the preferred model. However, growing evidence for irrationality or "bounded rationality" has now forced a fundamental re-think (Jones & Harris, 1967; Kahneman & Tversky, 2000), as massive violations of principles of rational thinking were demonstrated both in the laboratory, and in real life. Many of the failures in human reasoning also turn out to be highly resistant to monitoring and control (see also Fiedler, Chapter 7 this volume). Rather than simply demonstrating irrationality, such apparent cognitive failures can be better explained as having some adaptive functions (Gigerenzer, 2000; Simon, 1990).

In this section we shall briefly review some of the major cognitive mechanisms – many of which could also be conceived as evolutionary "mind modules" – that promote gullibility. These information processing mechanisms can be understood as representing either "cold" cognitive processes (such as limited processing capacity, reliance on heuristics or shortcuts, etc.), or by "hot" motivational tendencies where certain (often gullible) outcomes are preferred to others (see also Baumeister, Maxwell, Thomas, & Vohs, Chapter 2 this volume; Macrae, Olivier, Falbén, & Golubickis, Chapter 11 this volume; Dunning, Chapter 12 this volume; Mayo, Chapter 8 this volume).

The Search for Patterns and Meaning

The search for patterns, associations, and meaning is one of the most fundamental characteristics of the mental life of human beings, one that played a significant role in human adaptation and survival (von Hippel, 2018).

While sense-making is mostly adaptive and functional, the bias toward seeking and finding patterns and causation where there are none can also be a major source of gullibility. The bias toward meaning is particularly noticeable when people perceive order in objectively random (and hence, meaningless) events. Human beings tend to under-recognize randomness (see also Forgas, Chapter 10 this volume), a tendency often described as apophenia, a term that was originally used to label early stages of schizophrenia (e.g., Brugger, 2001).

A good example is the clustering illusion, a cognitive bias where people see patterns in randomly generated data (Chapman, 1967; Gilovich, 1991). Another well-known example is pareidolia, where people perceive patterns or familiar shapes and images in vague or otherwise random stimuli, such as the shapes of clouds, or, in shapeless inkblots as in the now discredited Rohrschach test. Meaningless, randomly generated word sequences when described as "psychology jargon," or as New Age wisdom can also be perceived as meaningful, a phenomenon Pennycook, Cheyne, Barr, Koehler, and Fugelsang (2015) labeled "bullshit receptivity" (see also Forgas, Chapter 10 this volume).

Over-perceiving patterns can be adaptive, as the cost of *not* perceiving a pattern where there is one is often higher than perceiving a pattern where there isn't one. Evolutionary psychologists suggest that pattern over-perception occurs because of the greater costs associated with Type II than Type I errors. Failing to make the connection between, for instance, a noise and the presence of the predator could easily result in death, but misperceiving a random noise as a threat has far less serious consequences. Adaptive fitness may thus be promoted by deviations from accuracy, for example, by over-perceiving the value of potential partners (see also Baumeister et al., Chapter 2 this volume), or by over-interpreting the welcoming behaviors of potential partners (Haselton & Buss, 2000).

However, the costs of over-perceiving patterns can also be significant by contributing not only to gullibility, but also to obsessive-compulsive disorders, and anxiety (Rachman, 1997). At a societal level, the tendency to infer causation in random or unrelated events often produces erroneous beliefs, superstition, mistaken inferences, causal mistakes, conspiracy theories, and often violence and aggression (Chapman, 1967; Hamilton & Gifford, 1976; see also Douglas et al., Chapter 4 this volume; van Prooijen, Chapter 17 this volume). Mistaken inferences are easily exploited by misleading political propaganda or advertising and play an important role in political judgment and decision-making (Myers, Chapter 5 this volume). Throughout history much cruelty and violence has been committed in the name of such deeply erroneous causal inferences (human sacrifice, witchcraft, etc.; Koestler, 1967; Pinker, 2012).

We reiterate, too, that one key innovation in human evolution involved deliberately shared information. Is it better to believe what everyone else believes, or to be ruthlessly skeptical? Religious skeptics may be superior at truth-seeking, compared to their more gullible fellow group members who embrace the religion – but the benefits of skepticism must be compared to the costs of being exiled or killed as punishment for deviating from the consensus. At the group level, much progress in human history, including nation-building, has depended on military success. And military discipline often required soldiers to put aside their own skepticism so as to follow orders, more or less without question. An army of gullible soldiers blindly obeying orders would probably prevail over an equally equipped enemy that encouraged each soldier to make up his own mind at each step.

The Acceptance Bias

Another potential source of gullibility is the near-universal tendency for humans to accept rather than reject incoming information. Following Spinoza's philosophical reasoning, there is now strong evidence to suggest that the human being is born a natural "believer" (Gilbert, 1991). Information received tends to first be coded as "true," and subsequent negation requires further time and effort (see Krueger et al., Chapter 6 this volume). There are several ways that this overwhelming bias can be interpreted. In one sense, this can be due to the adaptive value of trusting others in closely integrated ancestral societies. If comprehending a claim and believing it initially amount to the same thing, then the human being indeed approaches the world with a gullible mindset (see also Mayo, Chapter 8 this volume). Research shows that even if a claim is coded as potentially false, there are powerful internal motivational mechanisms designed to restore coherence not by revising our pre-existing system of mental representation, but by actively discrediting the offending claim (see also Cooper & Avery, Chapter 16 this volume; Dunning, Chapter 12 this volume), an important mechanism of gullibility maintenance.

The acceptance bias shows how gullibility occurs when people are distracted by other information, emotion, or time pressure. Disbelief is a second step, following the first step in which understanding is simultaneous with believing. If people do not get to the second step, they will be more likely to believe whatever they were told in the first step.

The Power of Heuristics

Human beings are more prone to believe interesting, captivating stories and narratives that are salient and easy to imagine (Kahneman & Tversky, 2000). When we are exposed to salient, frequent, and thus easily remembered information, due to a strange "mental bug" in our information processing system, such information will also be seen as more true, reliable, and valid (see also Strack, Chapter 9 this volume; Unkelbach & Koch, Chapter 3 this volume). These mental shortcuts exacerbate the human inability to see the world as it really is.

Typically, what is familiar, readily available, salient, focal, representative, and colorful captures our imagination and attention, and is given far more credence than it deserves. When information is easily accessible and fluid, it is more likely to be seen as true (see Oyserman, Chapter 14 this volume; Unkelbach & Koch, Chapter 3 this volume). Reliance on heuristics can also be promoted by such ephemeral factors as the mood we happen to be in (Forgas, 2013). However, as Krueger et al. (Chapter 6 this volume) note, the emphasis on heuristics as a source of gullibility only offers, at best, a partial understanding. Heuristics can account for many "false-positive" errors (believing something that isn't true), but tell us little about false negatives – not believing something that is true (see also Mayo, Chapter 8 this volume).

Overbelief in the Self

Self-serving biases and distortions can be a particularly powerful motivational source of misjudgments and gullibility (see also Dunning, Chapter 12 this volume; Macrae et al., Chapter 11 this volume). We are always more willing to believe flattering rather than unflattering information about ourselves, even when the manipulative intent is transparently obvious (Jones, 1964; Matovic & Forgas, 2018). Overconfidence in the self may have some adaptive evolutionary functions (von Hippel, 2018), but the very same ego-boosting mechanisms could also promote gullibility and produce distorted judgments and perceptions. Considerable evidence now shows that people often hold their beliefs with far greater certainty than is justified, believe that their judgments are more accurate than is the case, and overvalue their expertise compared to others (see also Dunning, Chapter 12 this volume; Macrae et al., Chapter 11 this volume). It seems that people are not so much intuitive scientists as intuitive lawyers and politicians, marshaling evidence that confirms their convictions while dismissing evidence that contradicts them. They overestimate their own knowledge, understanding, rectitude, competence, and luck (Pinker, 2018).

Social Mechanisms of Gullibility

Humans are thoroughly social creatures, and our views of the world are fundamentally shaped by what others think and do. In a profound sense, all symbolic knowledge is socially constructed and shared. Comparing our views and ideas with the views and ideas of others is the way all symbolic reality is constructed (Strack, Chapter 9 this volume). Social psychology offers countless examples of how such "social epistemology" processes work. In an inherently ambiguous and uncertain environment, humans will spontaneously construct shared norms and standards that, however arbitrary, will impose a semblance of consensual order and predictability on their view of reality (Sherif, 1936).

Further, such consensual norms, once established, turn out to be very resilient and difficult to change – almost as if human minds abhor ambiguity, disorder, and unpredictability (Jacobs & Campbell, 1961). What others think and do continues to have a powerful normative influence on human behavior, even if those norms are not internalized, and indeed, disbelieved (Asch, 1951). It turns out that the very process of openly discussing divergent views about reality can be a mechanism that promotes the acceptance of more extreme and biased views, as the voluminous research on group polarization phenomena shows (e.g., Forgas, 1977; see also Cooper & Avery, Chapter 16 this volume). It seems that human social evolution shaped human brains in such a way that we have become creatures who spontaneously monitor each other, and often construct and maintain a consensual rather than "true" representation of reality. Indeed, abundant research, dating back to the Asch conformity studies in the 1950s, has shown that people often favor getting consensus rather than pursuing the truth (for review, see Baumeister, Maranges, & Vohs, 2018).

Epistemological Failures to Monitor and Correct

These tendencies are exacerbated by a further epistemological failure as human beings fall far short from correctly evaluating incoming information in terms of its logical merits (see also Fiedler, Chapter 7 this volume; Krueger et al., Chapter 6 this volume). Models of formal reasoning, such as the ones proposed by Hume, Bayes, or Pascal, were developed to provide explicit (although not always mutually consistent) yardsticks by which human judgments can be corrected. However, these formal systems of reasoning are not a natural part of the way people typically think in everyday situations. This raises the question of why human brains evolved to process information in such an imperfect fashion. Is detecting the true state of affairs not always the most efficient and adaptive way to deal with reality? As we have seen, evolutionary psychology suggests that deviations from seeing the world as it is can indeed confer significant survival benefits. As Baumeister et al. (Chapter 2 this volume) argue, from the perspective of adaptive fitness, falling in love and perceiving our partners as more wonderful than they really are may be beneficial for reproduction and hence favored by natural selection, as it produces stronger pair bonds and better opportunities for raising successful offspring.

It seems that the human inability to recognize and correct such epistemological mistakes appears to be a built-in adaptation, a kind of metacognitive myopia. Metacognitive myopia refers to the apparently universal human inability to correctly evaluate the source, reliability, and validity of information we receive from others. Many reasoning deficits fail to be corrected at the metacognitive level, often indicating failures to monitor and control for the validity of incoming information, rather than simple failures of perception, encoding, memory, or information processing (Fiedler, Chapter 7 this volume). The role of metacognitive myopia as a contributing source of gullibility is still insufficiently recognized in psychology, as little attention is

12 *Joseph P. Forgas and Roy F. Baumeister*

given to the metacognitive task of monitoring and deciding what information to use or to ignore.

It turns out that judgmental errors often arise not because people are unable to process the information, but because they continue to accept and use false, misleading, unrepresentative, or even previously discredited sources of input. Most research concerned with heuristics and biases, including anchoring, representativeness, and availability effects (Kahneman, 2011; Kahneman & Tversky, 2000) tend to focus on faulty processing, neglecting the question of why humans seem unable to monitor, detect, and correct input biases. For example, people are notoriously poor in correcting for biased or unrepresentative sample sizes, and spurious experiences of repeated exposure to the same information will inevitably lead to the overestimation of the actual occurrence and validity of the event, even when judges are explicitly warned about such an effect (Fiedler, Chapter 7 this volume; see also Strack, Chapter 9 this volume).

Toward an Integration

As the previous sections show, there is now strong evidence in social and cognitive psychology showing that not seeing the world as it really is often turns out to be the baseline option for many human judgments. For a variety of reasons, evolution shaped human brains in such a way that they come equipped with information-processing programs that seem specifically designed to distort reality. While these "mind modules" may have been useful and adaptive in our ancestral environment, they can prove dangerous and dysfunctional in modern mass societies where interpersonal trust is often misplaced, and false information is easier to come by than ever (see also Myers, Chapter 5 this volume).

In the Stone Age context, where the world was stable and slow changing, trusting the messages and "memes" coming from well-known others to enhance one's limited experiences must have been of significant survival value, as most people were intimately known from birth to death, and as such, trustworthy. This is no longer the case in the modern, globalized world. Indeed, trust based on familiarity and the pressures of reputation began to erode with the spread of early cities, messages one gets from strangers or on the Internet are often explicitly designed to mislead us, for commercial, political, or personal reasons (see also Cooper & Avery, Chapter 16 this volume; Myers, Chapter 5 this volume). Human brains are poorly designed for fact checking, but are very good at accepting and incorporating secondary information (see Fiedler, Chapter 7 this volume).

These mental process, if not checked, can have very serious consequences in public life (see Cooper & Avery, Chapter 16 this volume; Myers, Chapter 5 this volume). For the last 300 years, since the triumph of the Enlightenment in Western civilization and the advent of the scientific age, seeking "truth" has become an act of faith in Western cultures. It is not coincidental that following the French Revolution, temples of "reason" and rational thinking were meant to replace conventional religion as the promoters of this religion. Philosophers like Spinoza, Hume, Bayes, and Pascal provided an epistemological framework for truth-seeking, and a veritable army of well-qualified experts and scientists were engaged in the daily task of discovering and communicating what is "true." This system of truth-checking and truth-filtering now appears to be breaking down. The technological revolution we are now experiencing has removed any distinction between "truth" and "information," and without expert filtering, any claim, by anyone, anywhere, about anything is now capable of reaching almost everybody on our planet. This book was designed to cover the latest research on many of the issues and processes we discussed so far in order to better understand contemporary gullibility. We shall now turn to a brief outline of the structure and contents of the book.

Overview of the Volume

Beyond this introductory chapter, the volume is organized into four complementary sections, containing four chapters each. Part I deals with the nature and functions of credulity. In Chapter 2 Baumeister, Maxwell, Thomas, and Vohs suggest that gullibility frequently occurs as an evolutionary adaptation with distinct survival advantages. Evolution has shaped people to form lasting alliances, and this is promoted by overvaluing their partners (a form of gullibility). When in passionate love, people overestimate their partner's positive qualities, and they themselves change so as to match those positive impressions. This is a largely unintentional process that evolution has shaped because it improves pair bonding and reproductive success. Men may be especially gullible in terms of entering into a long-term commitment based on false assumptions about the level of expected rewards.

Chapter 3 by Unkelbach and Koch shows that even though people often seem gullible according to standards of logic and rationality, these errors are often adaptive. The chapter highlights the tension between people's gullibility and their nevertheless high functioning using the example of information repetition in the formation of beliefs. Although mere repetition increases the apparent truth of information, from a functional perspective, believing repeated information may actually have adaptive advantages.

In Chapter 4 Douglas, Sutton, and Cichocka analyze the factors that attract people toward conspiracy theories and suggest that conspiracy beliefs are often driven by epistemic, existential, and social motives. Their review shows that people who believe in conspiracy theories will not simply believe *anything* they hear, but focus on conspiracy theories that appeal to important functional psychological motives. Thus conspiracy believers should not simply be dismissed as gullible, even though such beliefs may often distort reality.

In Chapter 5 Myers looks at how psychological science can contribute to our understanding of gullibility in public affairs. He surveys a broad range of evidence illustrating how misinformation and direct lies shape politics resulting in public beliefs about crime, migration, the economy, or climate change. Social-cognitive dynamics such as the persuasive power of mere repetition, the availability heuristic, confirmation bias, self-justification, statistical illiteracy, group polarization, and overconfidence all contribute to these effects. The role of objective, truth-supportive and evidence-based scientific scrutiny and education, and the promotion of critical thinking is also discussed in counteracting these effects.

Part II contains four chapters dealing with the role of cognitive processes in gullibility. Chapter 6 by Krueger, Vogrincic-Haselbacher, and Evans offers a conceptual overview of issues related to gullibility in order to ground it in psychological science. They consider gullibility from various perspectives on inductive reasoning (Humean, Bayesian, Pascalian). Although gullibility can be easily represented as a special case of heuristic reasoning and predictable irrationality, it is more difficult to embed gullibility in a theory that describes successes and failures of reasoning under lawful conditions. The issue of irrational trust plays an important role in explaining the cognitive mechanisms that produce gullibility.

In Chapter 7 Fiedler proposes the term "metacognitive myopia" to describe the common inability to evaluate the history, reliability, and validity of incoming information. Such naive reliance on received evidence irrespective of its source (gossip, hearsay, advertising, anecdotes) persists even when bias is obvious. The chapter reviews extensive evidence for metacognitive myopia showing that people are often unable to ignore irrelevant information, make inferences based on unrepresentative samples, and ignore base rates. Metacognitive myopia suggests that gullibility is not simply the product of faulty reasoning, but is caused by an inability to monitor and evaluate information sources, and points to the social responsibility to monitor and control our judgments at the metacognitive level.

In Chapter 8 Mayo explores the role of gullible versus skeptical mindsets in producing credulity. She reviews empirical research showing that incoming information can be processed using either a gullible mindset in which acceptance is the primary process or a skeptical mindset in which rejection is the primary process. Her research shows that the skeptical mindset offers a strong and successful negation process that diminishes gullibility such as false memory and misinformation effects. Contextual cues or personality dispositions may induce a skeptical mindset, and mindsets may fluctuate from one moment to the next, depending on individual differences and context.

In Chapter 9 Strack discusses the role of social comparison processes in promoting gullibility. Social comparison can be driven by the motivation to learn from others (upward comparison) or boost one's own self-esteem (downward comparison). From a cognitive perspective, comparisons can influence judgments by activating standards and standard-consistent information that selectively increase the accessibility of some information. Within the domain of behavioral economics, facilitating comparisons may affect people's utility assessments. Apparent gullibility may be due to such judgmental dynamics as illustrated by experimental results.

Part III of the volume features chapters dealing with affective and motivational processes in gullibility. Chapter 10 by Forgas explores the role of sub-conscious affective states and moods in producing gullibility. He describes several psychological mechanisms responsible for mood effects on gullibility and skepticism. A series of experiments are described showing that mild negative moods can decrease gullibility, including greater skepticism in truth judgments, reduced willingness to believe misleading information, the improved detection of deception, and reduced "bullshit" receptivity. The theoretical significance of these studies is discussed, and the practical implications of affectively induced gullibility will be considered.

In Chapter 11 Macrae, Olivier, Falbén, and Golubickis discuss how the self can bias information processing and gullibility. They suggest that the human mind may be easily deceived because it functions to optimize self-serving outcomes. For example, self-relevance is known to bias perceptual judgments. The chapter describes a series of experiments that explore the effects of self-relevance and ownership on decision-making, and the cultural determinants of self-prioritization. These analyses demonstrate that self-referential processing can trigger response biases and irrational or gullible decisions and judgments.

In Chapter 12 Dunning reviews an especially important phenomenon, self-gullibility, showing that people are particularly gullible as to their own capacities and beliefs. Research shows that people hold their opinions with too much confidence, endorse wrong answers with almost as much fervor as right ones, dismiss the opinions of others too much, and give greater credence to a belief when attributed to themselves. These failures are compounded by an inability to know when, how, and from whom to seek advice, and how to evaluate the quality of that advice. In order to overcome self-gullibility, people need to become more expert at weighing the credibility of internal beliefs and outside information rather than relying on the strength of their beliefs as a proxy for their validity.

Chapter 13 by Schwarz and Lee looks at a relatively little understood subliminal influence on credulity: olfactory signals. In most languages, suspicion is metaphorically linked with the sense of a foul, rotting smell, a link that is presumably adaptive, suggesting an evolutionary link to disgust and rejection. The chapter reviews experiments showing that incidental exposure to a fishy smell makes people more suspicious and curbs gullibility in a number of tasks. These effects do not emerge in response to other aversive smells. The results are discussed in the broader context of cognition as a situated, experiential, embodied, and pragmatic process.

Part IV presents chapters discussing the social and cultural aspects of gullibility. In Chapter 14 Oyserman examines the role of cultural fluency in promoting gullibility. Being part of a culture means knowing what to expect and this experience of *cultural fluency* makes daily life feel easy to process. In contrast, *cultural disfluency* arises in situations in which experiences mismatch predictions. Mismatch is a signal that elicits more deliberate thought. The cognitive ease arising from cultural fluency can increase credulity, and conversely, exposure to cultural disfluency can reduce gullibility.

In Chapter 15 Jussim, Stevens, Honeycutt, Anglin, and Fox look at one of the most embarrassing examples of gullibility: scientific gullibility, defined as cases when data or reasoning do not justify a scientific conclusion. The authors show that scientists, often influenced by ideological bias, frequently and systematically violate their own rules. This includes making unwarranted conclusions based on inadequate samples, presenting preferred opinions as facts not supported by data, engaging in motivated reasoning, and accepting evidence that supports preferred conclusions. They may fall prey to excessive scientism, assuming that a finding being published establishes it as scientific fact, and they may also fall victim to status quo bias, maintaining the scientific consensus. The chapter concludes with recommendations for limiting scientific gullibility.

In Chapter 16 Cooper and Avery discuss an important social psychological aspect of gullibility: that communications should be reasonably truthful, that is, fall within an *envelope of legitimacy*. When propositions lie outside the envelope of legitimacy, an aversive feeling of gullibility may result that threatens people's self-esteem. One way to reducing the discomfort is to "double down" on the false belief, convincing oneself that we have not been duped at all. In support of this hypothesis, Donald Trump voters who exhibited greater sensitivity to feelings of gullibility were significantly more likely to believe their candidate's campaign promises, especially those that seemed most unlikely.

Chapter 17 by van Prooijen looks at the social and psychological mechanisms that lead people to believe in conspiracy theories. Conspiracy believers often claim to be rational skeptics, and many conspiracy theories feature very complex and well-articulated explanations. The chapter shows that reasonable skepticism is not a cause for conspiracy beliefs, as such beliefs correlate positively with other implausible paranormal and pseudoscientific beliefs and bullshit receptivity. Conspiracy beliefs also predict increased susceptibility to a cognitive biases, suggesting that belief in conspiracy theories is rooted in heuristic rather than analytic thinking, indicating dispositional gullibility.

In summary, our aim with this volume is to contribute to a better understanding of the social psychology of gullibility, an issue of considerable topical relevance today. In this introductory chapter in particular we have tried to survey some of the most important historical, cultural, evolutionary, and psychological perspectives that may help to explain gullibility as a fundamental characteristic of our species. The chapters were selected to offer a broad and representative overview of the most recent research developments in this intriguing area. As editors, we are deeply grateful to our contributors for accepting our invitation to attend the 20th Sydney Symposium

On the Social Psychology of Gullibility   17

of Social Psychology, and sharing their valuable ideas with our readers. We sincerely hope that the insights contained in these chapters will contribute not only to the emerging science of human gullibility, but also to a better understanding of the role that credulity plays in human affairs.

References

Albright, M. (2018). *Fascism: A warning*. New York, NY: HarperCollins.

Asch, S. E. (1951). Effects of group pressure upon the modification and distortion of judgment. In H. Guetzkow (Ed.), *Groups, leadership and men* (pp. 177–190). Pittsburgh, PA: Carnegie Press.

Baumeister, R. F., Maranges, H. M., & Vohs, K. D. (2018). Human self as information agent: Functioning in a social environment based on shared meanings. *Review of General Psychology, 22*(1), 36–47.

Brugger, P. (2001). From haunted brain to haunted science: A cognitive neuroscience view of paranormal and pseudoscientific thought. In J. Houran & R. Lange (Eds.), *Hauntings and poltergeists: Multidisciplinary perspectives* (pp. 195–213). Jefferson, NC: McFarland & Company.

Chapman, L. (1967). Illusory correlation in observational report. *Journal of Verbal Learning and Verbal Behavior, 6*(1), 151–155.

Dahrendorff, R. (1975). *The new liberty*. London: Routledge, Kegan & Paul.

Dawkins, R. (1976). *The selfish gene*. Oxford: Oxford University Press.

Dennett, D (2017). *From bacteria to Bach*. New York, NY: W. W. Norton.

Deutsch, M., & Gerard, H. B. (1955). A study of normative and informational social influences upon individual judgment. *Journal of Abnormal and Social Psychology, 51*(3), 629–636.

Forgas, J. P. (1977). Polarisation and moderation of person perception judgements as a function of group interaction style. *European Journal of Social Psychology, 7*, 175–187.

Forgas, J. P. (2013). Don't worry, be sad! On the cognitive, motivational, and interpersonal benefits of negative mood. *Current Directions in Psychological Science, 22*(3), 225–232.

Forgas, J. P. (2017, March 31). Why are some people more gullible than others? *The Conversation*. Retrieved from http://theconversation.com/why-are-some-people-more-gullible-than-others-72412.

Gigerenzer, G. (2000). *Adaptive thinking: Rationality in the real world*. New York, NY: Oxford University Press.

Gilbert, D. T. (1991). How mental systems believe. *American Psychologist, 46*(2), 107–119.

Gilovich, T. (1991). *How we know what isn't so: The fallibility of human reason in everyday life*. New York, NY: The Free Press.

Goldberg, J. (2008). *Liberal fascism: The secret history of the American left*. New York, NY: Doubleday.

Greenspan, S. (2009). *Annals of gullibility: Why we get duped and how to avoid it*. Wesport, CT: Praeger.

Hamilton, D., & Gifford, R. (1976). Illusory correlation in interpersonal perception: A cognitive basis of stereotypic judgments. *Journal of Experimental Social Psychology, 12*(4), 392–407.

Harari, Y. N. (2014). *Sapiens: A brief history of humankind*. London: Vintage.

18   *Joseph P. Forgas and Roy F. Baumeister*

Haselton, M. G., & Buss, D. M. (2000). Error management theory: A new perspective on biases in cross-sex mind reading. *Journal of Personality and Social Psychology*, *78*(1), 81–91.

Heider, F. (1958). *The psychology of interpersonal relations*. New York, NY: John Wiley & Sons.

Jacobs, R. C., & Campbell, D. T. (1961). The perpetuation of an arbitrary tradition through several generations of a laboratory microculture. *Journal of Abnormal and Social Psychology*, *62*(3), 649–658.

Jones, E. E. (1964). *Ingratiation: A social psychologist analysis*. New York, NY: Appleton-Century-Croft.

Jones, E. E., & Harris, V. A. (1967). The attribution of attitudes. *Journal of Experimental Social Psychology*, *3*, 1–24.

Kahneman, D. (2011) *Thinking, fast and slow*. New York, NY: Farrar, Straus, & Giroux.

Kahneman, D., & Tversky, A. (Eds.) (2000) *Choices, values and frames*. New York, NY: Cambridge University Press.

Kelley, H. H. (1967). Attribution theory in social psychology. In D. Levine (Ed.), Nebraska symposium on motivation (Vol. 15, pp. 192–238). Lincoln, NE: University of Nebraska Press.

Koestler, A. (1967). *The ghost in the machine*. London: Penguin.

Koestler, A. (1978). *Janus: A summing up*. London: Hutchinson.

Lewandowsky, S., Oreskes, N., Risbey, J. S., Newell, B., & Smithson, M. (2015). Seepage: Climate change denial and its effect on the scientific community. *Global Environmental Change*, *33*, 1–13.

Matovic, D., & Forgas, J. P. (2018). Mood effects on ingratiation: Affective influences on producing and responding to ingratiating messages. *Journal of Experimental Social Psychology*, *76*, 186–197.

Pennycook, G., Cheyne, J. A., Barr, N., Koehler, D. J., & Fugelsang, J. A. (2015). On the reception and detection of pseudo-profound bullshit. *Judgment and Decision Making*, *10*(6), 549–563.

Piaget, J. (1950). *The psychology of intelligence*. London: Routledge & Paul.

Pinker, S. (2012). *The better angels of our nature*. New York, NY: Penguin Putnam.

Pinker, S. (2018). *Enlightenment now!* New York, NY: Allen Lane.

Pluckrose, H. Lindsay, J. A., & Boghossian, P. (2018, October 2). Academic grievance studies and the corruption of scholarship. *Aero*. Retrieved from https://areomagazine.com/2018/10/02/academic-grievance-studies-and-the-corruption-of-scholarship.

Popper, K. (1947). *The open society and its enemies*. London: Routledge.

Rachman, S. (1997). A cognitive theory of obsessions. *Behaviour Research and Therapy*, *35*(9), 793–802.

Rath-Vegh, I. (1963). *From the history of human folly*. Budapest: Corvina.

Sherif, M. (1936). *The psychology of social norms*. New York, NY: Harper.

Simon, H. A. (1990). Invariants of human behavior. *Annual Review of Psychology*, *41*, 1–19.

von Hippel, W. (2018). *The social leap*. New York, NY: Harper.

Part I

The Nature and Functions of Credulity

2 The Mask of Love and Sexual Gullibility

Roy F. Baumeister
UNIVERSITY OF QUEENSLAND

Jessica A. Maxwell
FLORIDA STATE UNIVERSITY

Geoffrey P. Thomas
FLORIDA STATE UNIVERSITY

Kathleen D. Vohs
UNIVERSITY OF MINNESOTA

One ideal in Western civilization is that a man and a woman discover that they were meant for each other, fall deeply and mutually in love, marry, and spend the rest of their lives together. They support each other through good and bad times, raise a family, share life's chores and burdens, and make each other happy, till death do them part. Love may change in some respects but lasts forever, expressed in kindness, concern, affection, and passionate, tender sex.

Not everyone's experience exactly lives up to that ideal. Yet the promise is powerful. The majority of young people say they want to marry (Wang & Parker, 2014), and most do (or at least enter into a long-term cohabitation; Stepler, 2017). Yet wedding vows promising lifelong devotion and fidelity will often be broken. Even though approximately 40% of U.S. marriages end in divorce (Schoen & Canudas-Romo, 2006), people are confident their own marriages will not reach the same fate (e.g., Fowers, Lyons, Montel, & Shaked, 2001; Klaczynski & Fauth, 1996; Weinstein, 1980). Many people even recite such confident vows at their second and third weddings, when presumably they should already know better. How could any person marrying for the third time really believe to be together "till death do us part"? Yet some do. Someone is awfully gullible.

This chapter considers forms of gullibility that help people make long-term commitments to romantic partners. The term *gullibility* is often used to refer to susceptibility to deliberate persuasion or deception (see also Cooper & Avery, Chapter 17 this volume; Krueger, Vogrincic-Haselbacher, & Evans, Chapter 6 this volume). That is not meant here.

We think men and women do mislead each other – but not knowingly or deliberately. Couples who managed to persuade each other that they were a great match may have left more offspring than their less gullible cohorts. In that way, romantic gullibility may increase reproductive fitness and spread through the gene pool. Our focus is not on intentional forms of deception in mating (such as faking orgasm; Kaighobadi, Shackelford, & Weekes-Shackelford, 2012), but rather on the subtle ways nature may mold people to present themselves as a better match than they truly are. Because we are taking an evolutionary approach, we focus here on hetero-sexual monogamous romantic relationships.

Clearly the human form of mating is an evolutionarily radical inno-vation. Other great ape males do not enter into long-term committed relationships in which they provide resources to an adult female and her offspring. From the perspective of other primates, human males would seem remarkably gullible.

Yet gullibility may be valuable, even crucial, for the species. Cooperative parenting is essential to our evolutionary and cultural success. The complex demands of human culture require a high level of intelligence and a large brain size, yet human infants must be born in a relatively altricial state to ensure passage of the head through the birth canal. It is only after a lengthy period of dependence on parents that a culturally competent adult emerges. Throughout much of human evolutionary, as a result of the greater biologi-cal demands of pregnancy and lactation on women occasioning prolonged periods of dependence on male support, the presence of a male providers significantly increased the survival fitness of their offspring. This depend-ence on male support has only recently been mitigated by the emergence of the welfare state in Western civilisations. In other words, humankind flourished because evolutionary sexual strategies and cultural norms set men up to be gullible enough to become long-term providers of resources to women and children.

In particular, sexual attraction and love serve functions in humans that extend beyond what other primates do: They are useful for forming and cementing interpersonal bonds between the partners who may well become parents (see reviews by Birnbaum, 2014; Fisher, 1998; Fletcher, Simpson, Campbell, & Overall, 2015). In modern times, the bond is reinforced by societal commitments, such as religious and legal obligations, but the need for cooperative parenting predated these institutional pressures.

Nobody is perfect, so mate selection requires the need to settle for an imperfect partner and make the best of it. Evolutionary theorizing assumes a large mating market with plenty of competition and a broad selection of possible mates. In practice, however, early humans (e.g., in hunter-gatherer societies for over 90% of human history) probably had relatively few options. If they were to reproduce, they had to select from among a very limited set of imperfect potential partners Committing to a long-term relationship with a flawed other person requires some gullibility and optimistic distortion.

Love and Irrationality

Passionate love was for a time regarded as a peculiar invention of Western culture, but subsequent scholarship concluded that it is found all over the world (Jankowiak & Fischer, 1992; Neto et al., 2000), and so constitutes a universal human experience. Love forges strong attachments between men and women, which are vital for raising human children (e.g., Fisher, 1998; 2004; 2006; Fisher, Aron, & Brown, 2006; Fletcher et al., 2015).

Humans seem to be evolutionarily predisposed to falling in love and maintaining lasting romantic pair-bonds. Feelings of euphoria, pleasure, arousal, compulsion, and addiction are dramatically increased by a romantic/passionate attraction (Fisher, 2004; Fisher, Xu, Aron, & Brown, 2016). Rejection and partner absence can send the person spiraling down to depression, doubt, anxiety, and jealousy (Baumeister & Wotman, 1992; Baumeister, Wotman, & Stillwell, 1993; Fisher et al., 2016).

Behaviors in the throes of romantic love are often extreme and irrational. Some cultures and some historical eras have recognized passionate love as an irrational state (Stone, 1988) and this has been an important justification for arranged marriages. Choosing a life partner while passionately in love would be like choosing all one's retirement investments while seriously drunk.

There is a long-standing recognition that love distorts how one perceives the love object. Lovers see the ones they love in idealized fashion, ignoring or overlooking flaws while exaggerating good traits (e.g., Conley, Roesch, Peplau, & Gold, 2009; Murray & Holmes, 1993; Murray, Holmes, & Griffin, 1996a, 1996b). Lovers regard their love objects as far more wonderful than do disinterested, objective observers (Barelds, Dijkstra, Koudenburg, & Swami, 2011) or even friends (Murray, Holmes, Dolderman, & Griffin, 2000). Moreover, an ironic truth is that many of the idiosyncratic qualities that attract partners initially are often viewed as the partner's worst flaws when the infatuation wears off (Felmlee, 2001; Pines, 1997). One may initially love a partner's relaxed laid-back attitude, only to later resent him or her for being irresponsible and unconscientious.

If conventional wisdom is correct and love distorts objective assessment of one's partner, this is one important form of gullibility. In a sense, nature has instilled a temporary state of gullibility into humans, so that they overestimate the quality of potential partners when deciding whether to enter into a long-term relationship. Obviously, idealizing the partner will increase the chances of commitment (see also Fletcher & Kerr, 2013; McKay & Dennett, 2009).

How the long the idealization lasts is debatable. One line of evidence in support of idealization is the pattern of partner-serving attributions

(Bradbury & Fincham, 1990; Fincham & Bradbury, 1993; Holtzworth-Munroe & Jacobson, 1985), such as taking credit for success and denying blame for failure (e.g., Mezulis, Abramson, Hyde, & Hankin, 2004; Zuckerman, 1979). People in strong loving relationships make attributions in ways that make the partner look even better than the self. This strategy is a useful aspect of sustaining a positive relationship (McNulty, 2010; McNulty, O'Mara, & Karney, 2008). People in troubled relationships do not show these patterns of partner-serving attributions (e.g., Fincham, Beach, & Baucom, 1987). Thus, if passionate love makes people idealize their partners, their cognitive strategies help to construe events in ways that maintain that idealized view.

The Mask of Love: Helping Gullibility Along

What natural selection presumably favored were cases in which a man and a woman forged a strong and lasting bond to each other, which sustained them through raising children into adulthood. Moreover, in the evolutionary past there were often not many alternative available partners: The hunter-gatherers did not have Match.com or eHarmony, nor did the early farming villagers, so they had to choose a mate from among a limited set of locally available candidates. When people have to settle for someone who is far from ideal, it helps to have gullibility. Love accomplished this partly by making the lovers see each other as better than they really are. This section develops the more radical idea that love has a second way of increasing mating among imperfect people. Love may temporarily make someone actually become a better person – a temporary change that will increase one's appeal to the potential partner.

The term "mask of love" refers to behavioral and personality changes during passionate love that increase the person's attractiveness. The person in love metaphorically (and unintentionally) puts on a mask that is far more attractive than the real face. The mask of love complements the perceptual biases that glorify the beloved person. To illustrate, if Harry loves Sally, he will see her as better than she really or normally is – *and* he becomes better than *he* really or normally is. If Sally is inclined to love him in return, then she too will become more lovable (thereby warranting his love all the more) and will see him in idealized form. Thus, each of them undergoes a double boost in attraction. Skepticism, the standard deterrent to gullibility, will be swept away (see also Dunning, Chapter 12 this volume; Mayo, Chapter 8 this volume).

Over time, individuals come to see themselves in the idealized way their partner does (Murray et al., 1996b). Research on the *Michelangelo phenomenon* suggests that one's romantic partners can help one become closer to one's ideal version of oneself (Drigotas, Rusbult, Wieselquist, & Whitton, 1999; see review by Rusbult, Finkel, & Kumashiro, 2009).

The Mask of Love and Sexual Gullibility   25

Combining the mask of love hypothesis with the Michelangelo effect suggests an intriguing form of human gullibility. When in love, Harry becomes temporarily a better person, and Sally's attentions help move him toward actually being that better person.

Still, sustaining this over a 50-year marriage must be difficult. Gullibility must therefore continue to help. When couples are committed to one another, their standards shift to fit their partner's existing characteristics (Fletcher & Kerr, 2013; Neff & Karney, 2003). In other words, if the mask comes off but you are already committed, you strive to be happy with what is actually behind the mask. From existing research it is hard to tell whether becoming the best version of oneself when in love is a permanent change. Because most studies rely on self and partner reports of traits, it is difficult to get an objective, unbiased assessment of partners' true traits (e.g., Murray et al., 1996a; Neff & Karney, 2003). Although self-concept may shift following relationship dissolution (Slotter, Gardner, & Finkel, 2010), there is no work on whether one's personality reverts to pre-love levels.

Longitudinal evidence shows that becoming involved in a romantic relationship is associated with lower alcohol and substance use (e.g., Rauer et al., 2016; Staff et al., 2010) and reductions in other undesirable behavior such as committing crimes (Barr & Simons, 2015). Passionate love appears to be a state of ongoing or frequent positive emotion. A cursory skim of Google images for "people in love" reveals abundant happy, smiling faces. The implication is that people in love exude positive emotion. Happier expressions make people more attractive (Golle, Mast, & Lobmaier, 2013), which would make them more appealing to partners. The smiling faces may also promote gullibility (see Mayo, Chapter 8 this volume) and reduce skepticism (Forgas, Chapter 10 this volume).

The reduction in depressive symptoms and pervasive positive emotions seems eminently well designed to improve someone's attractiveness in the mating market. Studies suggest that people generally dislike interacting with depressed people (e.g., Gotlib & Robinson, 1982; Hammen & Peters, 1978). Depression is also related to poorer romantic relationship quality (Segrin, Powell, Givertz, & Brackin, 2003) and can burden one's romantic partner (Coyne et al., 1987). Advice for getting others to like one typically emphasize smiling and showing positive emotion (e.g., Carnegie, 1936), and research on ingratiation confirms that positive emotions elicit liking (Jones & Wortman, 1973), as does humor (McGee & Shevlin, 2009). If being in love can reduce depression, it would facilitate bonding.

Careful laboratory studies by Gonzaga, Keltner, Londahl, and Smith (2001) found that love functions as a commitment-enhancing device. The effects of love were different from merely feeling happy or sexual desire. Feeling love led to more affiliative nonverbal behaviors and increased markers of commitment, such as trust, constructive conflict resolution, and mutual influence. Love motivates approach behaviors toward the love object and produces expressive behaviors that signal commitment to the other person.

Several other changes also involve gullibility (see next sections). The man in love should express how much he wants to improve her feelings and well-being. Once he has won her heart, however, his attention may shift to other priorities. This was one of the themes of Flaubert's prototypical novel *Madame Bovary* (1886): At first, Charles was obsessed with winning the heart of Emma and making her happy, but after the wedding his interests shifted back to business and other matters. Emma was disappointed that his over-riding concern with her happiness proved so temporary.

Perhaps even more important to the man is that he desires frequent and highly satisfying sex (Baumeister, Catanese, & Vohs, 2001; McNulty, Maxwell, Meltzer, & Baumeister, under review). The hypothesis that love increases female sexual desire seems uncontroversial, but we shall return to relevant evidence later in this chapter.

Female Gullibility?

Evolution works based on reproductive success. The analysis up until now has argued that human reproductive success depended substantially on forming lasting male–female partnerships, with women typically provid-ing direct care to children and men providing food and other resources to both. The next sections will discuss what sorts of gullibility would enhance reproductive success by making men and women enter into committed parenting partnerships.

Gullibility is a negative trait, and we respect contemporary norms in social science that hold that attributing negative traits to women is offen-sive and sexist. Our focus has therefore been on male gullibility. However, it is useful to consider whether in some respects nature made women vul-nerable as well, as there is well-documented evidence for female vulner-ability to judgmental errors when it comes to mating decisions (Haselton & Buss, 2000).

One issue relevant to our focus on sexuality concerns concealed ovula-tion. In most nonhuman primates, the female's ovulation is readily apparent. This encourages sexual behavior that leads to reproduction. It is a long-standing puzzle as to why evolution favored concealed ovulation in humans.

A gullibility explanation suggests that concealed ovulation makes women more willing to engage in sex even when they do not want to get preg-nant. In other words, concealed ovulation conceals the woman's current impregnability from her. Our ape ancestors presumably knew when they were ovulating, because of overt physical signs. As human intelligence and the symbolic ability to represent the future evolved, early human women became able to anticipate what sex during ovulation could do to them: months of pregnancy, a very painful birth process, and years of caring for a dependent child. Sensible women might avoid all of that and confine their sex lives to times when definitely wishing to become pregnant, if that is now their main motivation for wanting sex. But of course such women might not reproduce, so modern women are descended from those who were unable to tell whether they were fertile at the moment. Not knowing whether they are ovulating could also be regarded as a form of gullibility as elucidated by Dunning (Chapter 12 this volume).

Concealed ovulation meant that women could act on their sexual desires in the (sometimes mistaken) hope that sex would be safe from pregnancy. Throughout history, all over the world, women have engaged in sex and become pregnant against their wishes (e.g., Finer & Henshaw, 2006; Sedgh, Singh, & Hussain, 2014). The rate of unplanned, unwanted pregnancies would be much lower if ovulation were marked by unmistakable physical signs. Concealed ovulation has meant heartache and tragedy for countless individual women, but nature of course rewards reproduction, and so hominins with concealed ovulation out-reproduced those who knew when they were at high risk of impregnation.

Insofar as women use sex to entice men to form long-term relationships providing resources, then the woman would favor having sex with a man who seems a promising candidate. Above all, that would include him being in love with her. Phony declarations of love are sometimes considered a common feature of male seduction efforts. Female gullibility might mean being susceptible to such declarations. Buss (1989) found that one of women's principal complaints about men was that some of them declared love and interest in a lasting relationship – but then skedaddled after sex had been consummated. These cases presumably reflect a form of female gullibility. Women are aware of the pattern and can be appropriately skeptical.

Relevant findings by Ackerman, Griskevicius, and Li (2011) indicated that women reported feeling happier if their male partner first declared his love *after* sexual activity had occurred in a relationship rather than before, presumably because such declarations prior to sex were suspect. Men showed the opposite pattern, reacting more favorably to declarations of love *prior* to the commencement of sexual intercourse. Thus, women are often adaptively on guard against being gullible.

Male Gullibility

Our emphasis is on male gullibility, which is prominent in a mating context. The human male takes on a role and responsibility far beyond what most other primate males do, and he has to sacrifice and suffer a fair amount (though he also gets some benefits). He has to be rendered much more gullible than a chimpanzee or gorilla if he is to acquiesce in being a long-term steady provider of resources to his offspring (and even to their mother), as well as bodyguard and high-powered workhorse.

In that sense, gullibility could have abetted the acceptance of these new obligations. Let us imagine that in some prehistoric time, half the men were strongly gullible to female enticements and readily succumbed to providing for them for decades, while the other men remained like other "sensible" primate males and only sought food for themselves. From whom are today's human population descended? The ones who provided well and reliably were heavily favored by the women as sex partners and hence left copious offspring, while the non-gullible ones frequently removed themselves from the gene pool. Human men were heavily bred to be domesticatable and, well, suckers.

Clearly one adaptation was also to select men who came to love their children. Again, this may be evolutionarily novel, as most apes show no such feelings. Loving their children should make the men more willing to continue providing resources and protection over many years. This will not seem to him a form of gullibility. The gullibility is perhaps most apparent to the man whose wife divorces him and minimizes his subsequent contact with his children, often while continuing to extract resources. Farrell's (1993) observation epitomizes the man's discovery of how gullible he has been: He wrote that many a modern American divorced man feels that he is working his life away to provide money for people (ex-wife and children) who hate him.

Long-term emotional attachment to the woman would be another adaptation. The man may be so captivated by the experience of passionate love that he expects it to last forever and cannot understand why the woman no longer treats him with the heady mix of positive emotion, gratitude, hero worship, and sexual desire that marked their passionate love phase. If sufficiently gullible, he may cling on to his attachment to her and his love for her, even when objective observers could probably tell that all those positive things are gone for good. Research has found that men fall in love more rapidly than women (e.g., Ackerman et al., 2011), and women fall out of love more rapidly than men (Rubin, Peplau, & Hill, 1981). That pattern is consistent with the depiction of men as the more romantic – and more gullible – gender. Women initiate more divorces than men (Hewitt, Western, & Baxter, 2006; Kalmijn & Poortman, 2006), and men suffer poorer physical and mental health after divorce than women (Kõlves, Ide, & De Leo, 2010; Robards, Evandrou, Falkingham, & Vlachantoni, 2012) – again suggesting that men remain emotionally attached for longer. Male gullibility may thus be reflected in remaining emotionally attached to a woman beyond the point that is good for the man. Further supporting this notion is evidence that men report more experiences of unrequited love in young adulthood relative to experiences of mutual love, and more unrequited love than women (Hill, Blakemore, & Drumm, 1997; see also Baumeister et al., 1993); again suggesting men may naively remain attached to unreciprocating women.

One extension of this argument suggests that men's sense of fairness also constitutes a useful vulnerability. Whether women and men think differently about morality has been debated (cf. Gilligan, 1982; Jaffee & Hyde, 2000), but there is an empirical case that males are more concerned with abstract rules than females are. Gilligan (1982) noted that boys have developed complex group games with complex rules, and carry on debates about rules at an abstract level. In contrast, girls play less complex games, and if there is a dispute, the game ends abruptly and without resolution. Benenson (2014) found that girls' own games typically are no more complex than taking turns in jump-rope. When playing games borrowed from boys, girls show considerably less interest in rules (especially debating the rules). The reason might be that males evolved to work in larger groups with fairly shallow relationships, so that group performance depended on fairness and abstract rules. If so, then man's greater respect for notions of fairness makes him vulnerable to female requests couched in terms of fairness.

A meta-analysis on gender and cooperation by Balliet, Mulder, and van Lange (2011) found that there was no overall gender difference in cooperativeness and cooperative behavior, the patterns differed. In particular, women showed low cooperation with other women, whereas both men and women cooperated with men. Moreover, in multi-trial economic games, the gender difference in same-sex cooperation increased over trials. Male willingness to cooperate can survive an occasional bad action by the partner, whereas female cooperation ends abruptly if the partner disappoints her (as with the playground games, noted earlier). This also dovetails with the fact that women initiate more divorces than men (Kalmijn & Poortman, 2006).

Thus, another aspect of male gullibility may involve forgiving the occasional misdeed by the partner. This may have evolved to facilitate male–male cooperation but may be a form of gullibility in male–female relationships. Women have not developed such a pattern in their relationships with other women. From an adaptive perspective, a couple is more durable if at least one of them is inclined to forgive various misdeeds and conflicts. Prospects would be best if both partners are forgiving, but the benefit also arises from at least one being forgiving.

Above all, male gullibility may be driven by high sexual attraction to the woman. High sex drive has been shown to lead to various irrational patterns, such as future discounting (Wilson & Daly, 2004), greater risk-taking in a card game (Baker & Maner, 2008) and in skateboarding (Ronay & von Hippel, 2010). When males are sexually aroused they are more willing to engage in morally questionable behavior to obtain sex, and more willing to engage in unprotected sex (Ariely & Loewenstein, 2006). Like other primates, the male's primary interest in the female involves sexual opportunity. The woman can exploit this to entice him in to a committed sexual relationship. Male gullibility leads to believing that the sexuality enjoyed during the passionate love phase will be permanent.

Female Sex Drive as Mask of Love

In very general terms, men want sex from women. Women want long-term commitments from men. An ideal solution would be for the woman

30   *Roy F. Baumeister et al.*

to have boundless sexual desire for the man, who then gladly continues to provide resources. However, this may not be possible. In particular, once the relationship is established, the woman's energy may turn to focus on the children, so frequent sex may be an unaffordable distraction. This is consistent with theorizing that sexual desire serves to bond individuals long enough for both partners to raise their children together (Birnbaum, 2014; Birnbaum & Finkel, 2015; Hazan & Zeifman, 1994, 1999).

The core hypothesis here is that *female sexual desire is in substantial part an adaptation to facilitate recruiting a male provider,* that is, attracting him to form a long-term relationship in which he will provide for her. Once in this relationship, there is less use for female sexual desire, so it may diminish, having served its main function. There is indeed evidence that increased female sexual activity may serve to accomplish females' ultimate goal of securing partner resources (Rodríguez-Gironés & Enquist, 2001). Women are more likely to initiate sex if their partner is less invested in the relationship (Grebe, Gangestad, Garver-Apgar, & Thornhill, 2013). Taken together this evidence suggests that it was functional for a woman to have high desire early on in a relationship to promote her partner's commitment.

There are competing theories about female orgasms. Although all female mammals have a clitoris and are thus capable of sexual pleasure, and a few animals have been stimulated in the laboratory to the point of vaginal contractions, there is not much evidence of frequent orgasms occurring in the wild among nonhuman animals, and the brief, fairly rough nature of much animal copulation seems poorly suited to produce female orgasms. Human women may not be the first animals to have female orgasms, but they certainly have far more than other animals. There are various theories about this (see review by Puts, Dawood, & Welling, 2012), some of which emphasize the value of female orgasm for cementing bonds between man and woman (e.g., Eibl-Eibesfeldt, 1989; but see also Zietsch, Miller, Bailey, & Martin, 2011). The orgasm may intensify the woman's positive feelings and love for the man, and this may be reinforcing to him. This is likely multiplied by the human innovation of face-to-face intercourse. Face-to-face intercourse facilitates rapid and ongoing exchange of affection, including eye contact, talking, smiling, and kissing. One could say it seems well designed for turning sex into love.

In short, human evolution reshaped sexual intercourse in ways well suited to the communication of female pleasure to the man. This may well serve to strengthen the man's love for the woman and to encourage him to make the long-term commitment. Indeed there is evidence that men report feeling more masculine if a female partner orgasms in an imagined sexual encounter (Chadwick & van Anders, 2017). Both genders acknowledge a female's orgasm is a boost to the male's ego (Salisbury & Fisher, 2014).

Intense momentary pleasure is addictive to males. Men generally show much greater pursuit of such pleasures than women, including not just

The Mask of Love and Sexual Gullibility   31

sex but also obsessive involvement in music or sports, and even drugs. Men outnumber women in nearly all forms of alcohol and drug addiction (e.g., Brady & Randall, 1999; O'Malley & Johnston, 2002; Substance Abuse and Mental Health Services Administration, 2012). The male susceptibility to the pursuit of remembered pleasure is another key aspect of male gullibility and may have evolved to facilitate men becoming attached to their female sex partners.

The key point is that the communication of passionate sexuality is part of the woman's mask of love. That is, nature has selected in favor of women feeling and showing a strong sexual response for the sake of forming a long-term relationship. It almost appears as if high sexual desire and orgasmic responsiveness might be a transitory phase associated with securing a long-term provider. They are for closing the deal, not a permanent part of the deal. And he may not realize this (thus he is gullible).

Men may not always realize that in some cases, female sexual passion is a temporary condition perhaps designed by nature to entice him into a provider role. This is a key aspect of male gullibility. Presumably he believes that sex with her will always be the way it is during this passionate phase: thrilling, mutual, satisfying, and frequent. Indeed, a recent study of engaged men and women revealed that both sexes anticipated having sex approximately 11–12 times per month when married (Maxwell, Joel, & MacDonald, unpublished data), which is far above the typical frequency of sex in long-term relationships of once or twice per week (e.g., Blanchflower & Oswald, 2004; Call, Sprecher, & Schwartz, 1995).

A crucial prediction of the viewing of female sexuality as instrumental is that female desire for sex will drop off once the man is committed. The first author's own thinking along these lines was stimulated by Arndt's (2009) book, *The Sex Diaries*. Arndt, a journalist and sex therapist, developed a plan for a racy bestseller based on having an assortment of couples keep diary records of their sex lives. When she perused the diaries, she did find some titillating scenes. But far more frequent were scenes of men begging and groveling for sex, while the women refused and sometimes developed elaborate stratagems for avoiding sex. For example, one confided to her friends that it was often useful to start a small argument with her husband late in the evening, which would preempt any romantic mood or sexual overtures. Arndt concluded that some mysterious process causes many women to lose interest in sex as soon as they settle into a long-term relationship.

Archival data provide some support for that conclusion. Ard (1977) surveyed married couples across many ages. The women typically thought their marriages had about the right frequency of sex, whereas the men wished for much more (indeed twice as much) sex as they were having. This suggests that many couples adjusted their sexual frequency to the lower rate of desire by the wife. The feminist movement has encouraged women to be much more assertive about insisting that the husband

32   *Roy F. Baumeister et al.*

should wait for sex until the woman wants it too – which happens to be much less often. This change in behavioral expectations may well increase the need for couples to re-negotiate and re-define what they consider an acceptably coordinated and mutually acceptable sexual pattern. A survey by Byers and Lewis (1988) found that half their couples had a sexual disagreement at least once per month. They found no cases in which the wife complained about not enough sex. That was always the husband's complaint. Likewise, a survey of couples in sex therapy found that lack of sexual interest was a common problem among wives but rare among husbands (Hawton & Catalan, 1986; see Baumeister, Catanese, & Vohs, 2001, for broader review).

Probably the most thorough and rigorous data come from a pair of recent longitudinal studies that tracked newlywed couples across the first few years of marriage (McNulty, Maxwell, Meltzer, & Baumeister, under review). All couples began the study either just before or within a few months after their wedding day and were surveyed about twice per year for about five years. Right after the wedding, the men reported higher sexual desire than the women, but the difference, although significant, was not large. Over the subsequent years, the men's desire remained at about the same level – while their wives' sexual desire declined markedly and steadily. The effect remained significant after controlling for a host of other variables. In particular, it remained significant after controlling for childbirth, although childbirth increased the effect. This fits the view that once the woman has children, her energies are focused on childrearing rather than on her sex life with her husband. But even if she does not have children, her sex drive declines once the man is committed.

Why do men stay committed, once the wife loses interest in sex? One speculation is that natural selection has bred men to become addicted to powerful sources of pleasure, so that they continue to seek and expect satisfaction even as it dwindles. Another powerful insight was suggested by Cooper and Avery (Chapter 16 this volume), who note that when gullible people begin to think they have been duped, they "double down" on their commitment – that is, they believe ever more fervently in what the evidence suggests may have been a mistake, a kind of dissonance reduction effect. If the double-down hypothesis is correct, then when a man starts to realize that his wife is not acting like the sex goddess he perhaps rather naively and gullibly envisioned, this may well result in an intensification of his belief and expectation that eventually she may perhaps again become that (or, as he sees it, go back to being that; see Baumeister, Catanese, & Vohs, 2001). He may remain fixated on how wonderful it was before, and he fails to realize that things have changed – consistent with many patterns in which people do not realize that their knowledge is flawed or inadequate (see Dunning, Chapter 12 this volume; Fiedler, Chapter 7 this volume).

His and Her Gullibility

Our overarching hypothesis is that nature has instilled gullibility into men and women to bind them together. The mask of love hypothesis suggests that during the peaks of romantic attraction, men and women actually change so as to become more appealing partners to each other, in addition to viewing each other in idealized manner. Part of the female mask of love involves high sexual passion. This reflects the female's changes during love as well as the man's vulnerability to believing it will always be like this. The gullible male forms a strong attachment and provides her with resources for years to come.

In effect, nature has arranged a kind of "bait and switch" process that, like its marketing equivalent, functions to tempt people into commitments that they might not choose if fully informed and that can operate to their detriment. The mask of love entails that the person one comes to love and marry is not the same as the person with whom one ends up married, and the actual partner is a less appealing version than what one thought one was getting. The temporary flowering of the female sex drive is merely one of the more salient and problematic forms of the mask of love. But insofar as nature's goal is to promote reproductive success via partnered parenting, it works.

"Bait and switch" is legally prohibited in commerce as a deliberate deceptive technique, and we do not think that most men and women are deliberately deceptive. The term is used as an imperfect analogy. Still, it does introduce an economic perspective on mating. Before closing, we develop the economic analysis further.

Sexual Economics and Different Understandings

The mismatch in sexual desire that emerges over the early years of marriage points to further forms of gullibility in both men and women. When they negotiate and commit to a long-term relationship, they may have different understandings of what the commitment involves, even just in terms of sex. Both man and woman may exhibit some gullibility, albeit in different forms.

A conceptual scheme for analyzing these sexual negotiations is sexual economics theory. This is a decidedly unromantic approach to analyzing love and sex, but a vast amount of evidence fits it, as reviewed by Baumeister and Vohs (2004). The core idea is that sex functions as a resource or service that men want from women, and so men must give women some other resources in exchange. Male sexuality has no exchange value, whereas female sexuality can be traded for many things women want: not just money but also food, attention, drugs, respect, career advancement, forgiveness, reduced punishment for misdeeds, high grades for academic work, and more.

The theory was originally focused on forming a new sexual relationship, or commencing to have sex for the first time even if that is also the last time. Its applicability to marriage is unclear. In modern marriage, the wife already owns all the husband's assets (jointly), so there is not much more he can give her, thus there is no economic reason for her to give him sex. Insofar as her sex drive is based on extracting resources from him, it has no more utility once he has made a permanent commitment.

A revealing insight emerged from recent research on female competition. Women pass along gossip about their rivals, especially attractive ones (Reynolds, Baumeister, & Maner, in press). The content of the gossip is that the target woman is sexually unrestricted, that is, has plenty of sex with different partners. That seems to clash with the sexual economics analysis. To discredit a competitor, they say that she has a low price. Hardly any business marketers advertise that their rivals have lower prices. Why would this occur in the human mating market?

To resolve this dilemma (see Baumeister, Reynolds, Winegard, & Vohs, 2017), it is necessary to consider what is being traded. Sexual economics theory began by assuming that sexual intercourse and pleasure were what was traded. But human mating commitments often involve exclusivity, and female more often than male exclusivity. The man thinks he is getting sex, augmented by her promise of faithfulness. Perhaps she thinks the main thing she offers is exclusivity, augmented by a little bit of sex.

The couple can conceivably function just fine despite this difference in perspectival emphasis. They can make their commitment to each other, form a household as a cooperative team, start a family, and so forth.

However, the emerging sexual mismatch brings these different understandings to the fore. The man thought there would be plenty of sex, but his wife only wants to have sex occasionally. Many wives would be fine if sex were to stop altogether. Arndt (2009) told one story of a couple in which the man tried many different ways of initiating sex but received only angry rebuffs from his wife. Frustrated and exasperated, but trying to be respectful, he proposed that he should not be the one to initiate sex – that is, the next time they had sex would be up to her to initiate it. Nine years later, he was still waiting. For men in such a position, the marriage vow is a vow of chastity.

To the husband, then, it may seem that the wife is reneging on the deal. He married her partly in expectation of lots of sex, but she is not providing that.

From her perspective, however, she is fulfilling her part of the bargain that she would not have sex with anyone else, and she is succeeding at that. From her perspective, fidelity counts. That is precisely what she promised at the wedding. The church ceremony contained no vows about having sex when she did not desire it. During the passionate courtship, she felt abundant desire, but nowadays, not so much. Her sexual commitment likely assumed that sex would occur by mutual desire, not as an obligation. In sex, engaging in acts when one does not desire them has many negative connotations (e.g., Impett, Peplau, & Gable, 2005; Smith, 2007). As the woman fails to appreciate that her desire for her partner will dwindle over time she may not realize that sex will start to become more of a chore and less of a delight.

It is even possible that she thinks that he is the one who is not living up to the deal. If he accepts her unwillingness to have sex, he may resort to pornography and other outside stimulations – which to her may be a betrayal of the more important form of their commitment, namely to forsake all others. There are reports that some women object to their husband looking at pornography (e.g., Bridges, Bergner, & Hesson-McInnis, 2003), although admittedly women have a range of attitudes regarding their husband's porn use (Kohut, Fisher, & Campbell, 2017; Zitzman & Butler, 2009). Of course, many wives object to their husbands having sex with prostitutes or mistresses, even if the wife herself is largely disinclined to have sex. This is a moral and pragmatic dilemma: His partner is not interested in sex, but she objects to him finding alternative outlets. She has all but stopped sexual activity but his sex drive remains as strong as ever.

The problem thus arises because of bilateral gullibility. Each partner promises something and expects something in return, but these expectations do not quite match. The young couple in love are both happy with what they have and want to make it permanent, but they have different understandings of what it is they are making permanent.

Conclusion

Sexual gullibility is plausibly an innate tendency in humankind, because it likely improved reproductive success. It works differently in men and women. The gullibility helps them form a lasting attachment, which is optimal and adaptive for the babies that come along as a result of their having sex.

We emphasize again that the gullibility patterns do not at all imply deliberate deception. The mask of love hypothesis holds that these changes in behavior seem to occur naturally when in love, and the individual may not realize the misjudgment involved (see also Dunning, Chapter 12 this volume; Fiedler, Chapter 7 this volume; Krueger et al., Chapter 6 this volume). Powerful positive feelings may also increase gullibility (see also Forgas, Chapter 10 this volume). We suspect the wife may be as baffled as her husband at her loss of desire for sex across her early years of marriage. Explanations may focus on the stresses on her or on the newly visible faults in her husband (e.g., Sims & Meana, 2010). It is rarely realized that her high initial sexual response would have given him a misleading picture of what their future holds. In parallel, the man in love does everything to make her happy, and this too misrepresents what he might be as a husband. Neither are aware of their own fakery.

To commit to spending the rest of one's life with an imperfect person who may change in unpredictable and possibly unwelcome ways requires a major leap of faith, and a high degree of gullibility. Couples who successfully did this

36   Roy F. Baumeister et al.

left a larger footprint in the gene pool than those who avoided such a risky and dubious commitment. We have proposed that both men and women have been shaped by nature to be gullible so as to overestimate their partner's positive qualities during the commitment phase (passionate love).

References

Ackerman, J. M., Griskevicius, V., & Li, N. P. (2011). Let's get serious: Communicating commitment in romantic relationships. *Journal of Personality and Social Psychology, 100*(6), 1079–1094.

Ard, B. N. (1977). Sex in lasting marriages: A longitudinal study. *Journal of Sex Research, 13*, 274–285.

Ariely, D., & Loewenstein, G. (2006). The heat of the moment: The effect of sexual arousal on sexual decision making. *Journal of Behavioral Decision Making, 19*(2), 87–98.

Arndt, B. (2009). *The sex diaries: Why women go off sex and other bedroom battles.* Carlton, Australia: Melbourne University Press.

Baker, M. D., & Maner, J. K. (2008). Risk-taking as a situationally sensitive male mating strategy. *Evolution and Human Behavior, 29*(6), 391–395.

Balliet, D., Mulder, L. B., & van Lange, P. A. (2011). Reward, punishment, and cooperation: A meta-analysis. *Psychological Bulletin, 137*(4), 594–615.

Barelds, D. P., Dijkstra, P., Koudenburg, N., & Swami, V. (2011). An assessment of positive illusions of the physical attractiveness of romantic partners. *Journal of Social and Personal Relationships, 28*(5), 706–719.

Barr, A. B., & Simons, R. L. (2015). Different dimensions, different mechanisms? Distinguishing relationship status and quality effects on desistance. *Journal of Family Psychology, 29*(3), 360–370.

Baumeister, R. F., Catanese, K. R., & Vohs, K. D. (2001). Is there a gender difference in strength of sex drive? Theoretical views, conceptual distinctions, and a review of relevant evidence. *Personality and Social Psychology Review, 5*(3), 242–273.

Baumeister, R. F., Reynolds, T., Winegard, B., & Vohs, K. D. (2017). Competing for love: Applying sexual economics theory to mating contests. *Journal of Economic Psychology, 63*, 230–241.

Baumeister, R. F., & Vohs, K. D. (2004). Sexual economics: Sex as female resource for social exchange in heterosexual interactions. *Personality and Social Psychology Review, 8*(4), 339–363.

Baumeister, R. F., & Wotman, S. R. (1992). *Breaking hearts: The two sides of unrequited love.* New York, NY: Guilford Press.

Baumeister, R. F., Wotman, S. R., & Stillwell, A. M. (1993). Unrequited love: On heartbreak, anger, guilt, scriptlessness, and humiliation. *Journal of Personality and Social Psychology, 64*(3), 377–394.

Benenson, J. F. (2014). *Warriors and worriers: The survival of the sexes.* New York, NY: Oxford University Press.

Birnbaum, G. E. (2014). Sexy building blocks: The contribution of the sexual system to attachment formation and maintenance. In M. Mikulincer & P. R. Shaver (Eds.), *Mechanisms of social connection: From brain to group* (pp. 315–332). Washington, DC: American Psychological Association.

Birnbaum, G. E., & Finkel, E. J. (2015). The magnetism that holds us together: Sexuality and relationship maintenance across relationship development. *Current Opinion in Psychology, 1,* 29–33.

Blanchflower, D. G., & Oswald, A. J. (2004). Money, sex and happiness: An empirical study. *Scandinavian Journal of Economics, 106,* 393–415. doi:10.1111/j.1467-9442.2004.00369.x

Bradbury, T. N., & Fincham, F. D. (1990). Attributions in marriage: Review and critique. *Psychological Bulletin, 107,* 3–33.

Brady, K. T., & Randall, C. L. (1999). Gender differences in substance use disorders. *Psychiatric Clinics, 22*(2), 241–252.

Bridges, A., Bergner, R., & McInnis, M. (2003). Romantic partner's use of pornography: Its significance for women. *Journal of Sex and Marital Therapy, 29,* 1–14.

Buss, D. M. (1989). Conflict between the sexes: Strategic interference and the evocation of anger and upset. *Journal of Personality and Social Psychology, 56,* 735–747.

Byers, E. S., & Lewis, K. (1988). Dating couples' disagreements over the desired level of sexual intimacy. *Journal of Sex Research, 24,* 15–29.

Call, V., Sprecher, S., & Schwartz, P. (1995). The incidence and frequency of marital sex in a national sample. *Journal of Marriage and Family, 57,* 639–652.

Carnegie, D. (1936). *How to win friends and influence people.* New York, NY: Simon & Schuster.

Chadwick, S. B., & van Anders, S. M. (2017). Do women's orgasms function as a masculinity achievement for men? *Journal of Sex Research, 54*(9), 1141–1152.

Conley, T. D., Roesch, S. C., Peplau, L. A., & Gold, M. S. (2009). A test of positive illusions versus shared reality models of relationship satisfaction among gay, lesbian, and heterosexual couples. *Journal of Applied Social Psychology, 39*(6), 1417–1431.

Coyne, J. C., Kessler, R. C., Tal, M., Turnbull, J., Wortman, C. B., & Greden, J. F. (1987). Living with a depressed person. *Journal of Consulting and Clinical psychology, 55*(3), 347–352.

Drigotas, S. M., Rusbult, C. E., Wieselquist, J., & Whitton, S. W. (1999). Close partner as sculptor of the ideal self: Behavioral affirmation and the Michelangelo phenomenon. *Journal of Personality and Social Psychology, 77*(2), 293–323.

Eibl-Eibesfeldt. I. 1989. *Human ethology.* Hawthorne, NY: Aldine de Gruyter.

Farrell, W. (1993). *The myth of male power: Why men are the disposable sex.* New York, NY: Simon & Schuster.

Felmlee, D. H. (2001). From appealing to appalling: Disenchantment with a romantic partner. *Sociological Perspectives, 44*(3), 263–280.

Fincham, F. D., Beach, S. R., & Baucom, D. H. (1987). Attribution processes in distressed and nondistressed couples: IV. Self–partner attribution differences. *Journal of Personality and Social Psychology, 52*(4), 739–748.

Fincham, F. D., & Bradbury, T. N. (1993). Marital satisfaction, depression, and attributions: A longitudinal analysis. *Journal of Personality and Social Psychology, 64*(3), 442–452.

Finer, L. B., & Henshaw, S. K. (2006). Disparities in rates of unintended pregnancy in the United States, 1994 and 2001. *Perspectives on Sexual and Reproductive Health, 38*(2), 90–96.

Fisher, H. E. (1998). Lust, attraction, and attachment in mammalian reproduction. *Human Nature, 9*(1), 23–52.

Fisher, H. E. (2004). *Why we love: The nature and chemistry of romantic love*. New York, NY: Henry Holt.

Fisher, H. E. (2006). The drive to love. In R. Sternberg & K. Weis (Eds.), *The new psychology of love* (pp. 87–115). New Haven, CT: Yale University Press.

Fisher, H. E., Aron, A., & Brown, L. L. (2006). Romantic love: A mammalian brain system for mate choice. *Philosophical Transactions of the Royal Society B: Biological Sciences*, *361*(1476), 2173–2186.

Fisher, H. E., Xu, X., Aron, A., & Brown, L. L. (2016). Intense, passionate, romantic love: A natural addiction? How the fields that investigate romance and substance abuse can inform each other. *Frontiers in Psychology*, 7, 687.

Flaubert, G. (1886). *Madame Bovary: Provincial manners*. (E. Marx, Trans). London: W. W. Gibbings.

Fletcher, G. J. O., & Kerr, P. S. G. (2013). Love, reality, and illusion in intimate relationships. In J. A. Simpson & L. Campbell (Eds.), *Oxford handbook of close relationships* (pp. 306–320). New York, NY: Oxford University Press.

Fletcher, G. J. O., Simpson, J. A., Campbell, L., & Overall, N. C. (2015). Pair-bonding, romantic love, and evolution: The curious case of Homo sapiens. *Perspectives on Psychological Science*, *10*(1), 20–36.

Fowers, B. J., Lyons, E., Montel, K. H., & Shaked, N. (2001). Positive illusions about marriage among married and single individuals. *Journal of Family Psychology*, *15*(1), 95–109.

Gilligan, C. (1982). *In a different voice: Psychological theory and women's development*, Cambridge, MA: Harvard University Press.

Golle, J., Mast, F. W., & Lobmaier, J. S. (2013). Something to smile about: The interrelationship between attractiveness and emotional expression, *Cognition and Emotion*, *28*, 298–310. doi: 10.1080/02699931.2013.817383

Gonzaga, G. C., Keltner, D., Londahl, E. A., & Smith, M. D. (2001). Love and the commitment problem in romantic relations and friendship. *Journal of Personality and Social Psychology*, *81*(2), 247–262.

Gotlib, I. H., & Robinson, L. A. (1982). Responses to depressed individuals: Discrepancies between self-report and observer-rated behavior. *Journal of Abnormal Psychology*, *91*(4), 231–240.

Grebe, N. M., Gangestad, S. W., Garver-Apgar, C. E., & Thornhill, R. (2013). Women's luteal-phase sexual proceptivity and the functions of extended sexuality. *Psychological Science*, *24*(10), 2106–2110.

Hammen, C. L., & Peters, S. D. (1978). Interpersonal consequences of depression: Responses to men and women enacting a depressed role. *Journal of Abnormal Psychology*, *87*(3), 322–332.

Haselton, M. G., & Buss, D. M. (2000). Error management theory: A new perspective on biases in cross-sex mind reading. *Journal of Personality and Social Psychology*, *78*(1), 81–91.

Hawton, K., & Catalan, J. (1986). Prognostic factors in sex therapy. *Behaviour Research and Therapy*, *24*, 377–385.

Hazan, C., & Zeifman, D. (1994). Sex and the psychological tether. In K. Bartholomew & D. Perlman (Eds.), *Advances in personal relationships: Vol. 5. Attachment processes in adulthood* (pp. 151–177). London: Jessica Kingsley.

Hazan, C., & Zeifman, D. (1999). Pair-bonds as attachments: Evaluating the evidence. In J. Cassidy & P. R. Shaver (Eds.), *Handbook of attachment: Theory, research, and clinical applications* (pp. 336–354). New York, NY: Guilford Press.

Hewitt, B., Western, M., & Baxter, J. (2006). Who decides? The social characteristics of who initiates marital separation. *Journal of Marriage and Family*, *68*(5), 1165–1177.

Hill, C. A., Blakemore, J. E., & Drumm, P. (1997). Mutual and unrequited love in adolescence and young adulthood. *Personal Relationships*, *4*(1), 15–23.

Holtzworth-Munroe, A., & Jacobson, N. S. (1985). Causal attributions of married couples: When do they search for causes? What do they conclude when they do? *Journal of Personality and Social Psychology*, *48*(6), 1398–1412.

Impett, E. A., Peplau, L. A., & Gable, S. L. (2005). Approach and avoidance sexual motives: Implications for personal and interpersonal well-being. *Personal Relationships*, *12*(4), 465–482.

Jaffee, S., & Hyde, J. S. (2000). Gender differences in moral orientation: A meta-analysis. *Psychological Bulletin*, *126*(5), 703–726.

Jankowiak, W. R., & Fischer, E. F. (1992). A cross-cultural perspective on romantic love. *Ethnology*, *31*(2), 149–155.

Jones, E. E., & Wortman, C. B. (1973). *Ingratiation: An attributional approach*. Morristown, NJ: General Learning Press.

Kaighobadi, F., Shackelford, T. K., & Weekes-Shackelford, V. A. (2012). Do women pretend orgasm to retain a mate? *Archives of Sexual Behavior*, *41*(5), 1121–1125.

Kalmijn, M., & Poortman, A. R. (2006). His or her divorce? The gendered nature of divorce and its determinants. *European Sociological Review*, *22*(2), 201–214.

Klaczynski, P. A., & Fauth, J. M. (1996). Intellectual ability, rationality, and intuitiveness as predictors of warranted and unwarranted optimism for future life events. *Journal of Youth and Adolescence*, *25*(6), 755–773.

Kohut, T., Fisher, W. A., & Campbell, L. (2017). Perceived effects of pornography on the couple relationship: Initial findings of open-ended, participant-informed, "bottom-up" research. *Archives of Sexual Behavior*, *46*(2), 585–602.

Kõlves, K., Ide, N., & De Leo, D. (2010). Suicidal ideation and behaviour in the aftermath of marital separation: Gender differences. *Journal of Affective Disorders*, *120*(1), 48–53.

Maxwell, J. A., Joel, S., & MacDonald, G. (2018). *The sexual expectations of engaged men and women*. Unpublished manuscript.

McGee, E., & Shevlin, M. (2009). Effect of humor on interpersonal attraction and mate selection. *Journal of Psychology*, *143*(1), 67–77.

McKay, R. T., & Dennett, D. C. (2009). Our evolving beliefs about evolved misbelief. *Behavioral and Brain Sciences*, *32*(6), 541–561.

McNulty, J. K. (2010). When positive processes hurt relationships. *Current Directions in Psychological Science*, *19*(3), 167–171.

McNulty, J. K., Maxwell, J. A., Meltzer, A. L., & Baumeister, R. F. (under review). *The honeymoon is over: The widening gender gap in sexual desire during early marriage*.

McNulty, J. K., O'Mara, E. M., & Karney, B. R. (2008). Benevolent cognitions as a strategy of relationship maintenance: "Don't sweat the small stuff" . . . But it is not all small stuff. *Journal of Personality and Social Psychology*, *94*(4), 631–646.

Mezulis, A. H., Abramson, L. Y., Hyde, J. S., & Hankin, B. L. (2004). Is there a universal positivity bias in attributions? A meta-analytic review of individual, developmental, and cultural differences in the self-serving attributional bias. *Psychological Bulletin*, *130*(5), 711.

Murray, S. L., & Holmes, J. G. (1993). Seeing virtues in faults: Negativity and the transformation of interpersonal narratives in close relationships. *Journal of Personality and Social Psychology, 65*(4), 707.

Murray, S. L., Holmes, J. G., Dolderman, D., & Griffin, D. W. (2000). What the motivated mind sees: Comparing friends' perspectives to married partners' views of each other. *Journal of Experimental Social Psychology, 36*(6), 600–620.

Murray, S. L., Holmes, J. G., & Griffin, D. W. (1996a). The benefits of positive illusions: Idealization and the construction of satisfaction in close relationships. *Journal of Personality and Social Psychology, 70*(1), 79.

Murray, S. L., Holmes, J. G., & Griffin, D. W. (1996b). The self-fulfilling nature of positive illusions in romantic relationships: Love is not blind, but prescient. *Journal of Personality and Social Psychology, 71*, 1155–1180.

Neff, L. A., & Karney, B. R. (2003). The dynamic structure of relationship perceptions: Differential importance as a strategy of relationship maintenance. *Personality and Social Psychology Bulletin, 29*(11), 1433–1446.

Neto, F., Mullet, E., Deschamps, J. C., Barros, J., Benvindo, R., Camino, L., . . . Machado, M. (2000). Cross-cultural variations in attitudes toward love. *Journal of Cross-Cultural Psychology, 31*(5), 626–635.

O'Malley, P. M., & Johnston, L. D. (2002). Epidemiology of alcohol and other drug use among American college students. *Journal of Studies on Alcohol, Supplement,* (14), 23–39.

Pines, A. M. (1997). Fatal attractions or wise unconscious choices: The relationship between causes for entering and breaking intimate relationships. *Personal Relationship Issues, 4*, 1–6.

Puts, D. A., Dawood, K., & Welling, L. L. (2012). Why women have orgasms: An evolutionary analysis. *Archives of Sexual Behavior, 41*(5), 1127–1143.

Rauer, A. J., Pettit, G. S., Samek, D. R., Lansford, J. E., Dodge, K. A., & Bates, J. E. (2016). Romantic relationships and alcohol use: A long-term, developmental perspective. *Development and Psychopathology, 28*(3), 773–789.

Reynolds, T., Baumeister, R. F., & Maner, J. K. (in press). Competitive reputation manipulation: Women strategically transmit social information about romantic rivals. *Journal of Experimental Social Psychology.*

Robards, J., Evandrou, M., Falkingham, J., & Vlachantoni, A. (2012). Marital status, health and mortality. *Maturitas, 73*(4), 295–299.

Rodríguez-Gironés, M. A., & Enquist, M. (2001). The evolution of female sexuality. *Animal Behaviour, 61*(4), 695–704.

Ronay, R., & von Hippel, W. (2010). The presence of an attractive woman elevates testosterone and physical risk taking in young men. *Social Psychological and Personality Science, 1*(1), 57–64.

Rubin, Z., Peplau, L. A., & Hill, C. T. (1981). Loving and leaving: Sex differences in romantic attachments. *Sex Roles, 7*(8), 821–835.

Rusbult, C. E., Finkel, E. J., & Kumashiro, M. (2009). The michelangelo phenomenon. *Current Directions in Psychological Science, 18*(6), 305–309.

Salisbury, C. M., & Fisher, W. A. (2014). "Did you come?" A qualitative exploration of gender differences in beliefs, experiences, and concerns regarding female orgasm occurrence during heterosexual sexual interactions. *Journal of Sex Research, 51*(6), 616–631.

Schoen, R., & Canudas-Romo, V. (2006). Timing effects on divorce: 20th-century experience in the United States. *Journal of Marriage and Family, 68*(3), 749–758.

Sedgh, G., Singh, S., & Hussain, R. (2014). Intended and unintended pregnancies worldwide in 2012 and recent trends. *Studies in Family Planning, 45*(3), 301–314.

Segrin, C., Powell, H. L., Givertz, M., & Brackin, A. (2003). Symptoms of depression, relational quality, and loneliness in dating relationships. *Personal Relationships, 10*(1), 25–36.

Sims, K. E., & Meana, M. (2010). Why did passion wane? A qualitative study of married women's attributions for declines in sexual desire. *Journal of Sex & Marital Therapy, 36*(4), 360–380.

Slotter, E. B., Gardner, W. L., & Finkel, E. J. (2010). Who am I without you? The influence of romantic breakup on the self-concept. *Personality and Social Psychology Bulletin, 36*(2), 147–160.

Smith, C. V. (2007). In pursuit of "good" sex: Self-determination and the sexual experience. *Journal of Social and Personal Relationships, 24*(1), 69–85. http://doi.org/10.1177/0265407507072589

Staff, J., Schulenberg, J. E., Maslowsky, J., Bachman, J. G., O'Malley, P. M., Maggs, J. L., & Johnston, L. D. (2010). Substance use changes and social role transitions: Proximal developmental effects on ongoing trajectories from late adolescence through early adulthood. *Development and Psychopathology, 22*(4), 917–932.

Stepler, R. (2017). Number of U.S. adults cohabiting with a partner continues to rise, especially among those 50 and older. *Fact Tank: Pew Research Center.* Retrieved from www.pewresearch.org/fact-tank/2017/04/06/number-of-u-s-adults-cohabiting-with-a-partner-continues-to-rise-especially-among-those-50-and-older.

Stone, L. (1988). Passionate attachments in the West in historical perspective. In W. Gaylin & E. Person (Eds.), *Passionate attachments: Thinking about love.* New York, NY: The Free Press.

Substance Abuse and Mental Health Services Administration, Center for Behavioral Health Statistics and Quality. (2012). *Treatment episode data set (TEDS): 2002–2012: National admissions to substance abuse treatment services.* BHSIS Series S-71, HHS Publication No. (SMA) 14–4850. Rockville, MD: Substance Abuse and Mental Health Services Administration.

Wang, W., & Parker, K. (2014). Record share of Americans have never married. *Pew Research Center's Social & Demographic Trends Project.* Retrieved from www.pewsocialtrends.org/2014/09/24/record-share-of-americans-have-never-married.

Weinstein, N. D. (1980). Unrealistic optimism about future life events. *Journal of Personality and Social Psychology, 39*(5), 806–820.

Wilson, M., & Daly, M. (2004). Do pretty women inspire men to discount the future?. *Proceedings of the Royal Society of London B: Biological Sciences, 271* (Suppl. 4), S177–S179.

Zietsch, B. P., Miller, G. F., Bailey, J. M., & Martin, N. G. (2011). Female orgasm rates are largely independent of other traits: Implications for "female orgasmic disorder" and evolutionary theories of orgasm. *Journal of Sexual Medicine, 8*(8), 2305–2316.

Zitzman, S. T., & Butler, M. H. (2009). Wives' experience of husbands' pornography use and concomitant deception as an attachment threat in the adult pair-bond relationship. *Sexual Addiction & Compulsivity, 16*(3), 210–240.

Zuckerman, M. (1979). Attribution of success and failure revisited, or: The motivational bias is alive and well in attribution theory. *Journal of Personality, 47*(2), 245–287.

3   Gullible but Functional?

Information Repetition and the Formation of Beliefs

Christian Unkelbach and Alex Koch
UNIVERSITY OF COLOGNE

When considering how people come to form beliefs about the world they live in, they seem to be rather gullible (see Forgas & Baumeister, Chapter 1 this volume). People are convinced by weak arguments (Petty & Cacioppo, 1986; Petty, Wells, & Brock, 1976), they do not weight information properly (Dawes, 1979), and most critically, they fail to discount irrelevant information when forming beliefs (see Wilson & Brekke, 1994, for an overview). One of the most notorious ways people are influenced by irrelevant information is mere repetition. On first sight, simply repeating information should not change its informational value, should not increase its validity, change its veracity, or increase its influence on people's beliefs. However, simply repeating information *does* increase its subjective truth (Hasher, Goldstein, & Toppino, 1977; see Dechêne, Stahl, Hansen, & Wänke, 2010, for a review). This seemingly irrational tendency was already discussed and acknowledged by Wittgenstein in his *Philosohpische Untersuchungen* [Philosophical Investigations] (1955/1977). Wittgenstein famously stated that repeating informational input does not help to ascertain that information, and one cannot "buy several copies of the morning paper to ensure that the content is true" (p. 147). Similarly, Begg, Anas, and Farinacci (1992) stated that "there is no logical reason for repetition to affect rated truth or for earlier information to be trusted more than later information" (p. 447).

Repetition may thus seem "empty" from philosophical and logical perspectives; however, from a psychological perspective, repetition is a key element in learning and memory (Ebbinghaus, 1885/1971; Hintzman & Block, 1971; McClelland, McNaughton, & O'Reilly, 1995). It increases the subjective value of stimuli (Betsch, Plessner, Schwieren, & Gütig, 2001; Unkelbach, Fiedler, & Freytag, 2007; Zajonc, 1968), and it establishes and strengthens perceived links between stimuli as in associative and evaluative learning (De Houwer, Thomas, & Baeyens, 2001; Rescorla & Wagner, 1972). Considering this substantial impact of repetition on many psychological processes, it is less surprising that repetition also influences how people judge information's truth and impacts personal beliefs.

Repetition and Belief Formation 43

In experimental psychology, the phenomenon that simply repeating information increases its subjective truth (Dechêne et al., 2010; Hasher et al., 1977) is labeled the repetition-induced truth effect. This truth effect and its influence on the formation of beliefs is an empirically robust effect (see Dechêne et al., 2010, p. 239) and believing in the existence of this effect is certainly not a form of scientists fooling themselves (see Jussim, Stevens, Honeycutt, Anglin, & Fox, Chapter 15 this volume). It is also of great practical interest. For example, when information is ever more often shared, reposted online, or multiplied via social media, the increase in subjective truth due to mere repetition may explain the apparent increase in evidently false beliefs (see Myers, Chapter 5 this volume). Prominent examples are conspiracy theories (e.g., "9/11 was an inside job"; "Vaccinations cause autism"; see Douglas, Sutton, & Cichocka, Chapter 4 this volume; van Prooijen, Chapter 17 this volume), urban legends (e.g., "The hoover dam is built with dead bodies"; "Children tattoos contained LSD in the 1960s"), but also single pseudo facts (e.g., "The Great Wall of China is visible from the moon") or "fake" news (e.g., "FBI agent suspected in Hillary [Clinton] email leaks found dead in apartment murder-suicide"). Due to repetition, these statements might become more believable.

In the following, we will first provide examples of the effect and then explain its theoretical backgrounds. Based on these backgrounds, we will argue that repetition-induced truth has sometimes detrimental effects on what people believe to be true (e.g., pseudo facts, or "fake" news; see Myers, Chapter 5 this volume) when repetition comes from symbolic observations (e.g., social media, television, radio). Yet, we will argue that psychologically functional to believe repeated information more than novel information when repetition is based on direct observations.

Repetition-Induced Truth

The idea that repetition is a key variable in persuasion, subjective truth, and ultimately, the formation of beliefs about the world, is well recognized, not only in psychological journals. The classic treaty *The Crowd: A Study of the Popular Mind* by Gustave Le Bon (1895/1996), already stated:

> It was Napoleon, I believe, who said that there is only one figure in rhetoric of serious importance, namely, repetition. The thing affirmed comes by repetition to fix itself in the mind in such a way that *it is accepted in the end as a demonstrated truth.*
>
> (Le Bon, 1895/1996, bk II,
> ch. III: 2, n.p., italics added)

Similarly, in Aldous Huxley's (1932/2008) novel *Brave New World*, children are taught not only knowledge, but also moral lessons by repeating the same notions time and again while they sleep: "Sixty-two thousand four hundred repetitions make one truth (p. 47)."[1] And in general, people use the notion that repetition indicates information's truth with the simple rule of thumb that if they have learned something somewhere before, it is likely to be true. For sure, if someone remembers reading the information in the *Encyclopedia Britannica*, it is well justified to believe this information is true. However, as we will see, repetition effects extend well beyond what can be rationalized so easily. Repetition also influences people's beliefs if it comes from the identical source ("I told you, vaccinations cause autism"), if it is labeled as false ("It is false that vaccinations cause autism"), or even when the initial presentation is incompatible with the second presentation ("Vaccinations do not cause autism"; see below). So how does this strong influence of repetition on subjective truth and the formation of beliefs occur? Below, we provide a historical overview of the explanations for the repetition-induced truth effect.

A History of the Repetition-Induced Truth Effect

The Basic Effect

Hasher et al. (1977) presented the first empirical evidence of the repetition-induced truth effect in the psychological literature, and their basic design is still prevalent today. Participants heard statements from a large pool of topics and different subjects during a presentation phase (e.g., "The thigh bone is the longest bone in the human body") and were told that some of these are false and some are true. Factually, half of the statements were false, half were true. Two, four, and six weeks later, participants rated lists of "new" (not heard before) and "old" (heard before) statements on a scale from 1 ("definitely false") to 7 ("definitely true"). They found higher truth ratings for repeated compared to new statements even up to six weeks later. However, they provided no direct evidence for a psychological mechanism but concluded that people use mere frequency to attribute validity (i.e., "truth") to statements.

The Recognition Explanation

Going beyond the frequency-validity explanation, Bacon (1979) tested and offered the explanation that people may assign truth to repeated information simply because they remember the statements. Bacon showed that there is a correspondence between participants' recognition judgments (i.e., "old" vs. "new") and their rated truth; that is, whether they recognized a statement influenced the truth judgments. The data also contradicted the frequency explanation by Hasher and colleagues (1977) because the objective frequency status of a statement (i.e., repeated vs. novel) had less influence than the subjective repeated vs. novel status of that statement. Thus, Bacon

(1979) concluded that: "Consequently, the repetition effect is not really a repetition effect after all but a recognition effect" (p. 251). Please note that at this point, if recognition would be the sole correct explanation of the repetition-induced truth effect, then the effect would be indeed irrational and dysfunctional, as people might remember both lies and truths, and recognizing a lie should not increase its subjective truth. It would also be irrational for people to judge statements to be true just because they remember them from an experimental session two weeks earlier; because two weeks earlier, they also learned that they might be true or false (see above for the basic paradigm).

The Familiarity Explanation

Arkes, Boehm, and Xu (1991) offered and tested two explanations for the repetition-induced truth effect. The first mechanism underlying the effect the authors labeled as *referential validity*. If two independent sources provide the same information, that is, repeated information, then the information is more likely true, just because it is very unlikely that two independent sources provide the same false information. This follows because statements can be false in many different ways while there is usually only one true version of a statement. This is particularly true when it comes to statements about the physical world (see Alves, Koch, & Unkelbach, 2017, for a more general version of this argument). For example, Budapest may be a city in Romania or Argentina or Turkmenistan (all false), while there is only one correct statement: Budapest is a city in Hungary. This reasoning is also employed for judging the validity of eyewitness testimonies (i.e., two eyewitnesses independently reporting the same information makes it more likely true). It is also one of the most frequent strategies to assess validity when people search information online. For example, when two people independently praise the virtues of a given product in their reviews, or when two news sites independently report the same political events, they are more likely to be taken as true. For the repetition-induced truth effect, this implies that people recognize information but overlook that it comes from the same source as before (i.e., another experimental session rather than an independent outside source).

However, across their experiments, Arkes and colleagues (1991) found only evidence for their second suggested mechanism, namely that subjective familiarity with the statements determines judged truth. As familiarity also influences recognition judgments, subjective familiarity was a candidate for replacing recognition (Bacon, 1979) as the underlying mechanism of the repetition-induced truth effect. People may believe information if it feels familiar.

To pit recognition against familiarity, Begg et al. (1992) employed a so-called process dissociation procedure (see Jacoby & Kelley, 1992, for an easy introduction). Their participants heard statements from sources that were labeled as "true" or "false"; for example, given a male and a female speaker, participants learned that all statements by the male speaker would be false, and all statements by the female speaker would be true. Begg and colleagues (1992) found that repeated, and thus, more familiar statements from a "false" information source were more likely to be judged as true compared to new statements. Repeated, more familiar statements from a "true" information source, however, were most likely to be taken as true. Thus, the authors concluded that both familiarity and recognition independently contribute to judged truth.

The central role of familiarity was further supported by experiments showing that even statements labeled as blatant lies benefited from repetition (Brown & Nix, 1996), or that even information ("Crocodiles sleep with their eyes open") that directly contradicted the original information ("Crocodiles sleep with their eyes closed") became more believable due to the repetition of the semantic content (Garcia-Marques, Silva, Reber, & Unkelbach, 2015). These effects should not occur if people would factually remember the original encounter or recognize the statements.

The Fluency Explanation

The experiments by Begg and colleagues (1992) placed the repetition-induced truth effect into the larger category of effects caused by experiences (here: familiarity) elicited by the stimulus, such as the mere exposure effect (Mandler, Nakamura, & van Zandt, 1987; Zajonc, 1968), the revelation effect (Watkins & Peynircioglu, 1990; see also Topolinski & Reber, 2010), the false fame effect (Jacoby, Kelley, Brown, & Jasechko, 1989), or processing ease effects (see Strack, Chapter 9 this volume). Further, Whittlesea (1993) proposed that information familiarity is not a direct output from memory, but results from the automatic attribution that fluent processing of the respective information is due to a previous encounter. Thereby, processing fluency, which is the experienced ease of ongoing mental processes (Unkelbach & Greifeneder, 2013), became a candidate as the central explanatory construct for the repetition-induced truth effect.

Reber and Schwarz (1999) directly tested whether processing fluency (i.e., the experience of easy processing) influenced judged truth directly, without actually repeating information. Instead of repeating statements, they presented simple statements (e.g., "Osorno is a city in Chile") in fluent, easy-to-read colors (e.g., dark red or dark blue) or disfluent, difficult-to-read colors (e.g., green and yellow). Indeed, participants rated statements in difficult-to-read colors as less true compared to statements in easy-to-read colors. Similarly, McGlone and Tofighbakhsh (2000) showed that people believe aphorisms that rhyme and are thus fluently processed ("Woes unite foes") more than content-identical aphorisms that do not rhyme and are thus less fluently processed ("Woes unite enemies").

Repetition and Belief Formation   47

Fluency as the central explanatory construct for repetition–induced truth was further supported by experiments by Unkelbach (2007), which addressed two critical points: First, they showed that the repetition-induced truth effect it is not a mere exposure effect. Second, it is indeed processing fluency that mediates the effect. Concerning the first point, if repetition-induced truth is indeed due to subjective experiences elicited by a stimulus (e.g., a statement "feels" familiar), it might not be a fluency effect, but rather a mere exposure effect (Zajonc, 1968, 2001). The mere exposure effect is the acquisition of preferences due to the repeated exposure to stimuli; in other words, people like repeated things. The repetition-induced truth effect may then follow simply because people like repeated information more than novel information and express this preference with a positive truth rating. Alternatively, people might employ a "positive, therefore true" heuristic (Unkelbach, Bayer, Alves, Koch, & Stahl, 2011; but see Hilbig, 2012).

Unkelbach (2007) argued that fluency effects depend on the interpretation of the fluency experience (see also Unkelbach & Greifeneder, 2013), and a truth effect follows because people interpret fluent processing as a cue for a statement's truth. If people learn a different interpretation of processing fluency when judging truth (e.g., fluent processing as a cue for a statements falseness), a fluency explanation predicts that people should take repeated and thus fluently processed information as false instead of true. In contrast, mere exposure should unconditionally lead to higher rated truth of repeated information. Thus, participants encountered statements in a training phase for which truth correlated with their processing fluency. In a standard condition, truth and processing fluency were positively correlated; for example, true statements such as "Dolphins are mammals" were presented in dark blue or dark red and thus easy to read, while false statements such as "Lead is lighter than aluminum" were presented in light green or light yellow and thus difficult to read. In a reversed condition, *false* statements were easy to read and *true* statements were difficult to read. This latter condition reversed the color-based truth effect found by Reber and Schwarz (1999). In the following test phase, when participants judged the truth of easy or difficult to read statements, participants judged "easy" statements as false and "difficult" statements as true (see Olds & Westerman, 2012, for similar fluency reversals). The training with colors also reversed the repetition-induced truth based on repeated and novel statements that were both printed in black against a white background; that is, the fluency training transferred from one fluency source (i.e., color contrast) to another fluency source (i.e., repetition).

This finding clearly showed that it is people's interpretation of processing fluency that underlies the repetition-induced truth effect; otherwise standard vs. reversed training with color should not influence the effect of repetition on judged truth. Further, mere exposure would have predicted

48 *Christian Unkelbach and Alex Koch*

a main effect of repetition independent of standard vs. reversed training with color. Thus, processing fluency was established as the construct that explains both the repetition-based and non-repetition-based (e.g., color, rhyming) truth effect.

Yet, empirically, non-repetition-based fluency manipulations usually yield smaller truth effects than repetition-induced truth effects. For example, Hasher and colleagues (1977) reported a truth effect of $d = 0.84$ for repeated compared to new statements (estimated from Hasher et al., 1977, Table 1). The color-based truth effect by Reber and Schwarz (1999) was substantially smaller, namely $d = 0.13$. With some exceptions (e.g., Unkelbach, 2007, Experiment 2), stronger repetition-based truth effects are apparent in most data sets (e.g., compare Hansen, Dechêne, & Wänke, 2008, with Dechêne et al., 2010). Obviously, this could be due to fluency effects from repetition being stronger than fluency effects from, for example, color contrast. However, the pattern may also suggest that processing fluency and repetition influence truth via different processes. Addressing this issue, Silva, Garcia-Marques, and Mello (2016) directly compared perception-based and repetition-based fluency effects on truth and concluded that repetition and perceptual fluency influence truth judgments in different ways: "It seems that repetition has a stronger connection to truth, which is also less malleable than in the case of perceptual fluency [. . .] truth effects due to perceptual fluency are likely to have another origin" (p. 13).

Thus, on a functional level, repeating information increases its believability and subjective truth; on a process level, the specific cognitive mechanisms are still under investigation, and in the next section, we review an alternative explanation. While so far, repetition seems to be a path to gullibility, the following also suggests potential adaptive functions of people believing repeated information in particular, and easily processed information in general.

A Referential Theory

Besides smaller truth effects based on perceptual compared to repetition-induced fluency, the fluency explanation necessitated additional assumptions. In a nutshell: Why do people use fluency as a cue for truth rather than for falseness? One answer was provided by assuming that people learn to interpret processing fluency as "truth" (Unkelbach, 2006; Unkelbach & Greifeneder, 2013). For example, on the receptive side, people may learn that fluently processed information they hear is indeed true. Conversely, people may learn that telling the truth is easier (more fluent) than producing a lie. Another answer was that people have lay theories for the meaning of processing fluency (Greifeneder & Schwarz, 2014; Schwarz, 2004). That is, people either need to learn that fluent processing is indicative of truth, or they need a lay theory that makes the connection between truth and fluency (e.g., "If it feels fluent, it must be true"). This is non-trivial because one must assume benevolent learning environments that allow the link between truth and fluency to establish, or a source of a metacognitive theory that establishes the truth–fluency link.

To address the empirical difference between "pure" fluency effects and repetition-based fluency effects, and to address the additional assumptions about the source of the interpretation, Unkelbach and Rom (2017) proposed a *referential theory* of the repetition-induced truth effect. The theory starts from a philosophical point asking how people may in general judge the validity, veracity, or "truth" of a given piece of information. Most philosophical theories of truth incorporate two major elements for such judgments, namely correspondence and coherence (Kirkham, 1992).

Simplified, correspondence is the relation of information with physical reality. For example, if one hears "Mary is taller than Paul" and observes that Mary is taller than Paul in reality, the statement is true. Psychologically, one may thus see correspondence as references in memory that provide meaning for the elements of a given statement; upon hearing "Mary is taller than Paul," one may remember seeing those and judge the statement as true based on this reference in memory.

Coherence is then the relational consistency of these corresponding references. For example, one may have never seen Mary and Paul together, but one may remember Mary is a relatively small woman and Paul is a relatively tall man. Thus, the references that provide meaning for the labels "Mary" and "Paul" in memory might be incoherent with the statement "Mary is taller than Paul."

Similarly, the statement "The world's highest tree is a Sequoia tree in California" should have corresponding references in memory that provide meaning for the statement's elements. Upon hearing the statement, most people will have memory references for the elements "world," "Sequoia," "tree," and "California"; these elements correspond with physical reality. In addition, for most people, these corresponding references will be highly coherent. For example, California is a U.S. American state within the world, Sequoias are trees that grow in California, and Sequoias are also typically tall trees. Thus, the statement has corresponding references that are coherent and is thus likely to be judged as "true."

How correspondence and coherence may inform truth becomes apparent if one changes one element in the statement: "The world's highest tree is a Sequoia tree in Antarctica." Both statements have the same number of corresponding references. Yet, assuming that people have information in memory about California and Antarctica, the California statement is highly coherent, while the Antarctica statement is incoherent. Most people will have a memory representation of Antarctic that does not allow the growth of Sequoia trees. As a result, people on average should believe the California statement, but not the Antarctica one. Figure 3.1 illustrates this process.

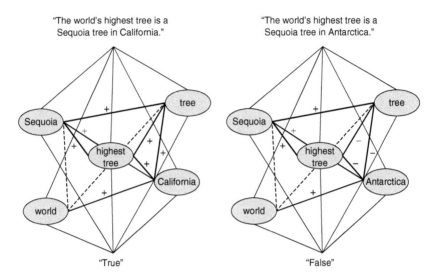

Figure 3.1 Illustration of how correspondence and coherence determine subjective truth. The solid grey lines indicate incoming information; here, a statement about trees. The grey circles ("tree") represent references in memory that provide meaning to the elements in the statement. Solid black lines indicate links between these references and the strength of the line indicates link strength. Dotted lines indicate links that are instigated by the incoming information. Finally, "plus" signs indicate an excitatory link and "minus" signs indicate inhibitory links. Coherence, defined as a parallel-constraint satisfaction solution (Kunda & Thagard, 1996), then defines the resulting subjective experience. If the statement's corresponding references form a coherent network, a "true" response follows, while an incoherent network of references results in a "false" response.

Source: Adapted from Unkelbach and Rom (2017, fig. 1a).

Figure 3.2 then illustrates the implications of this referential process for the repetition-induced truth effect. When people hear or read a novel piece of information or a novel statement (illustrated by the light grey lines), as in the typical exposure phase of a truth experiment in the tradition of Hasher and colleagues (1977), the statement activates corresponding references within memory (e.g., "California" etc.) and their respective links. For novel information in the statement (e.g., "Sequoia" for a person who does not know a Sequoia is a type of tree), a corresponding reference will be formed and – if no inconsistency is apparent – coherently linked to the activated corresponding references ("Sequoias are trees that grow in California"). In the subsequent test phase, repeated statements will thus have more corresponding references that are coherently linked (see the right panel of Figure 3.2) than new statements; this is why new statements will appear relatively less true than repeated statements.

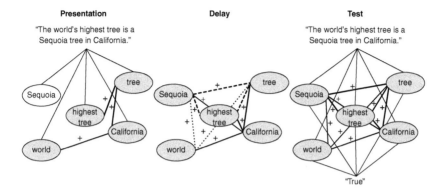

Figure 3.2 An illustration of the repetition-induced truth effect according to a referential explanation. The left panel shows the presentation phase when participants encounter a statement for the first time. If it is not incoherent with existing references (see Australia vs. Antarctica), the statement's corresponding references are linked within memory, as shown in the middle panel. At test, all of the repeated statements' elements are coherently linked, leading to a "true" judgment, as shown in the right panel. Novel statements at test are equivalent to the left panel. As the left panel has fewer coherently linked references compared to the right panel, a repetition-induced truth effect follows.

Source: Adapted from Unkelbach and Rom (2017, fig. 1b).

A truth effect based on fluent processing without repetition then occurs because many corresponding references that are coherently linked increase a statement's fluency of processing; thus, fluency is also a function of the coherently linked corresponding references, rather than the ultimate explanation why repetition increases judged truth. Conceptualizing processing fluency this way solves the theoretical challenge of how people learn to associate fluent processing with truth. The referential theory assumes that people believe statements and judge them to be true when they activate many coherently linked corresponding references. As many activated, coherently linked corresponding references increase both subjective truth and subjective processing fluency, people experience and learn that truth and fluency are correlated. This learned interpretation of processing fluency as a truth signal then leads to fluency-based truth illusions when fluency is manipulated independent of repetition (e.g., by color contrast or rhyming).

It is also important to emphasize that the referential theory predicts that new statements do not appear false, but simply as relatively less true, a boundary condition that is established for typical truth paradigms (Hansen et al., 2008; see also Wänke & Hansen, 2015). The theory thereby shares Gilbert's (1991) view that people by default believe incoming information the same way they believe the existence of physical objects upon seeing them. However, new statements will appear relatively less true than repeated statements because they have typically less corresponding references that are coherently linked.

The theory is consistent with philosophical considerations of how people judge truth, and it explains the available data on the repetition-induced truth effect; statements that have more coherently linked corresponding references will also be higher in recognition rates, higher in familiarity, and higher in fluent processing. And if one assumes that the links between items in memory constitute "knowledge" (e.g., a Sequoia is a tree), the theory also explains the interactions of knowledge and repetition when judging truth (Fazio, Brashier, Payne, & Marsh, 2015; Unkelbach & Stahl, 2009).

Finally, the referential theory also explains political and other kinds of partisanship or, in other words, why people with agendas and tastes maintain beliefs that contradict others' beliefs. For example, conservatives may repeatedly think about, talk with fellow conservatives about, or one-sidedly read or hear about positive but not necessarily true aspects of conservative politics. This should increase the amount of coherently linked corresponding references activated by statements conveying the same or related positive aspects (e.g., "Unemployment was at an all-time low during Reagan's presidency"). As a result, statements in favor of conservative, past society should become more and more believable, whereas due to an increased number of incoherent memory links and decreased processing fluency statements in favor of democratic views should become less believable (vice versa for democratic partisans, of course).

In sum, the referential theory thus suggests a cognitive mechanism of how repetition increases information believability and subjective truth. It also provides a cognitive explanation why people believe information that fits their own agendas and interests, and how these become self-reinforcing overtime. The localized nature of these networks also allows for conflicting beliefs within the same person. And most importantly for the present purposes, it explains why people may be gullible and believe information that they should not believe. Conspiracy theories, urban legends, pseudo facts, and "fake" news may become believable not due to motivated reasoning, political agendas, or simple stupidity (see Dunning, Chapter 12 this volume), but because repetition instigated local networks of coherent references that made this information more believable.

Why Repetition-Induced Truth May Be Functional

The repetition-induced truth effect exemplifies human gullibility and is also a good example how people are blind to the process that generates the data on which they base their judgments (see Fiedler, Chapter 7 this volume). Again, simply telling people the same thing twice should not make the message more believable, especially if the source is identical. But apparently it does. However, we want to argue that the repetition-induced truth effect might be functional after all, both from a fluency perspective as well as from a referential perspective.

To argue that such a truth effect might be functional necessitates a definition of what is functional, rational, or adaptive. This is not as trivial as it seems (see Reber & Unkelbach, 2010, for a more detailed treaty). For example, James (1909/1975) argued that a belief is justified if the belief increases utility for the believer. However, such a utilitarian notion of belief justification does not necessarily align with the factual state of affairs or what is commonly seen as "truth." For example, people with a family history of cardiovascular diseases might worry about their blood pressure, thereby increasing their blood pressure and increase the chance of cardiovascular malfunctions. Believing the factually false information that they have no such family history may actually have beneficial effects for their blood pressure and thus be functional from a utilitarian perspective (see Kirkham, 1992, for other justifications of belief).

Here, we do not follow such a utilitarian approach to belief justification, but follow a naïve empirical or rational approach. First, one needs to assume that there *exists* a true empirical state of affairs. Second, beliefs that correspond more with these true states are to be preferred over beliefs that correspond less with these true states. That is, the belief that "the earth is round" is preferable over the belief that "the earth is flat." Although the former is not a perfectly true description of the oblate spheroid form of the earth, it corresponds more with the empirically accessible facts about the earth's shape. Third, an effect, such as the repetition-induced truth effect, is functional if the existence of the effect leads on average to more beliefs that correspond with the assumed true state of affairs than when the effect would be non-existent. Put more simply, does the repetition-induced truth effect lead to more "true" beliefs or to more "false" beliefs? In the following, we address such a functionality both from a fluency perspective and the referential perspective.

Functionality from a Fluency Perspective

Unkelbach (2007) explicitly assumed that people use processing fluency in truth judgments because there is a correlation between factual truth and processing fluency. In other words, there should be a positive ecological correlation between people's fluency experiences and truth (see also Hertwig, Herzog, Schooler, & Reimer, 2008; Herzog & Hertwig, 2013). This positive correlation may exist for a normative as well as a practical reason. First, normatively, Grice (1975) proposed the maxims of quality and manner in interpersonal communications. That is, people following theses maxims should communicate truthfully (quality) and in a fluent, comprehensible way (manner). As people follow these two maxims differentially (e.g., people in a negative mood follow Grice's maxims more than people in a positive mood; Koch, Forgas, & Matovic, 2013; Forgas, Chapter 10 this volume), message receivers should observe a positive correlation between truth and processing fluency.

Practically, most people should communicate truthfully most of the time, as it is hard to imagine a functional society in which false information is more frequent than true information. Thus, true information should be more frequent compared to false information in the world. Higher frequency entails statistically a higher chance of redundancy and repetition (see also Alves, Koch, & Unkelbach, 2017; Koch, Alves, Krüger, & Unkelbach, 2016), also contributing to a correlation between truth and processing fluency. In addition, physical reality constrains truth such that there is only one way for information to be true, but many ways to be false. For example, one may state that the earth's shape is a plane, a cube, or sphere, but only one can be true. Similarly, the world's highest tree might be a spruce, a sequoia, or a Eucalyptus tree, but only one can be true. Thus, due to the high variety of potentially false information, true information is more likely to be repeated (leaving aside strategic miscommunication or false facts/fake news that are often repeated, see below).

One might reformulate this assumed positive correlation into the assumption that the conditional probability of truth given a fluently processed statement (or any information) is larger than 50% (see Reber & Unkelbach, 2010, for a full treaty). Given our definition above (i.e., beliefs are the more justified the more they correspond to truth), the repetition-induced truth effect is thus functional as long as $p(\text{true} \,|\, \text{fluent}) > .50$; that is, it is functional to believe fluently processed information as long as the probability that this fluently processed information is true is larger than 50%. Given the practical as well as the normative considerations outlined above, this relation is very likely to hold.

Functionality from a Referential Perspective

Again, from a fluency perspective, one might state that the effect is functional as long as fluency is an ecologically valid cue (see also Unkelbach & Greifeneder, 2013). The $p(\text{true} \,|\, \text{fluent}) > .50$ assumption, may remain untestable empirically, however. A similar empirical problem arises from the referential perspective, although one can also make a logical argument from this side with a simple thought experiment.

The sole necessary assumption to argue for the functionality of repetition-induced truth from a referential perspective is that experiences with regards to the physical world are consistent. If one imagines an environment in which information is only available from direct experiences and observations (e.g., immediately experiencing or observing information), but not from indirect or symbolic experiences or observations (e.g., language or pictures). Now imagine that someone in this environment directly observes that Person A gets sick after consuming Plant X. From a referential perspective, this should establish the according links between the corresponding references "Person A," "Plant X," and "sick." Now the observer sees that Person B, C, and D also get sick after eating Plant X. The resulting network of the established links will highlight "Plant X" and "sick," as these are the corresponding references in memory that are common to all the observations. Thus, there should be a strong association between "Plant X" and "sick," which might lead to an evaluation of the proposition that "Plant X is poisonous" as true.

However, if the observer has already seen many other people consuming Plant X and not getting sick, the proposition that Plant X is poisonous will be judged as false. Or, if the observer has consumed Plant B himself/herself and does not get sick, this would provide a strong incoherent corresponding reference (Kunda & Thaggard, 1996). As long as the informational input is based on direct observations and experiences, the referential network of corresponding references and their (in)coherence will approximate the "true" state of the world and the corresponding beliefs. In other words, assuming that there *is* a true state of the world, the present assumptions will lead to beliefs about the world that are approximately correct. The truth effect might thus be rooted in a direct, experience-based learning system that effectively approximates the truth about the world. And the same way the visual system is calibrated by haptic experiences (i.e., learning that the world is not upside down), people might learn that beliefs are true if they have a higher number of coherent compared to incoherent corresponding references in memory and can thus be processed fluently. Thus, the effect would be functional according to our definition (i.e., beliefs should approximate truth) as long as it is based on direct experiences and observations.

Detrimental Effects of Repetition–Induced Truth

The two caveats for the argument that repletion-induced truth might be functional are immediately apparent. From a fluency perspective, one might argue that in times of effortless automated online communication, false information is as likely to occur as true information. If Grice's (1975) quality but not manner maxim is strategically violated, and if the false information is strategically repeated, fluency might signal falsehood and the repetition-induced truth effect would no longer be functional. Such cases occur typically under what is labeled "propaganda," but might be generalized to any strategic communication attempt. Interestingly, Le Bon (1895/1996) already listed repetition in his chapter on how leaders might control the masses.

Second, from a referential perspective, truth by repetition may no longer functional if memory is no longer based on direct observations and experiences, but on symbolic experiences mediated by language because some information is more likely to be communicated than other information. For example, our observer of persons eating Plant X might not see himself/herself cases Person A–D but read about them in the newspaper, hear about them in the radio, or find out about them on the Internet. Why

56 Christian Unkelbach and Alex Koch

such symbolic experiences may reduce the functionality of inferring truth from coherence and fluency by repetition is immediately apparent: in an environment of direct observations, all persons eating the plant have an approximately equal chance to be observed. As a result, if the factual probability of getting sick after eating Plant X is low, one will observe few cases of sickness after consuming the plant but many cases of Plant X consumptions followed well-being. This will prevent the erroneous belief that Plant X is poisonous. In an environment of symbolic communication (i.e., social media, television) that prioritizes novel and exceptional news over representatively sampled news (see Fiedler, Chapter 7 this volume), all the consumption cases without sickness will be most likely not reported, preventing the corresponding references to be established and incoherently linked to "Plant X" and "sick." Rather, by all likelihood, the few sickness cases will get reported, and most likely repeatedly, increasing the probability that a proposition such as "Plant X causes sickness" will have many coherent corresponding references and thus will become an established belief.

The example parallels some of the most unfortunate false beliefs (here, we use "false" as improbable by any scientific standard; e.g., "Vaccinations cause autism"). All vaccinated children that never showed any signs of autism will not be symbolically represented (i.e., appear in the media); if anything, they may enter a medical summary statistic. Thus, a single case of autism though for a child who received a vaccination, without any causality implied, to be clear, that will get symbolic representation has almost the same impact and value as the summary statistic of all the cases where no evidence for autism after vaccinations was found (i.e., it may be represented as a single corresponding reference). In short, a pediatrician forming beliefs based on experience may not come to the belief that vaccinations cause autism. The layperson surfing the internet on the other hand may very well develop this belief, simply because it is repeated so frequently. Thus, although the referential perspective implies that the repetition-induced truth effect is functional if based on direct experiences and observations, it also provides a model for how symbolic communication may lead to the formation of false beliefs.

Is Repetition-Induced Truth Avoidable?

Assuming that repetition-induced truth is a form of gullibility, a final question is how one may avoid or ameliorate this form of gullibility. The present volume suggests some ways in which repetition-induced truth may be avoided. For example, a mindset of distrust (Mayo, Chapter 8 this volume) may lead people to consider the opposite and therefore lead to less impact of information repetition. Similarly, negative mood (Forgas, Chapter 10 this volume) might inoculate people against the influence of information repetition. Or most generally, any cue that might trigger more skepticism for internal signals such as bad smells (Schwarz & Lee, Chapter 13 this volume) or cultural disfluency (Oyserman, Chapter 14 this volume) may reduce repetition-induced truth. However, to the best of our knowledge, the attempts in the literature to curb the effects of repetition on judged truth were remarkably unsuccessful. For example, Fazio and colleagues (2015) selected statements for their truth effect paradigms for which participants should have knowledge. Nevertheless, the influence of repetition did not differ between such "possible-to-know" statements and "impossible-to-know" statements. Similarly, Unkelbach and Greifeneder (2018) found that when participants are given external advice whether a statement is true or not, the repetition influence remains stable, even when this advice is supposedly 100% valid. Thus, although the present volume suggests some paths to cure this form of gullibility, the empirical evidence so far suggests that the influence of repetition on judged truth will prevail.

Conclusion

The repetition-induced truth effect is a prime example of human gullibility. Whether it turns lies into truths, fiction to fact, or advertisements into successful persuasion, it is a seemingly easy-to-exploit effect. Based on the two explanations for the effect, the fluency explanation and the referential explanation, however, we argue that the effect is functional when information comes from direct experiences and observations. In an environment of direct experiences and observations, easily processed information is more likely true than false, and because nature does not contradict itself, networks of coherent references lead to the formation of correct beliefs. Thus, inferring truth from repetition may be an easy and useful shortcut to adequate truth judgment. However, in an environment of indirect and symbolic observations, repetition-induced truth may lead to the formation of incorrect beliefs. To the best of our knowledge, though, the belief that the highest tree in the world is a Sequoia tree in California, is correct.

Note

1 Please note that the character in whose train of thoughts this statement occurs, Bernard Marx, factually does not endorse this practice and reflects on the sentiment with the internal exclamation: "Idiots!"

References

Alves, H., Koch, A., & Unkelbach, C. (2017). The "common good" phenomenon: Why similarities are positive and differences are negative. *Journal of Experimental Psychology: General, 146,* 512–528.

Arkes, H. R., Boehm, L. E., & Xu, G. (1991). Determinants of judged validity. *Journal of Experimental Social Psychology, 27,* 576–605.

Bacon, F. T. (1979). Credibility of repeated statements: Memory for trivia. *Journal of Experimental Psychology: Human Learning and Memory, 5,* 241–252.

58 Christian Unkelbach and Alex Koch

Begg, I. M., Anas, A., & Farinacci, S. (1992). Dissociation of processes in belief: Source recollection, statement familiarity, and the illusion of truth. *Journal of Experimental Psychology: General, 121*, 446–458.

Betsch, T., Plessner, H., Schwieren, C., & Gütig, R. (2001). I like it but I don't know why: A value-account approach to implicit attitude formation. *Personality and Social Psychology Bulletin, 27*, 242–253.

Brown, A. S., & Nix, L. A. (1996). Turning lies into truths: Referential validation of falsehoods. *Journal of Experimental Psychology: Learning, Memory, and Cognition, 22*, 1088–1100.

Dawes, R. M. (1979). The robust beauty of improper linear models in decision making. *American Psychologist, 34*, 571–582.

Dechêne, A., Stahl, C., Hansen, J., & Wänke, M. (2010). The truth about the truth: A meta-analytic review of the truth effect. *Personality and Social Psychology Review, 14*, 238–257.

De Houwer, J., Thomas, S., & Baeyens, F. (2001). Association learning of likes and dislikes: A review of 25 years of research on human evaluative conditioning. *Psychological Bulletin, 127*, 853–869.

Ebbinghaus, H. (1885/1971). *Über das Gedächtnis. Untersuchungen zur experimentellen Psychologie [Concerning memory: Investigations in experimental psychology]*. Darmstadt, Germany: Wissenschaftliche Buchgesellschaft.

Fazio, L. K., Brashier, N. M., Payne, B. K., & Marsh, E. J. (2015). Knowledge does not protect against illusory truth. *Journal of Experimental Psychology: General, 144*, 993–1002.

Garcia-Marques, T., Silva, R. R., Reber, R., & Unkelbach, C. (2015). Hearing a statement now and believing the opposite later. *Journal of Experimental Social Psychology, 56*, 126–129.

Gilbert, D. T. (1991). How mental systems believe. *American Psychologist, 46*, 107–119.

Greifeneder, R., & Schwarz, N. (2014). Metacognitive processes and subjective experience. In J. W. Sherman, B. Gawronski, & Y. Trope (Eds.), *Dual-process theories of the social mind* (pp. 314–327). New York, NY: Guilford Press.

Grice, H. P. (1975). Logic and conversation. In P. Cole & J. L. Morgan (Eds.), *Syntax and semantics: Vol. 3. Speech acts* (pp. 41–58). New York, NY: Academic Press.

Hansen, J., Dechêne, A., & Wänke, M. (2008). Discrepant fluency increases subjective truth. *Journal of Experimental Social Psychology, 44*, 687–691.

Hasher, L., Goldstein, D., & Toppino, T. (1977). Frequency and the conference of referential validity. *Journal of Verbal Learning and Verbal Behavior, 16*, 107–112.

Hertwig, R., Herzog, S. M., Schooler, L. J., & Reimer, T. (2008). Fluency heuristic: A model of how the mind exploits a by-product of information retrieval. *Journal of Experimental Psychology: Learning, Memory, and Cognition, 34*, 1191–1206.

Herzog, S. M., & Hertwig, R. (2013). The ecological validity of fluency. In C. Unkelbach & R. Greifender (Eds.), *The experience of thinking: How the fluency of mental processes influences cognition and behaviour* (pp. 190–219). New York, NY: Psychology Press.

Hilbig, B. E. (2012). How framing statistical statements affects subjective veracity: Validation and application of a multinomial model for judgments of truth. *Cognition, 125*, 37–48.

Repetition and Belief Formation 59

Hintzman, D. L., & Block, R. A. (1971). Repetition and memory: Evidence for a multiple-trace hypothesis. *Journal of Experimental Psychology, 88*, 297–306.

Huxley, A. (1932/2008). *Brave new world*. Stuttgart, Germany: Ernst Klett Sprachen.

Jacoby, L. L., & Kelley, C. M. (1992). A process-dissociation framework for investigating unconscious influences: Freudian slips, projective tests, subliminal perception, and signal detection theory. *Current Directions in Psychological Science, 1*, 174–179.

Jacoby, L. L., Kelley, C., Brown, J., & Jasechko, J. (1989). Becoming famous overnight: Limits on the ability to avoid unconscious influences of the past. *Journal of Personality and Social Psychology, 56*, 326–338.

James, W. (1909/1975). *The meaning of truth* (Vol. 2). Cambridge, MA: Harvard University Press.

Kirkham, R. L. (1992). *Theories of truth: A critical introduction*. Cambridge, MA: Harvard University Press.

Koch, A. S., Alves, H., Krüger, T., & Unkelbach, C. (2016). A general valence asymmetry in similarity: Good is more alike than bad. *Journal of Experimental Psychology: Learning, Memory, and Cognition, 42*, 1171–1192.

Koch, A. S., Forgas, J. P., & Matovic, D. (2013). Can negative mood improve your conversation? Affective influences on conforming to Grice's communication norms. *European Journal of Social Psychology, 43*, 326–334.

Kunda, Z., & Thagard, P. (1996). Forming impressions from stereotypes, traits, and behaviors: A parallel-constraint-satisfaction theory. *Psychological Review, 103*, 284–308.

Le Bon, Gustave (1895/1996). *The crowd: A study of the popular mind / Psychologie des foules*. Project Gutenberg Etext. Retrieved from www.gutenberg.org/cache/epub/445/pg445.html.

Mandler, G., Nakamura, Y., & van Zandt, B. J. (1987). Nonspecific effects of exposure on stimuli that cannot be recognized. *Journal of Experimental Psychology: Learning, Memory, and Cognition, 13*, 646–648.

McClelland, J. L., McNaughton, B. L., & O'Reilly, R. C. (1995). Why there are complementary learning systems in the hippocampus and neocortex: Insights from the successes and failures of connectionist models of learning and memory. *Psychological Review, 102*, 419–457.

McGlone, M. S., & Tofighbakhsh, J. (2000). Birds of a feather flock conjointly (?): Rhyme as reason in aphorisms. *Psychological Science, 11*, 424–428.

Olds, J. M., & Westerman, D. L. (2012). Can fluency be interpreted as novelty? Retraining the interpretation of fluency in recognition memory. *Journal of Experimental Psychology: Learning, Memory, and Cognition, 38*, 653–664.

Petty, R. E., & Cacioppo, J. T. (1986). The elaboration likelihood model of persuasion. *Advances in Experimental Social Psychology, 19*, 123–205.

Petty, R. E., Wells, G. L., & Brock, T. C. (1976). Distraction can enhance or reduce yielding to propaganda: Thought disruption versus effort justification. *Journal of Personality and Social Psychology, 34*, 874–884.

Reber, R., & Schwarz, N. (1999). Effects of perceptual fluency on judgments of truth. *Consciousness and Cognition, 8*, 338–342.

Reber, R., & Unkelbach, C. (2010). The epistemic status of processing fluency as source for judgments of truth. *Review of Philosophy and Psychology, 1*, 563–581.

Rescorla, R. A., & Wagner, A. R. (1972). A theory of Pavlovian conditioning: Variations in the effectiveness of reinforcement and nonreinforcement. *Classical Conditioning II: Current Research and Theory, 2*, 64–99.

Schwarz, N. (2004). Meta-cognitive experiences in consumer judgment and decision making. *Journal of Consumer Research, 14*, 332–348.

Silva, R. R., Garcia-Marques, T., & Mello, J. (2016). The differential effects of fluency due to repetition and fluency due to color contrast on judgments of truth. *Psychological Research, 80*, 821–837.

Topolinski, S., & Reber, R. (2010). Gaining insight into the "Aha" experience. *Current Directions in Psychological Science, 19*, 402–405.

Unkelbach, C. (2006). The learned interpretation of cognitive fluency. *Psychological Science, 17*, 339–345.

Unkelbach, C. (2007). Reversing the truth effect: Learning the interpretation of processing fluency in judgments of truth. *Journal of Experimental Psychology: Learning, Memory, and Cognition, 33*, 219–230.

Unkelbach, C., Bayer, M., Alves, H., Koch, A., & Stahl, C. (2011). Fluency and positivity as possible causes of the truth effect. *Consciousness and Cognition, 20*, 594–602.

Unkelbach, C., Fiedler, K., & Freytag, P. (2007). Information repetition in evaluative judgments: Easy to monitor, hard to control. *Organizational Behavior and Human Decision Processes, 103*, 37–52.

Unkelbach, C., & Greifeneder, R. (2013). A general model of fluency effects in judgment and decision making. In C. Unkelbach & R. Greifeneder (Eds.), *The experience of thinking: How the fluency of mental processes influences cognition and behaviour* (pp. 11–32). New York, NY: Psychology Press.

Unkelbach, C., & Greifeneder, R. (2018). Experiential fluency and declarative advice jointly inform judgments of truth. *Journal of Experimental Social Psychology, 79*, 78–86.

Unkelbach, C., & Rom, S. C. (2017). A referential theory of the repetition-induced truth effect. *Cognition, 160*, 110–126.

Unkelbach, C., & Stahl, C. (2009). A multinomial modeling approach to dissociate different components of the truth effect. *Consciousness and Cognition, 18*, 22–38.

Wänke, M., & Hansen, J. (2015). Relative processing fluency. *Current Directions in Psychological Science, 24*, 195–199.

Watkins, M. J., & Peynircioglu, Z. F. (1990). The revelation effect: When disguising test items induces recognition. *Journal of Experimental Psychology: Learning, Memory, and Cognition, 16*, 1012–1020.

Whittlesea, B. W. (1993). Illusions of familiarity. *Journal of Experimental Psychology: Learning, Memory, and Cognition, 19*, 1235–1253.

Wilson, T. D., & Brekke, N. (1994). Mental contamination and mental correction: unwanted influences on judgments and evaluations. *Psychological Bulletin, 116*, 117–142.

Wittgenstein, L. (1955/1977). *Philosohpische Untersuchungen* [Philosophical investigations]. Frankfurt, Germany: Suhrkamp.

Zajonc, R. B. (1968). Attitudinal effects of mere exposure. *Journal of Personality and Social Psychology, 9*, 1–27.

Zajonc, R. B. (2001). Mere exposure: A gateway to the subliminal. *Current Directions in Psychological Science, 10*, 224–228.

4 Belief in Conspiracy Theories
Looking Beyond Gullibility

Karen M. Douglas, Robbie M. Sutton, and Aleksandra Cichocka
UNIVERSITY OF KENT

Conspiracy theories attribute significant social and political events to the actions of controlling and malevolent groups (e.g., Goertzel, 1994; Uscinski & Parent, 2014). For example, well known conspiracy theories suggest that the 9/11 attacks on the Twin Towers were an "inside job" orchestrated by the Bush administration to justify the war on terror, and that Diana, Princess of Wales was assassinated by the British Secret Service because she was a nuisance to the British establishment. Belief in conspiracy theories is more common than you might think. For example, over half of Americans believe that Lee Harvey Oswald did not act alone in the assassination of President John F. Kennedy (Jensen, 2013; Swift, 2013). Furthermore, recent polls suggest that nearly half of British people believe that the government is hiding information about the number of immigrants in the UK (Moore, 2016). There is therefore no doubt that conspiracy theories are popular. But are conspiracy believers gullible? Will they believe *anything* they hear? In this chapter, we argue that the research evidence to date does not support this conclusion. Instead, conspiracy theories seem to appeal to people when they need to satisfy important psychological motives.

Specifically, Douglas, Sutton, and Cichocka (2017) argued that people are drawn to conspiracy theories when – compared with nonconspiracy explanations – they seem to satisfy important social psychological motives that can be characterized as epistemic (e.g., the desire for understanding, accuracy, and subjective certainty), existential (e.g., the desire for control and security), and social (e.g., the desire to maintain a positive image of the self or group). We outline each of these motives in turn, highlighting evidence that people are drawn to conspiracy theories for these reasons in particular, and not because they will simply believe anything they hear. We also consider whether such psychological motives are met by believing in conspiracy theories. Finally, we take a broader perspective on how future research might expand this taxonomy, and directions that research on the psychology of conspiracy theories might take in future to further test the reasons why people believe in conspiracy theories.

Epistemic Motives

Heider (1958) argued that finding causal explanations for events is an important part of creating a consistent and accurate understanding of the world. People want to know the truth and be certain of that truth. They are also curious and want to find out new information. Furthermore, people are generally intolerant of uncertainty and want to find meaning even when events may seem random or very unlikely (Dugas, Gosselin, & Ladouceur, 2001). As causal explanations for events, conspiracy theories might appear to satisfy these motives. Specifically, they seem to provide broad, internally consistent explanations that allow people to maintain beliefs in situations of uncertainty and contradiction. They are often resistant to falsification by proposing that multiple actors coordinate and cover up their actions, and by implication that people who try to debunk them are part of the conspiracy (Lewandowsky et al., 2015). Conspiracy theories can also allow people to maintain consistency in their own beliefs (e.g., that climate change is not a serious issue) by characterizing evidence (e.g., scientific findings) as conspiracies themselves (Grimes, 2016; Lewandowsky, Oberauer, & Gignac, 2013).

Research supports this view that people turn to conspiracy theories for epistemic reasons. First, research consistently links conspiracy beliefs with uncertainty. Van Prooijen and Jostmann (2013) hypothesized that uncertainty should increase the extent to which people interpret signs suggesting that authorities are moral (or immoral) as evidence of conspiracy. In one of their experiments, the researchers manipulated uncertainty salience by asking people to think about the emotions they experience during times of uncertainty, or when they are watching television (control). Following the manipulation, they were presented with information about the morality or immorality of oil companies, before completing conspiracy-related questions about oil companies' involvement in the Iraq war. Van Prooijen and Jostmann (2013) found that people were only influenced by the morality information (i.e., conspiracy beliefs were heightened) when they were uncertain. Uncertainty seemed to be a pre-requisite for judging the plausibility of conspiracy theories even when information about morality was also prominent.

Research also links conspiracy beliefs with a search for patterns and meaning. For example, a study by Whitson and Galinsky (2008) found that the extent to which people saw patterns in noise was associated with belief in conspiracy theories. This suggests that belief in conspiracy theories is stronger among people are looking for patterns. A recent set of studies by van Prooijen, Douglas, and de Inocencio (2018) also showed that conspiracy beliefs are associated with pattern perception, but specifically, when patterns are illusory – that is there are no patterns and stimuli are completely random. In one of their studies, van Prooijen et al. (2018) asked participants to view sequences of random coin tosses (generated from a website called "random.org"), and to rate the extent to which the sequences were completely random, or completely determined. Participants were also asked to rate the extent to which they believed in well-known and fictitious conspiracy theories, as well as supernatural phenomena. Results revealed robust relationships between all variables, but most important for the current discussion that belief in both well-known and fictitious conspiracy theories were associated with illusory pattern perception.

Belief in conspiracy theories therefore appears to be a very basic cognitive response to the search for patterns where they do not, or are unlikely to, exist (but see Dieguez, Wagner-Egger, & Gauvrit, 2015 for evidence that this might not always occur). Furthermore, one recent set of studies demonstrated that belief in conspiracy theories is driven by a readiness to draw implausible causal connections even when stimuli are *not* random and *do* show a pattern (e.g., the case of real-life spurious correlations; van der Wal, Sutton, Lange, & Braga, 2018). Other research shows that conspiracy beliefs are stronger among people who seek other types of patterns in the environment, such as religious believers and believers in paranormal and supernatural phenomena (e.g., Bruder, Haffke, Neave, Nouripanah, & Imhoff, 2013; Darwin, Neave, & Holmes, 2011; Drinkwater, Dagnall, & Parker, 2012; Leiser, Duani, & Wagner-Egger, 2017; Oliver & Wood, 2014). Research also suggests that people are more likely to adopt conspiracy theories for events that are especially important or large scale. It is argued that the proportionality bias – that causes must be proportional to effects – means that small, mundane explanations for important events (e.g., that Princess Diana died because the driver of the car was drunk) are not as satisfying as larger and more elaborate explanations (e.g., that she was murdered by the British government; Leman & Cinnirella, 2007).

Beliefs in conspiracy theories have also been linked to the need for cognitive closure, which is the tendency to form quick judgments on any given topic (Kruglanski, 1990). Marchlewska, Cichocka, and Kossowska (2017) asked participants to complete a scale measuring the need for cognitive closure, and then some text relating the European Union's plans to finance refugees' stay in Poland. For some participants, this text introduced the idea of conspiracy by mentioning an alleged Internet conversation stating that the European Union's support for refugees in Poland was an attempt to gain control over Poland (vs. a control condition with irrelevant information). Participants were then asked to indicate their support for the conspiracy theory. Results revealed that the need for cognitive closure was associated with belief in the conspiracy theory, but that it was stronger when the conspiracy explanation was made salient. That is, people high in need for cognitive closure were more likely to believe the straightforward conspiracy explanation when it was available to them. Another experiment showed that this effect was especially important when events lacked a clear, official explanation (see also Leman & Cinnirella, 2013 for evidence of the link between need for cognitive closure and belief in conspiracy theories).

Evidence suggests that people might also turn to conspiracy theories as a result of cognitive errors or biases. For example, conspiracy beliefs have been linked to the conjunction fallacy (Brotherton & French, 2015; Dagnall, Denovon, Drinkwater, Parker, & Clough, 2017), which is an error of probabilistic reasoning in which people overestimate the likelihood of co-occurring events (Tversky & Kahneman, 1983). In two studies, Brotherton and French (2014) first examined people's tendency to commit conjunction errors. For example, in one scenario, participants were told that a group of students were visiting a beer garden after university and were asked to estimate the probability that (1) it is a warm summer's day, (2) that there are people sitting in the beer garden, and that (3) it is a warm summer's day and there are people sitting in the beer garden. A conjunction error occurs when participants rate the probability of (3) as being higher than one or both of (1) and (2). Brotherton and French found that the tendency to commit conjunction errors was significantly related to conspiracy beliefs. This occurred when the conjunctions were neutral, or had a conspiracy flavor.

Others have shown that projection of one's own personal beliefs onto others is associated with conspiracy beliefs. Douglas and Sutton (2011) found that people's tendency to believe in conspiracy theories is associated with the tendency to believe that – in the same situation – they would participate in the conspiracy themselves. That is, the belief that "they conspire" is in part the result of the belief that "I would conspire." Further, Douglas, Sutton, Callan, Dawtry, and Harvey (2016) found that hypersensitive agency detection – the tendency to attribute agency and intentionality where it does not (or is unlikely to) exist – was associated with conspiracy beliefs (see also Brotherton & French, 2014; van der Tempel & Alcock, 2015). Finally, McHoskey (1995) found that conspiracy beliefs may be in part a product of *biased assimilation* – carefully and critically analyzing information that disconfirms one's views but uncritically accepting information that confirms them (see also Thorson, 2015).

Various cognitive limitations have also been associated with conspiracy belief. For example, Swami, Voracek, Stieger, Tran, and Furnham (2014) found that lower levels of analytic thinking predicted conspiracy beliefs. In further experiments, Swami et al. (2014) asked participants to complete a range of tasks designed to elicit analytic thinking (e.g., verbal fluency, cognitive disfluency) and found that engaging in these tasks reduced belief in conspiracy theories. Conspiracy believers also tend to score lower in rational thinking style (Mikušková, 2018) and higher in intuitive thinking (Swami et al., 2014). Furthermore, people appear to look to conspiracy theories when they are bored (Brotheton & Eser, 2015), when they have lower levels of intelligence (Stieger, Gumhalter, Tran, Voracek, & Swami, 2013), and when they are less educated (Douglas et al., 2016). Perhaps conspiracy theories are adopted when knowledge – but also the ability to acquire knowledge – is lacking.

Belief in Conspiracy Theories 65

Other cognitive processes associated with belief in conspiracy theories involve a tendency to accept epistemically unjustified beliefs (Lobato, Mendoza, Sims, & Chin, 2014), and a general tendency toward religious or quasi-religious thinking (Franks, Bangerter, Bauer, Hall, & Noort, 2017). Finally, conspiracy beliefs tend to be positively correlated with factors such as non- or sub-clinical delusional thinking (Dagnall et al., 2017) and schizotypy, which describes a range of personality characteristics and experiences from normal to psychotic (Barron, Morgan, Towell, Altemeyer, & Swami, 2014; Bruder et al., 2013; Darwin et al., 2011; Swami, Pietschnig et al., 2013; van der Tempel & Alcock, 2015).

Overall, therefore, there is evidence that conspiracy theories appeal to individuals who seek accuracy and meaning (or both) but perhaps lack the cognitive tools or experience difficulties that prevent them from finding these via other means. Conspiracy theories therefore appeal to people who are looking for the truth but seem to lack the skills to look in the right places. This coheres with research showing that the most "unskilled" people are also the most prone to errors and misinformation, and at the same time they are the most "unaware" of the errors and misjudgments they are making (see Dunning, Chapter 12 this volume).

At this point, many readers would quite naturally draw the conclusion that conspiracy believers must therefore be gullible. They are cognitively limited, uneducated, prone to cognitive errors and biases, and they do not think analytically. They make irrational choices when evaluating different pieces of information (see also van Prooijen, Chapter 17 this volume). They must therefore believe anything they hear without critical evaluation. However, we feel that this conclusion would be premature. People will not believe anything they hear. Instead, they appear more likely to turn to conspiracy theories that could help them plug gaps in missing information, rather than believing anything at all. That is, they are seeking specific knowledge and not just anything will do. Furthermore, conspiracy believers often characterize themselves as truth seekers, defenders of the truth, and "skeptics." That is, they are skeptical of the information they receive from officialdom and are explicitly looking for facts and answers to critical questions. They are not blindly accepting what anyone will tell them – quite the opposite. They are perhaps just looking in the wrong places for these facts and answers. Also, cognitive factors are only one part of the picture that explain why people believe in conspiracy theories. There are other important motives that need to be considered (existential and social) as we explain in the remainder of this chapter.

Existential Motives

In addition to their epistemic purposes, causal explanations for events help people to feel safe and secure and also to be able to control things that happen to them and to their social groups (Tetlock, 2002). Early perspectives on conspiracy beliefs suggested that people turn to conspiracy theories for compensatory satisfaction when they do not feel safe and do not feel that they have control. For example, conspiracy theories may promise to make people feel safer because dangerous and deceitful individuals are identified and the threat they pose is countered (Bost & Prunier, 2013). Also, people who feel that they lack control may feel better when they adopt conspiracy theories because such theories allow them to feel that they possess an alternative, and non-official account (Goertzel, 1994).

Research supports the idea that people turn to conspiracy theories in a bid to fulfill existential motives. For example, studies have shown that people are likely to turn to conspiracy theories when they are anxious. Grzesiak-Feldman (2013) asked university students to complete a state-trait anxiety measure and found that both were associated with belief in conspiracy theories about Jewish people, Germans, and Arabs. In two further studies, Grzesiak-Feldman also showed that anxiety-inducing situations (i.e., waiting for exams) were associated with increased belief in conspiracy theories. People who feel powerless are also more likely to believe conspiracy theories (Abalakina-Paap, Stephan, Craig, & Gregory, 1999). People who have an insecure attachment style are also more likely to believe in conspiracy theories (Green & Douglas, 2018). Conspiracy beliefs are also strongly related to lack of sociopolitical control or lack of psychological empowerment (Bruder et al., 2013; see also Nyhan, 2017; Uscinski & Parent, 2014). Also, experiments have shown that conspiracy beliefs are greater when people feel unable to control outcomes, but that it is reduced when their sense of control is affirmed (van Prooijen & Acker, 2015).

Belief in conspiracy theories is also correlated with existential anxiety (Newheiser, Farias, & Tausch, 2011), and anomie – a feeling of personal unrest and lack of understanding of the social world (e.g., Abalakina-Paap et al., 1999; Bruder et al., 2013; Goertzel, 1994). Belief in conspiracy theories is also associated with a belief that the economy is getting worse (Parsons, Simmons, Shinhoster, & Kilburn, 1999). People may therefore feel that conspiracy theories will help them come to terms with their particular problems, enabling them to regain some of the psychological goods that they have lost (Franks et al., 2017). Specifically, Franks et al. (2017) argue that conspiracy theories help people make sense of unsettling events and provide optimism that things will change. In a similar vein, other researchers have demonstrated that conspiracy theories might buffer people from threats to the social system in which they live, such as a suffering economy, or negative social and political events (Jolley, Douglas, & Sutton, 2018).

There is therefore a convincing amount of evidence that people turn to conspiracy theories in an attempt to satisfy existential motives. This, however, does not mean that they are gullible. Believing in conspiracy theories to fulfill existential motives does not mean that people will believe simply anything they hear. Instead, the conspiracy beliefs are determined by the nature of the existential needs. For example, if people are feeling unsettled

Belief in Conspiracy Theories   67

about a particular issue, they might gravitate toward conspiracy theories to resolve the issue but they would not feel compelled to adopt conspiracy theories that are unrelated to that need. Using conspiracy theories to rationalize feelings of powerlessness is also not necessarily a gullible response. People will not simply believe anything – they will believe what helps them come to terms with the psychological goods that they are missing.

Social Motives

Causal explanations are also informed by a variety of social motivations, including the need to belong and to maintain a positive image of the self and the social groups that people belong to. Conspiracy theories may also be adopted in an effort to fulfill such social motives. For example, scholars have suggested that conspiracy theories may boost people's image of the self and the in-group by allowing blame for negative outcomes to be attributed to others. Thus, conspiracy theories may help to uphold people's image of the self and their in-group as capable and honest but as harmed or impaired by powerful and immoral others.

Research to date supports this argument. For example, Cichocka, Marchlewska, and Golec de Zavala (2016) found that conspiracy theories were particularly appealing to narcissists, who have an inflated yet insecure feeling of self-worth. Other studies have shown links between conspiracy beliefs and the social psychological need to feel unique to others (Imhoff & Lamberty, 2017; Lantian, Muller, Nurra, & Douglas, 2017). For example, in one experiment, Lantian et al. (2017) manipulated the need for uniqueness by asking participants to complete a task in which they were asked to think and write about the importance of individuality (vs. conformity), which is designed to increase (vs. decrease) the need to feel unique. Results revealed that participants in the individuality condition were more likely to believe conspiracy theories about a fictitious event than those in the conformity condition. It is argued that conspiracy theories allow people to feel that they are in possession of rare, important information that other people do not have, making them feel special and thus boosting their self-esteem.

Conspiracy theories are also important to the need to feel good about our social groups. Researchers have further found that conspiracy theories – in addition to appealing to individual narcissists – are also particularly appealing to *collective narcissists* who believe in the in-group's greatness paired with a belief that other people do not appreciate it enough. That is, the more narcissistic people are about their groups, the more they are likely to believe that other groups are conspiring against them. Specifically, Golec de Zavala and Cichocka (2012) found that national collective narcissism in Poland predicted endorsement of conspiracy stereotypes of Jews. Also, Cichocka, Marchlewska, Golec de Zavala, and Olechowski (2016) demonstrated that national collective narcissism in Poland was associated with the endorsement of conspiracy theories about Russian involvement in the Smolensk crash of

68 Karen M. Douglas et al.

2010 in which the Polish president and several officials died. However, ordinary identification with the national group without narcissism predicted *lower* likelihood of endorsing these conspiracy theories. This suggests that conspiracy explanations of intergroup events derive from a need to validate the group image by disparaging out-groups.

Other social motives appear relevant to conspiracy theories, including the need to belong. Graeupner and Coman (2017) considered the relationship between social exclusion and belief in conspiracy theories. Participants in one study were asked to think about a social interaction and rate how socially excluded they felt after the event. They were then asked to rate their agreement with a set of well-known conspiracy theories. Results revealed a relationship between social exclusion and belief in conspiracy theories, and a second (experimental) study showed that social exclusion also influenced superstitious beliefs. Graeupner and Coman argued that people turn to these beliefs to try to make sense of their negative social experiences. Furthermore, members of groups who have objectively low (vs. high) status because of their ethnicity (Crocker, Luhtanen, Broadnax, & Blaine, 1999) or income (Uscinski & Parent, 2014) appear more likely to believe in conspiracy theories. For example, Crocker et al. (1999) demonstrated that Black Americans (compared to White Americans) were more likely to believe in conspiracy theories about the American government conspiring against Blacks. Feeling socially disadvantaged and disenfranchised therefore appears to be a significant determinant of whether or not conspiracy theories appeal to people.

Related to this point, research from political science suggests that people on the losing (vs. winning) side of political processes are also more likely to believe conspiracy theories. Specifically, Uscinski and Parent (2014) argue – based on analyses of archival data from over 100 years of newspaper letters and also representative surveys – that people use conspiracy theories when they are powerless to defend themselves against the powerful. In other words, conspiracy theories are for "losers." Along this vein, conspiracy beliefs have also been linked to prejudice against powerful groups (Imhoff & Bruder, 2014) and groups that are viewed as enemies (Kofta & Sędek, 2005). Groups who feel that they have been victimized are also more likely to endorse conspiracy theories about other more powerful groups (Bilewicz, Winiewski, Kofta, & Wójcik, 2013; Mashuri & Zaduqisti, 2014).

Given such experiences, it is not gullible for people to believe that dominant groups have been (and probably still are) conspiring against them. When people believe in conspiracy theories, they are often responding to real threats, inequalities, and historical instances of threat and victimization. People therefore adopt beliefs that protect their own groups. To give another example, when left-wingers believe conspiracy theories that demonize right-wingers (and vice versa), they are endorsing beliefs that cohere with their political views, and indeed there is evidence that people do so at both ends of the political spectrum (Uscinski & Parent, 2014). If people were simply being gullible, they would believe in all conspiracy theories, but it is clear that they do not. Belief in conspiracy theories is motivated by people's group memberships and the beliefs that are associated with those group memberships.

In further support of this point, studies have shown that people are more likely to believe in conspiracies directed at their own group if they have personally experienced discrimination, such as being the victim of police harassment (Parsons et al., 1999), or race discrimination (Simmons & Parsons, 2005). Situational threats and crisis situations can also increase the likelihood of conspiracy beliefs (Kofta, Sędek, & Sławuta, 2011; Mashuri & Zaduqisti, 2014; van Prooijen & Douglas, 2017). It is therefore important to consider the political, social, and historical contexts that make conspiracy theories seem more believable to people than conventional explanations (see also Nattrass, 2013). People do not simply believe anything – they believe what they want to believe.

How Well Do Conspiracy Theories Satisfy Psychological Motives?

Relatively little research has addressed this question to date. However, the existing research suggests that conspiracy theories may be more appealing to people than actually satisfying their psychological motives. Taking existential motives first, some research suggests that rather than reducing uncertainty, conspiracy theories might even increase it. Specifically, Jolley and Douglas (2014a) asked people to read conspiracy theories about governments in one study, and about climate change in another. In each case, participants were asked how uncertain they felt and their responses were compared with participants who had either been in a control condition with no information, or an anti-conspiracy condition with material refuting the conspiracy theories. In each case, conspiracy theories – rather than making people feel more certain – made people feel even more uncertain.

There also seems to be little evidence that conspiracy theories satisfy existential motives. On the contrary, experimental exposure to conspiracy theories appears to immediately suppress people's sense of autonomy and control (Jolley & Douglas, 2014a, 2014b). For example, in the study mentioned in the previous paragraph by Jolley and Douglas (2014a), the researchers also measured feelings of powerlessness. These feelings increased – rather than decreased – as a result of being exposed to conspiracy theories. These same studies have also shown that conspiracy theories make people less inclined to take actions that, in the long term, might boost their autonomy and control. Specifically, after exposure to conspiracy theories, people are less inclined to commit to their workplaces (Douglas & Leite, 2017) and to engage in mainstream political processes such as voting and party politics (Jolley & Douglas, 2014a). Exposure to conspiracy theories may undermine people's control and power in another, more subtle way. Douglas and Sutton (2008) showed that people were effectively persuaded by conspiracy theories about the death of Princess Diana but were not aware that they had been persuaded. Instead, they falsely recalled that their previous beliefs were identical to their new beliefs. Being influenced without awareness is arguably not an empowering position.

Furthermore, although people are clearly drawn toward conspiracy theories in an attempt to satisfy their social motivations, it is not clear that this is a strategy that works. A typical feature of conspiracy theories is their negative, distrustful representation of others and out-groups. Thus, it is reasonable to suggest that they are not only an indication but also a cause of the feelings of alienation, disenfranchisement, and anomie with which they are associated (e.g., Abalakina-Paap et al., 1999). Experiments have also shown that exposure to conspiracy theories decreases trust in governmental institutions, even if the conspiracy theories are completely unrelated to those institutions (Einstein & Glick, 2015). It also causes people to trust politicians and scientists less, and to disengage with politics and scientific findings (Jolley & Douglas, 2014a). So far, research therefore suggests that conspiracy theories may further frustrate rather than satisfy people's social motives.

Summary and Future Directions

This does not mean that conspiracy believers are gullible, however. It *does* mean that the psychological crutch that people are using may not support them in the way they might hope. Beliefs in conspiracy theories may be ultimately self-defeating, but not straightforwardly a reflection of gullibility. We expect that further research will be undertaken to test the framework of Douglas et al. (2017) and to examine when conspiracy theories might satisfy people's psychological motives and when they might not.

Indeed, there are grounds to expect future research to show that conspiracy theories fulfill the motives of some people but not others. The experimental research conducted thus far has only sampled from populations such as undergraduate students and survey panelists who are not greatly disadvantaged or threatened. Furthermore, these populations tend to show quite low levels of conspiracy beliefs. Typically, on a seven-point scale, conspiracy beliefs are just above or below the midpoint of the scale (e.g., see Douglas & Sutton, 2011). These are people who therefore generally do not endorse conspiracy theories. For these people, conspiracy theories are likely to be experienced as bothersome or worrying, but not daily concerns that determine other activities in their lives.

These are not the people who scholars have in mind when they argue that conspiracy theories may sometimes help people satisfy their needs and motives. Instead, they are typically referring to groups and individuals who are already estranged from society and for whom conspiracy theories may offer some compensation for lost psychological goods. These include disempowered groups who may use conspiracy theories to destabilize

Belief in Conspiracy Theories 71

powerful groups and systems by formulating their own understanding of realities (Sapountzis & Condor, 2013) and by group cohesion and collective action (Adams, O'Brien, & Nelson, 2006). In these communities – and indeed in prominent online conspiracy communities such as the 9/11 Truth movement – conspiracy beliefs may offer an important source of belonging and shared reality.

Furthermore, it is clear that elites do conspire against public interests – that is, real conspiracies do happen. Conspiracy theories play an important role in making people aware of what has happened, and opening important information for discussion and debate. To be sure that conspiracy theories are harmful rather than helpful, further research needs to be conducted on people who have greater psychological motives to fulfill. That is, more detailed and longitudinal studies of disadvantaged populations are necessary.

Future research should also investigate other factors that might influence the extent to which people believe in conspiracy theories. For example, Forgas (Chapter 10 this volume) has demonstrated that everyday fluctuations in mood can influence people's levels of trust and acceptance of misinformation. No research to date has investigated how mood might influence conspiracy beliefs, however. It is plausible based on Forgas's research that a good mood could lead people to be less concerned about the fulfillment of social needs (i.e., they already feel good), and therefore make them more receptive to conspiracy theories. Future research could also consider the influence of the source of the conspiracy theories (see Cooper & Avery, Chapter 16 this volume). Taking into account the social motives associated with conspiracy beliefs, it is reasonable to suggest that people will believe conspiracy theories more if uttered by their peers than by outsiders. We also know little about the effects of repetition on conspiracy beliefs, but repetition of misinformation is likely to influence its acceptance (see Myers, Chapter 5 this volume; Unkelbach & Koch, Chapter 3 this volume). Finally, there is a limited amount of research on how conspiracy theories are processed when people come across them, and different levels of processing at the point of information encoding can influence information acceptance (Mayo, Chapter 8 this volume). In general, we call for a more detailed approach to the study of conspiracy theories than much of the current research (leading to the gullibility conclusion) has presented.

Finally, some conspiracy theories may indeed reflect believers' gullibility. Specifically, one cannot equate conspiracy theories about the 9/11 attacks or the assassination of President John F. Kennedy with conspiracy theories about lizard aliens ruling the world, or those proposing that the earth is flat. There are clearly distinctions between conspiracy theories and the people who believe them might therefore also differ on important dimensions. Although there is evidence that people who believe in one conspiracy theory also tend to believe in others (e.g., Goertzel, 1994; Wood, Douglas, & Sutton, 2012), studies have tested belief in well-known conspiracy theories

72 *Karen M. Douglas et al.*

rather than those that could be considered as more far-fetched. People who believe in the more far-fetched conspiracy theories may indeed show characteristics of gullibility. To date, there is no reliable typology of conspiracy theories but it clear that not all conspiracy theories are equal.

Closing Remarks

We have overviewed the recent taxonomy of conspiracy beliefs proposed by Douglas et al. (2017) in which it is argued that people are attracted to conspiracy theories in an attempt to fulfill epistemic, existential, and social motives. In reviewing the evidence for this argument, we also argue that conspiracy theories cannot simply be viewed as something that only the most gullible people will believe. Our framework supports this argument – people will not believe in just anything but they will believe what is likely to help them satisfy their motives. We therefore argue that conspiracy theories may be better viewed as a psychological prop that people lean on to alleviate specific psychological frustrations. More research is needed to determine when this strategy works and when it does not.

References

Abalakina-Paap, M., Stephan, W. G., Craig, T., & Gregory, L. (1999). Beliefs in conspiracies. *Political Psychology, 20*, 637–647.

Adams, G., O'Brien, L. T., & Nelson, J. C. (2006). Perceptions of racism in Hurricane Katrina: A liberation psychology analysis. *Analyses of Social Issues and Public Policy, 6*, 215–235.

Barron, D., Morgan, K., Towell, T., Altemeyer, B., & Swami, V. (2014). Associations between schizotypy and belief in conspiracist ideation. *Personality and Individual Differences, 70*, 156–159.

Bilewicz, M., Winiewski, M., Kofta, M., & Wójcik, A. (2013). Harmful ideas: The structure and consequences of anti-Semitic beliefs in Poland. *Political Psychology, 34*, 821–839.

Bost, P. R., & Prunier, S. G. (2013). Rationality in conspiracy beliefs: The role of perceived motive. *Psychological Reports, 113*, 118–128.

Brotherton, R., & Eser, S. (2015). Bored to fears: Boredom proneness, paranoia, and conspiracy theories. *Personality and Individual Differences, 80*, 1–5.

Brotherton, R., & French, C. C. (2014). Belief in conspiracy theories and susceptibility to the conjunction fallacy. *Applied Cognitive Psychology, 28*, 238–248.

Bruder, M., Haffke, P., Neave, N., Nouripanah, N., & Imhoff, R. (2013). Measuring individual differences in generic beliefs in conspiracy theories across cultures: Conspiracy mentality questionnaire. *Frontiers in Psychology, 4*(225). doi:10.3389/fpsyg.2013.00225

Cichocka, A., Marchlewska, M., & Golec de Zavala, A. (2016). Does self-love or self-hate predict conspiracy beliefs? Narcissism, self-esteem, and the endorsement of conspiracy theories. *Social Psychological & Personality Science, 7*, 157–166.

Cichocka, A., Marchlewska, M., Golec de Zavala, A., & Olechowski, M. (2016). "They will not control us": In-group positivity and belief in intergroup conspiracies. *British Journal of Psychology, 107*, 556–576.

Crocker, J., Luhtanen, R., Broadnax, S., & Blaine, B. E. (1999). Belief in U.S. government conspiracies against Blacks among Black and White college students: Powerlessness or system blame? *Personality and Social Psychology Bulletin*, *25*, 941–953.

Dagnall, N., Denovan, A., Drinkwater, K., Parker, A., & Clough, P. J. (2017). Urban legends and paranormal beliefs: The role of reality testing and schizotypy. *Frontiers in Psychology*, *8*(942). http://psycnet.apa.org/doi/10.3389/fpsyg.2017.00942

Darwin, H., Neave, N., & Holmes, J. (2011). Belief in conspiracy theories: The role of paranormal belief, paranoid ideation and schizotypy. *Personality and Individual Differences*, *50*, 1289–1293.

Dieguez, S., Wagner-Egger, P., & Gauvrit, N. (2015). Nothing happens by accident, or does it? A low prior for randomness does not explain belief in conspiracy theories. *Psychological Science*, *26*, 1762–1770.

Douglas, K. M., & Leite, A. C. (2017). Suspicion in the workplace: Organizational conspiracy theories and work-related outcomes. *British Journal of Psychology*, *108*, 486–506.

Douglas, K. M., & Sutton, R. M. (2008). The hidden impact of conspiracy theories: Perceived and actual impact of theories surrounding the death of Princess Diana. *Journal of Social Psychology*, *148*, 210–221.

Douglas, K. M., & Sutton, R. M. (2011). Does it take one to know one? Belief in conspiracy theories is influenced by personal willingness to conspire. *British Journal of Social Psychology*, *50*, 544–552.

Douglas, K. M., Sutton, R. M., Callan, M. J., Dawtry, R. J., & Harvey, A. J. (2016). Someone is pulling the strings: Hypersensitive agency detection and belief in conspiracy theories. *Thinking & Reasoning*, *22*, 57–77.

Douglas, K. M., Sutton, R. M., & Cichocka, A. (2017). The psychology of conspiracy theories. *Current Directions in Psychological Science*, *26*, 538–542.

Drinkwater, K., Dagnall, N., & Parker, A. (2012). Reality testing, conspiracy theories, and paranormal beliefs. *Journal of Parapsychology*, *76*, 57–77.

Dugas, M. J., Gosselin, P., & Ladouceur, R. (2001). Intolerance of uncertainty and worry: Investigating narrow specificity in a non-clinical sample. *Cognitive Therapy and Research*, *25*, 551–558.

Einstein, K. L., & Glick, D. M. (2015). Do I think BLS data are BS? The consequences of conspiracy theories. *Political Behavior*, *37*, 679–701.

Franks, B., Bangerter, A., Bauer, M. W., Hall, M., & Noort, M. C. (2017). Beyond "monologicality"? Exploring conspiracist worldviews. *Frontiers in Psychology*, *8*(861). doi: 10.3389/fpsyg.2017.00861

Goertzel, T. (1994). Belief in conspiracy theories. *Political Psychology*, *15*, 731–742.

Golec de Zavala, A., & Cichocka, A. (2012). Collective narcissism and anti-Semitism in Poland. *Group Processes and Intergroup Relations*, *15*, 213–229.

Graeupner, D., & Coman, A. (2017). The dark side of meaning-making: How social exclusion leads to superstitious thinking. *Journal of Experimental Social Psychology*, *69*, 218–222.

Green, R., & Douglas, K. M. (2018). Anxious attachment and belief in conspiracy theories. *Personality and Individual Differences*, *125*, 30–37.

Grimes, D. R. (2016). On the viability of conspiratorial beliefs. *PLOS ONE*, *11*(3), e0151003. doi:10.1371/journal.pone.0147905

Grzesiak-Feldman, M. (2013). The effect of high-anxiety situations on conspiracy thinking. *Current Psychology*, *32*, 100–118.

Heider, F. (1958). *The psychology of interpersonal relations.* New York, NY: John Wiley.

Imhoff, R., & Bruder, M. (2014). Speaking (un-)truth to power: Conspiracy mentality as a generalised political attitude. *European Journal of Personality, 28,* 25–43.

Imhoff, R., & Lamberty, P. K. (2017). Too special to be duped: Need for uniqueness motivates conspiracy beliefs. *European Journal of Social Psychology, 47,* 724–734.

Jensen, T. (2013). *Democrats and Republicans differ on conspiracy theory beliefs.* Retrieved from www.publicpolicypolling.com/polls/democrats-and-republicans-differ-on-conspiracy-theory-beliefs.

Jolley, D., & Douglas, K. M. (2014a). The effects of anti-vaccine conspiracy theories on vaccination intentions. *PLOS ONE, 9*(2), e89177. doi:10.1371/journal.pone.0089177

Jolley, D., & Douglas, K. M. (2014b). The social consequences of conspiracism: Exposure to conspiracy theories decreases the intention to engage in politics and to reduce one's carbon footprint. *British Journal of Psychology, 105,* 35–56.

Jolley, D., Douglas, K. M., & Sutton, R. M. (2018). Blaming a few bad apples to save a threatened barrel: The system-justifying function of conspiracy theories. *Political Psychology, 39,* 465–478.

Kofta, M., & Sędek, G. (2005). Conspiracy stereotypes of Jews during systemic transformation in Poland. *International Journal of Sociology, 35,* 40–64.

Kofta, M., Sędek, G., & Sławuta, P. N. (2011, July). *Beliefs in Jewish conspiracy: The role of situation threats to ingroup' power and positive image.* Paper presented at the 34th International Society of Political Psychology (ISSP) conference, Istanbul, Turkey.

Kruglanski, A. W. (1990). Motivations for judging and knowing: Implications for causal attribution. In E. T. Higgins, & R. M. Sorrentino (Eds.), *The handbook of motivation and cognition: Foundation of social behavior* (Vol. 2, pp. 333–368). New York, NY: Guilford.

Lantian, A., Muller, D., Nurra, C., & Douglas, K. M. (2017). "I know things they don't know!" The role of need for uniqueness in belief in conspiracy theories. *Social Psychology, 48,* 160–173.

Leiser, D., Duani, N., & Wagner-Egger, P. (2017). The conspiratorial style in lay economic thinking. *PLOS ONE, 12*(3), e0171238. doi: 10.1371/journal.pone.0171238

Leman, P. J., & Cinnirella, M. (2007). A major event has a major cause: Evidence for the role of heuristics in reasoning about conspiracy theories. *Social Psychological Review, 9,* 18–28.

Leman, P. J., & Cinnirella, M. (2013). Beliefs in conspiracy theories and the need for cognitive closure. *Frontiers in Psychology, 4*(378). doi:10.3389/fpsyg.2013.00378

Lewandowsky, S., Cook, J., Oberauer, K., Brophy, S., Lloyd, E. A., & Marriott, M. (2015). Recurrent fury: Conspiratorial discourse in the blogosphere triggered by research on the role of conspiracist ideation in climate denial. *Journal of Social and Political Psychology, 3,* 142–178.

Lewandowsky, S., Oberauer, K., & Gignac, G. E. (2013). NASA faked the moon landing – therefore, (climate) science is a hoax: An anatomy of the motivated rejection of science. *Psychological Science, 24,* 622–633.

Lobato, E., Mendoza, J., Sims, V., & Chin, M. (2014). Examining the relationship between conspiracy theories, paranormal beliefs, and pseudoscience acceptance among a university population. *Applied Cognitive Psychology, 28,* 617–625.

Marchlewska, M., Cichocka, A., & Kossowska, M. (2017). Addicted to answers: Need for cognitive closure and the endorsement of conspiracy beliefs. *European Journal of Social Psychology*. Advance online publication. doi:10.1002/ejsp.2308

Mashuri, A., & Zaduqisti, E. (2014). We believe in your conspiracy if we distrust you: The role of intergroup distrust in structuring the effect of Islamic identification, competitive victimhood, and group incompatibility on belief in a conspiracy theory. *Journal of Tropical Psychology*, 4, 1–14.

McHoskey, J. W. (1995). Case closed? On the John F. Kennedy assassination: Biased assimilation of evidence and attitude polarization. *Basic and Applied Social Psychology*, 17, 395–409.

Mikušková, E. B. (2018). Conspiracy beliefs of future teachers. *Current Psychology*, 37, 692–701.

Moore, P. (2016). *Little British believe in outlandish conspiracy theories*. Retrieved from https://yougov.co.uk/news/2016/05/27/conspiracies.

Nattrass, N. (2013). *The AIDS conspiracy: Science fights back*. New York, NY: Columbia University Press.

Newheiser, A., Farias, M., & Tausch, N. (2011). The functional nature of conspiracy beliefs: Examining the underpinnings of belief in the Da Vinci Code conspiracy. *Personality and Individual Differences*, 51, 1007–1011.

Nyhan, B. (2017). Why more Democrats are now embracing conspiracy theories. Retrieved from www.nytimes.com/2017/02/15/upshot/why-more-democrats-are-now-embracing-conspiracy-theories.html.

Oliver, J. E., & Wood, T. J. (2014). Conspiracy theories and the paranoid style(s) of mass opinion. *American Journal of Political Science*, 58, 952–966. doi: 10.1111/ajps.12084

Parsons, S., Simmons, W., Shinhoster, F., & Kilburn, J. (1999). A test of the grapevine: An empirical examination of the conspiracy theories among African Americans. *Sociological Spectrum*, 19, 201–222.

Sapountzis, A., & Condor, S. (2013). Conspiracy accounts as intergroup theories: Challenging dominant understandings of social power and political legitimacy. *Political Psychology*, 43, 731–752.

Simmons, W. P., & Parsons, S. (2005). Beliefs in conspiracy theories among African Americans: A comparison of elites and masses. *Social Science Quarterly*, 86, 582–598.

Stieger, S., Gumhalter, N., Tran, U. S., Voracek, M., & Swami, V. (2013). Girl in the cellar: A repeated cross-sectional investigation of belief in conspiracy theories about the kidnapping of Natascha Kampusch. *Frontiers in Psychology*, 4(297). https://dx.doi.org/10.3389%2Ffpsyg.2013.00297

Swami, V., Pietschnig, J., Tran, U. S., Nader, I. W., Stieger, S., & Voracek, M. (2013). Lunar lies: The impact of informational framing and individual differences in shaping conspiracist beliefs about the moon landings. *Applied Cognitive Psychology*, 27, 71–80.

Swami, V., Voracek, M., Stieger, S., Tran, U. S., & Furnham, A. (2014). Analytic thinking reduces belief in conspiracy theories. *Cognition*, 133, 572–585.

Swift, A. (2013). *Majority in US still believe JFK killed in a conspiracy*. Retrieved from www.gallup.com/poll/165893/majority-believe-jfk-killed-conspiracy.aspx.

Tetlock, P. E. (2002). Social-functionalist frameworks for judgment and choice: The intuitive politician, theologian, and prosecutor. *Psychological Review*, 109, 451–472.

Thorson, E. (2015). Belief echoes: The Persistent effects of misinformation and corrections. *Political Communication, 33*, 1–21.

Tversky, A., & Kahneman, D. (1983). Extensional vs. intuitive reasoning: The conjunction fallacy in probability judgment. *Psychological Review, 90*, 293–315.

Uscinski, J. E., & Parent, J. M. (2014). *American conspiracy theories*. New York, NY: Oxford University Press.

van der Tempel, J., & Alcock, J. E. (2015). Relationships between conspiracy mentality, hyperactive agency detection, and Schizotypy: Supernatural forces at work? *Personality and Individual Differences, 82*, 136–141.

van der Wal, R. C., Sutton, R. M., Lange, J., & Braga, J. P. N. (2018). Suspicious binds: Conspiracy thinking and tenuous perceptions of causal connections between co-occurring and spuriously correlated events. *European Journal of Social Psychology, 48*, 970–989.

van Prooijen, J.-W., & Acker, M. (2015). The influence of control on belief in conspiracy theories: Conceptual and applied extensions. *Applied Cognitive Psychology, 29*, 753–761.

van Prooijen, J.-W., & Douglas, K. M. (2017). Conspiracy theories as part of history: The role of societal crisis situations. *Memory Studies, 10*, 323–333.

van Prooijen, J.-W., Douglas, K., & De Inocencio, C. (2018). Connecting the dots: Illusory pattern perception predicts belief in conspiracies and the supernatural. *European Journal of Social Psychology, 48*, 320–335.

van Prooijen, J.-W., & Jostmann, N. B. (2013). Belief in conspiracy theories: The influence of uncertainty and perceived morality. *European Journal of Social Psychology, 43*, 109–115.

Whitson, J. A., & Galinsky, A. D. (2008). Lacking control increases illusory pattern perception. *Science, 322*, 115–117.

Wood, M. J., Douglas, K. M., & Sutton, R. M. (2012). Dead and alive: Beliefs in contradictory conspiracy theories. *Social Psychological and Personality Science, 3*, 767–773.

5 Psychological Science Meets a Gullible Post-Truth World

David G. Myers
HOPE COLLEGE

Gullibility poisons and polarizes today's public life. We live, declared the 2016 Oxford Dictionary with their word of the year, in a "post-truth" age. The Collins Dictionary seemingly concurred, by naming "fake news" – false information disseminated under the guise of news – its 2017 word of the year. And the Rand Corporation offered a 326-page report on *Truth Decay*, exploring "the diminishing role of facts and analysis" (Kavanagh & Rich, 2018).

In the United States, concerns for citizen gullibility cross party lines. In his farewell address, President Obama (2017) warned that a "threat to democracy" was growing from the lack of a "common baseline of facts" and from underappreciating "that science and reason matter." We have become, he lamented, "so secure in our bubbles that we start accepting only information, whether it's true or not, that fits our opinions, instead of basing our opinions on the evidence that is out there." His one-time opponent, Republican Senator John McCain (2017) expressed comparable alarm about "the growing inability, and even unwillingness, to separate truth from lies."

Concerns about gullibility and misinformation extend beyond politics. Is eating genetically modified (GM) foods safe? *Yes*, say 37% of U.S. adults, and 88% of 3,447 American Association for the Advance of Science members (Funk & Rainie, 2015). Is climate change "mostly due to human activity?" *Yes*, assume 62% of U.S. adults and nearly all climate science articles (Powell, 2015; Saad, 2017).

"This is not about Republicans versus Democrats," observed National Institutes of Health former director Harold Varmus (2017). "It is about a more fundamental divide, between those who believe in evidence . . . and those who adhere unflinchingly to dogma." And that divide is hugely important, reflected British historian Simon Schama (2017): "Indifference about the distinction between truth and lies is the precondition of fascism."

Gullibility and Misinformation Writ Large: The U.S. Example

Steven Pinker (2018) reminds us that human gullibility is long-standing: Unlike our medieval ancestors, few folks today "believe in werewolves, unicorns, witches, alchemy, astrology, bloodletting, miasmas, animal sacrifice, the divine right of kings, or supernatural omens in rainbows and eclipses" (p. 376). Yet gullibility endures. Its enduring extent and impact – and the impetus for this symposium – appear in Americans' striking misperceptions of social reality, with people's beliefs often divorced from facts. "Between the idea/and the reality/ . . . falls the shadow" (T. S. Eliot). Some examples:

> *Perception: Crime is rising.* "The murder rate in our country is the highest it's been in 47 years," said Donald Trump (2017) shortly after his inauguration. Most Americans nod their heads in agreement. Each recent year 7 in 10 Americans have told Gallup they believe that the United States has suffered more crime than in the previous year (Figure 5.1; Swift, 2016).
>
> *Reality: Crime is falling.* But FBI violent crime data (aggregated from local crime reports) reveals an alternative (actual) reality. Violent crime has plummeted (2017; Figure 5.2). This reality of *decreasing* crime is confirmed in people's self-reports to the Bureau of Justice Statistics (2016; Figure 5.3). Property crime rates and reports have similarly declined. Ergo, belief and fact have traveled in opposite directions. And when fear and fact conflict, fearmongering often wins.
>
> *Perception: Many immigrants are criminals.* "On the issue of crime," a Gallup survey (McCarthy, 2017) reveals, "Americans are five times more likely to say immigrants make the situation worse rather than

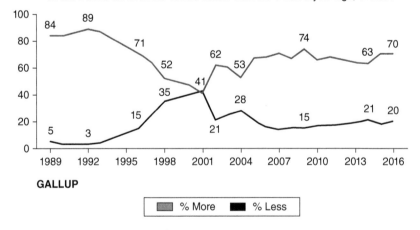

Figure 5.1 The perception: Americans perceive that crime is rising.

Source: Adapted from Gallup polls. https://news.gallup.com/poll/197318/americans-perceptions-crime-problem-steady.aspx.

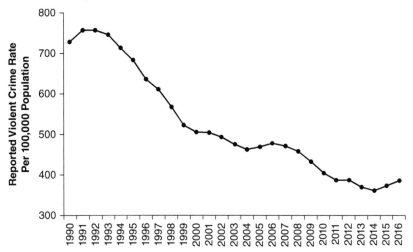

Figure 5.2 The reality: The American crime rate has been falling.

Source: Adapted from FBI data aggregated from local law enforcement. www.statista.com/statistics/191219/reported-violent-crime-rate-in-the-usa-since-1990 (Note, now available with 2017 data).

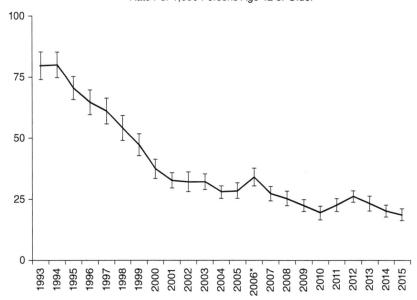

Figure 5.3 The reality: Crime victimization surveys confirm decreasing crime.

Source: Adapted from the National Crime Victimization Survey, Bureau of Justice Statistics. www.bjs.gov/content/pub/pdf/cv15.pdf.

better (45% to 9%, respectively)." The National Academy of Sciences (2015) reports that this perception of crime-prone immigrants "is perpetuated by 'issue entrepreneurs' who promote the immigrant–crime connection in order to drive restrictionist immigration policy" (p. 326).

Horrific rare incidents feed the narrative, as in the oft retold story of the Mexican national killing a young woman in San Francisco. Donald Trump's (2015a) words epitomized the perception: "When Mexico sends its people . . . they're bringing drugs. They're bringing crime. They're rapists." "If we don't get rid of these loopholes where killers are allowed to come into our country and continue to kill . . . if we don't change it, let's have a shutdown," said Trump (2018) as President. Much the same misinformation is spread by would-be dictators in Europe, such as Hungary's Prime Minister Viktor Orban.

Reality: Immigrants are not crime-prone. Immigrants who are poor and less educated may fit our image of criminals. Yet some studies find that, compared with native-born Americans, immigrants commit *less* violent crime (Adelman, Reid, Markle, Weiss, & Jaret, 2017; Butcher & Piehl, 2007; Riley, 2015). The same is true in Europe, in countries like Germany (Emery, 2016). "Immigrants are less likely than the native-born to commit crimes," confirms a National Academy of Sciences report (2015). After analyzing incarceration rates, the conservative Cato Institute (2017) confirmed that "immigrants are less likely to be incarcerated than natives relative to their shares of the population. Even illegal immigrants are less likely to be incarcerated than native-born Americans" (p. 327). Noncitizens are reportedly 7% of the U.S. population and 6% of state and federal prisoners (KFF, 2017; Rizzo, 2018). Moreover, as the number of unauthorized immigrants has tripled since 1990 (Krogstad, Passel, & Cohn, 2017), the crime rate, as we have seen, plummeted.

Perception: Unemployment worsened during the Obama presidency. In his presidential-bid announcement speech, Trump (2015b) declared that "Our real unemployment is anywhere from 18 to 20 percent." Two-thirds of his seemingly gullible supporters told Public Policy Polling (2016b) that, yes, unemployment had increased during the Obama years.

Reality: Following the recession-era doldrums that carried into Obama's first year, unemployment steadily and substantially dropped (Figure 5.4; BLS, 2017). By the time he left office, unemployment was down to 4.9% and some industries were facing a worker shortage.

Perception: The stock market fell during the Obama presidency (Figure 5.5). In the same Public Policy survey, Trump supporters were equally divided on whether the stock market had risen or fallen during the Obama years (4 in 10 believed each, with the remainder being unsure).

Reality: The stock market (S&P 500) nearly tripled during the Obama years.

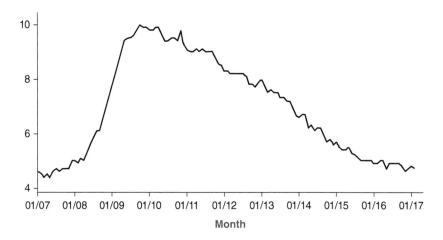

Figure 5.4 Unemployment rate during the Obama presidency.
Source: Adapted from the Bureau of Labor Statistics. https://data.bls.gov/timeseries/LNS 14000000 (Note: now updated a year).

Figure 5.5 Stock market during the Obama presidency.
Source: Adapted from S&P 500. www.barchart.com/stocks/quotes/$SPX/interactive-chart.

These recent U.S. examples have a partisan tinge. And it's true that several analyses found that the top fake news stories of the recent U.S. election, some planted by Russians, were similarly partisan (Hachman, 2017; Lee, 2016). Thus, all evidence to the contrary, President Obama finished his time in office with 42% of Republicans still believing he was born in Kenya, making him ineligible to have been president (Zorn, 2017).

82 *David G. Myers*

Much gullibility is not so overtly partisan (NASA faked the moon landing; crashed UFO spacecraft are stored at Nevada's Area 51; the Holocaust is a myth; see also on conspiracy theories Mayo, Chapter 8 this volume; van Prooijen, Chapter 17 this volume). Some bias is fostered by social scientists' eagerness to believe claims that suit their (mostly) progressive values (see Jussim, Stevens, Honeycutt, Anglin, & Fox, Chapter 15 this volume). And much political bias is bipartisan. Peter Ditto and his colleagues (2015, 2018) meta-analyzed the political bias literature and "found clear evidence of partisan bias in both liberals and conservatives, and at virtually identical levels." Thus, both Democrats and Republicans tend to believe that, when their party holds the presidency, the president cannot control gas prices; when the opposing party is in power they believe the president *can* do so (Vedantam, 2012). Or consider Democratic partisan bias in Larry Bartels' analysis (reported by FiveThirtyEight.com):

> [A] 1988 survey that asked "Would you say that compared to 1980, inflation has gotten better, stayed about the same, or gotten worse?" Amazingly, over half of the self-identified strong Democrats in the survey said that inflation had gotten worse and only 8% thought it had gotten much better, even though the actual inflation rate dropped from 13% to 4% during Reagan's eight years in office.
>
> (Gelman, 2009)

Other research teams have confirmed *mirror image bias* (Brandt, 2017; Chambers, Schlenker, & Collisson, 2013; Crawford, Kay, & Duke, 2015). Whatever supports our views, we tend to believe; whatever contradicts our views, we tend to dismiss (see Cooper & Avery, Chapter 16 this volume). This humbling finding is a reminder of how easy it is (paraphrasing Jesus) to "see the speck in our neighbor's eye" while not noticing the sometimes bigger speck in our own.

Explaining Gullibility and Misinformation

What explains the power of master manipulators, the striking embrace of false information, and various conspiracy theories (see Douglas, Sutton, & Cichocka, Chapter 4 this volume; van Prooijen, Chapter 17 this volume)?

Fake News

Some credulity feeds on plain fake news – what Nicholas Kristof (2016) called "lies in the guise of news." France, Britain, and the United States, have all accused Russia of aiming to sway public opinion and elections with legitimate-looking, falsehood-spouting websites. Hence, shortly after the 2016 election, Barack Obama (2016) warned that "If we can't discriminate between serious arguments and propaganda, then we have problems."

Pope Francis (2018) has deplored the infectious viral spread of fake news – "false information . . . meant to deceive and manipulate . . . by appealing to stereotypes and common social prejudices, and exploiting instantaneous emotions like anxiety, contempt, anger, and frustration." When emotion trumps evidence, gullibility ensues. And like the "crafty serpent" in the creation story, said Pope Francis, fake news uses mimicry (of real news) – a "sly and dangerous form of seduction that worms its way into the heart."

Some fake news spreads not from demagoguery, but less maliciously from mere satire that gullible people misinterpret, as in the Borowitz headline that "Trump Threatens to Skip Remaining Debates if Hillary is There," which Snopes (2016) felt compelled to explain was a spoof. A famous radio play about a Martian landing was believed as real by millions of people (see Cooper & Avery, Chapter 16 this volume). Snopes has also felt compelled to discount other satirical reports, some from *The Onion*, that, for example,

- "Mike Pence said that he was disappointed in husbands and fathers for allowing women to participate in the Women's March."
- "The Secret Service has launched an 'emotional protection' unit for President Trump."
- "Donald Trump announced plans to convert the USS *Enterprise* into a 'floating hotel and casino.'"

Mere Repetition

"Vaccines cause autism." "Climate change is a hoax." "Muslim terrorists pose a grave threat." Never mind the facts – that, for example, of 230,000 murders on U.S. soil since September 11, 2001, an infinitesimal proportion – 123 by 2017 – were terrorist acts by Muslim Americans, with none committed by terrorists born in the seven nations covered by Donald Trump's proposed anti-terrorist travel ban (Kristof, 2017). In 2015 and again in 2016, toddlers (with guns) killed more Americans than terrorists (Ingraham, 2016; Snopes, 2015).

Public gullibility about such myths is partly explained by "truth bias" – the disposition to believe others (Pantazi, Kissine, & Klein, 2018; Street & Kingstone, 2017) – and its amplification by the power of mere repetition.[1] (See also Krueger, Vogrincic-Haselbacher, & Evans, Chapter 6 this volume; Strack, Chapter 9 this volume; Unkelbach & Koch, Chapter 3 this volume). Much as mere exposure to unfamiliar stimuli breeds liking, so mere repetition can make things believable (Dechêne, Stahl, Hansen, & Wänke, 2010; Moons, Mackie, & Garcia-Marques, 2009; Schwarz, Newman, & Leach, 2017). In elections, advertising exposure helps make an unfamiliar candidate into a familiar one, which partially explain why, in U.S. congressional elections, the candidate with the most money wins 91% of the time (Lowery, 2014).

84   *David G. Myers*

Hal Arkes (1990) has called repetition's power "scary." Repeated lies can displace hard truths. Even repeatedly saying that a claim is *false* can, when discounted amid other true and false claims, lead older adults later to misremember it as *true* (Skurnik, Yoon, Park, & Schwarz, 2005). As we forget the discounting, our lingering familiarity with a claim can also make it seem credible.

In the political realm, repeated misinformation can have a seductive influence (Bullock, 2006; Nyhan & Reifler, 2008). Recurring clichés ("Crooked Hillary") can displace complex realities. George Orwell's *Nineteen Eighty-Four* harnessed the power of repeated slogans: "Freedom is slavery." "Ignorance is strength." "War is peace." Adolf Hitler understood: "All effective propaganda must be limited to a very few points and must harp on these in slogans" (*Mein Kampf*, 1926, ch. 6).

Moreover, falsehoods fly fast. On Twitter, lies have wings. In one analysis of 126,000 stories tweeted by 3 million people, falsehoods – especially false political news – "diffused significantly farther, faster, deeper, and more broadly than the truth" (Vosoughi, Roy, & Aral, 2018). Compared to true stories, falsehoods often are more emotionally dramatic, novel, and seemingly newsworthy. As Jonathan Swift (1710) anticipated, "Falsehood flies, and the truth comes limping after it" (or in later renditions, "A lie can travel halfway around the world while the truth is putting on its shoes").

Retractions of previously provided information also rarely work – people tend to remember the original story, not the retraction (Ecker, Lewandowsky, Swire, & Chang, 2011; Lewandowsky, Ecker, Seifert, Schwarz, & Cooke, 2012; see also Krueger et al., Chapter 6 this volume). Courtroom attorneys understand this, which is why they will say something that might be retracted on objection, knowing the jury will remember it anyway. Better than counteracting a falsehood is providing an alternative simple story – and repeating that several times (Ecker et al., 2011; Schwarz, Sanna, Skurnik, & Yoon, 2007; see also Mayo, Chapter 8 this volume; and van Prooijen, Chapter 17 this volume).

Mere repetition of a statement not only increases its *familiarity* and our *memory* of it, but also serves to increase the ease with which it spills off our tongue (Unkelbach & Koch, Chapter 3 this volume). And with this increased *fluency* comes a sense of coherence and increased believability (McGlone & Tofighbakhsh, 2000; see also Oyserman, Chapter 14 this volume, on cultural fluency). Other factors, such as rhyming, further increase fluency and believability. "Haste makes waste" says nothing more than "rushing causes mistakes," but it seems more true. What makes for fluency (familiarity, rhyming) also makes for believability. O. J. Simpson's attorney understood this when crafting his linguistic slam dunk: "If [the glove] doesn't fit, you must acquit."

Availability of Vivid (and Sometimes Misleading) Anecdotes

In his astonishingly perceptive *Novum Organuum*, published in 1620, Francis Bacon anticipated the modern science of gullibility by identifying

Psychological Science 85

"idols" or fallacies of the human mind. Consider, for example, his description of what today's psychological scientists know as *the availability heuristic* – the human tendency to estimate the commonality of an event based on its mental availability (often influenced by its vividness or distinctiveness):

> The human understanding is most excited by that which strikes and enters the mind at once and suddenly, and by which the imagination is immediately filled and inflated. It then begins almost imperceptibly to conceive and suppose that everything is similar to the few objects which have taken possession of the mind.
>
> (Bacon, 1620, n.p.)

As Gordon Allport (1954, p. 9) said, "Given a thimbleful of [dramatic] facts we rush to make generalizations as large as a tub." To persuade people of the perils of immigration and the need to "build the wall," Donald Trump repeatedly told the vivid story of the previously deported homeless Mexican who fired a gun killing a San Francisco woman. (The bullet actually ricocheted off the ground, and the man was found not guilty.) The political use of dramatic anecdotes is bipartisan, as illustrated when the wrongful detaining of Australian children's author Mem Fox at Los Angeles Airport triggered progressive's outrage over Trump administration border policies. But with 51 million nonresident tourists entering the United States each year, it behooved us to remember that, as we social scientists are fond of saying, "the plural of anecdote is not data."

The staying power of vivid images contributes to misperception that crime has been increasing. In 2015, six of the top ten Associated Press news stories were about gruesome violence (Bornstein & Rosenberg, 2016). "If it bleeds, it leads." Small wonder that Americans grossly overestimate their vulnerability to crime and terror. And not just Americans. In one survey of people across 30 countries, 1.8% of people reported experiencing a completed burglary in the prior year. And 29% of people thought they were likely or very likely to be burglarized during the next year (van Dijk, Kesteren, & Smit, 2007).

In other ways, too, we fear the wrong things. We exhibit *probability neglect* as we worry about unlikely possibilities while ignoring higher probabilities. As Bacon observed (1620), "Things which strike the sense outweigh things which do not immediately strike it, though they be more important" (n.p.). Thanks to cognitively available images of airplane crashes, we may feel more at risk in airplanes than in cars. In reality, from 2010 through 2014, U.S. travelers were nearly 2,000 times more likely to die in a car crash than on a commercial flight covering the same distance (National Safety Council, 2017). In 2017, there were no fatal commercial jet crashes anywhere in the entire world (BBC, 2018). For most air travelers, the most dangerous part of the journey is the un-scary drive to the airport.

After 9/11, as many people forsook air travel for driving, I estimated that if Americans flew 20% less (as airline data indicated) and instead drove half those unflown miles, we could expect an additional 800 traffic deaths in the ensuing year (Myers, 2001). Gerd Gigerenzer (2004, 2010) later checked that prediction against U.S. traffic accident data. The data confirmed an excess (compared to the prior five years) of some 1,595 deaths in the year following 9/11 – people who "lost their lives on the road by trying to avoid the risk of flying" (Gigerenzer, 2010, p. 96). Ergo, the terrorists appear to have killed, unnoticed, six times more people on America's roads than they did with the 265 fatalities of those flying on those four planes.

In 2018, school shootings understandably captured attention, leading some schools to have children practice huddling in closets during active shooter drills. Protecting children is appropriately a high priority. Yet Harvard risk expert David Ropeik (2018) calculates that the likelihood of any given school student being killed by a gun on any given day is incomprehensibly small – 1 in 614,000,000 – "far lower than almost any other mortality risk a kid faces, including traveling to and from school" or playing sports. "Statistics seem cold and irrelevant," acknowledges Ropeik. But, he argues, exaggerated fears of an "extraordinarily rare risk" do their own form of harm to children's security and well-being.

When estimating risks, reasonable people should, of course, seek data. Yet cognitive availability often predominates, as was illustrated one morning after I awoke at an airport hotel where I had been waylaid after a flight delay. The nice woman working the breakfast bar explained how, day after day, she met waylaid passengers experiencing weather problems, crew delays, and mechanical problems. Her conclusion (from her mentally available sample): Flying so often goes awry that if she needed to travel she would *never* fly.

Not-gullible people should likewise seek data when assessing global climate change: "Over time, are the planet air and seas warming? Are the polar ice caps melting? Are vegetation patterns changing? And should accumulating atmospheric CO_2 lead us to expect such changes?" Yet thanks to the availability heuristic, dramatic weather events make us gasp, while such global data we hardly grasp. Thus, people's recent weather experience contaminates their beliefs about the reality and threat of climate change (Kaufman et al., 2017). People express more belief in global warming, and more willingness to donate to a global warming charity, on warmer-than-usual days than on cooler-than-usual days (Li, Johnson, & Zaval, 2011; Zaval, Keenan, Johnson, & Weber, 2014). A hot spell increases people's worry about global warming, while a cold day reduces their concern. In one survey, 47% of Americans agreed that: "The record snowstorms this winter in the eastern United States make me question whether global warming is occurring" (Leiserowitz, Maibach, Roser-Renouf, & Smith, 2011). But then, after an ensuing blistering summer, 67% agreed that global warming helped explain the "record high summer temperatures in the U.S. in 2011" (Leiserowitz, 2011). A tweet from Comedian Stephen Colbert (2014) gets it: "Global warming isn't real because I was cold today! Also great news: world hunger is over because I just ate."

Confirmation Bias and Self-Justification

Bacon's (1620) *Novum Organum* human fallacies also included our tendency to welcome information that supports our views, and to discount what does not: "The human understanding, when any proposition has been once laid down (either from general admission and belief, or from the pleasure it affords), forces everything else to add fresh support and confirmation" (n.p.). Reflecting on his experiments demonstrating this human yen to seek self-supporting evidence (the *confirmation bias*), Paul Wason (1981) concludes that "Ordinary people evade facts, become inconsistent or systematically defend themselves against the threat of new information relevant to the issue" (p. 356). So, having formed a belief – that climate change is real (or a hoax), that gun control does (or does not) save lives, that people can (or cannot) change their sexual orientation – people selectively expose themselves to belief-supportive information (see also Cooper & Avery, Chapter 16 this volume). Our minds vacuum up supportive information. To believe is to see.

Confirmation bias and selective exposure give insight into the striking result of a May 2016 Public Policy Polling survey (2016a). Among voters with a favorable view of Donald Trump (a subset of Republicans), most believed Barack Obama was Muslim rather than Christian (65% vs. 13%). Among voters with an unfavorable view of Trump, the numbers were reversed (13% vs. 64%). Since both can't be right, the survey again displays gullibility writ large. And in the year after Trump's inauguration, anti- and pro-Trump people could read reports of Trump campaign contacts with Russia and reach similarly opposite conclusions of either "collusion" or "a nothing burger."

A sister phenomenon, *self-justification*, further sustains misinformation (see also Dunning, Chapter 12 this volume). To believe is also to justify one's beliefs. This was dramatically evident in U.S. national surveys surrounding the Iraq war. As the war began, 4 in 5 Americans supported the war – on the assumption that Iraq had weapons of mass destruction, though only 38% said the war would be justified if there were no such weapons (Duffy, 2003; Newport, Moore, Jones, & Saad, 2003). When the war was completed without any discovery of WMDs, 58% now justified the war even without such weapons (Gallup, 2003). "Whether or not they find weapons of mass destruction doesn't matter," suggested Republican pollster Frank Luntz (2003), "because the rationale for the war changed." As Daniel Levitin (2017) observed in *Weaponized Lies*, "The brain is a very powerful self-justifying machine" (p. 14).

88 *David G. Myers*

Confirmation bias and self-justification are both driven by people's motives. Motives matter, emphasize Stephen Lewandowsky and Klaus Oberauer (2016): "Scientific findings are rejected . . . because the science is in conflict with people's worldviews, or political or religious opinions" (p. 217). Thus, a conservative libertarian who cherishes the unregulated free market may be motivated to ignore evidence that government regulations serve the common good – that gun control saves lives, that mandated livable wages and social security support human flourishing, that future generations need climate-protecting regulations. A liberal may be likewise motivated to discount science regarding the toxicity of teen pornography exposure, the benefits of stable co-parenting, or the innovations incentivized by the free market. Again, Bacon (1620) foresaw the point: "The human understanding is no dry light, but receives an infusion from the will and affections . . . For what a man had rather were true he more readily believes" (n.p.).

Statistical Illiteracy

Our human powers of evolutionarily determined, automatic information processing feed our intuition (see Baumeister, Chapter 2 this volume). As car mechanics and physicians accumulate experience, their intuitive expertise often allows them to quickly diagnose a problem. Chess masters, with one glance at the board, intuitively know the right move. Japanese chicken sexers use acquired pattern recognition to separate newborn pullets and cockerels with instant accuracy. And for all of us, social experience enables us, when shown but a "thin slice" of another's behavior, to gauge their energy and warmth.

Human intuition has powers, but also perils. "The first principle," said physicist Richard Feynman (1974), "is that you must not fool yourself – and you are the easiest person to fool." In hundreds of experiments, people have overrated their eyewitness recollections, their interviewee assessments, and their stock-picking talents. Often we misjudge reality, and then we display *belief perseverance* when facing disconfirming information. As one unknown wag said, "It's easier to fool people than to convince them they have been fooled." For this gullibility, our statistical intuition is partly to blame.

Probability Neglect

Consider, for example, how statistical illiteracy and misinformation feed health scares (Gigerenzer, 2010). In the 1990s, the British press reported that women taking a particular contraceptive pill had a 100% increased risk of stroke-risking blood clots. This caused thousands of women to stop taking the pill, leading to many unwanted pregnancies and 13,000 additional abortions (which were also linked with increased blood-clot risk). A study

Psychological Science 89

indeed had found a 100% increased risk – but a nominal increase from 1 in 7,000 to 2 in 7,000.

In one study, Gigerenzer (2010) showed how gullibility crosses educational levels. He invited people to estimate the odds that a woman had breast cancer, given these facts: Among women in her age group, 1% had breast cancer. If a woman had breast cancer, the odds were 90% that a mammogram would show a positive result. Now imagine a woman had a positive mammogram. What is the probability that she had breast cancer? This simple question stymied even physicians, who greatly overestimated her risk.

But consider the same information framed with more transparent natural numbers: Of every 1,000 women in this age group, 10 had breast cancer. Of these 10, 9 will have a positive mammogram. Among the other 990 who don't have breast cancer, some 90 will have a false positive mammogram. So, again, what is the probability that a woman with a positive mammogram had cancer? Given the natural numbers, it becomes easier to see that among the 100 or so women receiving a positive result, only 10, or about 1 in 10, actually had breast cancer.

Perceiving Order in Random Events

"The human understanding," said Bacon (1620), is "prone to suppose the existence of more order and regularity in the world than it finds" (n.p.). In our eagerness to make sense of our world, we see patterns. People may perceive a face on the Moon, hear Satanic messages in music played backward, or perceive Jesus' image on a grilled cheese sandwich. It is one of the curious facts of life that even in random data, we often find order (Falk, & Ayton, 2009; Nickerson, 2002, 2005).

Random sequences seldom look random because, more than people expect, they contain streaks. Coin tosses have more runs of heads and of tails than people expect from random coin tosses. Likewise, basketball-shooting and baseball-hitting outcomes that mimic random coin tossing appear to have "hot" or "cold" streaks for which sports fans have ready explanations – as if there were something to explain (Gilovich, Tversky, & Vallone, 1985; Reifman, 2011). And as Burton Malkiel's many editions of *A Random Walk Down Wall Street* document, stock pickers are similarly tempted to see patterns in random data and to overestimate their ability to beat the efficient marketplace.

As determined pattern-seekers, we therefore sometimes fool ourselves. We see *illusory correlations*. We perceive causal links where there are none. We may even make sense out of nonsense, by believing that astrological predictions predict the future, that gambling strategies can defy chance, or that superstitious rituals will trigger good luck. As Bacon (1620) recognized, "All superstition is much the same . . . deluded believers observe events which are fulfilled, but neglect and pass over their failure, though it be much more common" (n.p.).

90 *David G. Myers*

Misinterpreting Regression Toward the Mean

Another common source of gullibility is our natural underappreciation of statistical regression. Because average results are more typical than extreme results, we may expect that, after an unusual event, things will tend to regress (return) toward their average level. Extraordinary events tend to be followed by more ordinary ones.

Failure to recognize such regression feeds superstitions and ineffective practices. When day-to-day behavior contains chance fluctuation, we may notice that others' behavior improves (regresses toward average) after we criticize them for an unusually bad performance, and that it worsens (regresses toward average) after we praise them for an exceptionally fine performance. Ironically, then, regression toward the average can mislead us into feeling rewarded for having criticized others and into feeling punished for having praised them (Tversky & Kahneman, 1974). Coaches who berate their teams at halftime after an exceptionally bad performance will tend to feel rewarded with a more normal second half performance, and vice versa for those who lavish praise after an outstanding first half performance.

Group Polarization

Human gullibility feeds on fake news, mere repetition, vivid anecdotes, self-confirming assessments, self-justification, and statistical misinformation, and is then further amplified as people network with like-minded others. In one of my early experiments with George Bishop, high- and low-prejudice high school students were grouped with kindred spirits for discussion of racial issues, such as a case of property rights clashing with open housing. Our finding, and that of many other experiments since, was that like minds polarize (Figure 5.6; Myers & Bishop, 1970). Separation + conversation → polarization.

This *group polarization phenomenon* – discussion magnifying a group's preexisting leanings – helps fuel both public good (when benevolent tendencies strengthen) and evil (from gang delinquency to terrorism). As with hot coals, like minds strengthen one another.

In communities, like minds are segregating more and more. Progressive places have attracted progressive people, and become more progressive. Ditto conservative places. Thus the percentage of Americans living in landslide counties – those with 60+% voting for the same presidential candidate – rose from 38% in 1992 to 60% in 2016 (Aisch, Pearce, & Yourish, 2016). And the proportion of entering collegians describing themselves as politically "middle of the road" dropped from 60% in 1983 to 42% in 2016 – with corresponding increases in those with "far left" and "far right" identities (Eagan et al., 2017; Twenge, Honeycutt, Prislin, & Sherman, 2016).

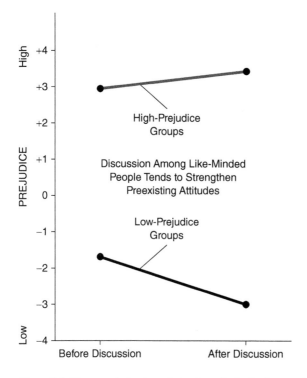

Figure 5.6 Group polarization. Attitudes polarized when students discussed racial issues in separated small groups of those with high and low prejudice.

Source: Myers and Bishop (1970).

As I cut my eyeteeth in social psychology with studies of group polarization, I did not foresee the creative possibilities or potential dangers of polarization enabled by social media, with liberal and conservative websites linking people mostly to kindred sites (Figure 5.7; Lazer et al., 2009). The Internet enables cancer survivors and conspiracy schemers to congregate with like-minded others and to share support for their shared aspirations and suspicions. With customized news feeds, retweets, and self-selections from a varied news buffet, we devour information – and misinformation (Bakshy, Messing, & Adamic, 2015; Barberá, Jost, Nagler, Tucker, & Bonneau, 2015). "Dear Satan," tweeted Steve Martin (2016), "thank you for having my internet news feed tailored especially for ME!"

Within this echo chamber of the like-minded, group polarization happens. Therefore, what begins as gullibility may become toxic. Views become more extreme. Suspicion may escalate into obsession. Disagreements with the other tribe can intensify to demonization. Disapproval may inflate to loathing.

Figure 5.7 Liberal and conservative websites network mostly with one another.
Source: Adapted from Lazer et al. (2009).

Overconfidence

The result of gullibility-producing biases and polarization is *overconfidence* in one's own wisdom. Such overconfidence – what researchers have called *cognitive conceit* – comes naturally. For example, when people's answers to factual questions – "Which is longer, the Panama or the Suez Canal?" "Is absinthe a liqueur or a precious stone?" – are correct 60% of the time, they will typically feel 75% confident (Fischhoff, Slovic, & Lichtenstein, 1977; Metcalfe, 1998; see also Dunning, Chapter 12 this volume).

Overconfidence – the bias that Daniel Kahneman (2015), if given a magic wand, would most like to eliminate – feeds political misjudgment. Philip Tetlock (1998, 2005) gathered 27,000+ expert predictions of world events, such as whether Quebec would separate from Canada, or the future of South Africa. His finding: Like stock brokers, gamblers, and everyday citizens, they were more confident than correct. The experts' predictions, made with 80% confidence on average, were right less than 40% of the time.

Citizens with a shallow understanding of complex proposals, such as cap-and-trade or a flat tax, may nevertheless express strong views. As the now-famous *Dunning–Kruger effect* reminds us, incompetence can ironically feed overconfidence (Kruger & Dunning, 1999; see also Dunning, Chapter 12 this volume). The less people know, the less aware they are of their own ignorance and the more definite they may sound. Asking them to explain the details of these policies exposes them to their own ignorance, which often leads them to express more moderate views (Fernbach, Rogers, Fox, & Sloman, 2013). "No one can see his own errors," wrote the Psalmist (19:12, GNB). But to confront one's own ignorance is to become wiser.

Conclusion: Gullibility and Humility

This enumeration of the roots of gullibility could be extended with explanations of the anchoring effect, belief perseverance, the false consensus phenomenon, issue framing, the fundamental attribution error, hindsight bias, illusory correlations, implicit associations, in-group bias, the just-world phenomenon, memory construction, mood-congruent memories, perceptual illusions, self-serving perceptions, implicit associations, in-group bias, the representativeness heuristic, and more. But this has been enough to appreciate that Pascal was right: "The human understanding is like a false mirror."

We can acknowledge human gullibility while still respecting our remarkable information-processing powers – appreciating, with Shakespeare's Hamlet, "in apprehension how like a god!" Our species is smart enough to have invented talking computers, cracked our genetic code, and traveled to the moon. Three cheers for our human brilliance.

Or maybe two cheers, because our mind's premium on efficiency enables us, with striking ease, to adapt successfully but also to form and sustain false beliefs. "The naked intellect," observed novelist Madeline L'Engle (1973, p. 87), "is an extraordinarily inaccurate instrument."

For this, science, education, and religion each offer remedies.

Science encourages a marriage of open curiosity with skepticism. "If you are only skeptical," noted Carl Sagan (1987), "then no new ideas make it through to you." But a smart mind also restrains gullibility by thinking critically. It asks, "What do you mean" and "How do you know"? "Openness to new ideas, combined with the most rigorous, skeptical scrutiny of all ideas, sifts the wheat from the chaff," Sagan (1996, p. 31) added.

Education is an antidote to what Sagan (1996) feared – a future for his grandchildren in which "our critical faculties in decline, unable to distinguish between what feels good and what's true, we slide, almost without noticing, back into superstition and darkness" (p. 25). Happily, education works. It can train people to recognize how errors and biases creep into their thinking (Nisbett, 2015; Nisbett & Ross, 1980). It can engage analytic thinking: "Activate misconceptions and then explicitly refute them," advise Alan Bensley and Scott Lilienfeld (2017; see also Chan, Jones, Hall Jamieson, & Albarracín, 2017). It can harness the powers of repetition, availability, and the like to teach true information (Schwarz et al., 2017). And thus, at the end of the day, it can and does predict decreased gullible acceptance of conspiracy theories (van Prooijen, 2017).

Finally, religion can provide a deep rationale for the humility that underlies science and critical thinking. All varieties of theism assume that (1) there is a God, and (2) it's not you or me. As fallible creatures we should therefore hold our own beliefs tentatively (our surest conviction can be that some of our beliefs err). We should assess others' ideas with open-minded skepticism. And when appropriate, we should use observation and experimentation to

94 *David G. Myers*

winnow truth from error. As St. Paul advised (1 Thessalonians 5:21), "Test everything, hold fast to what is good." Truth matters.

Note

1 As Ruth Mayo (Chapter 8 this volume) shows, in some contexts an opposite mistrust bias appears – leading people to discount valid information and to *dis*believe credible sources as fake news.

References

Adelman, R., Reid, L. W., Markle, G., Weiss, S., & Jaret, C. (2017). Urban crime rates and the changing face of immigration: Evidence across four decades. *Journal of Ethnicity in Criminal Justice, 15,* 52–77.

Aisch, G., Pearce, A., & Yourish, K. (2016, November 10). The divide between red and blue America grew even deeper in 2016. *New York Times.* Retrieved from www.nytimes.com/interactive/2016/11/10/us/politics/red-blue-divide-grew-stronger-in-2016.html.

Allport, G. W. (1954). *The nature of prejudice.* Cambridge, MA: Addison-Wesley.

Arkes, H. R. (1990). *Some practical judgment/decision making research.* Paper presented at the American Psychological Association convention, Chicago.

Bacon, F. (1620) *Novum Organum.* New York, NY: P. F. Collier & Son. Retrieved from www.gutenberg.org/files/45988/45988-h/45988-h.htm.

Bakshy, E., Messing, S., & Adamic, L. A. (2015). Exposure to ideologically diverse news and opinion on Facebook. *Science, 348,* 1130–1132.

Barberá, P., Jost, J. T., Nagler, J., Tucker, J. A., & Bonneau, R. (2015). Tweeting from left to right: Is online political communication more than an echo chamber? *Psychological Science, 26,* 1531–1542.

BBC. (2018, January 2). 2017 safest year for air travel as fatalities fall. Retrieved from www.bbc.com/news/business-42538053.

Bensley, D. A., & Lilienfeld, S. (2017). Psychological misconceptions: Recent scientific advances and unresolved issues. *Current Directions in Psychological Science, 26,* 377–382.

Bornstein, D., & Rosenberg, T. (2016, November 14). When reportage turns to cynicism. Retrieved from www.nytimes.com/2016/11/15/opinion/when-reportage-turns-to-cynicism.html.

Brandt, M. J. (2017). Predicting ideological prejudice. *Psychological Science, 28,* 712–722.

Bullock, J. (2006, March 17). *The enduring importance of false political beliefs.* Paper presented at the annual meeting of the Western Political Science Association, Albuquerque. Retrieved from www.allacademic.com/meta/p97459_index.html.

Bureau of Justice Statistics. (2016, October). *National crime victimization survey (NCVS), 1993–2015. Report NCJ* 250180.

BLS. (2017). *Labor force statistics from the Current Population Survey.* Bureau of Labor Statistics, Department of Labor. Retrieved from data.bls.gov/timeseries/LNS14000000.

Butcher, K. F., & Piehl, A. M. (2007). *Why are immigrants' incarceration rates so low? Evidence on selective immigration, deterrence, and deportation.* NBER Working Paper No. 13229. Retrieved from www.nber.org/papers/w13229.pdf.

Cato Institute. (2017, March 15). *Criminal immigrants: Their numbers, demographics, and countries of origin.* Immigration Research and Policy Brief No. 1. Retrieved from www.cato.org/publications/immigration-reform-bulletin/criminal-immigrants-their-numbers-demographics-countries.

Chambers, J. R., Schlenker, B. R., & Collisson, B. (2013). Ideology and prejudice: The role of value conflicts. *Psychological Science, 24,* 140–149.

Chan, M. S., Jones, C. R., Hall Jamieson, K., & Albarracín, D. (2017). Debunking: A meta-analysis of the psychological efficacy of messages countering misinformation. *Psychological Science, 28,* 1531–1546.

Colbert, S. (2014, November 18). [Tweet] Retrieved from https://twitter.com/stephenathome/status/534929076726009856?lang=en.

Crawford, J. T., Kay, S., & Duke, K. E. (2015). Speaking out of both sides of their mouths: Biased political judgments within (and between) individuals. *Social Psychological and Personality Science, 6,* 422–430.

Dechêne, A., Stahl, C., Hansen, J., & Wänke, M. (2010). The truth about the truth: A meta-analysis review of the truth effect. *Personality and Social Psychology Review, 14,* 238–257.

Ditto, P. H., Liu, B. S., Clark, C. J., Wojcik, S. J., Chen, E. E., Grady, R. H., . . . Zinger, J. F. (2018, in press). At least bias is bipartisan: A meta-analytic comparison of partisan bias in liberals and conservatives. *Perspectives on Psychological Science.*

Ditto, P. H., Wojcik, S. P., Chen, E. E., Grady, R. H., & Ringel, M. M. (2015). Political bias is tenacious. *Behavioral and Brain Sciences, 38,* 2.

Duffy, M. (2003, June 9). Weapons of mass disappearance. *Time,* 28–33.

Eagan, M. K., Stolzenberg, E. B., Zimmerman, H. B., Aragon, M. C., Whang Sayson, H., & Rios-Aguilar, C. (2017). *The American freshman: National norms Fall 2016.* Los Angeles, CA: Higher Education Research Institute, UCLA.

Ecker, U. K. H., Lewandowsky, S., Swire, B., & Chang, D. (2011). Correction false information in memory: Manipulating the strength of information encoding and its retraction. *Psychonomic Bulletin & Review, 18,* 570–578.

Emery, Jr., E. C. (2016, May 11). Donald Trump says Germany now riddled with crime thanks to refugees. *Politifact.* Retrieved from www.politifact.com/truth-o-meter/statements/2016/may/11/donald-trump/donald-trump-says-germany-now-riddled-crime-thanks.

Falk, R., Falk, R., & Ayton, P. (2009). Subjective patterns of randomness and choice: Some consequences of collective responses. *Journal of Experimental Psychology: Human Perception and Performance, 35,* 203–224.

Fernbach, P. M., Rogers, T., Fox, C. R., & Sloman, S. A. (2013). Political extremism is supported by an illusion of understanding. *Psychological Science, 24,* 939–946.

Feynman, R. (1974). Commencement address, California Institute of Technology. Retrieved from http://calteches.library.caltech.edu/3043/1/CargoCult.pdf.

Fischhoff, B., Slovic, P., & Lichtenstein, S. (1977). Knowing with certainty: The appropriateness of extreme confidence. *Journal of Experimental Psychology: Human Perception and Performance, 3,* 552–564.

Funk, C., & Rainie, L. (2015, January 29). *Attitudes and beliefs on science and technology topics.* Retrieved from www.pewinternet.org.

Gallup Organization. (2003, June 16). *Americans still think Iraq had weapons of mass destructions before war.* Retrieved from www.gallup.com/poll/8623/americans-still-think-iraq-had-weapons-mass-destruction-before-war.aspx.

Gelman, A. (2009, April 16). *Red and blue economies?* FiveThirtyEight.com. Retrieved from www.fivethirtyeight.com/features/red-and-blue-economies.

Gigerenzer, G. (2004). Dread risk, September 11, and fatal traffic accidents. *Psychological Science, 15,* 286–287.

Gigerenzer, G. (2010). *Rationality for mortals: How people cope with uncertainty.* New York, NY: Oxford University Press.

Gilovich, T., Tversky, A., & Vallone, R. (1985). The hot hand in basketball: On the misperception of random sequences. *Cognitive Psychology, 17,* 295–314.

Hachman, M. (2017, September 7). Just how partisan is Facebook's fake news? We tested it. *PC World.* Retrieved from www.pcworld.com/article/3142412/win dows/just-how-partisan-is-facebooks-fake-news-we-tested-it.html.

Hitler, Adolf. (1926). *Mein Kampf.* Retrieved from https://history.hanover.edu/courses/excerpts/111hitler.html.

Ingraham, C. (2016, October 20). Toddlers have shot at least 50 people this year. *Washington Post.* Retrieved from www.washingtonpost.com/news/wonk/wp/2016/10/20/toddlers-have-shot-at-least-50-people-this-year/?utm_term=.1088c471e74c.

Kahneman, D. (2015, July 18). "Daniel Kahneman: 'What would I eliminate if I had a magic wand? Overconfidence.'" *Guardian.* Retrieved from www.the guardian.com/books/2015/jul/18/daniel-kahneman-books-interview.

Kaufmann, R. K., Mann, M. L., Gopal, S., Liederman, J. A., Howe, P. D., Pretis, F., . . . Gilmore, M. (2017). Spatial heterogeneity of climate change as an experiential basis for skepticism. *PNAS, 114,* 67–71.

Kavanagh, J., & Rich, M. D. (2018). *Truth decay: An exploration of the diminishing role of facts and analysis in American public life.* Rand Corporation. Retrieved from www.rand.org/content/dam/rand/pubs/research_reports/RR2300/RR2314/RAND_RR2314.pdf.

KFF. (2017). *Population distribution by citizenship status.* Kaiser Family Foundation estimates based on the Census Bureau's March Current Population Survey (CPS: Annual Social and Economic Supplements). Retrieved from www.kff.org.

Kristof, N. (2016, November 12). Lies in the guise of news in the Trump era. *New York Times.* Retrieved from www.nytimes.com/2016/11/13/opinion/sunday/lies-in-the-guise-of-news-in-the-trump-era.html?_r=0.

Kristof, N. (2017, February 11). Husbands are deadlier than terrorists. *New York Times.* Retrieved from www.nytimes.com/2017/02/11/opinion/sunday/hus bands-are-deadlier-than-terrorists.html.

Krogstad, J. M., Passel, J. S., & Cohn, D. (2017, April 27). 5 facts about illegal immigration in the U.S. Pew Research Center. Retrieved from www.pewre search.org/fact-tank/2017/04/27/5-facts-about-illegal-immigration-in-the-u-s.

Kruger, J., & Dunning, D. (1999). Unskilled and unaware of it: How difficulties in recognizing one's own incompetence lead to inflated self-assessments. *Journal of Personality and Social Psychology, 77,* 1121–1134.

Lazer, D., Pentland, A., Adamic, L., Aral, S., Barbasi, A. L., Brewer, D., . . . van Alstyne, M. (2009). Life in the network: The coming age of computational social science. *Science, 323,* 721–723.

Lee, T. B. (2016, November 16). The top 20 fake news stories outperformed real news at the end of the 2016 campaign. *Vox.* Retrieved from www.vox.com/new-money/2016/11/16/13659840/facebook-fake-news-chart.

Leiserowitz, A. (2011, November 17). Do Americans connect climate change and extreme weather events? E-mail of Yale/GMU survey. New Haven, CT: Yale Project on Climate Change Communication, Yale University and George Mason University.

Leiserowitz, A., Maibach, E., Roser-Renouf, C., & Smith, N. (2011). *Climate change in the American mind: Americans' global warming beliefs and attitudes in May 2011*. New Haven, CT: Yale Project on Climate Change Communication, Yale University and George Mason University.

L'Engle, M. (1973). *The wind in the door*. New York, NY: Farrar Straus, & Giroux.

Levitin, D. J. (2017). *Weaponized lies: How to think critically in the post-truth era*. New York, NY: Dutton.

Lewandowsky, S., Ecker, U. K. H., Seifert, C. M., Schwarz, N., & Cooke, J. (2012). Misinformation and its correction: Continued influence and successful debasing. *Psychological Science in the Public Interest, 13*, 106–131.

Lewandowsky, S., & Oberauer, K. (2016). Motivated rejection of science. *Current Directions in Psychological Science, 25*, 216–222.

Li, Y., Johnson, E. J., & Zaval, L. (2011). Local warming: Daily temperature change influences belief in global warming. *Psychological Science, 22*, 454–459.

Lowery, W. (2014, April 4). 91% of the time the better-financed candidate wins. *Washington Post*. Retrieved from www.washingtonpost.com/blogs/the-fix/wp/2014/04/04/think-money-doesnt-matter-in-elections-this-chart-says-youre-wrong.

Luntz, F. (2003, June 10). Quoted by T. Raum, "Bush insists banned weapons will be found." Associated Press. Retrieved from www.ourmidland.com/news/arti cle/Bush-Insists-Banned-Weapons-Will-Be-Found-7186311.php.

Martin, S. (2016, 24 September). [Tweet] Retrieved from https://polititweet.org/tweet?account=14824849&tweet=779711357323137024.

McCain, J. (2017, February 17). Remarks by SASC chairman John McCain at the 2017 Munich Security Conference. Retrieved from www.mccain.senate.gov/public/index.cfm/2017/2/remarks-by-sasc-chairman-john-mccain-at-the-2017-munich-security-conference.

McCarthy, J. (2017, June 28). Americans more positive about effects of immigration. Gallup. Retrieved from http://news.gallup.com/poll/213146/americans-positive-effects-immigration.aspx.

McGlone, M. S., & Tofighbakhsh, J. (2000). Birds of a feather flock conjointly (?): Rhyme as reason in aphorisms. *Psychological Science, 11*, 424–428.

Metcalfe, J. (1998). Cognitive optimism: Self-deception or memory-based processing heuristics. *Personality and Social Psychology Review, 2*, 100–110.

Moons, W. G., Mackie, D. M., & Garcia-Marques, T. (2009). The impact of repetition-induced familiarity on agreement with weak and strong arguments. *Journal of Personality and Social Psychology, 96*, 32–44.

Myers, D. G. (2001, December). Do we fear the right things? *American Psychological Society Observer*, 3.

Myers, D. G., & Bishop, G. D. (1970). Discussion effects on racial attitudes. *Science, 169*, 778–789.

National Academies of Sciences, Engineering, and Medicine. (2015). *The integration of immigrants into American society*. Washington, DC: The National Academies Press. https://doi.org/10.17226/21746.

National Safety Council. (2017). Transportation mode comparisons: Passenger death and death rates, United States 2007–2014. *Injury Facts 2017 Edition*, 156. Itasca, IL: National Safety Council.

Newport, F., Moore, D. W., Jones, J. M., & Saad, L. (2003, March 21). *Special release: American opinion on the war*. Gallup Poll Tuesday Briefing. Retrieved from www.gallup.com/poll/tb/goverpubli/s0030325.asp.

Nickerson, R. S. (2002). The production and perception of randomness. *Psychological Review, 109*, 330–357.

Nickerson, R. S. (2005). Bertrand's chord, Buffon's needles, and the concept of randomness. *Thinking & Reasoning, 11*, 67–96.

Nisbett, R. E. (2015). *Mindware: Tools for smart thinking*. New York, NY: Farrar, Straus, & Giroux.

Nisbett, R. E., & Ross, L. (1980). *Human inference: Strategies and shortcomings of social judgment*. Englewood Cliffs, NJ: Prentice-Hall.

Nyhan, B., & Reifler, J. (2008). *When corrections fail: The persistence of political misperceptions*. Unpublished manuscript. Durham, NC: Duke University.

Obama, B. (2016, November 17). Remarks by President Obama and Chancellor Merkel of Germany in a Joint Press Conference. Retrieved from www.obamawhitehouse.archives.gov/the-press-office/2016/11/17/remarks-president-obama-and-chancellor-merkel-germany-joint-press.

Obama, B. (2017, January 10). Farewell address. Chicago, McCormick Place. Retrieved from www.obamawhitehouse.archives.gov/farewell.

Pantazi, M., Kissine, M., & Klein, O. (2018). The power of the truth bias: False information affects memory and judgment even in the absence of distraction. *Social Cognition, 36*, 167–198.

Pinker, S. (2018). *Enlightenment now: The case for reason, science, humanism, and progress*. New York, NY: Viking.

Pope Francis. (2018, January 24). *Message of his Holiness Pope Francis for World Communications Day: Fake news and journalism for peace*. The Vatican. Retrieved from https://w2.vatican.va/content/francesco/en/messages/communications/documents/papa-francesco_20180124_messaggio-comunicazioni-sociali.html.

Powell, J. L. (2015, November/December). The consensus on anthropogenic global warming. *Skeptical Inquirer*, 42–45.

Public Policy Polling. (2016a, May 10). *Clinton still has modest lead*. Retrieved from www.publicpolicypolling.com/polls/gop-quickly-unifies-around-trump-clinton-still-has-modest-lead.

Public Policy Polling. (2016b, December 9). *Trump remains unpopular: Voters prefer Obama on SCOTUS pick*. Retrieved from www.publicpolicypolling.com/wp-content/uploads/2017/09/PPP_Release_National_120916.pdf.

Reifman, A. (2011). *Hot hand: The statistics behind sports' greatest streaks*. Lincoln, NE: Potomac Books.

Riley, J. L. (2015, July 14). The mythical connection between immigrants and crime. *Wall Street Journal*. Retrieved from www.wsj.com/articles/the-mythical-connection-between-immigrants-and-crime-1436916798.

Rizzo, S. (2018, January 18). Trump's claim that immigrants bring "tremendous crime" is still wrong. *Washington Post*. Retrieved from www.washingtonpost.com/news/fact-checker/wp/2018/01/18/trumps-claim-that-immigrants-bring-tremendous-crime-is-still-wrong/?utm_term=.71c49a871044.

Ropeik, D. (2018, March 8). School shootings are extremely rare. What is fear of them driving policy? *Washington Post*. Retrieved from www.washingtonpost.com.

Saad, L. (2017, March 14). Global warming concern at three-decade high in U.S. Gallup. Retrieved from www.gallup.com/poll.

Sagan, C. (1987, Fall). The burden of skepticism. *Skeptical Inquirer, 12*(1). Retrieved from www.csicop.org/si/show/burden_of_skepticism.

Sagan, C. (1996). *The demon-haunted world*. New York, NY: Ballantine.

Schama, S. (2017, February 3). Tweet from @simon_schama.

Schwarz, N., Newman, E., & Leach, W. (2017). Making the truth stick & the myths fade: Lessons from cognitive psychology. *Behavioral Science & Policy, 2*, 85–95.

Schwarz, N., Sanna, L. J., Skurnik, I., & Yoon, C. (2007). Metacognitive experiences and the intricacies of setting people straight: Implications for debiasing and public information campaigns. *Advances in Experimental Social Psychology, 39*, 127–161.

Skurnik, I., Yoon, C., Park, D. C., & Schwarz, N. (2005). How warnings about false claims become recommendations. *Journal of Consumer Research, 31*, 713–724.

Snopes. (2015, December 17). *Kindergarten, stop*. Retrieved from www.snopes.com/toddlers-killed-americans-terrorists.

Snopes. (2016, September 27). *The great debate: Reports that Trump would not attend the final presidential debates if Hillary Clinton showed up originated with a satirical column*. Retrieved from www.snopes.com/trump-threatens-to-skip-debates.

Street, C. N. H., & Kingstone, A. (2017). Aligning spinoza with descartes: An informed cartesian account of the truth bias. *British Journal of Psychology, 108*, 453–466.

Swift, A. (2016, November 9). *Americans' perceptions of U.S. crime problem are steady*. Gallup News. Retrieved from www.news.gallup.com/poll/197318/americans-perceptions-crime-problem-steady.aspx.

Swift, J. (1710, November 2–9). *The Examiner, 15*, 2.

Tetlock, P. E. (1998). Close-call counterfactuals and belief-system defenses: I was not almost wrong but I was almost right. *Journal of Personality and Social Psychology, 75*, 639–652.

Tetlock, P. E. (2005). *Expert political judgement: How good is it? How can we know?* Princeton, NJ: Princeton University Press.

Trump, D. J. (2015a, June 16). Reported by I. Schwartz: Trump: Mexico not sending us their best; Criminals, drug dealers and rapists are crossing border. *Real Clear Politics*. Retrieved from www.realclearpolitics.com/video/2015/06/16/trump_mexico_not_sending_us_their_best_criminals_drug_dealers_and_rapists_are_crossing_border.html.

Trump, D. J. (2015b, June 16). Reported by L. Jacobson, Donald Trump says 'real' unemployment rate is 18 to 20 percent. *Politifact*. Retrieved from www.politifact.com/truth-o-meter/statements/2015/jun/16/donald-trump/donald-trump-says-real-unemployment-rate-18-20-per.

Trump, D. J. (2017, February 7). Roundtable discussion with county sheriffs. Retrieved from www.snopes.com/murder-rate-highest-in-47-years.

Trump, D. J. (2018, February 6). Trump says: "I'd love to see a shutdown" if no immigration law. *New York Times*. Retrieved from www.nytimes.com/reuters/2018/02/06/us/politics/06reuters-usa-congress-shutdown-trump.html.

Tversky, A., & Kahneman, D. (1974). Judgment under uncertainty: Heuristics and biases. *Science, 185*, 1124–1131.

100 David G. Myers

Twenge, J. M., Honeycutt, N., Prislin, R., & Sherman, R. A. (2016). More polarized but more Independent: Political party identification and ideological self-categorization among U.S. adults, college students, and late adolescents, 1970–2015. *Personality and Social Psychology Bulletin, 42*, 1364–1383.

van Dijk, D., Kesteren, J. V., & Smit, P. (2007). Criminal victimization in international perspective: key Findings from the 2004–2005 ICVS and EU ICS. Retrieved from www.unicri.it/services/library_documentation/publications/icvs/publications/ICVS2004_05report.pdf.

van Prooijen, J. (2017). Why education predicts decreased belief in conspiracy theories. *Applied Cognitive Psychology, 31*(1), 50–58.

Varmus, H. (2017, March 22). Why Trump's N.I.H. cuts should worry us. *New York Times*. Retrieved from www.nytimes.com/2017/03/22/opinion/why-trumps-nih-cuts-should-worry-us.html.

Vedantam, S. (2012, May 9). *Partiasan psychology: Why do people choose political loyalties over facts?*. Retrieved from www.npr.org/blogs/itsallpolitics/2012/05/09/152287372/partisan-psychology-why-are-people-partial-to-political-loyalties-over-facts.

Vosoughi, S., Roy, D., & Aral, S. (2018). The spread of true and false news online. *Science, 359*, 1146–1151.

Wason, P. C. (1981). The importance of cognitive illusions. *The Behavioral and Brain Sciences, 4*, 356.

Zaval, L., Keenan, E. A., Johnson, E. J., & Weber, E. U. (2014). How warm days increase belief in global warming. *Nature Climate Change, 4*, 143–147.

Zorn, E. (2017, January 5). Polls reveal sobering extent of nation's fact crisis. *Chicago Tribune*. Retrieved from www.chicagotribune.com/news/opinion/zorn/ct-polling-ignorance-facts-trump-zorn-perspec-0106-md-20170105-column.html.

Part II

Cognitive Processes and Gullibility

6 Towards a Credible Theory of Gullibility

Joachim I. Krueger
BROWN UNIVERSITY

Claudia Vogrincic-Haselbacher
UNIVERSITY OF GRAZ

Anthony M. Evans
TILBURG UNIVERSITY

Politicians are not known for putting a premium on truth, yet they seek to appear as if they did. George W. Bush famously asserted that "there's an old saying in Tennessee – I know it's in Texas, probably in Tennessee – that says, fool me once, shame on – shame on you. Fool me – you can't get fooled again."[1] Bush may have fooled his fellow Americans many times, but he did not fool everyone all the time. Occasionally, evidence contrary of what he asserted punched through. His claim that Iraq harbored weapons of mass destruction (WMD) at the time the United States was preparing for war was not substantiated – to the point that the absence of evidence amounted to evidence of absence (Hartnett & Stengrim, 2004). Of course, the evidence (or lack thereof) did not move all minds. Even today, some people feel that Saddam Hussein had such weapons stashed away somewhere (Hochschild & Einstein, 2015). These believers may point to the fact that Saddam did use WMD on citizens of his own country when unleashing poison gas on the Kurds. If WMD were found, dedicated minds might argue that the CIA had planted these weapons in order to reconcile ordinary American minds with the idea of war. As long as an idea is neither theoretically impossible nor empirically disproven, even David Hume or Thomas Bayes can only ask for skepticism but not outright disbelief.

As a low-stakes example, consider a social media post in which one of the authors (JIK) announced his departure from academia for the corporate world. Some of his friends wished him well, whereas others expressed puzzlement. Responding to a call from his superego, JIK eventually revealed his jocular intent. Humor is a risky form of gullibility play. The humorous guller must trust the gullees to "get it." The humorous guller must, in other words, temporarily disable the Gricean norm of truthfulness. By contrast, the serious guller strategically leverages the Gricean norm, thereby debasing it. Hence, the issue of gullibility can be framed as a dilemma or as a dialectic. This is the approach we take in this chapter.

The Gullibility Game

Parents tell their children – much as pastors, rabbis, schoolteachers, and insurance salespeople tell the rest of us – "thou shalt not lie!" Deontological imperatives are a culture's way of creating consent at low cost (Baron, 2012; see Forgas, Chapter 10 this volume; Oyserman, Chapter 14 this volume). These imperatives ask us not to think and reflect, but to engage the unquestioning, reflexive capacity of mind. This tends to work well enough to hold society together, but, as game theory teaches, being truthful is not a dominating strategy (Binmore, 2007). You will not be better off by being truthful irrespective of whether others lie. Nor is lying a dominating strategy in the way that defection is in the prisoner's dilemma. Kant solved the dilemma after a fashion by ignoring the material consequences and pronouncing truthfulness the moral choice.

Living humans, however, who worry about consequences, may consider the assurance game, also known as the "stag hunt" (Rousseau, 1754/1984), as a model of trust and gullibility (Krueger, Evans, & Heck, 2017). In the assurance game, the payoff matrix of which is shown in Figure 6.1, both players recognize that mutual cooperation (telling the truth) yields the best outcome for all. However, a player who believes that the other might defect (lie) will him- or herself defect, thereby confirming this very fear for the other. In other words, a player might doubt that the other will cooperate if the other player fears that this first player might have that fear, and so on. The assurance game has no dominating strategy, but in repeated play a strategy of tit for tat ("equivalent retaliation") is an effective way to settle into a mutually beneficial exchange of cooperative behavior (Axelrod, 1984). When speech acts are exchanged, tit for tat gives the benefit of the doubt. Speak the truth unless you are lied to. Alas, we often don't know at first whether we are being lied to. We must apply personal standards of how much credence to grant a claim when the claimant's intentions are veiled (Harris, Koenig, Corriveau, & Jaswal, 2018).

Player 2

		Stag	Hare
Player 1	Stag	2, 2	0, 1
	Hare	1, 0	1, 1

Figure 6.1 The assurance game in matrix form. Higher numbers indicate more preferred outcomes.

Gullibus Dialecticus

A dialectic is a potential intellectual impasse, a fanciful way of saying "it's complicated," but with a hope of resolution. If we cannot trust all claims all the time for fear of being gulled, how do we know the difference? If gullibility is the thesis and skepticism is the antithesis, how do we find a synthesis? To say "believe the credible" is to beg the question of how we know what is credible. Psychological science is flush with theories of animal learning (Church, 1963), deep learning (LeCun, Bengio, & Hinton, 2015), very deep learning (Simonyan & Zisserman, 2014), and machine learning (Rasmussen, 2004). All these theories assume the existence of honest feedback. The signal may come with noise, and perception and memory may be imperfect, but the feedback is rarely allowed to be strategic – unless experimenters lie to their participants.[2]

Epistemology and Induction

Being skeptical during the generally optimistic era of the enlightenment, Hume explored the phenomenon of gullibility. In his essay on miracles, he maintained that extraordinary claims require extraordinary evidence (Hume, 1748/1959). Setting this high standard for the verification of a miracle, he assigned it a low probability of occurring. For a claim of a miracle to be accepted, the probability of the claim being fake – by mistake or by design – must be lower still. Hume advised that we should not accept such claims lightly; the fact that beliefs in miracles are not uncommon suggests that Hume's rule has normative force (Hájek, 1995).

The same holds for Bayes' rule, although Bayes was not concerned with lying. Bayes' equation, which shows the relations among conditional and unconditional probabilities, is normative in the mathematical sense. Thou shalt not violate Bayes' theorem lest thou be incoherent. In psychological science, Bayes' theorem is often accepted as a norm of thinking (Edwards, Lindman, & Savage, 1963). Thou shalt think in the Bayesian way lest thou be irrational (Dawes, 1988). The psychological idea implicit in Bayes is seemingly beyond reproach. Belief – broadly defined as a person's subjective sense of the likelihood of an assertion being true – should be sufficiently determined by prior belief and evidence – in multiplicative fashion. The strength of the prior belief may be expressed as a likelihood or a probability, $p(B)$, and the strength of the evidence is expressed by the ratio of the likelihood of the evidence assuming that the belief in question is true, $p(D \mid B)$, over the cumulative likelihood of the evidence under all conceivable beliefs, $p(D)$. When only two mutually exclusive and exhaustive beliefs are in play ("The aliens either landed or they did not"), the latter term reduces to the sum of the likelihood of the evidence assuming that the belief is true plus the likelihood of the evidence assuming that the belief is false.

Bayes' theorem and the human judgment it informs work well when the numbers are on the table, either as probabilities or as frequencies (Gigerenzer

& Hoffrage, 1995). Basic rationality is assumed in that the human judges are not expected to bicker over the numbers. They only need to know how to divide and multiply. Although Bayesian theories model subjectivity, they demand consensus on what the data are. Subjectivity is placed in the term $p(B)$; it may vary over judges. The evidence, or the data, D, is objective. Thus, the term $p(D|B)$ is objective. The assumption that humans honor the objectivity of $p(D|B)$ shows the optimism of the enlightenment. Yet, human cognition and perception are subject to motivations and cognitive constraints, so much so that a value of, say, .05 for $p(D|B)$ means different things to different people (see Myers, Chapter 5 this volume).

A third approach is decision theoretic (Swets, Dawes, & Monahan, 2000). After Hume and Bayes, we meet Pascal (Hájek, 2003; Krueger, 2011b). Here too, we find a family of models and techniques, but the basic idea is simple. Decisions bisect reality so that the decision to endorse belief B amounts to a true positive, or a "hit," if that belief is true. If this belief is not true, the result is a false-positive error. If the decision is to reject B, but B is true, the result is a false-negative error, or "miss." If B is rejected and it is false, the result is a "correct rejection." A simple epistemic goal is to maximize accuracy by reducing the overall proportion of erroneous decisions. If, however, the relative values assigned to the four possible outcomes vary, so should the decision threshold or bias to endorse the belief. Following this logic, Pascal wagered to believe in God, considering it more painful to reject an existing god than to believe in a non-existing one. Pascal was a belief-liberal.

By contrast, conventional significance testing is belief-conservative as it is biased against beliefs in the non-existent. Here, the term $p(D|B)$ refers to the p value associated with the test statistic. Only if $p < .05$, the researcher rejects the idea of nothing, or nullness, tentatively inferring that there is systematic variance (an effect!) (Krueger et al., 2017). Significance testing is the researcher's way of checking gullibility. There is intense debate as to whether the protections against being gulled by the data (or naïve or nefarious investigators) are sufficient, which reinforces the idea that most people (lay and academic alike) tend to have a greater fear of believing something that is not there than of missing something that is (Ioannidis, 2014). Perhaps these fears are so strong because the evidence – mostly obtained with significance testing – suggests that people hold a far greater portfolio of beliefs than they should (see Jussim, Stevens, Honeycutt, Anglin, & Fox, Chapter 15 this volume).

The common subtext to these induction methods, be they Humean, Bayesian, and Neyman-Pearsonian (excepting Pascal himself), is that lay epistemology is too liberal, thereby underwriting gullibility. Formal methods of induction must teach the human observer to stick to the evidence. These formal methods have had a greater impact on scientific work than on everyday thinking. Ordinary thinking departs from formal epistemologies in two seemingly contradictory ways. One way is simple gullibility,

Towards a Credible Theory of Gullibility   107

which is the unreflective willingness to believe a claim. The other way is conditional gullibility, which is the tendency to assimilate evidence to preexisting beliefs. Let us consider the two in turn.

The Power of the Given Stimulus

Following Spinoza, Gilbert (1991) proposed that comprehending a claim and believing it are initially one and the same. To comprehend X, we must first believe X, if only for a moment. Middle school graffiteurs who write, "*Wer dies liest ist doof*" ("He – or she – who reads this is dumb") understand this (see Schwarz & Lee, Chapter 13 this volume). Doubt, skepticism, and eventual disbelief require mental work and thus time. The claim X must be situated within a mental network of relevant propositions, and the coherence of this network must be checked. If adding X to the network of beliefs reduces the network's coherence, X may be tagged as being negated. Psychologically, this tagging amounts to a verdict of "not true" rather than "false." Gilbert's theory is not statistical, but perceptual and cognitive. It treats gullibility as the result of the mental system's default operation, which can only be removed after careful consideration of contrary evidence.

Gilbert's (1991) dual-process approach captures only part of the general decision-theoretic model. As his approach focuses on the role of reflective cognition for the identification and the removal of false-positive errors, it limits good thinking to the transformation of false positive beliefs into correct rejections. False negatives remain unknown, and therefore any assessment of accuracy as the statistical association between belief (vs. unbelief) and reality (true vs. false) remains undefined. Gilbert's (1991) theory of belief was an early example of a dual-process theory, which has swept psychology since (see also Strack, Chapter 9 this volume; Unkelbach & Koch, Chapter 3 this volume). Many of the heuristics proposed in Kahneman and Tversky's groundbreaking work came to be reinterpreted in dual-process or dual-systems terms (Kahneman, 2011; but see Dawes, 1976, for an early dissent). A latecomer to dual systems, Kahneman suggested that fast, intuitive thinking is perceptual in nature, whereas slow, deliberative thinking represents what is ordinarily considered reasoning. Errors, and irrationality more generally, occur when the intuitive system generates a wrong response and when the deliberative system fails to correct it.

Viewed this way, gullibility flourishes where heuristic reasoning reigns. Anchoring is the effect of an initial stimulus on eventual judgment. The effect is dramatic, as it can occur even when the anchor is extreme or coming from randomness (Frederick & Mochon, 2012; Tversky & Kahneman, 1974). Gullers can use anchoring to induce gullees to accept beliefs that are more extreme than they would be or should be without the anchor. Deliberative thinking works to mitigate the anchor's effect, but insufficiently so (Epley & Gilovich, 2006; see Dunning, Chapter 12 this volume). Representative thinking is equally well documented. Gullers can induce false beliefs by using evocative imagery, which leads to false judgments if these images contradict statistical considerations. Magicians and charlatans are fond of providing audiences with visual, experiential demonstrations, seeking to disable slow thinking about coherence and probability. What Kahneman and Tversky (1982) called the simulation heuristic capitalizes on the power of story and narrative. Humans are gulled by good stories, that is, stories that have a dramatic arc, reveal causal relations, and tell about the reasons and intentions of human agents (Pennington & Hastie, 1993; Schank & Abelson, 1995). Narrative cognition bestows many benefits, not least among them boosted memory (Bartlett, 1932/1997). Again, however, gullers can exploit the human readiness for the narrative by weaving deceptive stories that satisfy these criteria but that happen to be utterly false. Belief is beggared if one cares to look.

If heuristics threaten rationality and foster gullibility, we begin to see the connection between the two. Both ought to be overcome by slow and careful thinking, but often are not. As Amos Tversky once put it in conversation with creativity scholar Victor Shamas, "the only thing that matters is what's on your mind – not what's in it" (Shamas, 2018, p. 162). The stress is to be imagined on the preposition "on." Tversky was alluding to the dominance of the salient stimulus (cf. Dawes, 1988). Many judgmental heuristics – with the exception of the story heuristic perhaps – may be bundled due to this critical feature. People are liable to be gullible if they fail to go beyond whatever stimulus is right in front of them (Posner, 1973). Uncorrected, their judgments show focalism and nonregressiveness (Fiedler & Krueger, 2012). Social and cognitive psychology has produced a wealth of evidence for a variety of processes that can be subsumed under this rubric. To name a few; stimuli become more salient (and thus gulling) if they are novel, surprising, or familiar (Pennycook & Rand, 2017), if they are vividly imagined or causally explained (Gregory, Cialdini, & Carpenter, 1982), or if people fail to question them (mindlessness; Langer, Blank, & Chanowitz, 1978; see also Forer, 1949). Through various associative processes, salient stimuli affect judgment and inference more broadly. Salient stimuli become emotionally significant through evaluative conditioning (Hütter, Sweldens, Stahl, Unkelbach, & Klauer, 2012) and diagnostic (or pseudo-diagnostic) of other dimensions through statistical contingency (Fiedler, Freytag, & Meiser, 2009; Rothbart, 2015/1981).

Whatever makes a stimulus salient and focal is not necessarily indicative of truth, although there may be probabilistic relationships. If a correction is needed, how can it be achieved? This is a problem that still awaits an elegant solution. Consider the anchoring heuristic. Kahneman, Tversky, and the investigators they inspired, offer no normative model of adjustment. The error arising from the use of this heuristic is seen in the post-adjustment difference in the estimates made by those starting with a high anchor and those starting with a low one. Even if this difference were closed, the result might be wildly inaccurate (Krueger, Freestone, & MacInnis, 2013).

This limitation highlights a shortcoming of the dual-systems approach, namely the lack of an explicit decision-theoretic framework. There is a built-in neglect of false-negative errors as no provision is made for cases in which people would have fared better had they used an intuition-based heuristic (Fiedler, Kutzner, & Krueger, 2012). Research in the fast-and-frugal-heuristics framework addresses this issue by abandoning the intuition-plus-correction template (Gigerenzer & Gaissmaier, 2011). This framework asks questions of ecological validity to distinguish the conditions under which intuitive responses work well from the conditions under which they do not. From this perspective, there is no generic issue of gullibility; instead there is a readiness to believe that may be modulated by contextual conditions, with positive or negative consequences depending respectively on the match or the mismatch of the person's psychological capacities with environmental structure.

Both, the heuristics-and-biases approach and the fast-and-frugal-heuristics approach leave important questions unanswered. Whereas the former often fails to advise human judges just how much to correct their intuitions, the latter offers little assistance in how to choose the best heuristic in a given setting (Rieskamp & Otto, 2006). The human judge has two options, which have only begun to receive research attention. The first option is to turn to processes that stimulate creativity when formal models are mute on how to go beyond the focal stimulus. Turning to a mindset of foraging, the judge can open up associate networks (Baror & Bar, 2016; Colzato, Ozturk, & Hommel, 2012). This tactic may not be sufficient to restore rationality, but it can help prepare the ground. Mental foraging has the potential to dilute or transform claims that might otherwise gull the person. The second option is to strategically choose ignorance over information, when there is reason to believe that the information is tainted or gulling (Hertwig & Engel, 2016). *Homo ignorans* cannot be *Homo credulans*. Aischylos (2014), the greatest tragedian of the Western canon, dramatized the value of not knowing (e.g., the time and circumstances of one's death) in *Prometheus Bound*. Perhaps for us humans, blind hope beats foreknowledge at least some of the time.

A core assumption of belief-correction models is that the person must want to correct the biasing effect of the focal stimulus (Evans & Stanovich, 2013; but see Krueger, 2012b; Kruglanski, 2013). Sometimes, people just don't want to. Times of distress, uncertainty, and despair are fertile ground for the unchecked growth of belief and superstition (Keinan, 2002). Practices of questionable scientific credibility enjoy popularity when other options have been exhausted (e.g., homeopathy, dowsing, use of charms. Practitioners and their clients alike use the heuristic "It can't hurt," and shift the burden of proof to the skeptics (Vyse, 1997/2014). Practitioners can become self-gullers, gathering enough positive evidence to convince themselves that the practice works (Hyman, 1981). Focusing on the co-occurrences of the focal stimulus ("the practice") and a desired outcome ("success"), pseudo-contingencies (Fiedler et al., 2009; see Fiedler, Chapter 7

110 *Joachim I. Krueger et al.*

this volume) and illusory correlations (Dawes, 1989) take in the unwary. Self-gulling becomes a case of self-enhancement and overconfidence (Heck & Krueger, 2015; Moore & Healy, 2008; see also see Dunning, Chapter 12 this volume; Macrae, Olivier, Falbén, & Golubickis, Chapter 11 this volume).

The Return of the Prior Belief

From a Bayesian perspective, the power of the focal stimulus over the belief *du jour* shows the power of diagnostic or pseudo-diagnostic information over judgment, to the neglect and detriment of prior belief. Tversky and Kahneman (1974) famously asserted that focalism is so strong that it cannot be understood as a poor form of Bayesian thinking but that it is something entirely different. Humans are utterly blind, or at least myopic in some of their judgments (see Fiedler, Chapter 8 this volume). Yet, closing the book on reasoning would itself be an example of focalism. There is more.

The idea of gullibility as a losing battle against the focal stimulus misses an important psychological point. It is not the case that people believe everything and anything at any time. Gullibility can be highly conditional. Some people categorize claims into the credible and the incredible a priori. Consider popular conspiracy theories. There are a number of ways in which such theories can be developed and maintained (see Douglas, Sutton, & Cichocka, Chapter 4 this volume). The simplest heuristic is to divide claims into two categories: conventional and subversive. A person applying this distinction may believe any claim falling in the latter class and reject all others. Epistemology, evidence, and truth aside, this tactic can yield motivational benefits. Subscribers may feel "clued in," privileged, and being members of a select few who have peered behind the veil (Krueger, 2010). An acceptance of all breaks with convention can lead to grotesque contradictions. With this strategy, reports of moon landings will be considered fake, while reports of aliens brought to earth by Apollo 20 (twenty!) ring true (see also Myers, Chapter 5 this volume). More poignantly, a person with this contrarian mindset may claim that climate change is a hoax, while believing that the government manipulates the weather to subdue the population (Lewandowsky, Oberauer, & Gignac, 2013). The common denominator is the idea that the government and traditional news outlets lie by default (Pennycook, Cannon, & Rand, 2017). Ironically, conspiracy theorists of this type can cultivate a self-image of ingullibility. They come to believe that it is the ordinary people who live behind a veil of ignorance and deception because of their gullibility. Again, gullibility begets self-enhancement. A conspiracy theorist may see no contradiction in the belief that the government practices mind control, but that his or her own mind has not thus been controlled (van Prooijen, Chapter 17 this volume).

An extreme variant of conditional gullibility is "gaslighting," further amplified in self-gaslighting. To gaslight someone is to insist on a falsehood with such conviction that the victim begins to doubt his or her own sanity (Abramson, 2014). Some claims of miracles my require gaslighting (Mayo, Chapter 8 this volume). A communicator may boldly claim that Nelson Mandela died in prison until some listeners begin to consider this as a possibility, if only in a parallel universe (Krueger, 2016). Church father Tertullian raised gaslighting to a principle of religious belief when declaring "*credo quia absurdum*" ("I believe it because it is absurd") (Bühler, 2008). Variants of gaslighting can be observed on the political scene on a daily basis ("The crowd at my rally was the largest ever!").

A more sophisticated tactic points to a higher order or deeper logic of things, which only the discerning few can appreciate. In esoteric circles, the clichés that "the universe does not make mistakes," that there is a "cosmic balance" to things, or that "everything happens for a reason" have great power to gull the mind and fill it with nonsense (Ayer, 1936). Instead of setting up conditions for disbelief, this heuristic "liberates" the person from such conditions if they were suggested. Consider the case of Robert Betz, a self-help promoter and impresario. In a workshop JIK attended, Mr. Betz asserted that disease is the way of the universe to keep score (Krueger, 2008). Leaving open the question of whether misbehavior eventually begets disease, Betz claimed that disease is always caused by misbehavior. The universe lets us know that this is so by making the disease representative of the offense. Parkinson's disease, by this logic, both reveals and punishes the afflicted person's earlier quests for control. When asked by a woman in the audience how he explains birth defects, Betz responded with the only argument left: the baby's misbehavior lay in a past life. When asked by JIK how he knew this to be so, Betz put his hand on his chest and declared that he knew this in his heart. Belief had become untethered from reality. No other challenges were made.

While Mr. Betz holds a master's degree in marketing, Professor Justin Barrett has contributed to the empirical literature on child development, and in particular the genesis of the belief in god (Barrett, 2012). Yet, Barrett puts belief before reason (Krueger, 2011a, 2012a). His proof of the existence of god goes like this: "If god exists, we may assume that He created man in such a way that man is prepared to believe in god. Now that I believe in god, I conclude that god exists." This is a case of the reverse-inference fallacy (Krueger, 2017). Barrett's argument uses its conclusion as evidence for its own truth.

Gullibility, in this world, is self-sustaining. Illogic and irrationality provide multiple psychological tools, but the greater context is social. False and destructive beliefs survive in part when the public, even if enlightened, is excessively polite. It is generally difficult to challenge bad ideas, especially in public (Asch, 1956; Krueger & Massey, 2009). Conformity and acquiescence are powerful forces, evolved to support social cohesion and peace. To confront lies, deception, and bad ideas, and do so assertively, requires skill and strength of mind (see von Horváth, 1937/2015, for a literary treatment of this issue). Professional gullers know what they can get away with, and it tends to be a lot. One particularly potent device is to tap an audience's affect by linking a (false) claims to core values. Core values stir the emotions much like sacred possessions do (Tetlock, 2003), and it is a crude breach of social convention to question them. In an atmosphere, in which appeals to tribal values, mythic group identities, or other divisive themes are commonplace, genteel acquiescence is the handmaiden of propaganda with deleterious consequences for larger human society (Bernays, 1928). In the face of false or exploitative claims, resistance is needed, not acquiescence.

As an example of personal failure in this regard, consider another visitation of the conspiracy scene (Krueger, 2015a, 2015b). In this instance, JIK attended a "congress" of Russian "scientists" billed as "mindfully into the future." One of the presenters, a certain Professor Sergej Sall, asked who benefits from the antagonism between the Western and the Islamic worlds. The answer would appear to be obvious to those with an adequately prepared mind, but Sall added, for good measure, an oracular sign right out of the heuristics-and-biases toolbox. Hidden truths reveal themselves in surface similarities. Hence, Sall presented the claim – without commentary – that ISIS is an acronym for "Israel Secret Intelligence Service." The skeptical and rational mind might wonder why, if this service were so secret, would it leave such an obvious hint. There was no open resistance from the audience (including JIK), only polite applause (not from JIK).

Evidence Checked

"Evidence checked" is a double entendre. When presented with wild claims, people can check the relevant evidence to regulate their beliefs, or they can "check" the evidence as they might check (i.e., resist) an enemy's advance. At one pole of this continuum, the pure form of enlightenment thinking demands the admittance and fair evaluation of all relevant evidence, and a principled updating of one's beliefs, perhaps in Bayesian fashion. At the other pole, there is outright neglect or rejection of the evidence, as described in the previous section. Most human psychology plays out in the middle ground where evidence is entertained, but selectively so.

Beginning with Festinger's (1957) theory of cognitive dissonance, the strategic selectivity of the social mind has been a stock presence in research on attitudes and attitude change as well as judgment and decision-making more general (Cooper & Avery, Chapter 16 this volume; Fischer, 2011; Frey, 1986). Whether this selective sampling of information (Fiedler & Juslin, 2006; Fiedler, Chapter 7 this volume) and its biased assimilation (Ditto, Scepansky, Munro, Apanovitch, & Lockhart, 1998; Lord, Ross, & Lepper, 1979) is motivated or a built-in feature of the cognitive process is not of concern here. Rather, we note that selective processing provides a self-reinforcing set of mechanisms that have the potential of locking in false beliefs originating from focal stimuli. In other words, selective processing exacerbates gullibility (Myers, Chapter 5 this volume).

Traditionally, social psychology has been concerned with the effects of (potentially insincere) individual communicators (Cialdini, 2016) or the effects of institutionalized propaganda (Lewandowsky, Stritzke, Freund, Oberauer, & Krueger, 2013). In today's digital world, social media play a big role in shaping beliefs on just about any topic. Here, both the individual's biased choices and the platform's tailored algorithms converge on highly selective exposure to news and stories (Bakshy, Messing, & Adamic, 2015). Users find themselves in "echo chambers" and "filter bubbles" that amplify rather than test or modulate initial beliefs. Lack of awareness of this skew, besides a lack of will or capacity to correct it, raises concerns about gullibility to a higher level (Knobloch-Westerwick, Mothes, & Polavin, 2017).

Susceptibility to "fake news" has become the postmodern face of gullibility par excellence. Defined as news items that are "intentionally and verifiably false" (Allcott & Gentzkow, 2017, p. 4), or that "contradict the best available evidence" (Flynn, Nyhan, & Reifler, 2017, p. 2), the term fake news has been popularized by politicians who themselves hold dubious records of truthfulness. Because of its pervasiveness and resistance to correction, fake news compromises a democracy's functioning (Pennycook et al., 2017). Fake news contaminates public discourse on the economy (Bartels, 2002), foreign policy (Kull, Ramsay, & Lewis, 2003), gun control (Aronow & Miller, 2016), climate change (McCright & Dunlap, 2011), vaccination (Freed, Clark, Butchart, Singer, & Davis, 2010), and genetically modified food (Gaskell et al., 2004). At a time when anything presented or represented on the Internet qualifies as "information," psychological limitations to the person's ability or willingness to correct false beliefs is not the only or even the central concern. Even an educated and willing mind is easily gulled because it does not even know which items require correction or dismissal. "Bullshit," to use Harry Frankfurt's (2005) technical term, is as hard to detect as it is to correct. Contemporary society is called upon to find new ways of creating and maintaining trusted authorities for the dissemination of credible and evidence-based information in the public interest.

Gullibility Without a Guller: The Case of Irrational Trust

It is hard to imagine gullibility without someone who is doing the gulling. The Hebrew creation myth features a serpentine guller praying on human vanity, thereby introducing gullibility as part of the original sin. Yet, we have seen examples of self-gulling (see also Dunning, Chapter 12 this volume), and we have argued that a wholesale condemnation of susceptibility to social influence is not the answer. Humans need to rely on the testimony of others to some extent; excessive cynicism is not effective (Gaertig & Simmons, 2018), nor is it the case that cynical individuals are generally more intelligent than others (Stavrova & Ehlebracht, 2018). Like gullibility more generally, interpersonal trust presents a dilemma. Without trust, life is poor; with excessive trust, it might be a disaster (Krueger & Evans, 2013). Collectively, humans flourish if they trust one another (Johnson & Mislin, 2011), but those who are being trusted have an incentive to defect, especially if the interaction is short-lived.

In the experimental trust game, the issue of gullibility manifests as naivité (Evans & Krueger, 2009). The game does not require a gulling agent. Players decide if they wish to transfer money to another person, knowing that the transfer creates value (typically, the transferred amount is tripled), and knowing that the other person may not reward by keeping all the money (see Figure 6.2 for a display of the extensive form of the game). If the problem of gullibility is that people believe too much, the problem of naivité is that people trust too much. Conventional game theory asserts that any act of trust is irrational because the trustee has no real (i.e., material) incentive to give back. This understanding of rational choice is too restrictive, however. The break-even point is a more realistic criterion. If people invest more than they receive back, their trust seems exaggerated.

Some have argued that trust is inflated because people perceive and enact it as a default of cooperation (Dunning, Anderson, Schlösser, Ehlebracht, & Fetchenhauer, 2014; Rand, 2016). They think it is the socially correct thing to do, and pay the price in lost returns (Krueger, Massey, & DiDonato, 2008). On this view, trusting is a social norm, on a par with the norm of reciprocity (Gouldner, 1960). This hypothesis is only partly valid. People are

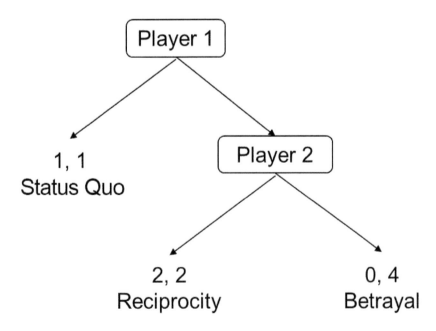

Figure 6.2 The trust game in its extensive form. Higher numbers indicate more preferred outcomes. In this depiction, the entrusted amount is quadrupled.

willing to punish those who fail to reciprocate trust, but refuse to punish those who fail to trust in the first place (Bicchieri, Xiao, & Muldoon, 2011). It is indeed implausible that parents and padres enjoin their charges to trust blindly. They rather seek to instill awareness that trust is a dilemma that can only be mitigated by figuring out who and when to trust. Individuals who have this kind of discriminative ability are perceived not only as competent but also as moral (Evans & van de Calseyde, 2018).

The trust dilemma is hard, yet people have some success solving it (Evans & Krueger, 2016). Although they are sensitive to their own potential gains and losses, people do not pay much attention to the other person's (the trustee's) incentives. These incentives predict behavioral trustworthiness well, but those who trust – or decide not to – neglect this source of information. As a result, their decisions are insufficiently regressive. Both, strong trust and strong distrust, should be tempered (Evans & Krueger, 2017). People are not only too impressed by their own potential payoffs as focal stimuli (Evans & Krueger, 2011), they also rely too much on the physical attractiveness of others when deciding whether to trust (Bonnefon, Hopfensitz, & De Neys, 2013; Olivola, Funk, & Todorov, 2014). Instead of being a generic default, trust is cue-dependent; and some of the cues are bad. But people learn. Trust decisions mature during childhood (Evans, Athenstaedt, & Krueger, 2013) and they are correlated with intelligence and reflective reasoning (Corgnet, Espín, Hernán-González, Kujal, & Rassenti, 2016).

Outlook

We have considered elements of a credible theory of gullibility without fully developing such a theory. The challenges to such an endeavor are considerable. To be unique, a credible theory of gullibility would have to treat gullibility as a psychological phenomenon that cannot be reduced to general principles of learning, persuasion, and belief change. Such a theory would have to ensure that usage of the term gullibility is not judgmental, moralistic, or subject to outcome bias (Baron & Hershey, 1988; Heck & Krueger, 2016). We submit that a fruitful way of theorizing about gullibility is within the context of broader perspectives on inductive reasoning (Humean, Bayesian, Pascalian, as well as dual-processes approaches). Another theoretical challenge is to account for special cases of self-gulling or of being gulled in the absence of communication. We considered the phenomenon of irrational trust to explore the border region between gullibility proper and a related but overlapping concept.

Notes

1 The quote may be found here: www.washingtonexaminer.com/news/george-w-bush-flubs-winston-churchill-quote.
2 Experimental social psychology traditionally relies on deception, and thus on participants' gullibility.

References

Abramson, K. (2014). Turning up the lights on gaslighting. *Philosophical Perspectives*, *28*, 1–30. doi:10.1111/phpe.12046

Aischylos. (2014). *Prometheus bound* (J. Agee, Trans.). New York, NY: New York Review of Books Classics.

Allcott, H., & Gentzkow, M. (2017). Social media and fake news in the 2016 election. *NBER Working Paper Series, Working Paper 23089.*

Aronow, P. M., & Miller, B. T. (2016). Policy misperceptions and support for gun control legislation. *Lancet*, *387*(10015), 223. https://doi.org/10.1016/S0140-6736(16)00042-8

Asch, S. E. (1956). Studies of independence and conformity: I. A minority of one against a unanimous majority. *Psychological Monograph*, *70*(9), 1–70.

Axelrod, R. (1984). *The evolution of cooperation.* New York, NY: Basic Books.

Ayer, A. J. (1936). *Language, truth & logic.* London: Gollancz.

Bakshy, E., Messing, S., & Adamic, L. A. (2015). Political science. Exposure to ideologically diverse news and opinion on Facebook. *Science*, *348*(6239), 1130–1132. https://doi.org/10.1126/science.aaa1160

Baron, J. (2012). Where do nonutilitarian moral rules come from? In J. I. Krueger (Ed.), *Social judgment and decision making* (pp. 261–278). New York, NY: Psychology Press.

Baron, J., & Hershey, J. C. (1988). Outcome bias in decision evaluation. *Journal of Personality and Social Psychology*, *54*, 569–579. http://dx.doi.org/10.1037/0022-3514.54.4.569

Baror, S., & Bar, M. (2016). Associative activation and its relation to exploration and exploitation in the brain. *Psychological Science*, *27*, 776–789. doi:10.1177/0956797616634487

Barrett, J. L. (2012). *Born believers: The science of children's religious belief.* New York, NY: Free Press.

Bartels, L. M. (2002). Beyond the running tally: Partisan bias in political perceptions. *Political Behavior*, *24*, 117–150.

Bartlett, F. C. (1932/1997). *Remembering: A study in experimental and social psychology.* Cambridge: Cambridge University Press.

Bernays, E. L. (1928). *Propaganda.* New York, NY: Liveright.

Bicchieri, C., Xiao, E., & Muldoon, R. (2011). Trustworthiness is a social norm, but trusting is not. *Politics, Philosophy & Economics*, *10*, 170–187. https://doi.org/10.1177/1470594X10387260

Binmore, K. (2007). *Game theory: A very short introduction.* Oxford: Oxford University Press.

Bonnefon, J.-F., Hopfensitz, A., & De Neys, W. (2013). The modular nature of trustworthiness detection. *Journal of Experimental Psychology: General*, *142*, 143–150. http://dx.doi.org/10.1037/a0028930

Bühler, P. (2008). Tertullian: The teacher of the credo quia absurdum. In J. Stewart (Ed.), *Kierkegaard research: Sources, reception and resources, Vol. 4: Kierkegaard and the patristic and medieval traditions* (pp. 131–138). Aldershot, UK: Ashgate.

Church, R. M. (1963). The varied effects of punishment on behavior. *Psychological Review*, *70*, 369–402. http://dx.doi.org/10.1037/h0046499

Cialdini, R. (2016). *Pre-suasion: A revolutionary way to influence and persuade.* New York, NY: Simon & Schuster.

Colzato, L. S., Ozturk, A., & Hommel, B. (2012). Meditate to create: The impact of focused-attention and open-monitoring training on convergent and divergent thinking. *Frontiers in Psychology*, *3*, 116. doi: 10.3389/fpsyg.2012.00116

Corgnet, B., Espín, A. M., Hernán-González, R., Kujal, P., & Rassenti, S. (2016). To trust or not to trust: Cognitive reflection in trust games. *Journal of Behavioral and Experimental Economics*, *64*, 20–27. https://doi.org/10.1016/j.socec.2015.09.008

Dawes, R. M. (1976). Shallow psychology. In J. S. Carroll & J. W. Payne (Eds.), *Cognition and social behavior* (pp. 3–12). Oxford: Lawrence Erlbaum.

Dawes, R. M. (1988). *Rational choice in an uncertain world*. San Diego, CA: Harcourt Brace Jovanovich.

Dawes, R. M. (1989). Experience and validity of clinical judgment: The illusory correlation. *Behavioral Sciences & The Law*, *7*, 457–467. doi: 10.1002/bsl.2370070404

Ditto, P. H., Scepansky, J. A., Munro, G. D., Apanovitch, A. M., & Lockhart, L. K. (1998). Motivated sensitivity to preference-inconsistent information. *Journal of Personality and Social Psychology*, *75*, 53–69. https://doi.org/10.1037/0022-3514.75.1.53

Dunning, D., Anderson, J. E., Schlösser, T., Ehlebracht, D., & Fetchenhauer, D. (2014). Trust at zero acquaintance: More a matter of respect than expectation of reward. *Journal of Personality and Social Psychology*, *107*, 122–141.

Edwards, W., Lindman, H., & Savage, L. J. (1963). Bayesian statistical inference for psychological research. *Psychological Review*, *70*, 193–242. http://dx.doi.org/10.1037/h0044139

Epley, N., & Gilovich, T. (2006). The anchoring-and-adjustment heuristic: Why the adjustments are insufficient. *Psychological Science*, *17*, 311–318. https://doi.org/10.1111/j.1467-9280.2006.01704.x

Evans, A. M., Athenstaedt, U., & Krueger, J. I. (2013). The development of trust and altruism during childhood. *Journal of Economic Psychology*, *36*, 82–95. doi.org/10.1016/j.joep.2013.02.010

Evans, A. M., & Krueger, J. I. (2009). The psychology (and economics) of trust. *Social and Personality Psychology Compass: Intrapersonal Processes*, *3*, 1003–1017. doi:10.1111/j.1751-9004.2009.00232.x

Evans, A. M., & Krueger, J. I. (2011). Elements of trust: Risk taking and expectation of reciprocity. *Journal of Experimental Social Psychology*, *47*, 171–177. doi:10.1016/j.jesp.2010.08.007

Evans, A. M., & Krueger, J. I. (2016). Bounded prospection in dilemmas of trust and reciprocity. *Review of General Psychology*, *20*, 17–28. doi.org/10.1037/gpr0000063

Evans, A. M., & Krueger, J. K. (2017). Ambiguity and expectation-neglect in dilemmas of trust. *Judgment & Decision Making*, *12*, 584–595. http://journal.sjdm.org/17/17131/jdm17131.pdf.

Evans, A. M., & van de Calseyde, P. F. M. (2018). The reputational consequences of generalized trust. *Personality and Social Psychology Bulletin*, *44*, 492–507. doi: 10.1177/0146167217742886

Evans, J. St. B. T., & Stanovich, K. E. (2013). Dual-process theories of higher cognition: Advancing the debate. *Perspectives in Psychological Science*, *8*, 223–241. https://doi.org/10.1177/1745691612460685

118 *Joachim I. Krueger et al.*

Festinger, L. (1957). *A theory of cognitive dissonance.* Evanston, IL: Row Peterson.

Fiedler, K., Freytag, P., & Meiser, T. (2009). Pseudocontingencies: An integrative account of an intriguing cognitive illusion. *Psychological Review, 116,* 187–206.

Fiedler, K., & Juslin, P. (2006). *Information sampling and adaptive cognition.* New York, NY: Cambridge University Press.

Fiedler, K., & Krueger, J. I. (2012). More than an artifact: Regression as a theoretical construct. In J. I. Krueger (Ed.), *Social judgment and decision-making* (pp. 171–189). New York, NY: Psychology Press.

Fiedler, K., Kutzner, F., & Krueger, J. I. (2012). The long way from α-control to validity proper: Problems with a short-sighted false-positive debate. *Perspectives on Psychological Science, 7,* 661–669. doi: 10.1177/1745691612462587

Fischer, P. (2011). Selective exposure, decision uncertainty, and cognitive economy: A new theoretical perspective on confirmatory information search. *Social and Personality Psychology Compass, 5,* 751–762. https://doi.org/10.1111/j.1751-9004.2011.00386.x

Flynn, D. J., Nyhan, B., & Reifler, J. (2017). The nature and origins of misperceptions: Understanding false and unsupported beliefs about politics. *Political Psychology, 38,* 127–150.

Forer, B. R. (1949). The fallacy of personal validation: A class-room demonstration of gullibility. *Journal of Abnormal and Social Psychology, 44,* 118–123.

Frankfurt, H. G. (2005). *On bullshit.* Princeton, NJ: Princeton University Press.

Frederick, S. W., & Mochon, D. (2012). A scale distortion theory of anchoring. *Journal of Experimental Psychology: General, 141,* 124–133. doi: 10.1037/a0024006

Freed, G. L., Clark, S. J., Butchart, A. T., Singer, D. C., & Davis, M. M. (2010). Parental vaccine safety concerns in 2009. *Pediatrics, 125,* 654–659. https://doi.org/10.1542/peds.2009-1962

Frey, D. (1986). Recent research on selective exposure to information. In L. Berkowitz (Ed.), *Advances in experimental social psychology* (Vol. 19, pp. 41–80). New York, NY: Academic, Press.

Gaertig, C., & Simmons, J. P. (2018). Do people inherently dislike uncertain advice? *Psychological Science, 29,* 504–520. doi: 10.1177/0956797617739369

Gaskell, G., Allum, N., Wagner, W., Kronberger, N., Torgersen, H., Hampel, J., & Bardes, J. (2004). GM foods and the misperception of risk perception. *Risk Analysis: An Official Publication of the Society for Risk Analysis, 24,* 185–194. https://doi.org/10.1111/j.0272-4332.2004.00421.x

Gigerenzer, G., & Gaissmaier, W. (2011). Heuristic decision making. *Annual Review of Psychology, 62,* 451–482. doi:10.1146/annurev-psych-120709-145346

Gigerenzer, G., & Hoffrage, U. (1995). How to improve Bayesian reasoning without instruction: Frequency formats. *Psychological Review, 102,* 684–704.

Gilbert, D. (1991). How mental systems believe. *American Psychologist, 46,* 107–119. http://dx.doi.org/10.1037/0003-066X.46.2.107

Gouldner, A. W. (1960). The norm of reciprocity: A preliminary statement. *American Sociological Review, 25,* 161–178. doi: 10.2307/2092623

Gregory, W. L., Cialdini, R. B., & Carpenter, K. M. (1982). Self-relevant scenarios as mediators of likelihood estimates and compliance: Does imagining make it so? *Journal of Personality and Social Psychology, 43,* 89–99.

Hájek, A. (1995). In defense of Hume's balancing of probabilities in the miracles argument. *Southwest Philosophy Review, 11,* 111–118. doi: 10.5840/swphilreview199511111

Hájek, A. (2003). Waging war on Pascal's wager. *The Philosophical Review, 112,* 27–56.

Harris, P. L., Koenig, M. A., Corriveau, K. H., & Jaswal, V. K. (2018). Cognitive foundations of learning from testimony. *Annual Review of Psychology, 69,* 251–273.

Hartnett, S. J., & Stengrim, L. A. (2004). "The whole operation of deception": Reconstructing President Bush's rhetoric of weapons of mass destruction. *Cultural Studies: Critical Methodologies, 4,* 152–197. https://doi.org/10.1177/1532708603262787

Heck, P. R., & Krueger, J. I. (2015). Self-enhancement diminished. *Journal of Experimental Psychology: General, 144,* 1003–1020. http://dx.doi.org/10.1037/xge0000105

Heck, P. R., & Krueger, J. I. (2016). Social perception of self-enhancement bias and error. *Social Psychology, 47,* 327–339. doi: 10.1027/1864-9335/a000287

Hertwig, R., & Engel, C. (2016). *Homo ignorans*: Deliberately choosing not to know. *Perspectives on Psychological Science, 11,* 359–372. https://doi.org/10.1177/1745691616635594

Hochschild, J. L., & Einstein, K. L. (2015). Do facts matter? Information and misinformation in American politics. *Political Science Quarterly, 130,* 585–624. doi: 10.1002/polq.12398

Hume, D. (1748/1959). *Enquiry concerning human understanding.* New York, NY: Dover.

Hütter, M., Sweldens, S., Stahl, C., Unkelbach, C., & Klauer, K. C. (2012). Dissociating contingency awareness and conditioned attitudes: Evidence of contingency-unaware evaluative conditioning. *Journal of Experimental Psychology: General, 141,* 539–557. doi: 10.1037/a0026477

Hyman, R. (1981). The psychic reading. *Annals of the New York Academy of Sciences, 364,* 169–181. doi: 10.1111/j.1749-6632.1981.tb34471.x

Ioannidis, J. P. A. (2014). How to make more published research true. *PLoS Med 11*(10): e1001747. https://doi.org/10.1371/journal.pmed.1001747

Johnson, N. D., & Mislin, A. A. (2011). Trust games: A meta-analysis. *Journal of Economic Analysis, 32,* 865–889. https://doi.org/10.1016/j.joep.2011.05.007

Kahneman, D. (2011). *Thinking, fast and slow.* New York, NY: Farrar, Straus, & Giroux.

Kahneman, D., & Tversky, A. (1982). The simulation heuristic. In D. Kahneman, P. Slovic, & A. Tversky (Eds.), *Judgment under uncertainty: Heuristics and biases* (pp. 201–208). New York, NY: Cambridge University Press.

Keinan, G. (2002). The effects of stress and desire for control on superstitious behavior. *Personality and Social Psychology Bulletin, 28,* 102–108. https://doi.org/10.1177/0146167202281009

Knobloch-Westerwick, S., Mothes, C., & Polavin, N. (2017). Confirmation bias, ingroup bias, and negativity bias in selective exposure to political information. *Communication Research, 7,* 1–21. https://doi.org/10.1177/0093650217719596

Krueger, J. I. (2008). Report on a self-help workshop. *Psychology Today Online.* Retrieved from www.psychologytoday.com/blog/one-among-many/200812/report-self-help-workshop.

Krueger, J. I. (2010). Die "Grosse Verschwörungstheorie" aus psychologischer Sicht [The "great conspiracy theory" from a psychological perspective]. *Zeitschrift für Anomalistik, 10,* 6–16.

Krueger, J. I. (2011a). Belief is not evidence. *Psychology Today Online*. Retrieved from www.psychologytoday.com/blog/one-among-many/201112/belief-is-not-evidence.

Krueger, J. I. (2011b). Don't bet on Pascal's wager. *Psychology Today Online*. Retrieved from www.psychologytoday.com/blog/one-among-many/201112/don-t-bet-pascal-s-wager.

Krueger, J. I. (2012a). Barrett's banalogies. *Psychology Today Online*. Retrieved from www.psychologytoday.com/blog/one-among-many/201204/barretts-banalogies.

Krueger, J. I. (2012b). The (ir)rationality project in social psychology: A review and assessment. In J. I. Krueger (Ed.), *Social judgment and decision-making* (pp. 59–75). New York, NY: Psychology Press.

Krueger, J. I. (2015a). Gullibility gulag. *Psychology Today Online*. Retrieved from www.psychologytoday.com/blog/one-among-many/201511/gullibility-gulag.

Krueger, J. I. (2015b). Gulliber's travails. *Psychology Today Online*. Retrieved from www.psychologytoday.com/blog/one-among-many/201512/gullibers-travails.

Krueger, J. I. (2016). How not to believe. *Psychology Today Online*. Retrieved from www.psychologytoday.com/blog/one-among-many/201611/how-not-believe.

Krueger, J. I. (2017). Reverse inference. In S. O. Lilienfeld & I. D. Waldman (Eds.), *Psychological science under scrutiny: Recent challenges and proposed solutions* (pp. 110–124). New York, NY: Wiley.

Krueger, J. I., & Evans, A. M. (2013). Fiducia: Il dilemma sociale essenziale/Trust: The essential social dilemma. *In-Mind: Italy, 5*, 13–18. http://it.in-mind.org/article/fiducia-il-dilemma-sociale-essenziale.

Krueger, J. I., Evans, A. M., & Heck, P. R. (2017). Let me help you help me: Trust between profit and prosociality. In P. A. M. van Lange, B. Rockenbach, & T. Yamagishi (Eds.), *Social dilemmas: New perspectives on trust* (pp. 121–138). New York, NY: Oxford University Press.

Krueger, J. I., Freestone, D., & MacInnis, M. L. (2013). Comparisons in research and reasoning: Toward an integrative theory of social induction. *New Ideas in Psychology, 31*, 73–86. http://dx.doi.org/10.1016/j.newideapsych.2012.11.002

Krueger, J. I., & Massey, A. L. (2009). A rational reconstruction of misbehavior. *Social Cognition, 27*, 785–810. doi:10.1521/soco.2009.27.5.786

Krueger, J. I., Massey, A. L., & DiDonato, T. E. (2008). A matter of trust: From social preferences to the strategic adherence to social norms. *Negotiation & Conflict Management Research, 1*, 31–52. doi:10.1111/j.1750-4716.2007.00003.x

Kruglanski, A. (2013). Only one? The default interventionist perspective as a unimodel – commentary on Evans & Stanovich (2013). *Perspectives on Psychological Science, 8*, 242–247. https://doi.org/10.1177/1745691613483477

Kull, S., Ramsay, C., & Lewis, E. (2003). Misperceptions, the media, and the Iraq war. *Political Science Quarterly, 118*(4), 569–598.

Langer, E. J., Blank, A., & Chanowitz, B. (1978). The mindlessness of ostensibly thoughtful action: The role of "placebic" information in interpersonal interaction. *Journal of Personality and Social Psychology, 36*(6), 635–642. http://dx.doi.org/10.1037/0022-3514.36.6.635

LeCun, Y., Bengio, Y., & Hinton, G. (2015). Deep learning. *Nature, 521*, 436–444. doi:10.1038/nature14539

Lewandowskyy, S., Oberauer, K., & Gignac, G. E. (2013). NASA faked the moon landing – therefore, (climate) science is a hoax: An anatomy of the motivated rejection of science. *Psychological Science, 24*, 622–633. https://doi.org/10.1177/0956797612457686

Lewandowsky, S., Stritzke, W. G. K., Freund, A. M., Oberauer, K., & Krueger, J. I. (2013). Misinformation, disinformation and violent conflict: From Iraq and the "War on Terror" to future threats to peace. *American Psychologist, 68*, 487–501. doi: 10.1037/a0034515

Lord, C. G., Ross, L., & Lepper, M. R. (1979). Biased assimilation and attitude polarization: The effects of prior theories on subsequently considered evidence. *Journal of Personality and Social Psychology, 37*, 2098–2109. https://doi.org/10.1037/0022-3514.37.11.2098

McCright, A. M., & Dunlap, R. E. (2011). Cool dudes: The denial of climate change among conservative white males in the United States. *Global Environmental Change, 21*, 1163–1172. https://doi.org/10.1016/j.gloenvcha.2011.06.003

Moore, D. A., & Healy, P. J. (2008). The trouble with overconfidence. *Psychological Review, 115*, 502–517. http://dx.doi.org/10.1037/0033-295X.115.2.502

Olivola, C. Y., Funk, F., & Todorov, A. (2014). Social attributions from faces bias human choices. *Trends in the Cognitive Sciences, 18*, 566–570. https://doi.org/10.1016/j.tics.2014.09.007

Pennington, N., & Hastie, R. (1993). Reasoning in explanation-based decision-making. *Cognition, 49*, 123–163. https://doi.org/10.1016/0010-0277(93)90038-W

Pennycook, G., Cannon, T. D., & Rand, D. G. (2017). Prior exposure increases perceived accuracy of fake news. *SSRN Electronic Journal*. Retrieved from https://papers.ssrn.com/sol3/papers.cfm?abstract_id=2958246.

Pennycook, G., & Rand, D. G. (2017). Who falls for fake news? The roles of analytic thinking, motivated reasoning, political ideology, and bullshit receptivity. *SSRN Electronic Journal*. Retrieved from https://ssrn.com/abstract=3023545.

Posner, M. I. (1973). *Cognition: An introduction.* Glenview, IL: Scott, Foresman.

Rand, D. R. (2016). Cooperation, fast and slow: Meta-analytic evidence for a theory of social heuristics and self-interested deliberation. *Psychological Science, 27*, 1192–1206. https://doi.org/10.1177/0956797616654455

Rasmussen C. E. (2004). Gaussian processes in machine learning. In O. Bousquet, U., von Luxburg, & G. Rätsch (Eds.), *Advanced lectures on machine learning. Lecture notes in computer science* (Vol. 3176, pp. 63–71). Heidelberg, Germany: Springer-Verlag.

Rieskamp, J., & Otto, P. E. (2006). SSL: A theory of how people learn to select strategies. *Journal of Experimental Psychology: General, 135*, 207–236.

Rothbart, M. (1981/2015). Memory processes and social beliefs. In D. L. Hamilton (Ed.), *Cognitive processes in stereotyping and intergroup behavior* (pp. 145–182). New York, NY: Psychology Press.

Rousseau, J.-J. (1754/1984). *A discourse on inequality.* (M. Cranston, Trans.). New York, NY: Penguin.

Schank, R. C., & Abelson, R. P. (1995). Knowledge and memory: The real story. In R. S. Wyer (Ed.), *Advances in social cognition* (Vol. 8, pp. 1–85). Hillsdale, NJ: Erlbaum.

Shamas, V. (2018). *Deep creativity: Inside the creative mystery.* New York, NY: Morgan James.

122 Joachim I. Krueger et al.

Simonyan, K., & Zisserman, A. (2014). Very deep convolutional networks for large-scale image recognition. *Proceedings of the International Conference on Learning Representations*. Retrieved from http://arxiv.org/abs/1409.1556.

Stavrova, O., & Ehlebracht, D. (2018). The cynical genius illusion: Exploring and debunking lay beliefs about cynicism and competence. *Personality and Social Psychology Bulletin*. https://doi.org/10.1177/0146167218783195

Swets, J. A., Dawes, R. M., & Monahan, J. (2000). Psychological science can improve diagnostic decisions. *Psychological Science in the Public Interest, 1*, 1–26. http://dx.doi.org/10.1111/1529-1006.001

Tetlock, P. E. (2003). Thinking the unthinkable: sacred values and taboo cognitions. *Trends in Cognitive Science, 7*, 320–324. https://doi.org/10.1016/S1364-6613(03)00135-9

Tversky, A., & Kahneman, D. (1974). Judgment under uncertainty: Heuristics and biases. *Science, 185*, 1124–1131. doi: 10.1126/science.185.4157.1124

von Horváth, Ö. (1937/2015). *Jugend ohne Gott*. Berlin, Germany: Holzinger.

Vyse, S. (1997/2014). *Believing in magic: The psychology of superstition*. New York, NY: Oxford University Press.

7 Metacognitive Myopia

Gullibility as a Major Obstacle in the Way of Rational Behavior

Klaus Fiedler
UNIVERSITY OF HEIDELBERG

Introduction

For more than half a century, psychological research has been concerned with unwanted consequences and serious costs of irrational judgments and decisions. This provocative research topic emerged in the late 1960s and in the early 1970s, shortly after a rationalist view on *Homo sapiens* had been established in developmental research (Piaget, 1950), reasoning (Sarbin, Taft, & Bailey, 1960), and in the social psychology of attribution (Jones & McGillis, 1976; Kelley, 1967). This rationalist picture of the human mind had to be drastically revised in the light of growing evidence for irrationality: Wason's (1968) seminal studies on the inability to solve even the simplest logical reasoning problems; Goldberg's (1968, 1970) disarming demonstrations of shortcomings in expert judgments; Oskamp's (1965) early work on overconfidence; Dawes, Faust, and Meehl's (1989) provocative comparison of clinical and actuarial judgments; and of course Tversky and Kahneman's (1974) groundbreaking work on heuristics and biases. From a social psychological viewpoint, the list can be supplemented with Janis' (1972) groupthink analysis of insufficient political decision making, Weinstein's (1980) notion of unrealistic optimisms, sunk-cost (Arkes & Blumer, 1985), the planning fallacy (Buehler, Griffin, & Ross, 1994), and the persistence of the fundamental attribution bias (Jones & Harris, 1967).

All these massive violations of rational principles were not just observed in artificial experimental settings but also in the context of highly consequential and existential problems, such as estimations of lethal risks, trust in expert advice, attribution of responsibility and guilt, and political decisions. Perhaps the most scaring conclusion from countless studies is that strong motivation, incentives, and careful debriefing hardly eliminate the deficits in human reasoning.

Gullibility and the Attribution of Responsibility for Irrational Behavior

Admittedly, this somewhat pessimistic sketch may be not quite representative of the recent literature, which underwent a shift from irrationality to

124 *Klaus Fiedler*

adaptive functions of ecological and social rationality (Gigerenzer, 2000). Fast and frugal heuristics (Gigerenzer & Todd, 1999) may not accord to formal logic but nevertheless help the individual to get around in an uncertain world. Preference reversals and fallacies (like the conjunction fallacy) may reflect pragmatic misunderstandings of the probability concept (McKenzie & Nelson, 2003). Unrealistic optimism may be justified under specific conditions (Harris & Hahn, 2011). Logical reasoning seems to be intact when reasoning tasks are framed as social contracts (Cosmides & Tooby, 1992). Human perception is remarkably consistent with Bayesian calculus (Trommershäuser, Maloney, & Landy, 2008; see also Krueger, Vogrincic-Haselbacher, & Evans, Chatper 6 this volume). And, anomalies can be conceived as fully normal side effects of seemingly mild and realistic constraints or bounded rationality (Simon, 1982). No one would contest that working memory is limited, that people are sometimes under-motivated, that information costs may exceed benefits from accuracy, and that optimistic biases can increase self-worth and happiness – but nobody would take this as a dramatic deficit of the mind.

This perspectival shift in the psychology of judgment and decision making can be characterized as a shift from irrationality to gullibility (Greenspan, 2009; Rotter, 1980; Yamagishi, Kikuchi, & Kosugi, 1999) – the focus of the present volume. Gullibility is an ambivalent concept that allows for different attributions of malfunctioning and failure. Is the individual too simple-minded and naïve to solve intricate problems that exceed the individual's evolved capacities? Does the mobilization of existing capacities depend on incentive structures and opportunity costs? Do apparent violations of normative rules serve some useful adaptive function? Or does failure originate in careless mistakes and negligence of available knowledge for which the individual can be blamed? The notion of gullibility may suggest innocence or blameworthiness, excessive demands or carelessness, external or internal attributions.

While much recent research emphasizes the individual's "innocence," suggesting external attributions for mistakes and biases to wicked environments, a different perspective is taken in the present chapter. Although illusions and biases can originate in the environment and seemingly irrational behaviors may serve an adaptive function (Pleskac & Hertwig, 2014; see also Baumeister, Maxwell, Thomas, & Vohs, Chapter 2 this volume; Unkelbach & Koch, Chapter 3 this volume), this should not be misunderstood as a generalized acquittal. Serious attempts and progress in understanding the biological origins and the adaptive value of bounded rationality should not prevent us from noting clearly irrational behaviors such as absurd beliefs about death panels (Nyhan, 2010), grossly biased risk estimates (Swets, Dawes & Monahan, 2000), or catastrophic losses in sunk-cost situations (Arkes & Blumer, 1985). Allusions to bounded rationality can hardly undo the cost and hardship caused by such misdeeds, for which a mature social agent must be blamed (see Dunning, Chapter 12 this volume).

Metacognition Highlights the Individual's Responsibility

Individuals are particularly responsible for those quality control functions of their own cognitive processes that are commonly called metacognition. Metacognition is all about monitoring and control. Monitoring functions are concerned with the assessment of information validity and permissibility of cognitive operations. The monitoring results then provide the input for control functions: basing action on valid information and discarding or correcting for invalid evidence. The remainder of this chapter is concerned with metacognitive myopia – a major source of irrationality that originates in conspicuous deficits in both monitoring and control functions.

Metacognitive Myopia: Major Impediment of Rationality

A growing body of evidence on metacognitive myopia (MM), as reviewed in Fiedler (2012), suggests that many reasoning deficits arise at the metacognitive level – reflecting failures to monitor and control for the validity of the information given, rather than at the primary cognitive level of perception, encoding, and memory functions. People are remarkably accurate in processing even complex arrays of stimulus information, and there is no cogent evidence for restricted capacity or motivational biases as causes of strong violations of logical rules. Most striking anomalies arise in spite of sufficient capacity and mastery of logical rules because people are notoriously uncritical and naïve regarding the validity of the information given. This short-sightedness (myopia) is not due to people's lack of interest or insensitivity to information but, ironically, to their being too sensitive to information, which is taken for granted when it can be suspected to be invalid and even when its invalidity is obvious.

MM at Varying Degrees of Blatancy

Experimental evidence for MM can be organized on a continuum of task intricacy. On one end of this continuum are highly intricate tasks that render MM effects unsurprising, making validity hard to evaluate. For instance, when observing small and large samples of behaviors (exhibited by in-groups and out-groups, respectively) laypeople will hardly take the reduced variance of smaller samples into account (Linville, Fischer, & Salovey, 1989). Consequently, observers can hardly correct for an out-group-homogeneity bias (Ostrom & Sedikides, 1992), that is, for the stereotypical tendency to perceive out-groups as more homogenous and less differentiated than in-groups.

At the other end of the continuum, the naive reliance on given evidence (hearsay, social media tweet, gossip, advertising, others' opinions) is most conspicuous if the invalidity or deceptive nature of stimulus input is crystal clear. For instance, even when an explicit debriefing instruction tells people that a statement is wrong, or when people themselves correctly deny the

126 *Klaus Fiedler*

validity of propositions and correctly recognize the input to be wrong, they nevertheless continue to be influenced by such misinformation.

Some Provocative Evidence to Start With

Let us first illustrate the MM syndrome with some examples from social psychology, which illustrate the latter type of blatant MM effects. In a later section, we will turn to other evidence from experimental cognitive psychology, which is better suited to explain the psychological origins of the metacognitive deficit.

One striking example, to start with, can be found in Jones and Harris' (1967) seminal demonstration of correspondence bias. Participants were asked to infer an essay writer's political orientation from an essay that was either in favor of or against the communist spirit of the Cuban leader Fidel Castro. Communist attitudes were inferred from pro-Castro essays and anti-communist attitudes from anti-Castro essays, even when participants knew that essay writers were not free to express their true opinion but were randomly assigned to either the pro- or to the anti-condition. They continued to exhibit correspondent inferences (of attitudes from essay contents) even though essays were written on demand and hence fully undiagnostic.

In Jones and Harris' (1967) paradigm, invalidity is obvious but it remains implicit. In a perseverance paradigm (Ross, Lepper, & Hubbard, 1975), participants are explicitly debriefed of the invalidity of an alleged feedback about their test performance. Nevertheless, the perseverance effect shows that the influence of such clearly discredited fake information is not fully reversible (see also Cooper & Avery, Chapter 16 this volume; Douglas, Sutton, & Cichocka, Chapter 4 this volume; Myers, Chapter 5 this volume).

In two experiments by Fiedler, Armbruster, Nickel, Walther, and Asbeck (1996), participants who had watched a video clip of a talk show first responded to a series of questions asking either whether the protagonist had shown positive behaviors (Did he praise others? Did he delight others?) or whether he had shown negative behaviors (Did he neglect others? Did he attack others?), depending on the experimental condition. Even when participants correctly denied having seen these behaviors that were actually not presented in the film, their subsequent trait ratings were systematically biased towards the misleading and correctly denied question contents. For instance, denying "attacking" led to higher ratings of "aggressive." Thus, participants continued to rely on information that they had themselves correctly classified as false.

Decades later than Ross et al.'s (1975) intriguing perseverance effects, a modern research program on debunking conveys more or less the same message about the inability to correct for misinformation (Chan, Jones, Hall Jamieson, & Albarracín, 2017; Lewandowsky, Ecker, Seifert, Schwarz, & Cook, 2012). Meta-analyses provide strong evidence for the persistence, despite convincing counterevidence, of erroneous beliefs in such myths as genetically modified mosquitoes causing the outbreak of the Zika virus in Brazil (Schipani, 2016), the existence of mass destruction weapons in Iraq before the U.S. invasion (Newport, 2013), or the alleged causal impact of the rubella vaccine on autism, measles, and mumps. The effect size of perseverance effects proved remarkable (d ranging from 0.75 to 1.06; see Chan et al. (2017).

In all these articles, the idea of MM was never mentioned. This conspicuous lack of interest in metacognition might itself be interpreted as a reflection of MM among scientists (see also Jussim, Stevens, Honeycutt, Anglin, & Fox, Chapter 15 this volume). Apparently, the need to critically monitor and control the validity of information is hardly appreciated as a central module of adaptive behavior. In social cognition as in behavioral decision research, the individual is conceived as an agent who processes the given stimulus data, not as a critically minded, emancipated censor who decides what information to use or to discard. Chan et al.'s (2017) meta-analysis refers to additional stimulus input as a remedy, rather than to metacognitive reflection of the original input: "A detailed debunking message correlated positively with the debunking effect. Surprisingly, however, a detailed debunking message also correlated positively with the misinformation-persistence effect" (p. 1531).

Understanding the Origins of MM

Maybe the aforementioned social-psychological studies are too complex and value-laden to trigger proper metacognitive reasoning. Even pre-assigned essays may be diagnostic about true attitude if a social norm obliges essay writers to be authentic. Indeed, while some norm, heuristic, or motive can be found to justify almost every biased inference, such rationalizing explanations are incomplete. A complete theoretical account must also explain why an upcoming bias is not detected by the monitoring function and why it is not corrected by the control function. The failure to go beyond the mere emergence of heuristic-and-bias phenomena and to explain why arising biases are not detected and corrected at the metacognitive level is typical of four decades of heuristics-and-biases research (Tversky & Kahneman, 1974). Virtually all research is confined to anchoring, availability effects, base-rate neglect, or insensitivity to sample size (Tversky & Kahneman, 1971) as causes of initial biases. Hardly any research has ever tried to explain why *Homo sapiens* do not detect and correct for upcoming biases.

In the subsections to follow, I will discuss five distinct subtypes of MM, each of which constitutes a challenging psychological research program in its own right. In the final section, I will summarize the evidence and discuss the implications of MM research for the gullibility debate and for the attribution of responsibility in the domain of rationality.

128   *Klaus Fiedler*

Inability Not to Learn

A basic insight from a century of experimental psychology is that learning curves have positive slopes; learning strength increases with increasing number of trials. In an animal conditioning context, the more often a neutral conditional stimulus (1,000 Hertz tone) is paired with the presentation of an unconditional stimulus (food), the stronger will be the conditioned reaction (saliva production elicited by the tone). In foreign language acquisition, vocabulary learning increases with repeated rehearsal. The same holds for training in sports, singing, and handcraft. That learning increases with repeated practice is not only obvious; it is inevitable. It is easy to see that we cannot tell our autonomous nervous system not to learn from repeated pairings of signals and electrical shocks. We can also not tell our memory system to stop profiting from repetition. What is experienced many times will be increasingly kept in memory. As obvious as this truism might appear, this commonsense insight is systematically neglected in task settings that call for the exclusion of merely repeated, redundant stimuli.

Participants in a series of experiments by Unkelbach, Fiedler, and Freytag (2007) saw on each trial of a computerized task a simulated TV program, which informed them in a running text line about the stocks that were the daily winners on the stock market. After 16 simulated days, their task was to estimate the frequency with which each stock was among the daily winners. The actual winning rates for subsets of stocks were 4, 6, or 8, respectively. However, on some days they saw two perfectly redundant TV programs about the same day on the stock market, so that the presentation frequencies could diverge from the actual winning frequencies. For instance, given an actual winning frequency of 8, the presentation frequency for a given stock could be 8, 12, or 16, respectively, depending on how often these winning outcomes were repeated. Although judgments were generally quite sensitive to the true winning rates, the judges were strongly misled by the selective repetition manipulation. Repetitions had a similarly strong influence on frequency estimates and preferences for the ten stocks as independent winning outcomes. This finding persisted after an explicit warning that some of the stock market news would be repeated and that selective repetition may distort frequency estimates.

Given this warning, participants might have closed their eyes during repeated news programs, or they might have monitored and assessed what shares profited most from selective repetition. However, they were apparently not interested in monitoring and correcting for unwarranted repetition biases. They presumably did not expect repetitions to influence their frequency estimates. By the way, the same biases were not just evident in numerical frequency estimates but also in ratings of the willingness to invest in the various shares.

Apparently, the underlying learning process is sensitive to every stimulus item presenting a share as a daily winner, regardless of whether the stimulus represents a new winner or a repetition of an already noted winner. Just as

Gullibility and Rationality   129

in Pavlovian conditioning the impact of an electrical shock is quite independent of whether a shock was intentional, or planned by design, all observations that link specific shares to winning support the evaluative-learning process. In other words, evaluative learning reflects the accrual of evaluative experience rather than a frequentist inference.

Detecting Proportional Changes

Support for this contention, and further evidence on why we cannot not learn from mere repetition, comes from recent evidence on the detection of proportional change (Fiedler et al., 2016). Assessing the proportion of a focal outcome is of eminent importance in reality: Is there a change in a student's rate of correct responses, in a football team's record of successful matches, or in the acceptance rate of a political party? To investigate performance on such tasks, Fiedler et al. (2016) developed a sequential paradigm in which each trial provides participants with a binary sample of two symbols (* and o). They were asked to decide whether the current sample was drawn from the same universe as the preceding sample or from a different universe in which the probability p(*) of a focal symbol * had increased or decreased. Again, change judgments were sensitive to actual changes. However, despite this general sensitivity to p-changes, change judgments were strongly influenced by changes in absolute sample size n. Increases in relative p were readily detected when absolute n increased as well, for instance, when 4* out of 8 increased to 10* out of 16. However the same proportional change from 8* out of 16 to 5* out of 8 was hardly recognized. Conversely, decreases in p were only noticed readily when n also decreased but not when absolute sample size increased. When p remained unchanged (i.e., successive samples were drawn from the same universe), increasing n misled participants to believe that p had increased and decreasing n led them to believe p had decreased.

These often replicated anomalies in detection of change were not due to misunderstandings of task instructions. Participants did not simply count the cardinal number of critical * symbols in the numerator. This was evident from the fact that when n (i.e., the denominator) was held constant a change from, say, 4* out of 8 to 5* out of 8 was not different from a change from 8* out of 16 to 10* out of 16. It is also insufficient to explain the anomalies as ratio bias (Denes-Raj, Epstein, & Cole, 1995) or denominator neglect (Reyna & Brainerd, 2008), because it was easy to keep p independent of n when *-proportions were described numerically, as normalized percentage (Fiedler et al., 2016, experiment 2). The anomalies were only observed when proportional quantities had to be extracted inductively from experienced samples.

Indeed, logical reflection shows that the inductive assessment of p must be sensitive to n. Imagine a highly motivated and perfectly unbiased participant who sincerely wants to assess the proportion of * symbols experienced in a binary sample, or else, the rate of pro arguments in a political debate, or

130 *Klaus Fiedler*

different students' proportions of correct responses in the virtual classroom. In any case, the task calls for a continuous update of a sample proportion $p*$ of the frequency f of focal elements divided by the total number n of all elements. The question, however, is what positive increment or negative increment must be added to the growing sample proportion for each new observation of a focal or non-focal element. Logically, the incremental weight given to each elementary observation should be $1/n$. In a very long list of 100 observations, each element should be given a weight of $1/100$. But if n is only 2 or 3, the elementary observation must be given a much higher weight of $1/2$ or $1/3$, respectively.

But what should our ideally motivated, unbiased assessor do when n is undefined, that is, when the overall number of political votes or student answers is not known beforehand? Indeed, under most natural task conditions sample sizes n are unknown and uncontrollable. Nobody knows in advance how many pro and con arguments will be produced in a political debate, how often different students in a school class raise their hands and provide responses to knowledge questions. Moreover, n is often fully undetermined; it may be impossible to say when a sample started and when it will end. Apart from the fact that n is unknown beforehand, it may be impossible to administrate the impact of all n's belonging to hundreds of sampling tasks in which we are involved at any point in time, recalculating growing $_np*$ (after n observations) from the preceding estimate $_{n-1}p*$ (after $n-1$ observations) according to the normative updating rule $_np* = [(1/n) \cdot n_{th}$ element$] + [(n-1)/n \cdot {}_{n-1}p*]$. As n increases, such an updating rule would become more and more demanding in terms of numerical precision and replete with cumulative error.

Still, even though it is impossible to divide the number of focal outcomes by an exact count of n, our rational agent is quite sensitive to proportions, that is, he or she will somehow relate the number of focal outcomes (in the numerator) to a crude feeling (in the denominator) of n in the stimulus context. The same number of focal features in the current sample may thus be worth more (less) if a small (large) preceding sample suggests a smaller (larger) denominator.

Note that such context sensitivity might actually account for the full pattern of anomalies reported in the preceding section. If the size of the former sample triggers the expectation of the (uncertain) size of the current sample size (denominator), then indeed the same number of * observations in the current sample should be worth more (less) when a small (rather than a large) preceding sample decreases the expected denominator and thereby increases the weight given to elementary * observations.

Responsibility for Sample-Size Insensitivity

The preceding causal explanation for the impossibility to assess proportions whose denominators are unknown should not be mistaken as an excuse for all the massive biases we have found in detection-of-change tasks. Although the foregoing discussion might help to explain the origin of MM for sample size, it does not explain why the MM lethargy carries over to many situations in which the biasing impact and unfairness of unequal n are crystal clear. My cognitive analysis of the impossibility of assessing p independently of n is not meant as an acquittal for other, hard-to-believe consequences of MM for the impact of sample size. For an illustration, let us return to a social psychological perspective on clearly irrational and unnecessary biases and shortcomings for which mature human beings must be held responsible.

One memorable example can be found in criteria based statement analysis (CBSA; Steller & Köhnken, 1989; Vrij & Mann, 2006), the diagnostic method used by expert witnesses to evaluate the credibility of witness reports. CBSA is typically applied in criminal (rape or sexual abuse) trials in which no physical evidence is available so that court decisions with existential consequences for the defendant depend on the validity of the credibility analysis. As the presumption of innocence implies the null hypothesis that an aggregating witness statement is wrong, the CBSA method consists in a one-sided search for linguistic truth criteria in the transcribed report. An expert witness' review and recommendation thus depend on how many truth criteria can be found in the report, such as amount of detail, spontaneous self-correction, or structured presentation. The CBSA count of linguistic symptoms of veracity very often determines whether the defendant goes to jail, loses his family, his job, and his existence. However, although CBSA counts have been shown to be higher when reported experiences are real, they are also subject to a detrimental artifact, text length. A long report of 15 or 20 pages is more likely to include a reasonable number of truth criteria than a short report of only 2 pages. Although so much is at stake and the flagrant bias is easy to understand and might be corrected in a straightforward manner, this problem is widely ignored in legal practice (Fiedler, 2019).

In a similar vein, the inability to perfectly monitor and control for n generalizes to many other situations, in which unfair evaluations depend on sample size and appropriate corrections suggest themselves: teachers' evaluations of students providing unequal numbers of responses (Fiedler, Wöllert, Tauber, & Hess, 2013), self-serving biases due to larger samples of self-related than other-related experience (Moore & Healy, 2008), in-group-serving biases, or devaluation of minorities relative to majorities showing identical rates of positive behavior (Fiedler, 2000a, 2000b, 2008). Or, for an example from the allegedly rational domain of science (see Jussim et. al., Chapter 15 this volume), evidence for distinct hypotheses is strongly contaminated with the biasing impact of the popularity and the number of conducted studies. Validity concerns and critical assessments of whether manipulations have been effective or whether mediation tests are logically appropriate (Fiedler, Harris, & Schott, 2018) are hardly ever considered, reflecting a strong syndrome of MM in scientific practice.

132   Klaus Fiedler

Pitfalls of Conditional Reasoning

A similar story can be told about a long tradition of research on conditional reasoning. To illustrate, consider the conditional probability $p(\text{HIV}|\text{positive test})$ that people have actually contracted the HIV virus given a positive HIV test. Estimates of this conditional are highly inflated if participants are told that the base rates of HIV is $p(\text{HIV}) = 0.1\%$, that the base rate of positive test results is $p(\text{positive test}) = 1\%$, and that the reverse conditional, or hit rate of HIV-infected people who are tested positively is $p(\text{positive test}|\text{HIV}) = 100\%$. To provide a correct estimate of $p(\text{HIV}|\text{positive test})$, Bayes' theorem prescribes that the reverse conditional must be multiplied with the ratio of the two base rates: $p(\text{HIV}|\text{positive test}) = p(\text{positive test}|\text{HIV}) \cdot p(\text{HIV})/p(\text{positive test}) = 100\% \cdot 0.1\%/1\% = 10\%$. The conditional probability of HIV given a positive HIV test is indeed in the range of 10%.

That most judges grossly overestimate this remarkably low figure is easy to "explain" or to justify, by simply admitting that lay people are not in full command of Bayesian calculus. Understanding that the ratio of two inverse conditional probabilities $p(\text{HIV}|\text{positive test})/p(\text{positive test}|\text{HIV})$ is identical to the ratio $p(\text{HIV})/p(\text{positive test})$ of corresponding base rates sounds like higher mathematics that ordinary people cannot be expected to understand. So nobody would come to blame ordinary people who dramatically overestimate risks expressed as conditional probabilities.

However, again, the strong anomalies persist under conditions that make it easy to recognize and overcome the underlying base-rate neglect (Bar-Hillel, 1984). For instance, consider an experiment (cf. Fiedler, Brinkmann, Betsch, & Wild, 2000) in which participants who know the HIV base rate is very low (say, 1 out of 1,000) are presented with an index-card file with two slots, one containing very few HIV cases and another slot with a huge number of (1,000 times more) not-HIV cases. Each index card has the diagnosis (HIV vs. not HIV) on one side and the test result (positive vs. negative) on the other side. Participants can sample as many cards from the file as they feel appropriate to make an accurate estimate of $p(\text{HIV}|\text{positive test})$. A typical search pattern would be that participants sample all (rare) HIV cases plus a similar number of not-HIV cases. Noting that the test result is positive for 100% of all HIV cases but only for very few not-HIV cases, most people infer that a positive test result is a very good predictor of HIV.

The serious flaw does not lie in a failure to apply Bayesian calculus. It lies in the obvious fact that a sample of roughly equal numbers of HIV and non-HIV cases is extremely biased. While it contains all HIV cases, it only contains a vanishingly small subset of not-HIV cases. Basing a conditional estimate of HIV on such a dramatically biased sample, which grossly over-represents the true rate of HIV cases is reflective of an incredibly blatant version of MM, for which mature adult people can be held responsible. It is easy to see that a raffle that selectively includes all unattractive items is not attractive or that a forecast of a football team's winning record should not rely on a sample that draws heavily on only the worst matches in the past.

Yet, as a consequence of MM, people continue to make important inferences from such extremely biased samples, the invalidity of which is not at all beyond the scope of human intelligence. When given a forced choice between a biased and an unbiased sample, MM often prevents *Homo sapiens* from choosing correctly. Thus, keeping with the previous example, when highly educated students can choose between (1) a biased sample that contains equal numbers of HIV and not-HIV cases and (2) an unbiased sample that contains proportionally more not-HIV cases, they typically prefer to base their estimate on the former sample. Apparently, MM gives more attention to the superficial advantage of an equal-n design than to a critical or thoughtful check on whether the very attribute to be estimated is misrepresented in the sample.

Impoverished Causal Reasoning

Causal impact judgments provide another example of MM that at first sight appears to reflect an adaptive property of the human mind. Logically, the impact of a manipulated change Δx in a causal condition x on an observed change Δy in an effect dimension y can be quantified by a ratio $\Delta y/\Delta x$. Causal impact is highest when a minimal causal input (small denominator) produces a maximal effect (high numerator). For instance, if a very small dosage of a poison (small Δx) is sufficient to kill a huge elephant (strong Δy), the causal impact is higher than if the same dosage only kills a tiny mouse (smaller Δy), or if a much higher dosage (larger Δx) is required to kill an elephant.

This ratio principle underlying the notion of causal impact – dividing the size of an effect by the amount of causal input that was required to produce the effect – appears logically sound and not too complicated for the human mind. It affords a plausible solution of many practical problems. Given that 10 grams of a substance have a nutrition value of 50 calories, we can infer that 100 grams of the same substance have 500 calories. Or, if 5 grams of another substance have 50 calories, its nutrition value must be twice as high. Yet, actual judgments of causal influences are not sensitive to this obvious ratio principle. Oftentimes, judges are exclusively sensitive to effect sizes and largely ignore the causal input, taking the experienced effect for granted, while MM prevents them from deeper thinking about the causal story behind. We assess whether a patient's depression is mild or severe, but hardly ever relate the degree of depression to the strength of the stressors in a patient's life that brought about the depression. Or, in science, we praise studies with high effect sizes, but we hardly ever consider how strong an experimental manipulation was necessary to produce an effect. In empirical

134   *Klaus Fiedler*

science, we definitely do not downgrade an effect (Δy) if it was caused by too strong a treatment (Δx). While it is difficult to publish a study producing a very weak effect, reviewers and editors will hardly ever reject a paper because a causal treatment was too strong.

When causal origins cannot be fully ignored as in science, causal reasoning does not follow the ratio principle. Rather, researchers base their causal-impact judgments on the covariance principle: The causal impact demonstrated in experiment is considered maximal if a strong cause produces a strong effect (not if weak input managed to produce strong output). The same holds for lay judgments of causal impact (Hansen, Rim, & Fiedler, 2013): If "45-minute waiting time causes an increase in customer anger of 10 scale points," the subjective causal impact is stronger than if "14-minute waiting time causes an increase in customer anger of 10 scale points."

Again, one might justify the covariance principle as an adaptive strategy (Fiedler, Freytag, & Unkelbach, 2011): In reality adaptive agents not only face the task of quantifying the impact of a single cause; they typically have to detect the influence of a cause in the context of many different causes $a, b, c,$ $\ldots w$ that vary at the same time. When in such a multi-causal setting an effect Δy co-occurs with changes in several causal factors, a very subtle change in, say, Δa, will be much less detectable than a massive change in, say, Δw. A loud and attention-grabbing provocation is more detectable and will thus appear to have a stronger causal impact on an aggressive act or crime than a hardly detectable, subtle insulting gesture.

Still, although covariance looks like an adaptive rule that maximizes detectability, it hardly justifies the maladaptive neglect of the ratio principle and the widespread tendency to focus on salient effects while ignoring causal origins. It cannot be adaptive only to evaluate the performance of a car, without considering the amount of fuel required to reach that performance. Indeed, ignoring the causes of many ecological, economical, and political effects represents a cardinal case of MM.

Divergent Trends at Different Aggregation Levels

Last but not least, a prominent final example is MM for existing differences between aggregation levels. On one hand, the vicissitudes of aggregation levels are intrinsically counter-intuitive, and one is tempted to excuse their neglect. It is hard to understand, for instance, that the correlation between Black skin color and illiteracy is negligible at the level of individual people but close to perfect at the level of large geographic districts. Black individuals are hardly more likely than White people to be illiterate, but the correlation between the proportion of Black people and the proportion of illiterates in different U.S. districts is very high ($r > .80$ for very large districts). This may be hard to understand at first sight. One has to recognize that the genetic influences underlying individuating correlations are fully independent of the economic factors producing the ecological correlation at high district level (Robinson, 1950).

Gullibility and Rationality   135

However, on the other hand, the notion of divergent trends at varying aggregation levels does not exceed our intelligence; we are familiar with many pertinent examples. Rich nations may have high poverty rates; what is pleasant in the short run may be unpleasant in the long run; or research findings obtained at group level need not hold for individual participants. Because of these and many other plausible experiences, the human mind is not bound to myopic confusion of aggregation levels. The gender stereotype that leadership ability is more typical of males than of females is true at the level of vocational environments (Eagly & Steffens, 1984). In vocational fields with the highest rate of leadership ability (top management in organizations) the rate of males is highest. Yet, at the individual level, it is possible that the few female leaders working in top management positions outperform the majority of males, thus creating an inverse correlation at individuating level. Regardless of whether females are actually superior or inferior, the point here is simply that confusing correlations observed at different aggregation levels is a serious category mistake.

Conclusions: Gullibility, Myopia, and Social Responsibility

Thus, a review of MM effects reveals that rationality research is intimately related to the ambivalent concept of gullibility, the meaning of which implies both innocence and negligence. A good deal of recent work on judgment and decision-making highlights the normal origins and the adaptive functions served by many apparent violations of rational norms. Biases and illusions can be explained as normal consequences of ordinary laws of learning, properties of the probabilistic environment, and intrinsic difficulties of some inference tasks. However, even when the origins of irrational behavior can be understood and rationalized, this does not exempt the individual of his or her social responsibility. In spite of bounded rationality, the individual remains blameworthy. Not all deficits in metacognitive functions can be attributed to unavoidable constraints. Some MM effects are unbelievably blatant and naïve and not enforced by task demands that exceed our cognitive capacities. We perfectly understand that selective repetition may bias impressions, that the probability that males are millionaires is much lower than the probability that millionaires are male, that highly concentrated poison has more causal power than diluted poison, or that happiness of nations is not happiness of people. And yet, we fall prey to repetition biases, fail on highly meaningful conditional reasoning tasks, we misunderstand the ratio principle of causal inference, and we are completely confused by divergent trends observed at different aggregation levels.

The MM perspective on rationality points to missed opportunities to utilize insights and critical analyses that are easily understood and hard to contest. It appears as if, for some reason, we are simply not interested or motivated to engage in critical assessment, or to cast the validity of a flawed sample into question. For an illustrative example, consider the recent "me too" debate on the social media, and its echo in the mass media. Regardless of what part of the information solicited in this public debate is true, semi-true, exaggerated, or even faked, and regardless of whether part of the reported transgressions are harmless and manifestations of normal mating behavior, the sampling procedure or "research design" underlying this media game is sorely biased. The debate relies on a retrieval prompt that exclusively refers to the worst exemplars of norm-violating behaviors represented in the extreme part of the distribution of (male) human conduct. The amount and strength of evidence solicited by such a sampling process do not tell us anything about the relative rate of such misbehaviors, because normal and nice behavior is ignored. All we can infer from such a lop-sided sampling process is that a large number of social media agents (maybe more than a billion) have been reached by the "me too" prompt. Although we fully understand that such a "research design" is biased, we nevertheless continue to be impressed by the pessimistic results. It is somehow comparable to persisting illusions that continue to fool our perception in spite of perfect debriefing.

Nevertheless, an ultimate goal of a gullibility debate must be to counter this MM lethargy and to remind people of their responsibility to engage in critical monitoring and control. Neither restricted working memory nor lack of incentives nor any other aspect of bounded rationality restricts our ability, and our obligation to monitor and control the quality of the information that impinges on our mind. For some inference problems, to be sure, there may be no patent remedies at the metacognitive level. Repetition biases cannot be turned off, the base rates needed to deal with conditional inference problems may be unknown, and information may not be available at the appropriate aggregation level. Even then, however, we can still recognize dangerous situations in which stimulus samples are flawed, an information source is untrustworthy, or unequal sample size must lead to unfair and lop-sided comparisons. And we can decide not to act or to discard information that is obviously flawed.

Recent work on nudging (Thaler & Sunstein, 2008) and prudent default setting (Johnson & Goldstein, 2003) emphasizes environmental design and external decision aids as key interventions. The MM perspective suggests an opposite, self-determined and internally controlled approach, namely, critical assessment and emancipation at the metacognitive level (Hertwig & Grüne-Yanoff, 2017). Which of the two opposite approaches turns out to be superior is a matter of future research, but for the moment, the gullibility debate can help to articulate the psychological underpinnings of both positions.

References

Arkes, H. R., & Blumer, C. (1985). The psychology of sunk cost. *Organizational Behavior and Human Decision Processes*, *35*(1), 124–140.

Bar-Hillel, M. (1984). Representativeness and fallacies of probability judgment. *Acta Psychologica*, *55*(2), 91–107.

Gullibility and Rationality 137

Buehler, R., Griffin, D., & Ross, M. (1994). Exploring the "planning fallacy": Why people underestimate their task completion times. *Journal of Personality and Social Psychology, 67*(3), 366–381.

Chan, M. S., Jones, C. R., Hall Jamieson, K., & Albarracín, D. (2017). Debunking: A meta-analysis of the psychological efficacy of messages countering misinformation. *Psychological Science, 28*(11), 1531–1546.

Cosmides, L., & Tooby, J. (1992). Cognitive adaptions for social exchange. In J. H. Barkow, L. Cosmides, & J. Tooby (Eds.), *The adaptive mind: Evolutionary psychology and the generation of culture* (pp. 163–228). New York, NY: Oxford University Press.

Dawes, R. M., Faust, D., & Meehl, P. E. (1989). Clinical versus actuarial judgment. *Science, 243,* 1668–1674.

Denes-Raj, V., Epstein, S., & Cole, J. (1995). The generality of the ratio-bias phenomenon. *Personality and Social Psychology Bulletin, 21*(10), 1083–1092.

Eagly, A. H., & Steffen, V. J. (1984). Gender stereotypes stem from the distribution of women and men into social roles. *Journal of Personality and Social Psychology, 46*(4), 735–754.

Fiedler, K. (2000a). Beware of samples! A cognitive-ecological sampling theory of judgment biases. *Psychological Review, 107,* 659–676.

Fiedler, K. (2000b). On mere considering: The subjective experience of truth. In H. Bless & J. P. Forgas (Eds.), *The message within: The role of subjective experience in social cognition and behavior* (pp. 13–36). New York, NY: Psychology Press.

Fiedler, K. (2008). The ultimate sampling dilemma in experience-based decision making. *Journal of Experimental Psychology: Learning, Memory & Cognition, 34,* 186–203.

Fiedler, K. (2012). Meta-cognitive myopia and the dilemmas of inductive-statistical inference. *Psychology of Learning and Motivation, 57,* 1–55.

Fiedler, K. (2019). A missed opportunity to improve on credibility analysis in criminal law. In R. S. Sternberg (Ed.), *My biggest research mistake* (pp. 201–203). New York, NY: Sage.

Fiedler, K., Armbruster, T., Nickel, S., Walther, E., & Asbeck, J. (1996). Constructive biases in social judgment: Experiments on the self-verification of question contents. *Journal of Personality and Social Psychology, 71*(5), 861–873.

Fiedler, K., Brinkmann, B., Betsch, T., & Wild, B. (2000). A sampling approach to biases in conditional probability judgments: Beyond base rate neglect and statistical format. *Journal of Experimental Psychology: General, 129,* 399–418.

Fiedler, K., Kareev, Y., Avrahami, J., Beier, S., Kutzner, F., & Hütter, M. (2016). Anomalies in the detection of change: When changes in sample size are mistaken for changes in proportions. *Memory & Cognition, 44*(1), 143–161.

Fiedler, K., Freytag, P., & Unkelbach, C. (2011). Great oaks from giant acorns grow: How causal-impact judgments depend on the strength of a cause. *European Journal of Social Psychology, 41*(2), 162–172.

Fiedler, K., Harris, C., & Schott, M. (2018). Unwarranted inferences from statistical mediation tests: An analysis of articles published in 2015. *Journal of Experimental Social Psychology, 75,* 95–102.

Fiedler, K., Wöllert, F., Tauber, B., & Hess, P. (2013). Applying sampling theories to attitude learning in a virtual school class environment. *Organizational Behavior and Human Decision Processes, 122,* 222–231.

138   *Klaus Fiedler*

Gigerenzer, G. (2000). *Adaptive thinking: Rationality in the real world*. New York, NY: Oxford University Press.

Gigerenzer, G., & Todd, P. M. (1999). Fast and frugal heuristics: The adaptive toolbox. In *Simple heuristics that make us smart* (pp. 3–34). New York, NY: Oxford University Press.

Goldberg, L. R. (1968). Simple models or simple processes? Some research on clinical judgments. *American Psychologist, 23*(7), 483–496.

Goldberg, L. R. (1970). Man versus model of man: A rationale, plus some evidence, for a method of improving on clinical inferences. *Psychological Bulletin, 73*(6), 422–432.

Greenspan, S. (2009). *Annals of gullibility: why we get duped and how to avoid it.* Westport, CT: Praeger.

Hansen, J., Rim, S., & Fiedler, K. (2013). Psychological distance and judgments of causal impact. *Journal of Experimental Social Psychology, 49*, 1184–1189.

Harris, A. L., & Hahn, U. (2011). Unrealistic optimism about future life events: A cautionary note. *Psychological Review, 118*(1), 135–154.

Hertwig, R., & Grüne-Yanoff, T. (2017). Nudging and boosting: Steering or empowering good decisions. *Perspectives on Psychological Science, 12*(6), 973–986.

Janis, I. L. (1972). *Victims of groupthink: A psychological study of foreign-policy decisions and fiascoes*. Oxford: Houghton Mifflin.

Johnson, E. J., & Goldstein, D. G. (2003), "Do defaults save lives?" *Science, 302* (5649), 1338–1339.

Jones, E. E., & Harris, V. A. (1967). The Attribution of Attitudes. *Journal of Experimental Social Psychology, 3*(1), 1–24.

Jones, E. E., & McGillis, D. (1976). Correspondent inferences and the attribution cube: A comparative reappraisal. *New Directions in Attribution Research, 1*, 389–420.

Kelley, H. H. (1967). Attribution theory in social psychology. Nebraska Symposium on Motivation, *15*, 192–238.

Lewandowsky, S., Ecker, U. K. H., Seifert, C. M., Schwarz, N., & Cook, J. (2012). Misinformation and its correction: Continued influence and successful debiasing. *Psychological Science in the Public Interest, 13*, 106–131.

Linville, P. W., Fischer, G. W., & Salovey, P. (1989). Perceived distributions of the characteristics of in-group and out-group members: Empirical evidence and a computer simulation. *Journal of Personality and Social Psychology, 57*(2), 165–188.

McKenzie, C. M., & Nelson, J. D. (2003). What a speaker's choice of frame reveals: Reference points, frame selection, and framing effects. *Psychonomic Bulletin & Review, 10*(3), 596–602.

Moore, D. A., & Healy, P. J. (2008). The trouble with overconfidence. *Psychological Review, 115*(2), 502–517.

Newport, F. (2013). *Americans still think Iraq had weapons of mass destruction before war*. Retrieved from www.gallup.com/poll/8623/americans-still-think-iraqhad-weapons-mass-destruction-before-war.aspx.

Nyhan, B. (2010). Why the "death panel" myth wouldn't die: Misinformation in the health care reform debate. *The Forum, 8*(1), 5.

Oskamp, S. (1965). Overconfidence in case-study judgments. *Journal of Consulting Psychology, 29*(3), 261–265.

Ostrom, T. M., & Sedikides, C. (1992). Out-group homogeneity effects in natural and minimal groups. *Psychological Bulletin, 112*(3), 536–552.

Piaget, J. (1950). *The psychology of intelligence.* Oxford: Harcourt Brace.

Pleskac, T. J., & Hertwig, R. (2014). Ecologically rational choice and the structure of the environment. *Journal of Experimental Psychology: General, 143*(5), 2000–2019.

Reyna, V. F., & Brainerd, C. J. (2008). Numeracy, ratio bias, and denominator neglect in judgments of risk and probability. *Learning and Individual Differences, 18*(1), 89–107.

Robinson, W. S. (1950). Ecological correlations and the behavior of individuals. *American Sociological Review, 15,* 351–357.

Ross, L., Lepper, M. R., & Hubbard, M. (1975). Perseverance in self-perception and social perception: Biased attribution processes in the debriefing paradigm. *Journal of Personality and Social Psychology, 32,* 880–892.

Rotter, J. B. (1980). Interpersonal trust, trustworthiness, and gullibility. *American Psychologist, 25*(1), 1–7.

Sarbin, T. R., Taft, R., & Bailey, D. E. (1960). *Clinical inference and cognitive theory.* Oxford: Holt, Rinehart, & Winston.

Schipani, V. (2016). *GMOs didn't cause Zika outbreak.* Retrieved from www.factcheck.org/2016/02/gmosdidnt-cause-zika-outbreak.

Simon, H. A. (1982). *Models of bounded rationality.* Cambridge, MA: MIT Press.

Steller, M., & Köhnken, G. (1989). Criteria-based statement analysis. Credibility assessment of children's statements in sexual abuse cases. In D. C. Raskin (Ed.), *Psychological methods for investigation and evidence* (pp. 217–245). New York, NY: Springer.

Swets, J. A., Dawes, R. M., & Monahan, J. (2000). Psychological science can improve diagnostic decisions. *Psychological Science in the Public Interest, 1*(1), 1–26.

Thaler, R. H., & Sunstein, C. R. (2008). *Nudge: Improving decisions about health, wealth, and happiness.* New Haven, CT: Yale University Press.

Trommershäuser, J., Maloney, L. T., & Landy, M. S. (2008). Decision making, movement planning and statistical decision theory. *Trends in Cognitive Sciences, 12,* 291–297.

Tversky, A., & Kahneman, D. (1971). Belief in the law of small numbers. *Psychological Bulletin, 76,* 105–110.

Tversky, A., & Kahneman, D. (1974). Judgment under uncertainty: Heuristics and biases. *Science, 185*(4157), 1124–1131.

Unkelbach, C., Fiedler, K., & Freytag, P. (2007). Information repetition in evaluative judgments: Easy to monitor, hard to control. *Organizational Behavior and Human Decision Processes, 103,* 37–52.

Vrij, A., & Mann, S. (2006). Criteria-based content analysis: An empirical test of its underlying processes. *Psychology, Crime & Law, 12*(4), 337–349.

Wason, P. C. (1968). Reasoning about a rule. *Quarterly Journal of Experimental Psychology, 20*(3), 273–281.

Weinstein, N. D. (1980). Unrealistic optimism about future life events. *Journal of Personality And Social Psychology, 39*(5), 806–820.

Yamagishi, T., Kikuchi, M., & Kosugi, M. (1999). Trust, gullibility, and social intelligence. *Asian Journal of Social Psychology, 2*(1), 145–161.

8 The Skeptical (Ungullible) Mindset

Ruth Mayo
THE HEBREW UNIVERSITY OF JERUSALEM

Did the Americans really land on the moon? Opinion polls suggest that between 6% and 20% of Americans surveyed believe that the manned landings were faked. The claim purports that the famous moon landing was staged, either in Hollywood or in Area 51, with the aim of defeating the Russians in the space race while avoiding any risk of failure. The money for the moon landing was supposedly given to many people who took part in this scam to do their job and forever keep this a secret. Don't believe it? Take a look at the famous picture of the landing. Why is the flag moving when we know there is no wind on the moon? Where are the stars? And why is there no crater where the Lunar Module has landed (https://en.wikipedia. org/wiki/Moon_landing_conspiracy_theories)? Reading these claims and looking at the picture with these questions in mind, on a scale from 0 (didn't land) to 10 (definitely landed), think for a minute and note how sure are you that indeed the Americans landed on the moon?

Psychology theories and research suggest that even if you were completely certain that the Americans landed on the moon, now, after reading the above claims, you are a bit less sure, choosing 9 or 8 on the scale rather than 10. Why? How does reading some alternative theory, a conspiracy theory, affect us in the sense of considering it as a possibility? If someone thinks that the Americans did land on the moon, and after being exposed to the above conspiracy theory s/he is a bit less sure about it, then this suggests how gullible our mind is, being affected by any passing information even when we think or know this information is wrong.

The Gullible Mind

The advocated cognitive basis for the gullible mind is the spontaneous nature of belief in contrast with the secondary nature of disbelief. The basic assertion is that the process of understanding any information entails belief. In other words, understanding is believing. And while belief is the spontaneous primary process, negating information is a secondary process, demanding motivation, ability, and cognitive resources (Deutsch, Gawronski, & Strack, 2006; Gilbert, 1991; Gilbert, Pelham, & Krull, 1988; Gilbert, Tafarodi, &

	Cartesian Procedure	Spinozan Procedure (Gullible Mindset)
Representation Stage	Comprehension	Comprehension and Acceptance
Assessment Stage	Acceptance OR Rejection	Certification (of Acceptance) OR Unacceptance

Figure 8.1 The Cartesian and Spinozan models.

Source: Adapted from Gilbert (1991).

Malone, 1993; Trope, 1986). The "understanding equals believing" model dates back to Spinoza and is presented in contrast to the Cartesian model (see Figure 8.1). While the latter suggests that people can comprehend information without tagging it as true or false, the Spinozan model theorizes that comprehension entails immediate acceptance that may be overturned only with a secondary processes of evaluation that results in the endorsement of the initial acceptance or a lack of acceptance.

The most direct set of studies aiming to test the Spinozan model was conducted by Daniel Gilbert and colleagues (Gilbert, 1991; Gilbert et al., 1988; Gilbert et al., 1993), who demonstrated that if participants are constrained cognitively – for example, by having to do multiple tasks – they keep using in their judgments and decisions information that they know is false. These findings are interpreted as a demonstration of the primary belief model, showing that interfering with the secondary process can leave one holding a belief about even clearly false information. Importantly, studies have demonstrated that even without interference, people have a difficult time negating explicitly false information (Begg, Anas, & Farinacci, 1992; Gilbert, Krull, & Malone, 1990). For example, people do not remember clear negations and end up recalling as true the information that was clearly negated (e.g., remembering that "the side effects of the flu vaccine are more dangerous than the flu itself" even though this information was explicitly tagged as false; Schwarz, Sanna, Skurnik, & Yoon, 2007). One of the more extreme examples of this failure of negation is the false-memory effect whereby events that are correctly rejected at first become "true" memories of real events (Fiedler, Walther, Armbruster, Fay, & Naumann, 1996; Loftus, 2005; see also Fiedler, Chapter 7 this volume; Forgas, Chapter 10 this volume; Schwarz & Lee, Chapter 13 this volume). Thus, if you are asked if you saw a coat hanger in an apartment, and you didn't, you will initially correctly answer "no," but after some time has passed and you are

142   *Ruth Mayo*

asked again, chances are significantly higher that you will think that you saw a coat hanger in the apartment and say "yes" compared to a situation in which you did not see a coat hanger and were not asked about it before. In other words, negating correctly in an initial instance may lead to incorrect affirmation at a later time (Fiedler et al., 1996).

Other effects are endorsed as supporting the Spinozan model from the belief aspect; one example is the acquiescence inclination, as people tend to say "yes" to everything (Knowles & Condon, 1999). Again, the idea is that when one is asked "Were you satisfied with your first year at college?" then one thinks of good things that happened, things that one is satisfied with, and therefore respond in the affirmative; but if one is asked "Were you disappointed with your first year at college?" one now thinks about disappointing things that happened and therefore affirm again. In other words, we tend to affirm as we accept and think in a congruent way with whatever concept we are exposed to. A related phenomenon is the most basic confirmation bias whereby people tend to search for, perceive, and interpret information that confirms rather than falsifies their preexisting thoughts (see also Dunning, Chapter 12 this volume; Snyder & Swann, 1978; Wason & Johnson-Laird, 1972).

Thus, decades of research conclude that believing, affirming, and accepting is primary, while negating, falsifying, and rejecting is secondary. One must have the motivation, time, and cognitive resources in order to be able to negate. Comprehension means acceptance, and that is the basis for our gullible mind that first believes and accepts any given information and is able to reject only as a secondary, demanding process. If this is the case, then how can we explain our spontaneous, immediate rejection of certain suggestions, such as to click on a link that promises we will win a million-dollar prize? Or the offer of a ride home from a complete stranger who stopped his car next to us? Do we need motivation, time, and cognitive resources to reject the "click here," "get in" messages? The current chapter proposes that the answer is "no" and aims to demonstrate that negation can also be (a) successful and (b) a primary process.

The Condition for Successful Negation

As outlined above, most research portrays negation as a secondary process that is prone to fail, leading to gullibility. The explanation given for this "weak" negation lies in the way we process and encode negation: We first process the core of the negated sentence and then add negation to it (Clark & Chase, 1972; Just & Carpenter, 1976). For example, if one is told, "Tim is not a tidy person," the concept of "tidiness" is activated in one's mind, together with congruent associations such as tidy behaviors (e.g., keeping a daily schedule) and other related traits (e.g., pedant). Only at the next stage does one negate the concept of tidiness by giving these activated associations a negation tag, and therefore one will correctly negate at that point (see also

The Skeptical (Ungullible) Mindset   143

Krueger, Vogrincic-Haselbacher, & Evans, Chapter 6 this volume). But, and this "but" is important, because the negation tag is a separate cognitive construct added to the core and its congruent associations, the two (i.e., core and negation tag) might get separated due to many reasons, including simply the passage of time, leaving one, in the end, falsely remembering that s/he was told that "Tim is a tidy person." We termed this model of negation processing and encoding the "schema–plus–tag model" (Mayo, Schul, & Burnstein, 2004). Important consequences of this model include immediate activation of the schema associations that actually represent the opposite meaning of negating the statement (or other stimuli), with the end result that we might lose the negation tag and have only the schema remain in our mind, again, with the opposite meaning of the original message. One can easily see how the schema–plus–tag model is congruent with the Spinozan model – accepting a concept first and negating it later with the risk of being left only with the concept. The schema–plus–tag model explains why negation is secondary and prone to failure.

However, studies suggest another model by which we may process and encode negation (Brewer & Lichtenstein, 1975; Gannon & Ostrom, 1996; Horn, 1989; Lea & Mulligan, 2002; Lyons, 1995; MacDonald & Just, 1989). We term this model the "fusion model" because it fuses the core of the negation with its negation tag into an alternative affirmative schema that carries the meaning of the negation (Mayo et al., 2004). Thus for the statement "Tim is not a tidy person," we activate an affirmative alternative schema that communicates the meaning of the negation of "tidy," which is "messy." Messy is an affirmative schema that means "not tidy." In this case, the concept of "messy" is activated in one's mind together with congruent associations such as messy behaviors (e.g., having piles of paper on the desk) and other related traits (e.g., confused). Hence, in the fusion model we process and encode negation within a schema that is congruent with the negation's meaning, suggesting a successful negation both in the immediate moment as well as in memory. We will remember that Tim is messy. If the fusion model enables successful negation, why don't we use it at all times?

In order for the fusion model to be available for us to use, there must be an alternative affirmative schema that represents and connotes the negation meaning. If there is not, we are stuck with the schema–plus–tag model. Our work demonstrates this critical role of the alternative affirmative schema in an experiment using bipolar characteristics (e.g., having clear opposites, such as happy/sad, smart/stupid) in one condition, and unipolar characteristics (e.g., characteristics that don't have a simple opposite, such as romantic, adventurous, and responsible) in the other condition (Mayo et al., 2004).[1] For each characteristic we created three behavior probes: one that is congruent with the characteristic but not with the characteristic's negation (i.e., for "Tim is tidy": "Tim's clothes are folded neatly in his closet"); one that is congruent with the characteristic's negation but not with the characteristic (i.e., "Tim forgets where he leaves his car keys"); and one that is irrelevant to the characteristic (i.e., "Tim likes to have long conversations on the phone"). The participants read the description of the person and then received the behavioral probe and had to decide as accurately and quickly as possible if the behavior is congruent, incongruent, or irrelevant to the description read before. We measured how long it took to make these judgments. Each participant saw half of the descriptions appear in affirmation and the other half in negation, and responded to all three types of behaviors that appeared in a random order between blocks. The findings indicated that for affirmative descriptions, responses for both bipolar and unipolar descriptions were faster for the congruent behaviors than the incongruent ones, suggesting that people have in mind associations that fit the description and therefore are quicker to respond to congruent types of behaviors than incongruent ones. However, for the negated phrasing, given bipolar characteristics, participants were faster to respond to congruent than incongruent associations, while the opposite was true for unipolar characteristics. For the latter, participants were actually faster to respond to incongruent associations than to congruent ones. Thus, while for both unipolar and bipolar characteristics participants correctly negate, they think of the negation-congruent meaning for the negation of bipolar characteristics, and they think of the negation core meaning for the unipolar ones. We also tested participants' memory of the descriptions in a surprise quiz at the end of the study. Memory for the affirmatively phrased descriptions was high for both the bipolar terms (91%) and the unipolar descriptions (93%). However, correct memory of the negated descriptions was much better for the bipolar terms (83%) compared to the unipolar terms (62%). Specifically, the case of losing the negation tag and remembering in error only the core of the message was significantly more prevalent for the unipolar descriptions (38%) compared to the bipolar descriptions (14%). Thus, in order to negate successfully, one must have an alternative affirmative schema.

Exploring research that demonstrates the weakness and failure of negation leads to the conclusion that in these studies the negation concerned a unipolar type of information. For example, for the false-memory phenomenon, there is no opposite for getting lost in the mall when you were 5 years old – you either got lost or you didn't. Thus, properly negating getting lost leads one to have an image of getting lost, and although one correctly denies it, still the image and congruent associations (e.g., crying) remain, and thus one may lose the negation tag and succumb to false memory. This is also true for negating seeing a coat hanger in the apartment, or negating false information in general, such as circulating concepts that the MMR vaccine causes autism. In all of these instances, there is no an alternative affirmative schema, and this may be the reason for the failed negation process and encoding. Indeed, research now has demonstrated repeatedly that having an affirmative alternative schema enables a successful negation (Chiu & Egner, 2015; Horne, Powell, Hummel, & Holyoak, 2015; Isberner & Richter, 2013; Orenes, Beltrán, & Santamaría, 2014; Rapp, Hinze, Slaten, & Horton,

The Skeptical (Ungullible) Mindset   145

2014; Richter, Schroeder, & Wöhrmann, 2009; Tettamanti et al., 2008; Vandeberg, Eerland, & Zwaan, 2012; see also Douglas, Sutton, & Cichocka, Chapter 4 this volume; van Prooijen, Chapter 17 this volume, on how such a process might apply to conspiracy theories). It is important to note that, as in the study of Horne et al. (2015), the alternative schema does not need to be a semantic construction. If one has any alternative schema that serves him or her for the negation, s/he will negate successfully. Specifically, Horne et al. (2015) offered an alternative affirmative schema for the false casualty posited between the MMR vaccine and autism by activating the alternative image of the illness that the vaccine eradicates.

A wonderful example may be found in the study regarding the paradoxical effects of thought suppression (Wegner, Schneider, Carter, & White, 1987): "Don't think of white bears." Reporting this effect, all that is usually said is that once you are told not to think of white bears, you keep thinking of them. However, in the same research, in the second experiment, Wegner et al. (1987) offered their participants an affirmative alternative schema: "If you do happen to think of a white bear, please try to think of a red Volkswagen instead." In this experimental condition, participants were less likely to demonstrate the preoccupation with white bears.

Of course, having an alternative schema doesn't guarantee that one will use it. Various factors may affect whether we choose the schema–plus-tag model or the fusion model. For example, we found that participants who suffer from rumination tend to negate with a negative schema: using the schema–plus-tag model for negation of negative information (for "Tim is not stupid") but the fusion model for negating positive information" (for "Tim is not smart"). This pattern suggests the possibility of the negative schemas being chronically activated, thus leading to their use when they are negated or when their affirmative counterpart is negated (Haran, Mor, & Mayo, 2011). Hence the schema we use may depend on who we are, what we are thinking about, and more. For example, before a medical procedure if the doctor says that the "procedure is not dangerous," even though there is an alternative affirmative schema for "not dangerous" (i.e., safe), given that the patient is likely prone to being worried, chances are high of using the schema–plus-tag model and continuing to think mainly of danger.

Interestingly, most negative behaviors don't have an alternative affirmative schema – you either did them or you didn't. Therefore, negating a negative behavior actually leads others to think of that negative behavior, its congruent associations, and probably remembering it as something you did. If you want to successfully negate it, you must come up with an alternative affirmative schema. For example, instead of saying, "I did not steal," one may consider saying, "The police are trying to set me up." Returning to the opening example of conspiracy theories, the interesting point is that usually conspiracy theories suggest claims that don't have an alternative schema (for many examples in this volume, see Cooper & Avery, Chapter 16; Douglas et al., Chapter 4; Myers, Chapter 5; van Prooijen, Chapter 17). But if one

146   *Ruth Mayo*

has such a schema, then s/he can negate these theories. Thus, knowing the explanation for the doubts raised by the picture of the moon landing will lead people to be less influenced by the suggestion that the Americans never landed on the moon (i.e., the landing was done gradually and this is why there is no crater, the angle of the photo leads to not seeing the stars, and the movement created when putting the flag in the ground on the moon actually led to its apparent fluttering, which continues even more because there is no atmosphere on the moon). Of course, there could be a competition between the negated false information and the truth. Many times the false information is much more interesting and vivid than the boring truth. This may also affect the type of negation model used and therefore its end result. These factors and many others should be further tested to better understand when and why people process and encode negation with the successful versus unsuccessful model.

Negation as a Primary Process

Accepting the two models of negation and their role in successful negation still leaves the possibility that negation begins with the schema-plus-tag model, and if conditions are right, the fusion model is applied in a later stage of processing (Kaup, Lüdtke, & Zwaan, 2006). This conceptualization is congruent with the Spinozan model. The schema-plus-tag model is the first phase – one thinks of the core of the negation. Only in the second phase might one move to the fusion model and encode with the alternative affirmative schema. Any interruption or a shortage of resources or time will leave us with the first phase only, the schema-plus-tag, which means thinking of the core of the negation rather than its actual negation and possibly forgetting the negation. However, if this is the case, then it implies that when you are standing in the rain, waiting for your bus, and a stranger stops his car next to you, opens the window and says, "Hop in! I will take you home," you first consider this offer, thinking for example of getting home faster and getting out of the rain, and only later (even if it's only few milliseconds later) will you think of the possible danger. The claim made in this chapter is that in such a circumstance you immediately think of the alternative schema that exist for this stranger's offer (being robbed or worse), and you don't consider getting home faster, even for a millisecond. In other words, in this case negation with the fusion model is a primary process. Still, clearly in this example the rejection is thought of as a strategic response. However, the current chapter's conjecture is that the specific reaction – primary negation – that occurs in this particular example of distrusting a specific source takes place in a general mindset of distrust, which is termed here *the skeptical mindset*. This mindset may be activated by a specific source, by a contextual cue one is not aware of, or by a general chronic tendency to distrust others.

As thinking is for doing (James, 1890) and thought is situated (Schwarz, 2002; Smith & Semin, 2004; see also Fiedler, Chapter 7 this volume), the

The Skeptical (Ungullible) Mindset   147

cognition of each mindset should adjust accordingly. Thus, if trust means taking things at "face value," cognition should be of a congruent type. If distrust means not taking things at "face value," cognition should be of an incongruent type. Therefore, the hypothesis suggested in this chapter is that the spontaneous reaction of rejection is the primary process of the skeptical mindset, and negation will take place regarding any incoming stimuli, even if it is completely unrelated to trust or distrust. Hence, the primary process of negation cannot be considered the result of any strategic, effortful, directed type of process. This suggests that there is a gullible mindset that has acceptance as its primary process, and there is also a skeptical mindset that has rejection as its primary process (see Figure 8.2). Because people tend to trust others unless they have reasons not to (Berg, Dickhaut, & McCabe, 1995; Légal, Chappé, Coiffard, & Villard-Forest, 2012; McKnight, Cummings, & Chervany, 1998), the gullible/trusting mindset is considered the default mindset. The skeptical/distrust mindset will be evoked by any external (processed consciously or unconsciously; Mayer & Mussweiler, 2011; for a possible interesting instance, see Oyserman, Chapter 14 this volume) or internal cue of distrust, given that some people can be characterized as being habitually distrusting (Rotter, 1967, 1971).

To test the hypothesis of a skeptical mindset that is characterized by a primary negation process, we aimed to demonstrate its resulting associations, processes, and finally reaction to incoming information. To avoid any specific strategic explanation, in all studies, distrust – assumed to be the trigger for the skeptical mindset – is manipulated incidentally or measured as a personality trait. The effect tested is always regarding a task that is unrelated to distrust. Hence, the effect is not a strategic response. The proposition is that in a skeptical mindset, compared to a gullible mindset, one considers alternative associations rather than the congruent ones, and negates rather than accepts; and as a result of these processes one is less influenced by incoming information – in other words, less gullible.

Associations

In our studies, we have hypothesized that whereas in a gullible mindset a congruent flow of activation takes place, thereby activating congruent cognitions, in a skeptical mindset, the flow of activation changes and triggers incongruent cognitions. Therefore, in a skeptical mindset, a message will spontaneously activate a meaning that is incongruent with the original message. To test this, we created 40 sets of three words: a target word (i.e., empty) and two possible primes for it; one that is congruent with the target (i.e., hollow); and one that is incongruent with the target (i.e., full). The participants' task in the study was to decide if a target word is an adjective or a noun (Schul, Mayo, & Burnstein, 2004). We told the participants that to create a visual load, we had inserted a face and an additional word. Their task concerned only the second word that appeared. Each trial started with the presentation of a face that was trustworthy or untrustworthy for 800 ms. Then a prime word was superimposed on the face, below the eyes. After being shown for 82 ms, the prime word was replaced by a target word, which remained on the screen until a response was made or until a 2-s response window closed. The priming word was either congruent or incongruent with the target.

The known effect is that people are faster to decide about the target word if a congruent prime preceded it, compared to an incongruent prime (for a review, see McNamara, 2005). In time measurement this means faster responses for targets that appear following a congruent prime compared to an incongruent prime. If a distrust contextual cue, such as an untrustworthy face, activates the skeptical mindset that spontaneously considers alternatives rather than going with the congruent flow of the prime, then the congruency effect should overturn and participants should be faster in responding to the target following an incongruent prime compared to a congruent one. This is exactly the pattern of results found in our studies: a significant interaction between the type of prime (congruent vs. incongruent) and the face (trustworthy/untrustworthy).

Participants were faster to respond following a congruent prime if the word appeared on a trustworthy face, but they were faster to respond to the target following an incongruent prime if the face upon which the words appeared was untrustworthy. This finding suggests that indeed an unrelated contextual cue for distrust (i.e., an untrustworthy face) leads the mind to an incongruent type of activation rather than a congruent one. It is easier to think of "empty" following "full" rather than "hollow." The activation of incongruent associations was not the result of a conscious processing strategy, because the prime–target interval was very short (less than 100 ms; see Neely, 1977) and because the respondents were unlikely to come up with a theory linking the un/trustworthy faces to the facilitation of congruent and incongruent targets.

Hence, we concluded that whereas in a gullible mindset the type of active association is of a congruent nature, in a skeptical mindset it is of an incongruent nature. As the un/trustworthy faces were a within-subject factor, changing from one trial to the next, the findings suggest that the two mindsets switch easily and that in the skeptical mindset the negation process can happen spontaneously. This finding was replicated using different types of distrust manipulations and even when testing the activation using a free association task in which people said out loud the first word that came to their mind and we recorded their responses. Following a trustworthy face, the free association was of a congruent type, but following an untrustworthy face, that free association was of an incongruent type (Schul et al., 2004).

These findings suggest that the skeptical mindset spontaneously activates incongruent associations, which we perceive as the end result of a negation process. Next we tested the negation process itself.

The Underlying Process

In order to determine whether the skeptical mindset processes information differently than the gullible mindset, we turned to a basic bias that is all about accepting information rather than rejecting it – the confirmation bias. This refers to the human tendency to seek, interpret, and create information in ways that verify existing beliefs (Snyder & Swann, 1978; Wason & Johnson-Laird, 1972; see also Cooper & Avery, Chapter 16 this volume; Dunning, Chapter 12 this volume; Krueger et al., Chapter 6 this volume; Myers, Chapter 5 this volume). Is the skeptical mind free from this bias? To test this hypothesis we turned to a classic task demonstrating the confirmation bias, the Wason's (1960) rule-discovery task. In this task participants see the series "2 4 6" and are asked to offer what is the underlying rule for creating this series. Most participants think that the rule is "+2." Next, participants are given a chance to check out their rule by writing six series that will be checked to see if they fit the rule. Most people write other series that are congruent with the "+2" rule (Klayman & Ha, 1987; Oswald & Grosjean, 2004), such as "10 12 14." These series conform with the rule "+2" and they will be given a check mark, and therefore the participant will think that s/he got it right and that the rule is "+2." However, the rule is actually any ascending number. One may find this out only by thinking of series that do not fit the "+2" rule, such as "5 6 7" that would be marked with a check or "9 7 5" that would be marked with an "X." Putting forth this type of series that does not fit the rule one initially generated is called negative testing, as one is testing whether his or her rule is incorrect, in contrast to positive testing that confirms only with information that fits one's hypothesis. In order to alter the mindset from gullible to skeptical, before the Wason rule-discovery task, we (Mayo, Alfasi, & Schwarz, 2014) asked our participants to create an impression regarding a person whose face they saw. In one condition that face was trustworthy, and in the other condition the face was untrustworthy. We asked our participants to keep their impression in mind because they will be asked about it at the end of the study. The rule-discovery task was presented as a filler task to make it more difficult to remember their impression. The hypothesis was that after viewing an untrustworthy face, participants will think of more disconfirming series, compared to following the trustworthy face. This is exactly what we found. Only 16.67% of participants exposed to a trust-inducing face generated at least one incongruent series, that is, reasoned with negative testing. However, 60% of participants exposed to a distrust-inducing face did so. Thus, incidental distrust – a face of a person that has nothing to do with the task in hand – tripled the proportion of participants who generated at least one negative test. Overall, 27.5% of all series in the distrust condition, but only 7.4% in the trust condition, were coded as negative tests of participants' own hypotheses (for a replication of this effect with a different type of distrust manipulation see also Schwarz and Lee, Chapter 13 this volume).

150   *Ruth Mayo*

We conducted another study where we did not manipulate trust or distrust but rather measured the chronic individual disposition of trusting, termed "generalized trust." This is our general orientation towards the social world and the people in it, reflecting an overall conviction that people are likely to be reliable, sincere, cooperative, benevolent, and truthful with benign intentions (Acar-Burkay, Fennis, & Warlop, 2014; Christie & Geis, 1970; Rotter, 1967, 1971; Wrightsman, 1974, 1991). Members of an online panel were asked to complete allegedly unrelated tasks online. They first responded to Yamagishi and Yamagishi's (1994) six-item trust scale (e.g., "Most people are trustworthy"; 1 = strongly agree, 7 = strongly disagree). Next they completed the Wason's (1960) rule-discovery task. The findings replicated the contextual mindset study: Whereas more than two-thirds (68.82%) of participants in the lowest-trust quartile generated at least one negative test, less than half (48.86%) of those in the highest-trust quartile did so. Thus, low-trust participants were more likely to generate negative tests than were high-trust participants. This was our first time finding that the skeptical mindset may be a personality trait or disposition. We continued to find that the effects of the skeptical/gullible mindsets apply to both a contextually primed mindset as well as a more stable personality mindset in subsequent studies (Kleiman, Sher, Elster, & Mayo, 2015).

The Skeptical Mind: Not Being Influenced by Incoming Information

The findings reported so far demonstrate a skeptical mindset that entails a spontaneous negation process with the activation of alternatives to the original accessible concept. This effect suggests that in such a mindset, the effect of any given concept should be diluted, as it is negated with the consideration of its incongruent alternatives rather than congruent ones. In other words, incoming information should have less of a congruent influence. Thus the gullible/skeptical mindsets may influence the accessibility of mental constructs, which in turn can affect cognitions, feelings, and actions (Aarts, Gollwitzer, & Hassin, 2004; Bargh, Chen, & Burrows, 1996; Bargh, Gollwitzer, Lee-Chai, Barndollar, & Trötschel, 2001; Bargh & Pietromonaco, 1982; Dijksterhuis & van Knippenberg, 1998; Higgins, 1996; Lerner, Small, & Loewenstein, 2004; Schwarz, 2009; Schwarz, Strack, & Mai, 1991; Srull & Wyer, 1979). We proposed that the skeptical mindset, resulting either from a chronic disposition or from a contextual factor, should attenuate or completely eliminate accessibility effects.

For example, in the basic priming paradigm, famously known as the "Donald paradigm," Higgins, Rholes, and Jones (1977) primed their participants either with positive characteristics (e.g., adventurous, confident, independent, persistent) or with negative characteristics (e.g., reckless, conceited, aloof, stubborn) and then asked them to read an ambiguous paragraph describing a person named Donald. The paragraph could lead to a

The Skeptical (Ungullible) Mindset   151

more or less positive impression. The main finding of Higgins et al. (1977) was that being primed with positive characteristics led to a significantly more positive impression of Donald compared to being primed with negative trait words, meaning that judgments are affected in a congruent way by the priming words.

We (Kleiman et al., 2015) tested the exact same paradigm with the single addition of measuring dispositional trust (Yamagishi & Yamagishi, 1994) at the end of the study. For participants high in dispositional trust, we found a significant accessibility effect such that they rated Donald more negatively in the negative-characteristics priming condition than in the positive-characteristics priming condition. However, for participants low in dispositional trust, the accessibility effect disappeared; the trait primes did not inform participants' judgments as there was no difference between the two priming conditions. Importantly, we did not find that the level of generalized trust affected the way Donald was judged in general; that is, the effect is not due to people low in trust judging Donald overall less or more favorably than participants who are high in trust. Rather, the accessibility effect of the positive/negative words did not occur. An interesting related example of the attenuation of the accessibility effect is the finding that distrust reduces stereotyping (Posten & Mussweiler, 2013). A stereotype usually leads to congruent judgments of the stereotyped person; however, because distrust leads to a spontaneous activation of alternatives – or in Posten and Mussweiler's (2013) terminology, a dissimilarity-focus – the congruent effect of the accessible stereotype is reduced.

Next we turn to embodiment, "bodily priming," based on the theoretical stance that mental representations of concepts are grounded in sensorimotor experiences (Barsalou, 1999; see also Schwarz & Lee, Chapter 13 this volume). Embodiment has been shown to affect impression formation, judgments, and decisions, as well as behaviors that correspond to the abstract concept that the sensorimotor experience makes accessible (e.g., Ackerman, Nocera, & Bargh, 2010; Jostmann, Lakens, & Schubert, 2009; Lee & Schwarz, 2012; Schnall, 2011; Schubert, 2005; Slepian, Young, Rule, Weisbuch, & Ambady, 2012; Williams & Bargh, 2008b; Zhong & Liljenquist, 2006; for an elaborate theoretical discussion, see Barsalou, 1999; Lakoff & Johnson, 1999). We (Kleiman et al., 2015) replicated the 2008 study of Williams and Bargh in which participants felt a warm or cold therapeutic pack, judged its quality, and then moved on to a seemingly separate task of creating an impression regarding an abstract person. Williams and Bargh's (2008a) finding is that participants who touched a hot therapeutic pack created a significantly warmer impression regarding the abstract person compared to participants who touched a cold pack. The idea is that the physical warmth is translated to the social trait of warmth.

This time, we did not measure trust but manipulated it. Before touching and evaluating the therapeutic pack, participants wrote about an event that happened to them in which they could trust/not trust another person. They were asked to remember this event because they would be asked about it at the end of the study. This request was made with the aim of keeping the distrust–skeptical mindset activated throughout the study. We replicated Williams and Bargh's (2008a) embodiment effect in the trust condition: Participants who wrote about a trust event judged the abstract person as warmer after touching the hot pack compared to the cold pack. However, this effect disappeared in the condition of writing about a distrust event. In the distrust condition there was no significant effect for touching the hot versus cold pack. It was not the case that the person was judged generally better or worse in the trust vs. distrust condition. Also, the evaluation of the therapeutic pack was not affected by the dis/trust condition, only translation of the physical experience into its social meaning in the trust condition (i.e., gullible mindset) but not in the distrust condition (i.e., skeptical mindset) (Kleiman et al., 2015). This suggests that in a trust context, the gullible mind is affected by the physical warmth in a congruent way, thereby transforming the bodily sensation into its metaphoric cognitive concept (Gallese & Lakoff, 2005). However, in a distrust context, the skeptical mind is not affected by the physical warmth in the sense that it does not lead to a congruent social judgment.

As a last example, think of the context of advertising. Ads are embedded within content articles on the web, to be seen by consumers in order to bring a specific brand to mind, thus making it accessible. Will this accessibility effect of an ad fade in a skeptical mindset? An identical set of two different static ads for a well-known brand of diapers was planted in two different "online" articles, which varied in the dimension of trust (but were similar in shape and length). In the control condition the article was about a person's unique hobby of raising homing pigeons. In the skeptical condition the article presented findings of a recently published State Comptroller report listing the ways in which citizens are being deceived by government institutions. Participants thought that the study was about reading and comprehension of web articles. They read the article, scrolling down as the two ads appeared, one in the middle of the article and one at the end. Then they were told that in order for some time to pass before being tested about the article, they are requested to answer a business school survey.

The survey began by asking the participant to name a familiar brand of toothpaste, followed by several evaluation questions regarding the brand. The next question was to name a brand of diapers one is familiar with, again followed again by several evaluation questions about the brand. The findings were that 62.5% of the participants in the baseline condition named the advertised "brand A" as a brand they were familiar with, but only 18.7% of the participants in the skeptical condition did so (Kleiman et al., 2015). Thus, within a control context, exposure to an ad makes the advertised brand more accessible. However, in the context of distrust (skeptic mindset), this accessibility effect diminishes, as the advertised brand loses its advantage over possible alternatives (i.e., competing brands).

Conclusion: The Gullibility of the Mind Is Context-Dependent

The current chapter's main claim is that negation can be a successful primary process reducing gullibility. First, one needs an affirmative alternative schema that carries the meaning of the negation in order to be able to successfully negate. Second, if the mind is in a context of distrust, due to situation or personality, then a skeptical mindset emerges, one of primary rejection. Specifically, the accompanying default result of the comprehension process is likely to be context-dependent. A mind may be gullible, in which comprehension equals acceptance and rejection is a secondary process, or skeptical, in which comprehension equals rejection and acceptance is a secondary process (see Figure 8.2).

Beyond the primary mode and ease of the negation process in a skeptical mindset, the fact that the mindset is pre-activated may be a critical factor in the ability to negate. When negation is explicitly communicated in a semantic manner, such as "the umbrella is not open" (Deutsch et al., 2006; Kaup et al., 2006), or in an explicit instruction to negate, ignore, discount, or correct information (DeCoster & Claypool, 2004; Fazio, Barber, Rajaram, Ornstein, & Marsh, 2013; Gilbert et al., 1993; Martin, Seta, & Crelia, 1990; Nisbett & Wilson, 1977; Skurnik, Yoon, Park, & Schwarz, 2005; for a review regarding misinformation, see Lewandowsky, Ecker, Seifert, Schwarz, & Cook, 2012; Rapp & Braasch, 2014), it makes sense that the person first activates the original information and then considers its negation. In the skeptical mindset, in contrast, negation is not explicitly presented but is rather self-generated. Critically, the claim is that for the skeptical mindset, negation is the primary, default process. One of the main factors enabling successful negation and correction is being prepared to negate before receiving the information (Lewandowsky et al., 2012; Schul Burnstein, & Bardi, 1996). Accordingly, one could naturally and easily correct for information received when one is already in a skeptical mindset. To conclude, the claim presented is that when we know better (equipped with an alternative schema and context), we are utterly non-gullible.

	Cartesian Procedure	Spinozan Procedure (Gullible Mindset)	Skeptical Mindset
Representation Stage	Comprehension	Comprehension and Acceptance	Comprehension and Rejection
Assessment Stage	Acceptance OR Rejection	Certification (of Acceptance) OR Unacceptance	Certification (of Rejection) OR Acceptance

Figure 8.2 The Cartesian and Spinozan models.

Source: Adapted from Gilbert (1991) with the addition of the skeptical mindset outlined in this chapter.

154 Ruth Mayo

Note

1 This study was conducted in Hebrew, in which there are no prefixes or suffixes; rather, a negation is communicated only by use of the separated word "not" (e.g., "not happy," "not responsible").

References

Aarts, H., Gollwitzer, P. M., & Hassin, R. R. (2004). Goal contagion: Perceiving is for pursuing. *Journal of Personality and Social Psychology, 87*, 23–37.

Acar-Burkay, S., Fennis, B. M., & Warlop, L. (2014). Trusting others: The polarization effect of need for closure. *Journal of Personality and Social Psychology, 107*, 719–735.

Ackerman, J. M., Nocera, C. C., & Bargh, J. A. (2010). Incidental haptic sensations influence social judgments and decisions. *Science, 328*, 1712–1715.

Bargh, J. A., Chen, M., & Burrows, L. (1996). Automaticity of social behavior: Direct effects of trait construct and stereotype activation on action. *Journal of Personality and Social Psychology, 71*, 230–244.

Bargh, J. A., Gollwitzer, P. M., Lee-Chai, A., Barndollar, K., & Trötschel, R. (2001). The automated will: Nonconscious activation and pursuit of behavioral goals. *Journal of Personality and Social Psychology, 81*, 1014–1027.

Bargh, J. A., & Pietromonaco, P. (1982). Automatic information processing and social perception: The influence of trait information presented outside of conscious awareness on impression formation. *Journal of Personality and Social Psychology, 43*, 437–449.

Barsalou, L. W. (1999). Perceptions of perceptual symbols. *Behavioral and Brain Sciences, 22*, 637–660.

Begg, I. M., Anas, A., & Farinacci, S. (1992). Dissociation of processes in belief: Source recollection, statement familiarity, and the illusion of truth. *Journal of Experimental Psychology: General, 121*(4), 446.

Berg, J., Dickhaut, J., & McCabe, K. (1995). Trust, reciprocity, and social history. *Games and Economic Behavior, 10*, 122–142.

Brewer, W. F., & Lichtenstein, E. H. (1975). Recall of logical and pragmatic implications in sentences with dichotomous and continues antonyms. *Memory & Cognition, 3*, 315–318.

Chiu, Y. C., & Egner, T. (2015). Inhibition-induced forgetting when more control leads to less memory. *Psychological science, 26*(1), 27–38.

Christie, R., & Geis, F. (1970). *Studies in Machiavellianism.* San Diego, CA: Academic Press.

Clark, H. H., & Chase, W. G. (1972). On the process of comparing sentences against pictures. *Cognitive Psychology, 3*, 472–517.

DeCoster, J., & Claypool, H. M. (2004). A meta-analysis of priming effects on impression formation supporting a general model of informational biases. *Personality and Social Psychology Review, 8*, 2–27.

Deutsch, R., Gawronski, B., & Strack, F. (2006) At the boundaries of automaticity: Negation as reflective operation. *Journal of Personality and Social Psychology, 91*, 385–405.

Dijksterhuis, A., & van Knippenberg, A. (1998). The relation between perception and behavior, or how to win a game of trivial pursuit. *Journal of Personality and Social Psychology, 74*, 865–877.

Fazio, L. K., Barber, S. J., Rajaram, S., Ornstein, P. A., & Marsh, E. J. (2013). Creating illusions of knowledge: Learning errors that contradict prior knowledge. *Journal of Experimental Psychology: General, 142*(1), 1.

Fiedler, K., Walther, E., Armbruster, T., Fay, D., & Naumann, U. (1996). Do you really know what you have seen? intrusion errors and presuppositions effects on constructive memory. *Journal of Experimental Social Psychology, 32*(5), 484–511.

Gallese, V., & Lakoff, G. (2005). The brain's concepts: The role of the sensory-motor system in conceptual knowledge. *Cognitive neuropsychology, 22*(3–4), 455–479.

Gannon, K. M., & Ostrom, T. M. (1996). How meaning is given to rating scales: The effects of response language on category activation. *Journal of Experimental Social Psychology, 32*, 337–360.

Gilbert, D. T. (1991). How mental systems believe. *American Psychologist, 46*, 107–119.

Gilbert, D. T., Krull, D. S., & Malone, P. S. (1990). Unbelieving the unbelievable: Some problems in the rejection of false information. *Journal of Personality and Social Psychology, 59*(4), 601.

Gilbert, D. T., Pelham, B. W., & Krull, D. S. (1988). On cognitive busyness: When person perceivers meet persons perceived. *Journal of Personality and Social Psychology, 54*(5), 733.

Gilbert, D. T., Tafarodi, R. W., & Malone, P. S. (1993). You can't not believe everything you read. *Journal of Personality and Social Psychology, 65*, 221–233.

Haran, D., Mor, N., & Mayo, R. (2011) Negating in order to be negative: The relationship between depressive rumination, message content and negation processing. *Emotion, 11*, 1105–1111.

Higgins, E. T. (1996). Knowledge activation: Accessibility, applicability, and salience. In E. T. Higgins & A. Kruglanski (Eds.), *Handbook of social psychology: Basic principles* (pp. 133–168). New York, NY: Guilford Press.

Higgins, E. T., Rholes, W. S., & Jones, C. R. (1977). Category accessibility and impression formation. *Journal of Experimental Social Psychology, 13*, 141–154.

Horn, L. R. (1989). *A natural history of negation.* Chicago, IL: University of Chicago Press.

Horne, Z., Powell, D., Hummel, J. E., & Holyoak, K. J. (2015). Countering anti-vaccination attitudes. *Proceedings of the National Academy of Sciences, 112*(33), 10321–10324.

Isberner, M. B., & Richter, T. (2013). Can readers ignore implausibility? Evidence for nonstrategic monitoring of event-based plausibility in language comprehension. *Acta Psychologica, 142*(1), 15–22.

James, W. (1890). *The principles of psychology* (Vol. 2). New York, NY: Henry Holt.

Jostmann, N. B., Lakens, D., & Schubert, T. W. (2009). Weight as an embodiment of importance. *Psychological Science, 20*, 1169–1174.

Just, M. A., & Carpenter, P. A. (1976). Eye fixations and cognitive processes. *Cognitive Psychology, 8*, 441–480.

Kaup, B., Lüdtke, J., & Zwaan, R. A. (2006). Processing negated sentences with contradictory predicates: Is a door that is not open mentally closed? *Journal of Pragmatics, 38*(7), 1033–1050.

Klayman, J., & Ha, Y.-W. (1987). Confirmation, disconfirmation, and information in hypothesis testing. *Psychological Review, 94*, 211–228.

Kleiman, T., Sher, N., Elster, A., & Mayo, R. (2015). Accessibility is a matter of trust: Dispositional and contextual distrust blocks accessibility effects. *Cognition, 142*, 333–344.

156 *Ruth Mayo*

Knowles, E. S., & Condon, C. A. (1999). Why people say "yes": A dual-process theory of acquiescence. *Journal of Personality and Social Psychology, 77*(2), 379.

Lakoff, G., & Johnson, M. (1999). *Philosophy in the flesh: The embodied mind and its challenge to Western thought.* New York, NY: Basic Books.

Lea, R. B., & Mulligan, E. J. (2002). The effect of negation on deductive inferences. *Journal of Experimental Psychology, 28,* 303–317.

Lee, S. W. S., & Schwarz, N. (2012). Bidirectionality, mediation, and moderation of metaphorical effects: The embodiment of social suspicion and fishy smells. *Journal of Personality and Social Psychology, 103,* 737–749.

Légal, J. B., Chappé, J., Coiffard, V., & Villard-Forest, A. (2012). Don't you know that you want to trust me? Subliminal goal priming and persuasion. *Journal of Experimental Social Psychology, 48*(1), 358–360.

Lerner, J. S., Small, D. A., & Loewenstein, G. (2004). Heart strings and purse strings carryover effects of emotions on economic decisions. *Psychological Science, 15,* 337–341.

Lewandowsky, S., Ecker, U. K., Seifert, C. M., Schwarz, N., & Cook, J. (2012). Misinformation and its correction continued influence and successful debiasing. *Psychological Science in the Public Interest, 13*(3), 106–131.

Loftus, E. F. (2005). Planting misinformation in the human mind: A 30-year investigation of the malleability of memory. *Learning & Memory, 12*(4), 361–366.

Lyons, J. (1995). *Linguistic semantics: An introduction.* Cambridge: Cambridge University Press.

MacDonald, M. C., & Just, M. A. (1989). Changes in activation levels with negation. *Journal of Experimental Psychology, 15,* 633–642.

Martin, L. L., Seta, J. J., & Crelia, R. A. (1990). Assimilation and contrast as a function of people's willingness and ability to expend effort in forming an impression. *Journal of Personality and Social Psychology, 59,* 27–37.

Mayer, J., & Mussweiler, T. (2011). Suspicious spirits, flexible minds: When distrust enhances creativity. *Journal of Personality and Social Psychology, 101,* 1262–1277.

Mayo, R., Alfasi, D., & Schwarz, N. (2014). Distrust and the positive test heuristic: Dispositional and situated social distrust improves performance on the Wason Rule Discovery Task. *Journal of Experimental Psychology: General, 143,* 985–990.

Mayo, R., Schul, Y., & Burnstein, E. (2004). "I am not guilty" vs. "I am innocent": Successful negation may depend on the schema used for its encoding. *Journal of Experimental Social Psychology, 40*(4), 433–449.

McKnight, D. H., Cummings, L. L., & Chervany, N. L. (1998). Initial trust formation in new organizational relationships. *Academy of Management Review, 23,* 473–490.

McNamara, T. P. (2005). *Semantic priming: Perspectives from memory and word recognition.* New York, NY: Psychology Press.

Neely, J. H. (1977). Semantic priming and retrieval from lexical memory: Roles of inhibitionless spreading activation and limited-capacity attention. *Journal of Experimental Psychology: General, 106,* 226–254.

Nisbett, R. E., & Wilson, T. D. (1977). Telling more than we can know: Verbal reports on mental processes. *Psychological Review, 84,* 231–259.

Orenes, I., Beltrán, D., & Santamaría, C. (2014). How negation is understood: Evidence from the visual world paradigm. *Journal of Memory and Language, 74,* 36–45.

Oswald, M. E., & Grosjean, S. (2004). Confirmation bias. In R. F. Pohl (Ed.), *Cognitive illusions: A handbook on fallacies and biases in thinking, judgment, and memory* (pp. 79–96). New York, NY: Psychology Press.

Posten, A. C., & Mussweiler, T. (2013). When distrust frees your mind: The stereotype-reducing effects of distrust. *Journal of Personality and Social Psychology, 105*, 567–584.

Rapp, D. N., & Braasch, J. L. (2014). *Processing inaccurate information: Theoretical and applied perspectives from cognitive science and the educational sciences.* Cambridge, MA: MIT Press.

Rapp, D. N., Hinze, S. R., Slaten, D. G., & Horton, W. S. (2014). Amazing stories: Acquiring and avoiding inaccurate information from fiction. *Discourse Processes, 51*(1–2), 50–74.

Richter, T., Schroeder, S., & Wöhrmann, B. (2009). You don't have to believe everything you read: Background knowledge permits fast and efficient validation of information. *Journal of Personality and Social Psychology, 96*(3), 538.

Rotter, J. B. (1967). A new scale for the measurement of interpersonal trust. *Journal of Personality, 35*, 651–665.

Rotter, J. B. (1971). Generalized expectancies for interpersonal trust. *American Psychologist, 26*, 443–452.

Schnall, S. (2011). Embodiment in affective space: Social influences on the perception of spatial layout. In A. Maas & T. Schubert (Eds.), *Spatial dimensions of social thought* (pp. 129–152). Berlin, Germany: Mouton De Gruyter.

Schubert, T. W. (2005). Your highness: Vertical positions as perceptual symbols of power. *Journal of Personality and Social Psychology, 89*, 1–21.

Schul, Y., Burnstein, E., & Bardi, A. (1996). Dealing with deceptions that are difficult to detect: Encoding and judgment as a function of preparing to receive invalid information. *Journal of Experimental Social Psychology, 32*, 228–253.

Schul, Y., Mayo, R., & Burnstein, E. (2004). Encoding under trust and distrust: the spontaneous activation of incongruent cognitions. *Journal of Personality and Social Psychology, 86*, 668–679.

Schwarz, N. (2002). Situated cognition and the wisdom of feelings: Cognitive tuning. In L. Feldman Barrett & P. Salovey (Eds.), *The wisdom in feelings* (pp. 144–166). New York, NY: Guilford.

Schwarz, N. (2009). Mental construal in social judgment. In F. Strack & J. Förster (Eds.), *Social cognition: The basis of human interaction* (pp. 121–138). Philadelphia, PA: Psychology Press.

Schwarz, N., Sanna, L. J., Skurnik, I., & Yoon, C. (2007). Metacognitive experiences and the intricacies of setting people straight: Implications for debiasing and public information campaigns. *Advances in Experimental Social Psychology, 39*, 127–161.

Schwarz, N., Strack, F., & Mai, H. P. (1991). Assimilation and contrast effects in part–whole question sequences: A conversational logic analysis. *Public Opinion Quarterly, 55*, 3–23.

Skurnik, R., Yoon, C., Park, D. C., & Schwarz, N. (2005). How warnings about false claims become recommendations. *Journal of Consumer Research, 31*, 713–724.

Slepian, M. L., Young, S. G., Rule, N. O., Weisbuch, M., & Ambady, N. (2012). Embodied impression formation: Social judgments and motor cues to approach and avoidance. *Social Cognition, 30*, 232–240.

Smith, E. R., & Semin, G. R. (2004). Socially situated cognition: Cognition in its social context. *Advances in Experimental Social Psychology, 36*, 53–117.

Snyder, M., & Swann, W. B. (1978). Hypothesis-testing processes in social interaction. *Journal of Personality and Social Psychology, 36*(11), 1202.

Srull, T. K., & Wyer, R. S. (1979). The role of category accessibility in the interpretation of information about persons: Some determinants and implications. *Journal of Personality and Social Psychology, 37*, 1660–1672.

Tettamanti, M., Manenti, R., Della Rosa, P. A., Falini, A., Perani, D., Cappa, S. F., & Moro, A. (2008). Negation in the brain: Modulating action representations. *Neuroimage, 43*, 358–367.

Trope, Y. (1986). Identification and inferential processes in dispositional attribution. *Psychological Review, 93*(3), 239.

Vandeberg, L., Eerland, A., & Zwaan, R. A. (2012). Out of mind, out of sight: Language affects perceptual vividness in memory. *PloS one, 7*(4), e36154.

Wason, P. C. (1960). On the failure to eliminate hypothesis in a conceptual task. *Quarterly Journal of Experimental Psychology, 12*, 129–140.

Wason, P. C., & Johnson-Laird, P. N. (1972). *Psychology of reasoning: Structure and content* (Vol. 86). Cambridge, MA: Harvard University Press.

Wegner, D. M., Schneider, D. J., Carter, S. R., & White, T. L. (1987). Paradoxical effects of thought suppression. *Journal of Personality and Social Psychology, 53*(1), 5.

Williams, L. E., & Bargh, J. A. (2008a). Experiencing physical warmth promotes interpersonal warmth. *Science, 322*, 606–607.

Williams, L. E., & Bargh, J. A. (2008b). Keeping one's distance: The influence of spatial distance cues on affect and evaluation. *Psychological Science, 19*, 302–308.

Wrightsman, L. S. (1974). *Assumptions about human nature: A social psychological analysis*. Monterey, CA: Brooks/Cole.

Wrightsman, L. S. (1991). Interpersonal trust and attitudes toward human nature. In J. P. Robinson, P. R. Shaver, & L. S. Wrightsman (Eds.), *Measuring of personality and social psychological attitudes* (pp. 373–412). San Diego, CA: Academic Press.

Yamagishi, T., & Yamagishi, M. (1994). Trust and commitment in the United States and Japan. *Motivation and Emotion, 18*, 129–166.

Zhong, C. B., & Liljenquist, K. (2006). Washing away your sins: Threatened morality and physical cleansing. *Science, 313*, 1451–1452.

9 Comparing Is Believing

Ease of Comparison as a Means to Induce Gullibility

Fritz Strack
UNIVERSITY OF WÜRZBURG

Approaching Gullibility

In its German translation, "gullibility" means "leichtgläubig," literally translated: "eager to believe," in a more social context "easy to be convinced."

Of course, the easiest way – perhaps another type of gullibility – is to consider this characteristics as a feature of *personality*. Within the framework of the "big five" (e.g., Borgatta, 1964), gullibility might perhaps be described as a blend of high "openness" and low "conscientiousness."

The second approach is more *social* in nature. One may ask about persuasive techniques that promote the acceptance of a message without being convinced by its content, a persuasion that is based on impression management (Hass & Mann, 1976; see also Cooper & Avery, Chapter 16 this volume; Myers, Chapter 5 this volume).

Finally, one may go one more step in a *reductionist* direction and ask about the psychological processes that facilitate believing. And of course, social cognition is the discipline that may provide insights that may help to understand the underlying mechanisms (see also in this volume: Fiedler, Chapter 7; Forgas, Chapter 10; Krueger, Vogrincic-Haselbacher, & Evans, Chapter 6; Unkelbach & Koch, Chapter 3).

Gullibility: Heuristically Generated

It is obvious that gullibility can be produced by heuristics (Tversky & Kahneman, 1974; see also Strack & Deutsch, 2002). As it is well known, heuristics describe ways in which judgments can be simplified. If judgments express beliefs, heuristics can be understood as promoters of gullibility. Indeed, at the beginning of this research program, heuristics had a pejorative flavor and were often described as judgmental fallacies resulting from deviations from normative rules. This was particularly reinforced by efforts to link psychological biases with judgmental heuristics (e.g., Nisbett & Ross, 1980).

Subsequently, however, heuristics were increasingly seen as strategies that simplify judgments by reducing their complexity with the goal of making them easier, less effortful and faster to execute. In fact, it has been argued that under specific circumstances, heuristics may even improve human judgment (Gigerenzer & Gaissmaier, 2011). As a consequence, one may wonder if the negative associations elicited by "gullibility" due to heuristic use deserve to be examined more closely.

As much as heuristics are candidates as determinants of gullibility, there is one severe problem: Heuristics do not share a single, common psychological property. As much as they converge in their consequences, namely facilitating and accelerating the judgmental process, their operation cannot be reduced to a joint mechanism. As Kruglanski and Thompson (1999) had pointed out in their "unimodel," simplified judgments are cut from the same psychological cloth as their more systematic counterparts, because they are based on syllogistic inferences. Of course, the various bases of such inferences may differ and this may depend on the goal of the judgment. Thus, assessments of frequency or probability may be built on the experienced ease with which a given content can be retrieved (Schwarz et al., 1991) or recognized (Goldstein & Gigerenzer, 2002; see also Oyserman, Chapter 14 this volume; Unkelbach & Koch, Chapter 3 this volume) while the similarity with a prototype may be harnessed to consider a category membership (e.g., Tversky & Kahneman, 1982). In an attempt to reach an overarching understanding of the operation of heuristics, Kahneman and Frederick (2002) have proposed "attribute substitution" as a common denominator. For example, while systematic judgments are based on normative parameters of logic or probability, heuristic simplification may replace them with peripheral assessments that are, imperfectly though, related to them. The similarity of a target with the prototype of a category is one prominent example. Linda, whose characteristics fitted that of a liberal activist was less likely to be seen as a banker than as a banker who is active in the feminist movement. The neglect of the most basic rule of probability theory led to the so-called "conjunction fallacy" (Tversky & Kahneman, 1982).

However, if heuristics are not defined as deviations from normative rules but as simplifications of comparatively complex and effortful judgmental procedures, the heuristic nature of a judgmental procedure is defined in contrast to a less heuristic way of generating a judgment. For example, to estimate the relative size of cities, the recognition heuristic is a simplification compared to searching for the relevant information in an encyclopedia, which may be characterized as "systematic." At the same time, to be even more precise, one might consult the official statistics. Thus, depending on the reference point, searching the encyclopedia may be described as a strategy that is both systematic and heuristic in nature, depending on the basis of comparison.

This suggests that the terms "heuristic" and "systematic" do not describe psychologically defined categories of human judgment but are synonyms for "simple" and "complex" as endpoints of a scale of judgmental complexity.

To be sure, if the additional time and effort does not increase the adaptive value of accuracy, there is no reason to assume that complex is always better. As a consequence, the search for the determinants of gullibility must continue and focus on the psychological mechanisms involved. One way would be to generate a list of those cues and mechanisms that are involved in various heuristics. This strategy, however, runs the risk of coming up with an infinite number of specific procedures, which are employed with the intention to simplify one's judgment. Alternatively, one might take a closer look at the general dynamics of human judgment and identify overarching psychological/cognitive principles that facilitate beliefs with or without a concomitant intention.

From Heuristics to Social Influence: Exploiting Gullibility

Social influence is typically understood as a type of compliance and conformity (Cialdini & Goldstein, 2004). Motivational forces were typically associated with the positive consequences of complying and conforming and/or the negative consequences of failing to do so. Thus, the influence was seen to be mediated by rewards or punishments as a function of the target's behavior.

Frequently, however, social influence may be more effective if it affects the targets' judgments in ways that are not immediately obvious. This is the case if it is not the outcome that causes pleasure or pain but the process that itself varies in pleasantness. This applies if the generation of a judgment requires little or much effort. And this is exactly what heuristics are all about: simplifying judgments. Thus, social influence may be effectively achieved by offering heuristics that result in the desired outcome.

This is exactly what Robert Cialdini has described in his book, *Influence: Science and Practice* (1985). Instead of using external reward and punishment, Cialdini identified tendencies within the individual to be harnessed for the purposes of the influencer. This "jujitsu" strategy includes the reliance on simple rules (e.g., reciprocity) and the simplification of judgments. Comparison plays a crucial role. For once, there is "perceptual contrast" that is driven by the deviance from an adapted state of experience, like the felt temperature of lukewarm water after having held one's hand in ice water. However, the perceptual nature that presupposes adaptation is not necessary. Mere judgmental mechanisms will suffice. Perhaps best known, Cialdini (1985) describes the letter of a young female college attendant who makes her parents believe that she was pregnant and about to bring home a socially unacceptable husband, only to reveal that these stories had been invented to justify her receiving poor grades in her studies. As much as adaptation may intensify experiences of contrast, the judgmental effect and its behavioral consequences do not need a perceptual representation (Kahneman, 1999). As we shall argue, the accessibility of the standard and the ease comparison will play a crucial role.

162 *Fritz Strack*

The second type of comparison discussed by Cialdini is assimilative in nature. It describes a type of social comparison (Festinger, 1954) that validates people's own assessments based on the judgment and behaviors of others (see also Cooper & Avery, Chapter 16 this volume). Interestingly, this assimilation affect also has a perceptual component when it comes to social contagion, e.g., when laughing or yawning by others functions as cues guiding a response. Most important, it provides a "social proof" that releases judges from assessing the situation and allows them to facilitate the process by simply following the others. Often, the validity of an assumption may be quantitatively evaluated by the number of others who behave in a cue-consistent manner. However, to the degree that their behavior was socially based as well, the validity assessment may be misleading. Also, others' preferences may differ from one's own. Even if "millions of flies can't be wrong," the proof of the observation depends on its transferability across individuals.

To overcome the traps of mere frequency, authority and expertise are identified as characteristics that further validate social influences. Even if such "peripheral" (e.g., Petty & Cacioppo, 1986) cues do not differ in the basic psychological mechanisms that result in the judgment (Kruglanski & Thompson, 1999), they facilitate the process compared to a more elaborate evaluation of the "central" aspects of the facts.

Of course, the existence of these judgmental facilitators or cues suggests that their presence liberates judges from weighing pros and cons. Even if there exist no pertinent data, it can be assumed that these simplifying aspects contribute to gullibility.

Social Cognition

As a basic model, the paradigm of information processing provides a framework in which human judgments are generated. They are understood as the result of information processing, which consists of the encoding, categorization, storage in memory, retrieval, and syllogistic inferences. In a more elaborate variant of the basic model, we (Strack & Deutsch, 2004, 2015) attempted to integrate different modes of information processing and link them to affect and behavior.

Specifically, we identified two processing systems that follow distinct principles. The *impulsive system (IS)* directs behavior by linking external cues to behavioral schemata based on previously learned associations. The internal responses that are generated during its operation can be conceived within the *reflective impulsive model (RIM)* as a network in which information is processed automatically through a fast and parallel spread of activation along the associative links between contents. In contrast, processes of rule-based reasoning and of symbol manipulation are assumed to be carried out in the *reflective system (RS)*. Although this enables greater flexibility, the reflective system operates slowly, tends to be disrupted by other processes, and depends on intention and effort.

The Impulsive System

Specifically, the *IS* represents environmental regularities as patterns of activation in an associative network. Links are created or strengthened if stimuli are presented in close temporal or spatial proximity. The *IS* works like a simple memory system (see Johnson & Hirst, 1991) that slowly forms enduring, non-propositional representations of the typical properties of the environment (see McClelland, McNaughton, & O'Reilly, 1995; Smith & DeCoster, 2000). Propositional knowledge cannot be represented in the impulsive system.

Processes in the impulsive system may be accompanied by an experiential mode of awareness. Specifically, processing a stimulus elicits three types of feelings. First, it triggers feelings related to the physical senses, such as colors, sounds, or tastes (see also Schwarz and Lee, Chapter 13 this volume). Second, based on innate or learned links, it triggers positive or negative affective feelings (see also Forgas, Chapter 10 this volume). Third, it triggers cognitive feelings, such as familiarity or ease (see also Unkelbach & Koch, Chapter 3 this volume). Generally, these feelings are assumed to result from strong stimulation of specific perceptual and affective structures within the impulsive system. Sources of activation are external perception of a stimulus, reflection about the stimulus, and spreading activation to stimulus representations from associated representations.

Consider, for example, an individual who repeatedly sees, smells, and finally buys and eats a piece of cake in a bakery. On the basis of the described principles, all sensory and motor representations that take place during the episodes will be linked, and an associative cluster that relates to cake will be created. When the person encounters a similar situation and engages in thinking about cakes or related concepts, this cluster will be activated again and lead to anticipatory sensations of taste and smell, as well as to the anticipation of the pleasure of sweet taste. Likewise, behavioral schemata that are related to eating will be activated. One striking example is the phenomenon of "impulse buying," when consumer behavior is not determined by rational choice but by affective determinants (see Hofmann, Strack, & Deutsch, 2008).

The Reflective System

In contrast, the *RS* serves regulatory and representational goals that complement the operation of the impulsive system. It is in charge of generating explicit judgments and decisions and of performing executive functions such as overcoming habits or putting together action plans in new situations (Lieberman, 2003). To fulfill these functions, reflective processes are based on symbolic representations, which are momentary re-representations of the concepts stored in the impulsive system. Only the reflective system can combine symbols flexibly by syllogistic operations. This flexibility, however, comes at the cost of slow processing and a great instability of representations in the *RS*. Such representations need to be rehearsed during

164 *Fritz Strack*

operation, which activates the corresponding concepts in the impulsive system. Representations of this kind are a prerequisite for generating explicit, propositional judgments and decisions, as well as for correcting judgments to increase their accuracy and or socially desirability. Of course, motivational as well as situational factors may affect the accessibility of information, which may subsequently bias inferences in a direction that meets the desires of either the person or an outside influencer.

If knowledge has been generated, syllogistic rules allow inferences that "go beyond the information given" (Bruner, 1973). Through reflection, the person exposed to a cake may link the perceptual input to a suitable category (i.e., cake, pie). In addition, elements that are associated with the category (e.g., sweet) may be activated and used for further reasoning. For instance, from the property of sweetness a high calorie content and a damaging potential may be inferred. These inferential processes are fundamentally different from the mere activation of associations in memory described above because they connect the activated contents, resulting in propositional knowledge, or beliefs. While the mere activation of the concept facilitates the inference, it does not create knowledge about cakes being high in calories. This knowledge, in turn, may be employed to form a behavioral decision (e.g., not to buy the cake).

This distinction is particularly important to understand negations. They are cognitive operations that only occur in the reflective system (see also Krueger et al., Chapter 6 this volume). Importantly, if they do not involve the cognitive creation of a concomitant affirmative representation, they will create associative traces in the impulsive system that correspond to the non-negated information. As a consequence, just saying "no" is not sufficient to create stable representations that reflect the content of a negation (Deutsch, Gawronski, & Strack, 2006; Gawronski, Deutsch, Mbirkou, Seib, & Strack, 2008; see also, Mayo, Chapter 8 this volume; Douglas, Sutton, & Cichocka, Chapter 4 this volume; van Prooijen, Chapter 17 this volume).

Operations of the reflective system may be accompanied by an awareness that something is or is not the case. Such *noetic* states of awareness may be accompanied by *experiential* states of awareness. For example, trying to answer an almanac question may be accompanied by a feeling of knowing (Koriat, 1993) that is not the same as actually knowing that something is the case. This feeling may be triggered by peripheral characteristics of the answer that are unrelated to the required information, for example, that the answer starts with a certain letter. A particularly striking example comes from Alter and Oppenheimer (2006) who found that at the stock exchange, newly emitted shares were more successful if their names were easily pronounceable.

Gullibility from the Perspective of the Reflective Impulsive Model (*RIM*)

The *RIM* provides a theoretical framework that allows us to look at the cognitive determinants of gullibility from a more systematic perspective.

Specifically, it describes several psychological routes on which judgments can be simplified and thus increase the likelihood of belief and the possibility of gullibility.

It is important to note that judgments are based on beliefs that are propositional in nature. That is, we assign a characteristic to a target and assign a truth value to the resulting characterization. From the vantage point of the *RIM*, this is produced by the *RS*. However, its effortful operations can be simplified in different ways. Moreover, existing heuristics can be understood in their underlying psychological dynamics.

Accessibility of Information (and Anchoring)

Most importantly, the mere accessibility of information in the *IS* operates as a major judgmental determinant. Prior activation in close temporal distance is the best guarantee that a piece of applicable information will simplify and shortcut the search for further information. U.S. President Trump, who is frequently described as highly impulsive in his decisions, is known to be influenced the most by those advisors with whom he has spoken most recently, which illustrates the influence of accessibility in a natural setting (see also Cooper & Avery, Chapter 16 this volume; Myers, Chapter 5 this volume). Priming research has demonstrated the operation of accessibility in a great number of studies showing that the influence may operate automatically without an awareness of the priming episode (see Cheesman & Merikle, 1984).

At the same time, reflective operations may affect the ease with which an information comes to mind. An example is judgmental anchoring that was mentioned as a heuristic by Tversky and Kahneman (1974) next to "availability" and "representativeness." The phenomenon is an assimilation of an absolute judgment toward the standard of a preceding comparative judgment. Best known is a study by Tversky and Kahneman (1974) in which participants were provided with a randomly generated number that served as a standard to decide if the proportion of African nations in the UN was higher or lower. Subsequently, when judges had to assess the true proportion, their judgments were distorted into the direction of the previous standard.

Of course, providing a standard in a natural conversation typically suggests that the true value is somewhere in the vicinity. Thus, gullibility is influenced by the intention of the communicator. Tversky and Kahneman (1974), however, excluded this possibility by openly generating the standard in a random fashion. The resulting assimilation effect must be explained without invoking communicative influences. The original authors proposed "insufficient adjustment" as an underlying mechanism. However, this explanation seems to beg the question without suggesting a psychological mechanism. As a consequence, Thomas Mussweiler and I (Mussweiler & Strack, 1999; Strack & Mussweiler, 1997) approached the phenomenon from an information-processing perspective. Specifically, we assumed anchoring to be the result of semantic priming. This assumption gave rise to a more elaborate "selective accessibility model" that was corroborated in a number of experiments. The model assumes that to generate a comparative judgment, relevant information must be retrieved from memory. Simultaneously, the provided standard operates like a baseline hypothesis to be tested. That is, people who were asked if the proportion of African states in the UN is higher or lower than a high anchor of 65% are assumed to have tested the possibility that the proportion is 65% and then responded by providing information about the direction in which the retrieved information deviated from the standard. However, research on hypothesis testing has shown that this information search is selective such that hypothesis-consistent information (e.g., "Many African nations that are members of the UN come easily to mind") will be more likely to be retrieved than inconsistent information. Even if the hypothesis is rejected, this type of activation in the *RS* will cause the consistent information to remain accessible and enter into the absolute judgment as a source of potential gullibility.

This conceptualization of anchoring as a knowledge accessibility effect is supported by a large body of evidence demonstrating that anchoring effects share many of the qualities that are typical for knowledge-accessibility effects in general. First, anchoring effects depend on the applicability of the knowledge that was rendered accessible by the comparative task. A second aspect is the similarity in use of the accessible information. Research on the judgmental effects of accessibility has repeatedly demonstrated that the direction of an influence depends on how similar the accessible knowledge is to the judgmental target. If an accessible concept is similar, it is typically used as a basis for the judgment, which leads to assimilation and possible gullibility. If, however, an accessible concept differs largely from the target, it will be used as a standard of comparison, which produces a contrast effect. For example, comparing the mean winter temperature in the Antarctic to a high versus low anchor (20 °C versus 50 °C) produced an assimilation effect on absolute judgments of temperatures in the maximally similar Antarctic while the same comparison produced a contrast effect on absolute judgments of temperatures on maximally dissimilar Hawaii. Thus, the direction of anchoring effects appears to depend on the similarity of the activated concept and the judgmental target, just as is true for knowledge-accessibility effects in general.

A third feature that anchoring and knowledge-accessibility effects have in common is that the degree of accessibility of judgment-relevant knowledge determines the time and effort that is needed to make a judgment. This pattern was replicated in the anchoring domain where response latencies for the absolute judgment depended on the extent to which the accessibility of relevant knowledge had been increased during the preceding comparative task.

However, different levels of accessibility do not only influence the speed of absolute judgments, but also their content. That is, judges who generate more anchor-consistent knowledge during the comparative task because they are in a sad mood, which is typically associated with more elaborate processing, should show larger anchoring effects than judges in a neutral mood.

A final characteristic of knowledge accessibility effects that is shared by anchoring is its temporal robustness. Knowledge accessibility effects are typically long-lasting, provided they are not superimposed by other applicable information. The same temporal robustness also characterizes judgmental anchoring. In particular, it has been demonstrated that anchoring effects still occur if the comparative and absolute questions are separated by one week.

In summary, this line of research demonstrates how the dynamics of basic cognitive processes can be harnessed to understand heuristics whose underlying mechanisms have not been sufficiently understood. Moreover, it sheds light on mechanisms of comparison that simplify social judgments in many domains. That is, they show how comparisons may ease and distort categorical judgments and they explain how people can be manipulated by being induced to engage in specific comparisons. As a consequence, the analysis of the cognitive processes underlying heuristics and comparative judgments may contribute to a better understanding of the resulting gullibility.

Comparisons in Social Settings as a Source of Gullibility

One of the first theories of modern social psychology was Festinger's (1954) theory of social comparison processes. It was a seminal attempt to understand interindividual processes by identifying their underlying intraindividual, cognitive dynamics. Its first hypothesis identifies individuals' needs to evaluate their opinions and abilities. More important, its second hypothesis is about social facilitation. Specifically, it claims that "to the extent that objective, non-social means are not available, people evaluate their opinions and abilities by comparison . . . with the opinions and abilities of others" (p. 118). Festinger has not only pointed at the readiness to be influenced by others, he has also pointed at the determinants that initiate or prevent comparisons. In particular, he has identified the difference between one's own characteristics and those of the comparison person to be a main obstacle for comparisons. Importantly, he has identified a motivational component that he calls a "unidirectional drive upward," which applies if abilities are compared, but not if the comparison is about opinions. Finally, comparisons are terminated if they turn out to be unpleasant.

Festinger's (1954) theory was the starting point of a social psychology that is based on cognitive operations. Even if their structure was more in the focus than their temporal dynamics, social judgments have occupied a focal point ever since in social psychology (Suls & Wills, 1991). As Festinger (1954) has aptly observed, these judgments were driven by two motives that might occasionally stand in conflict: truth and positive feelings about oneself. Under the label "downward comparison" the latter has subsequently

168 *Fritz Strack*

(e.g., Wills, 1981, 1987) stimulated a new research program that proved to have even therapeutic implications (Taylor & Lobel, 1989).

In social-cognition research, comparative judgments were often embedded in more basic mechanisms of priming. Specifically, the activation of information was found to influence the generation of judgments. However, this influence may occur in two directions, assimilation and contrast, depending on the similarity of the target and the prime. That is, if information about others is sufficiently similar to the target, it may serve as a cue to elicit related information that will become the basis of the judgment, which will become more similar. However, if the accessible information is very dissimilar to the target, it may serve as a standard and generate a contrast effect (Herr, Sherman, & Fazio, 1983).

Similarity may also be created by superordinate categories. That is, if a category is activated that causes the target and the standard to belong to together, the target will be judged to be more similar. However, if the context suggests that the two belong to different categories, they will be judged to be more different. As a consequence, the same piece of information can produce both assimilation and contrast effects and thereby foster gullibility.

Assimilation versus Contrast Explained

Schwarz and Bless (1992; see also Bless & Schwarz, 2010) have proposed an "inclusion/exclusion model" that describes the underlying mechanisms. It assumes that evaluative judgments require mental representations of both the target of judgment and a standard against which the target is evaluated. Both representations draw on information that is most accessible at the time of judgment. The degree of accessibility. However, the way accessible information influences the judgment depends on its use. If the information is used in forming a representation of the target, assimilation will occur such that the features in the representation of the target result in a corresponding representation and, as a consequence, in a corresponding judgment. The size of the assimilation effect is assumed to increase with the amount and the extremity of relevant information that is included in the representation of the target.

According to the model, contrast effects can take two forms. First, excluding a corresponding attribute results in a less converging representation of the target and hence in a less converging judgment. Like assimilation effects, this subtraction-type of contrast effect is based on changes in the representation of the target and therefore limited to evaluations of this specific target. Subtraction-based contrast effects are assumed to increase with the amount and extremity of converging information that is excluded from the representation of the target.

Second, the inclusion/exclusion model states that if information has been excluded from the representation of the target it may also be used in constructing a representation of a standard. If this information is converging, it results in a more positive representation of the standard, relative to which the target is evaluated more differently. These comparison-based contrast effects generalize to all targets to which the standard is applied. Their size increases with the amount of converging information that is used in constructing the standard. Thus, the model predicts the direction (i.e., assimilation versus contrast) and size of context effects, as well as their generalization across targets. More importantly, It demonstrates how easy is to influence judgments in opposite directions.

While assimilation versus contrast can be elicited by a variety of variables (Bless & Schwarz, 2010), one determinant seems to be particularly important. It is the categorization of the standard that allows the target to be subsumed or not. In an early study, Bless and Schwarz (1998) had asked participants different questions about their political knowledge, one of them about Richard von Weizsäcker who was a highly respected (formal figure head) president of Germany and a member of the Christian Democratic Union (CDU), a party that was held in very low regard at the time. Depending on conditions, the participants were either asked about the name of the party Weizsäcker had belonged to for more than 20 years or about his office that sets him aside from party politics. As predicted by the inclusion/exclusion model, participants' subsequent evaluations of Weizsäcker's party were more positive if the preceding question triggered his inclusion in, rather than his exclusion from, the representation they had formed of his party. This suggests that through mere accessibility of different characteristics, a target may influence judgments in opposing directions.

The Ease of Forming Comparative Judgments

This research shows that contrast effects may not only be the results of outright comparisons. They may also be caused by selective accessibility. To trigger and facilitate comparisons, commensurability must be created. Popular knowledge has it that you cannot compare apples with oranges. Much less should it be possible to relate buying a car to forgoing an overseas family vacation. In economics, however, such comparisons are believed to be the basis for the assessment of subjective utility. Under the name of "opportunity costs" (e.g., Rieskamp & Hoffrage, 2008), economic agents are assumed to compare what they are willing to give up or do without if they acquire a new good. Opportunity costs are often defined as "the next best choice" or the "loss of other alternatives when one alternative is chosen." Thus, the value of the loss or the waiver can be taken to assess the utility of a purchase.

Psychologically, however, it is highly questionable if such a comparative assessment is commonly taking place. To be sure, important decisions that involve major expenses may trigger purchases one has to renounce. In daily life, however, assessing the opportunity costs to generate a comparison standard seems to be rare. For once, the "next best alternative" is not

170 *Fritz Strack*

really a loss but can be acquired as well. More important, perhaps, is the fact that preferential comparisons need a common dimension on which the target and the standard can be allocated. This may require some effort and involve ambiguities that need to be resolved. If a decision has to be made between a new kitchen and a family vacation, it involves comparisons on many dimensions that need to be weighed in order to enter into a global preferential decision.

At the same time, providing such a dimension greatly facilitates comparisons and induces people to reach desired conclusions. Perhaps, the most effective facilitator of comparisons is the dimension of money. On an interval scale with a natural zero point, the value of a good can be described with any desired numerical exactness. However, the result of comparing different targets on the same value dimension may have been caused by different characteristics and preferences implies a comparison of these characteristics. If I like alterative A better than B, it is not necessarily due to the fact that A has more of what I like than B. Instead, it may be the case that the two alternatives have different characteristics and I like that of A more than that of B, which may require some serious deliberating.

Thus, the easiest way of comparing is when the same target causes different losses. If the same product is cheaper in outlet A than in outlet B, the evaluator may consider a purchase from A good deal. Of course, B may try to reduce the commensurability by pointing at peripheral characteristics that may revalue the product, such as the location of the shop or consulting and support. Therefore, the ease of comparison can be further increased by comparing the target with itself at different times. Such an intra-target comparison typically occurs on a temporal dimension such that the current price has been reduced compared to a higher price some time ago. Alternatively, the current price is offered for only a limited period of time and it will be increased in the future. Advantageous monetary comparisons are often advertised as "saving." Ironically, its definition as "income not spent" is turned into its opposite "saving by spending." Obviously, the arbitrary use of comparison standards combined with the ease of comparing on the joint evaluative dimension provides an ideal instrument of social influence. Thus, even if the recipients are convinced to have achieved a "good deal," it has induced a type of gullibility that was produced by directing the evaluation from the characteristics of the target to the relative utility of the purchase. The arbitrariness of the standard affords influencing people's choices in a powerful way that effectively obscures the lack of rationality by making them believe that they have made a good decision.

Comparative Judgments in the Ultimatum Game

Such judgments and decisions deviate from assumptions of economic rationality if the standard is merely a reference point but not an actual alternative to be chosen. It is therefore not surprising that comparisons play a major role in the so-called anomalies in microeconomics (Thaler, 1988; see also Krueger, Vogrincic-Haselbacher, & Evans, Chapter 6 this volume). Perhaps best known is the "ultimatum game," where players have to agree on the distribution of a given sum of money. Specifically, proposers suggest the proportion that they want to keep for themselves and the resulting proportion for the responders. If the responder agrees, the money will be distributed as proposed. If, however, the responder does not accept the proposed distribution, nobody will receive anything.

From the vantage point of economic rationality, responders should accept any offer that gives them a share above zero. However, numerous studies (see Güth, 1995) have demonstrated that offers resulting in shares below 40% are frequently rejected. This "anomalous" and irrational behavior has been explained by invoking the concept of fairness (Fehr & Schmidt, 1999). Specifically, it has been argued that proposers violate the social norm, which should be sanctioned to maintain it.

Whatever explanation is preferred, the irrational choice is always driven by a comparison standard, namely 50% standing for an equal distribution. It generates a conflict between the rationally prescribed acceptance of anything above zero and the relatively disadvantageous outcome.

More generally, however, comparative assessments can be aggravated if relative judgments are in conflict with the possibility of consumption, which is the basis of rational choice. This will be intensifies if the responder's focus is directed on the consummatory consequences of deal. In other words, if responders are primed with what they can do with the money, its relative value is less important.

This was shown in two studies (Zürn & Strack, 2017) in which participants in the ultimatum game were induced to think about what they would do with the money (or a corresponding gift voucher) they were to earn. Specifically, to activate specific consumption opportunities, these participants had to contemplate for 1 minute what they could buy with the gift voucher. Therefore, we presented them with the ten main product categories offered by Amazon.com and asked them to select the category from which they would most likely buy something.

We predicted that responders would be less likely to engage in comparative assessments and accept more disadvantageously unequal offers if consumption was primed and therefore more accessible than in the control condition where the deviation from the standard was assumed to be more important. This results indicated that this was the case. That is, the acceptance rate of responders for whom the consumption was primed was significantly higher than that for the no-priming control group.

In a second, replication study, the conflict between the two types of judgments (consumption versus distribution based) was assessed by recording responders' response latencies. Indeed, responders for whom the consumption possibilities had been primed took longer to decide than the no-priming control group. That is, if conflict is an indication of reduced gullibility, aggravating comparative judgments may be a means in that direction.

In another set of experiments (Zürn, Schmidt, Hewig, & Strack, unpublished) we manipulated their difficulty in a more direct fashion. Specifically, we told responders in the ultimatum game that the game would be played with foreign currencies whose value would be converted into euro cents. As a consequence, both the amount to be distributed by the proposer and the share offered to the respondent were uneven numbers, which made it difficult to calculate the exact proportion or deviation from the mean. This manipulation was innovative because in previous publications, the full amounts were typically reported as multiples of ten, which made deviations from the mean rather obvious. As Figure 9.1 shows, while we replicated the typical rejection of unfair offers, the response latencies were significantly increased for the converted currencies were increased when it was more difficult to calculate the proportions.

Moreover, responders were more likely to accept offers below an equal distribution if the amount could be easily converted into proportions than if this was more difficult (see Figure 9.2). This is another example how the

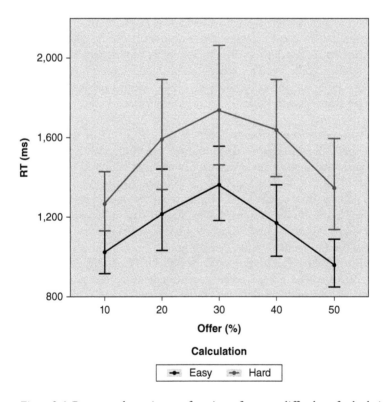

Figure 9.1 Response latencies as a function of ease or difficulty of calculating proportions.

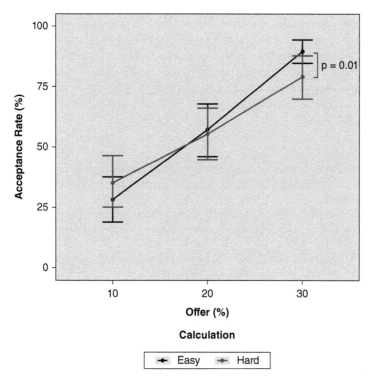

Figure 9.2 Acceptance rates as a function of ease or difficulty of calculating proportions.

ease of generating a judgment induces judges to respond in a way that is in the interest of the actor who provides the response frame.

Conclusions

In summary, this chapter argues that the human tendency to accept one of many judgmental alternatives depends not only on their convincingness but also on the ease with which they can be generated, and this can be an important source of gullibility in everyday life (see also Fiedler, Chapter 7 this volume; Myers, Chapter 5 this volume; Unkelbach & Koch, Chapter 3 this volume). As a consequence, offering heuristic routes affects the believability of various outcomes and serves as a powerful means of social influence. Heuristics are pragmatically defined in relation to some more difficult (systematic) ways of processing while the types of simplification are numerous and even unlimited. A psychological understanding of the ease versus difficulty of generating a judgment requires a deeper exploration of the underlying mechanisms. As a theoretical orientation, the reflective impulsive model was introduced.

174 *Fritz Strack*

Based on both this model and evidence from the domains of social influence and social comparison, we have argued that other than directing people's attention toward a favorable outcome, judgmental facilitation may be caused by the accessibility of an arbitrary standard and the ease of comparison. This has been recognized as a powerful means of influence in the marketing domain. Beyond that, the ease of comparison deserves a more basic exploration as a fundamental mechanism of gullibility and social influence.

References

Alter, A. L., & Oppenheimer, D. M. (2006). Predicting short-term stock fluctuations by using processing fluency. *Proceedings of the National Academy of Sciences, 103*, 9369–9372.

Bless, H., & Schwarz, N. (1998). Context effects in political judgement: Assimilation and contrast as a function of categorization processes. *European Journal of Social Psychology, 28*, 159–172.

Bless, H., & Schwarz, N. (2010). Mental construal and emergence of assimilation and contrast effects: The inclusion/exclusion model. *Advances in Experimental Social Psychology, 42*, 319–374.

Borgatta, E. F. (1964). The structure of personality characteristics. *Systems Research and Behavioral Science, 9*, 8–17.

Bruner, J. S. (1973). *Beyond the information given: Studies in the psychology of knowing.* New York, NY: Norton.

Cialdini, R. B. (1985). *Influence: Science and practice.* Glenview, IL: Scott, Foresman, & Co.

Cialdini, R. B., & Goldstein, N. J. (2004). Social influence: Compliance and conformity. *Annual Review of Psychology, 55*, 591–621.

Cheesman, J., & Merikle, P. M. (1984). Priming with and without awareness. *Perception & Pychophysics, 36*, 387–395.

Hass, R. G., & Mann, R. W. (1976). Anticipatory belief change: Persuasion or impression management? *Journal of Personality and Social Psychology, 34*, 105.

Herr, P. M., Sherman, S. J., & Fazio, R. H. (1983). On the consequences of priming: Assimilation and contrast effects. *Journal of Experimental Social Psychology, 19*, 323–340.

Deutsch, R., Gawronski, B., & Strack, F. (2006). At the boundaries of automaticity: Negation as reflective operation. *Journal of Personality and Social Psychology, 91*, 385–405.

Fehr, E., & Schmidt, K. M. (1999). A theory of fairness, competition, and cooperation. *Quarterly Journal of Economics, 114*, 817–868.

Gawronski, B., Deutsch, R., Mbirkou, S., Seibt, B., & Strack, F. (2008). When "just say no" is not enough: Affirmation versus negation training and the reduction of automatic stereotype activation. *Journal of Experimental Social Psychology, 44*, 370–377.

Gigerenzer, G., & Gaissmaier, W. (2011). Heuristic decision making. *Annual Review of Psychology, 62*, 451–482.

Goldstein, D. G., & Gigerenzer, G. (2002). Models of ecological rationality: The recognition heuristic. *Psychological Review, 109*, 75.

Güth, W. (1995). On ultimatum bargaining experiments: A personal review. *Journal of Economic Behavior & Organization, 27*, 329–344.

Festinger, L. (1954). A theory of social comparison processes. *Human Relations, 7*, 117–140.

Hofmann, W., Strack, F., & Deutsch, R. (2008). Free to buy? Explaining self-control and impulse in consumer behavior. *Journal of Consumer Psychology, 18*, 22–26.

Johnson, M. K., & Hirst, W. (1991). Processing subsystems of memory. In R. G. Lister & H. J. Weingartner (Eds.), *Perspectives on cognitive neuroscience* (pp. 197–217). New York, NY: Oxford University Press.

Kahneman, D. (1999). Objective happiness. In D. Kahneman, E. Diener, & N. Schwarz (Eds.), *Subjective Well-being: The foundations of hedonic psychology* (pp. 3–25). New York, NY: Russell Sage.

Kahneman, D., & Frederick, S. (2002). Representativeness revisited: Attribute substitution in intuitive judgment. In T. Gilovich, D. Griffin, & D. Kahneman (Eds.), *Heuristics and biases* (pp. 49–81). New York, NY: Cambridge University Press.

Koriat, A. (1993). How do we know that we know? The accessibility account of the feeling of knowing. *Psychological Review, 100*, 609–639.

Kruglanski, A. W., & Thompson, E. P. (1999). Persuasion by a single route: A view from the unimodel. *Psychological Inquiry, 10*, 83–109.

Lieberman, M. (2003). Reflexive and reflective judgment processes: A social cognitive neuroscience approach. In J. P. Forgas, K. D. Williams, & W. von Hippel (Eds.), *Social judgments: Explicit and implicit processes* (pp. 44–67). New York, NY: Cambridge University Press.

McClelland, J. L., McNaughton, B. L., & O'Reilly, R. C. (1995). Why there are complementary learning systems in the hippocampus and neocortex: Insights from the successes and failures of connectionist models of learning and memory. *Psychological Review, 102*, 419–457.

Mussweiler, T., & Strack, F. (1999). Hypothesis-consistent testing and semantic priming in the anchoring paradigm: A selective accessibility model. *Journal of Experimental Social Psychology, 35*, 136–164.

Nisbett, R. E., & Ross, L. (1980). *Human inference: Strategies and shortcomings of social judgment.* New York, NY: Prentice Hall.

Petty, R. E., & Cacioppo, J. T. (1986). The elaboration likelihood model of persuasion. In L. Berkowitz (Ed.), *Advances in experimental social psychology* (Vol. 19, pp. 123–203). New York, NY: Academic Press.

Rieskamp, J., & Hoffrage, U. (2008). Inferences under time pressure: How opportunity costs affect strategy selection. *Acta Psychologica, 127*, 258–276.

Schwarz, N., & Bless, H. (1992). Constructing reality and its alternatives: An inclusion/exclusion model of assimilation and contrast effects in social judgment. In L. L. Martin & A. Tesser (Eds.), *The construction of social judgments* (pp. 217–245). Hillsdale, NJ: Lawrence Erlbaum.

Schwarz, N., Bless, H., Strack, F., Klumpp, G., Rittenauer-Schatka, H., & Simons, A. (1991). Ease of retrieval as information: Another look at the availability heuristic. *Journal of Personality and Social Psychology, 61*, 195–202.

Smith, E. R., & DeCoster, J. (2000). Dual-process models in social and cognitive psychology: Conceptual integration and links to underlying memory systems. *Personality and Social Psychology Review, 4*, 108–131.

Strack, F., & Deutsch, R. (2002). Urteilsheuristiken. In D. Frey & M. Irle (Eds.), *Theorien der Sozialpsychologie Bd. 3* (pp. 352–384). Bern: Huber.

Strack, F., & Deutsch, R. (2004). Reflective and impulsive determinants of social behavior. *Personality and Social Psychology Review, 8,* 220–247.

Strack, F., & Deutsch, R. (2015). The duality of everyday life: Dual-process and dual system models in social psychology. *APA Handbook of Personality and Social Psychology, 1,* 891–927.

Strack, F., & Mussweiler, T. (1997). Explaining the enigmatic anchoring effect: Mechanisms of selective accessibility. *Journal of Personality and Social Psychology, 73,* 437.

Suls, J. E., & Wills, T. A. E. (1991). *Social comparison: Contemporary theory and research.* Hillsdale, NJ: Lawrence Erlbaum Associates.

Taylor, S. E., & Lobel, M. (1989). Social comparison activity under threat: Downward evaluation and upward contacts. *Psychological Review, 96,* 569.

Thaler, R. H. (1988). Anomalies: The ultimatum game. *Journal of Economic Perspectives, 2,* 195–206.

Tversky, A., & Kahneman, D. (1974). Judgment under uncertainty: Heuristics and biases. *Science, 185,* 1124–1131.

Tversky, A., & Kahneman, D. (1982) Judgments of and by representativeness. In D. Kahneman, P. Slovic, & A. Tversky (Eds.), *Judgment under uncertainty: Heuristics and biases* (pp. 84–98). Cambridge, UK: Cambridge University Press.

Wills, T. A. (1981). Downward comparison principles in social psychology. *Psychological Bulletin, 90,* 245–271.

Wills, T. A. (1987). Downward comparison as a coping mechanism. In C. R. Snyder & C. Ford (Eds.), *Coping with negative life events: Clinical and social-psychological perspectives* (pp. 243–268). San Diego, CA: Academic Press.

Zürn, M., Schmidt, B., Hewig, J., & Strack, F. (unpublished) *Making sense of anomalies: The utilitarian logic of irrational choice.* Würzburg, Germany: University of Würzburg.

Zürn, M., & Strack, F. (2017). When more is better: Consumption priming decreases responders' rejections in the ultimatum game. *Frontiers in Psychology, 8,* 2226.

Part III

Affective and Motivational Processes and Gullibility

10 On the Role of Affect in Gullibility

Can Positive Mood Increase, and Negative Mood Reduce Credulity?

Joseph P. Forgas
UNIVERSITY OF NEW SOUTH WALES

Introduction

What is the role of affect in gullibility? Does mood influence the way we examine and evaluate more or less suspicious or doubtful information? For example, could a happy mood predispose people to be more trusting and credulous, and conversely, could negative mood function as a subconscious warning signal, producing a more cautious and critical evaluation of information? We do know that *Homo sapiens* is a rather moody species (Forgas & Eich, 2013), and credulity is also a fundamental characteristic of humankind (see also Baumeister, Maxwell, Thomas, & Vohs, Chapter 2 this volume; Cooper & Avery, Chapter 16 this volume; Dunning, Chapter 12 this volume; Fiedler, Chapter 7 this volume; Krueger, Vogrincic-Haselbacher, & Evans, Chapter 6 this volume; Myers, Chapter 5 this volume). How do these two qualities, mood and gullibility, interact? This chapter will review experiments indicating that mild, everyday moods can have a marked influence on gullibility. Most of us are intuitively aware that our feelings might have some influence on our judgments and behaviors, but the nature of this influence remains incompletely understood.

Gullibility versus Skepticism

The unique human ability to create, share, and act upon second-hand, fictional information as real is one of the most remarkable evolutionary achievements of our species (Harari, 2014). Most social organisation and integration is based on the unique human capacity to accept and trust shared systems of beliefs as "real." But there is also a significant cost associated with this remarkable cognitive ability to treat fiction as reality. The tendency to accept fiction as real is also the basis of human gullibility and superstition (see also Krueger et al., Chapter 6 this volume; Myers, Chapter 5 this volume; Strack, Chapter 9 this volume). Belief in witches, magic potions, exorcism, and human sacrifice is now rare, but conspiracy theories,

180 *Joseph P. Forgas*

pyramid schemes, alternative therapies, and miracle diets are still with us today (see also Douglas, Sutton, & Cichocka, Chapter 4 this volume; Myers, Chapter 5 this volume; van Prooijen, Chapter 17 this volume). In everyday life, knowing what to believe and what to reject remains a challenging cognitive task. Rejecting valid information as false (excessive skepticism) is just as dangerous as accepting invalid information as true (excessive gullibility; see also Mayo, Chapter 8 this volume).

Affect and Credulity

Affect has long been suspected as a source of irrationality and bias in judgments. Ever since antiquity, many great philosophers such as Plato, Aristotle, St. Augustine, Descartes, Pascal, Kant, and others considered affect to be a primitive and invasive but sovereign human faculty that can subvert human reason (Hilgard, 1980). As Pascal (1643/1966) argued, "the heart has its reasons which reason does not understand" (p. 113). Social theorists such as Machiavelli identified affect as a powerful subversive influence on effective thinking, and proposed elaborate schemes to exploit this human weakness for political gain (Machiavelli, 1961). Machiavelli anticipated much of what passes for everyday political practice in autocratic countries, such as Hungary, where the Western virtues of democracy and its psychological foundation in rationality and individual autonomy have not yet taken root (Albright, 2018; Forgas, Kelemen, & László, 2015; see also Cooper & Avery, Chapter 16 this volume; Myers, Chapter 5 this volume).

Psychologists have also often assumed that whenever emotions are "directly involved in action, they tend to overwhelm or subvert rational mental processes" (Elster, 1985, p. 379). Psychoanalytic theories were especially influential in in casting affective states as "noisome, irrational agents in the decision-making process" (Toda, 1980, p. 133). Supporting this dynamic view, Feshbach and Singer (1957) found that attempts to suppress fear, paradoxically, increased the tendency to see "another person as fearful and anxious" indicating that "suppression of fear facilitates the tendency to project fear onto another social object" (p. 286). The recurring thread of irrationality and violence in human history was seen by some writers as evidence of a fatal flaw in the evolution of our species (Koestler, 1978), due to the poor structural integration between the archaic emotional and more rational neocortical structures of the brain.

A contrary view, however, suggests that affect can also serve as a useful, and even essential input to effective social thinking (Damasio, 1994; de Sousa, 1987; Oatley & Jenkins, 1996). This chapter presents evidence that mild affective states and moods can indeed influence gullibility by regulating the information processing strategies people adopt. What are the psychological mechanisms that might link affect to gullibility? We shall turn to this question next.

Can Mood Influence Gullibility?

Affective experiences penetrate every aspect of our lives, and influence many of our cognitive and behavioral strategies (Fiedler, 2001; Forgas, 2013; Zajonc, 1980, 2000; see also Fiedler, Chapter 7 this volume; Schwarz & Lee, Chapter 13 this volume). First, affective states can exert a strong *affect-congruent* influence on the valence of thinking (Forgas & Eich, 2013). Affective states can also regulate the kinds of *information processing strategies* people adopt in social situations (Bless, 2001; Bless & Fiedler, 2006; Fiedler, 2001; Forgas, 1994, 2002). Surprisingly, the role of affect in gullibility has received insufficient prior attention. Our interest here is in mild mood states rather than emotions, as subconscious moods have been found to have more uniform, enduring, and reliable cognitive and behavioral consequences than is the case with intense and highly conscious and context-specific emotions (Forgas, 2006, 2013).

For our purposes, we may define moods as low-intensity, diffuse, and relatively enduring affective states without a salient antecedent cause and therefore little cognitive content. In contrast, emotions are more intense, short-lived and usually have a definite cause and clear cognitive content (Forgas, 1995, 2002). There are two complementary cognitive mechanisms that are responsible for the infusion of mood states into thinking and judgments: (1) informational effects (influencing the content and valence of cognition), and (2) processing effects (influencing the process of cognition).

Informational Effects

Moods may influence gullibility versus skepticism by selectively priming the accessibility of positively or negatively valenced information in memory (Bower, 1981; Forgas, 1995). Thus positive mood should prime a more positive, trusting evaluation, and negative mood should prime more negative and skeptical evaluations. Consistent with this affect-priming model, numerous studies found a mood-congruent bias in memory and social judgments (Bless & Fiedler, 2006; Fiedler, 2001; Forgas, 1994, 1995; Forgas, Bower, & Krantz, 1984; Niedenthal, Halberstadt, Margolin, & Innes-Ker, 2000). In some cases, the prevailing mood state may also function as a direct heuristic cue, informing evaluative reactions to a stimulus or a situation (Clore, Schwarz, & Conway, 1994; Schwarz & Clore, 1983).

Subsequent integrative theories of affect and cognition such as the affect infusion model (AIM; Forgas, 1995, 2002) specifically predict that affect congruence in thinking and judgments should be greatest when more open, elaborate, and constructive processing is required to perform a task. Most veracity and credulity judgments involve uncertainty and thus require such open and constructive processing (Fiedler, 2001; Forgas, 1995, 2002). Because credulity judgments require judges to go beyond the information given (Bond & DePaulo, 2006; Kraut, 1980; O'Sullivan, 2003), there should be a mood-congruent influence on gullibility.

182   *Joseph P. Forgas*

Processing Effects of Mood

In addition, moods may also influence the way information is processed (*processing effects*). Negative mood may function as a mild evolutionary alarm signal, triggering a more accommodative, detailed, and systematic processing style. Positive mood in turn signals safety and familiarity, promoting a more heuristic, assimilative, and top-down processing style (Bless, 2001; Bless & Fiedler, 2006; Fiedler, 2001). Accordingly, negative mood should reduce credulity and facilitate the more accurate detection of deceptive communications (Bless & Fiedler, 2006). Consistent with such a mood-induced processing dichotomy, people in a negative mood think less heuristically and tend to use more detailed schemas, process persuasive messages more systematically (Bless, 2001; Forgas, 2007), rely more on new, external information (Fiedler, Fladung, & Hemmeter, 1987), show fewer judgmental errors (Forgas, 2011, 2013) and have better memory (Fiedler, Lachnit, Fay, & Krug, 1992; Forgas, Laham, & Vargas, 2005). Extrapolating from this evidence, we expect here that negative mood should also inhibit gullibility by promoting a more careful, accommodative processing style.

In contrast, positive mood may enhance gullibility by recruiting a more heuristic, and assimilative thinking style (see also Fiedler, Chapter 7 this volume; Krueger et al., Chapter 6 this volume; Strack, Chapter 9 this volume; Unkelbach & Koch, Chapter 3 this volume). We investigated these predictions in a series of studies, exploring mood effects on (1) bullshit detection, (2) the truth bias when evaluating urban myths, (3) the detection of verbal and nonverbal deception, and (4) gullibility in eyewitness recollections. Overall, we expected increased gullibility in positive mood, and greater skepticism in negative mood.

Mood Effects on Bullshit Receptivity

Perceiving Meaning Where There Is None

Perhaps the purest form of gullibility occurs when people infer meaning in meaningless, randomly generated information. In a now famous hoax the physicist Alan Sokal submitted an intentionally meaningless text to a postmodernist theoretical journal to investigate whether a leading North American journal of postmodern cultural studies would publish an article liberally salted with nonsense if (a) it sounded good and (b) it flattered the editors' ideological preconceptions (Sokal, 1996). The article was duly accepted and published (Sokal, 1994). When Sokal subsequently revealed the hoax, it became obvious that in many academic departments in the humanities and social sciences infested by postmodernism and meaningless verbiage can be easily passed off as a valuable intellectual product. A recent study "On the reception and detection of pseudo-profound bullshit" by

Pennycook, Cheyne, Barr, Koehler, and Fugelsang (2015, p. 559) nicely confirmed the same effect, showing that people often perceive vacuous, pseudo-profound "bullshit" text as potentially meaningful.

In a recent study we examined the possibility that induced mood can influence bullshit receptivity (Forgas, Matovic, & Slater, 2018). We asked participants in a positive or negative induced mood to rate the meaningfulness and profundity of two kinds of verbal "bullshit" text. The first kind, New Age "bullshit," was taken from a spoof website randomly combining words from the banal pronouncements of Deepak Chopra: http://wisdom ofchopra.com (e.g., "Imagination is inside exponential space time events" and "Good health imparts reality to subtle creativity"). Another source of bullshit was meaningless psychological jargon constructed by randomly combining various psychological jargon words (Forgas, 1985). As moods can influence information processing strategies (Forgas, 2013), we expected positive mood to increase, and negative mood to reduce bullshit receptivity.

Mood indeed had a significant influence. Those in a positive mood saw more "meaning" than those in the neutral and negative mood groups (see Figure 10.1). Gullibility was also significantly greater for New Age sentences than for scientific jargon terms. However, the mood × sentence type interaction was not significant, indicating a relatively uniform and content-independent mood effect on gullibility. Response times and memory data (recall and recognition) were also collected, and confirmed the predicted processing differences. Positive mood judges took less time than those in the neutral and negative mood conditions to produce a judgment. As expected,

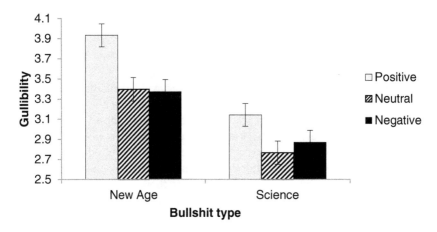

Figure 10.1 Means and standard errors for mood effects on interpreting New Age and scientific nonsense sentences: participants in the positive mood condition were more gullible than those in the neutral and negative mood conditions in assessing the meaningfulness of nonsense sentences across both New Age and scientific content.

184 *Joseph P. Forgas*

there was a trend towards an inverse correlation between response latency and gullibility, $r(79) = -.15$, $p = .169$. Participants in a positive mood also had worse recall and recognition memory for sentence details than did those in the neutral and negative mood conditions. A d' analysis confirmed that participants in the positive mood condition were significantly less able to discriminate between correct and distractor items than those in the negative mood condition (Bless & Fiedler, 2006).

Paradoxically, more gullible participants were also more confident in their responses, $r(79) = .23$, $p = .036$, especially in positive mood (Forgas & Cromer, 2004; Forgas et al., 2005). It seems that judges had little insight into their own biases (see also Dunning, Chapter 12 this volume). A subsequent mediational analysis suggested that positive mood was associated with greater self-confidence and ultimately, greater gullibility (Bower, 1981; Forgas, 1995; Schwarz & Clore, 1983). Considering the response latency, memory, and self-confidence findings together, these results suggest that shorter processing latencies and less accommodative processing in positive mood increased bullshit receptivity, impaired recall, but also produced greater self-confidence.

Mood Effects on Visual Bullshit Receptivity

Seeing meaning where there may be none is not limited to verbal statements, but may also occur when people evaluate ambiguous or indeterminate visual information. Images showing what may appear as random patterns of shapes and colors may be interpreted as children's work, computer generated images, or even modern art. In one recent study, we asked participants in public places who received a prior mood induction (reminiscing about positive or negative life episodes) to judge the meaningfulness of four different examples of complex visual images. The target images were four abstract expressionist paintings taken from Internet sites (for example, by Jackson Pollock, and others; Forgas et al., 2018).

A clear mood effect on perceiving meaning was obtained. Participants in a positive mood were significantly more likely to perceive meaning in these abstract expressionist images than were negative mood participants. Although these results show a clear mood effect, further work is needed to explore the psychological mechanisms responsible. Together with our earlier results showing a clear mood effect on perceiving meaning in meaningless verbal text, these findings suggest that there is a powerful human tendency to infer meaning in meaningless stimuli, and that this tendency is accentuated by positive, and reduced by negative mood.

Mood Effects on the Truth Bias in Believing Urban Myths

Much everyday information we come across such as "urban myths" are ambiguous, confusing, and potentially unreliable. As investigating every

On the Role of Affect in Gullibility 185

claim is inherently impossible (Fiedler & Wänke, 2009), people often rely on simple heuristics such as ease of processing (fluency) to decide whether to believe or disbelieve new information. In one experiment we investigated the joint effects of *ease of processing (fluency)*, and the *affective state* of the judge on believing the truth of a variety of urban myths (Koch & Forgas, 2012). We expected that negative affect should reduce, and positive affect should increase reliance on fluency cues as a heuristic in truth judgments.

Considerable evidence suggests that easy to process or *fluent* information is often more likely to be accepted as true, and *disfluent* information is more often rejected as false (Begg, Anas, & Farinacci, 1992; Reber & Schwarz, 1999; Unkelbach, 2006; see also Oyserman, Chapter 14 this volume; Unkelbach & Koch, Chapter 3 this volume). This so-called *truth effect* (Dechêne, Stahl, Hansen, & Wänke, 2009) occurs regardless of a statement's content. The experience of fluency itself is determined by a variety of factors, such as familiarity, frequency, or even the visual clarity of the information (see Alter & Oppenheimer, 2009; Unkelbach, Bayer, Alves, Koch, & Stahl, 2011). However, fluency cues can also be readily discounted when people "explicitly or implicitly recognize that it stems from an irrelevant source" (Alter & Oppenheimer, 2009, p. 231), or when a more elaborate and attentive processing style is adopted (Hawkins, Hoch, & Meyers-Levy, 2001). As negative moods are expected to recruit a more vigilant processing style (Bless & Fiedler, 2006; Forgas, 1998, 2010, 2011), mood should be a significant moderator of the truth effect.

Participants in this experiment first received a mood induction (viewed positive or negative film clips) and then judged the truth of 30 ambiguous "urban myth" type statements presented with either high or low perceptual fluency (high or low contrastive background; see Reber, Winkielman, & Schwarz, 1998). The "urban myths" comprised ten *neutral* claims (e.g., "Instead of iron, horseshoe crabs have copper in their blood"), ten *positively valenced* claims (e.g., "Gelotology is the study of laughter and its beneficial effects on the body"), and ten *negatively valenced* claims (e.g., "The suicide rate in Nunavut is four times higher than in the rest of Canada"). Within each valence category, five statements, although highly obscure, were actually true, and five statements were factually false.

Fluently presented urban myths (high-contrast script) were indeed judged as more true than disfluent myths. However there was also a significant interaction between fluency and mood, such that negative mood actually reversed this fluency effect (Figure 10.2). We also obtained some direct evidence for the predicted processing differences, as judges in a negative mood paid greater attention to and were more influenced by relevant stimulus features such as the level of concreteness and abstraction of the urban myths, unlike those in a positive mood. Thus, positive mood maintained, but negative mood eliminated the heuristic reliance on visual fluency as a subliminal truth cue when evaluating urban myths. Such affective influences on truth judgments may also be important in real-life truth judgments (such

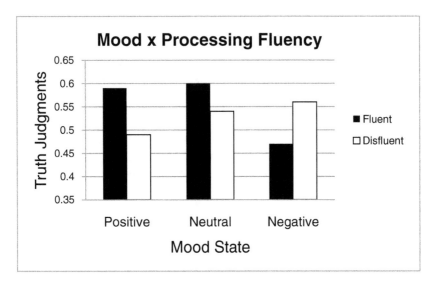

Figure 10.2 The interactive effects of mood and fluency on truth judgments: positive mood maintains, and negative mood reduces reliance on fluency as an indicator of truth.

Source: Adapted from Koch and Forgas (2012).

as believing or disbelieving one's partner) that usually occur in affect-rich contexts (Ciarrochi, Forgas, & Mayer, 2006).

Mood Effects on Detecting Deception

Believing or disbelieving social messages is another important domain of gullibility, and can be particularly difficult when facing intentional deception by others. Detecting deception is also of practical importance in forensic, judicial, and investigative domains (cf. Lane & DePaulo, 1999), and such decisions often occur in affectively charged contexts, such as when evaluating the credibility of a romantic partner, a friend, a child, or an employee.

Past research suggests that people are often overly trusting when assessing truthfulness, and are not very good at detecting deception (Bond & DePaulo, 2006; Ekman & O'Sullivan, 1991; Levine, Park, & McCornack, 1999; see also Krueger et al., Chapter 6 this volume; Mayo, Chapter 8 this volume; Strack, Chapter 9 this volume). Many people hold incorrect naïve theories about cues to deception, and focus on the wrong behaviors to detect lies (Fiedler, 1989; Fiedler & Walka, 1993). The confirmation bias, the correspondence bias, the "truth bias," and the implicit tendency to trust others further compromise our detection efficacy (McCornack & Parks, 1986; O'Sullivan, 2003).

Several experiments now suggest that positive moods increase and negative moods decrease judgmental biases such as the correspondence bias (Forgas, 1998). In one series of our experiments (Forgas & East, 2008a, 2008b) we predicted that negative mood should reduce gullibility and increase skepticism, as dysphoric individuals should form less positive and optimistic inferences about the veracity of social messages and should be better at detecting deception (Forgas, 1995, 2002; Forgas et al., 1984).

In one study (Forgas & East, 2008a), participants viewed mood-inducing films, and then watched video clips of males and females who were either truthful or deceptive in denying an alleged theft, and judged the target's guilt or innocence, and their truthfulness. Half the targets were truthful in denying the theft, and half were deceitful. They were motivated to be convincing by the promise of free movie tickets if their denials are believed (whether their denials were true or not). The mood manipulation was successful, and as expected, mood did have a significant effect on judgments of guilt. Negative mood participants made more guilty judgments than happy or neutral judges (see Figure 10.3).

Interestingly, there was also a significant interaction between mood and deceptiveness. Mood effects on guilt judgments were greater when targets were deceptive rather than truthful (Figure 10.3). Those in a negative mood

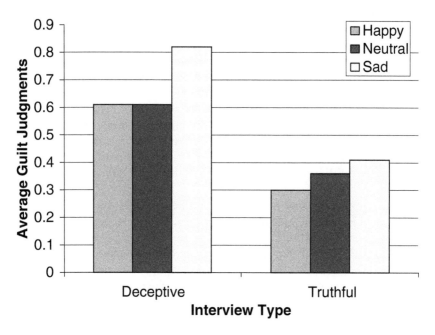

Figure 10.3 The effects of mood and the target's veracity (truthful, deceptive) on judgments of guilt of targets accused of committing a theft (average proportion of targets judged guilty in each condition.

Source: Adapted from Forgas and East (2008a).

188 *Joseph P. Forgas*

correctly formed more guilty judgments of deceptive (guilty) rather than honest (innocent) targets, while those in a happy and neutral mood were more credulous and less able to discriminate between innocent and guilty targets. Overall, detection of deception rates were significantly better than chance only by those in negative mood, whereas neutral and happy mood participants did not detect guilt above chance level.

A follow-up signal detection analysis confirmed that negative mood actually improved detection accuracy compared to neutral or happy judges (d' = 1.15, vs. .64, vs. .81, respectively), and also produced a higher overall skeptical, conservative bias (C = .53, .35, .22, respectively). In other words, negative mood has a dual effect on credulity, increasing accuracy and discrimination, and also producing a stricter and more conservative criterion for acceptance. Honesty ratings showed a similar pattern. Truthful targets were rated as more honest than deceptive targets in negative rather than positive mood.

Mood Effects on Nonverbal Credulity

Gullibility and credulity are also important when deciding whether nonverbal signals such as facial displays (by a partner, a child, or a manager) are genuine or deceptive (Jones, 1964). Facial expressions serve important interpersonal functions, as reliable cross-cultural signals indicating emotions, attitudes, and motivational states (Darwin, 1872; Ekman, Friesen, & Ellsworth, 1972). As facial expressions may be easily faked, differentiating between honest and deceptive displays is difficult and usually performed at a level only slightly above chance (Bond & DePaulo, 2006; Kraut, 1980; Levine et al., 1999).

Nonverbal credulity is also subject to various contextual influences (McCornack & Parks, 1986), such as the correspondence bias (DePaulo, 1992), and also the possibility of mood effects (Schiffenbauer, 1974). Poor ability to decode facial signals seems associated with depression and relationship problems (Bouhuys, Geerts, Mersch, & Jenner, 1996; Carton, Kessler, & Pape, 1999).

One relevant experiment by Forgas and East (2008b) examined if happy mood could promote, and negative mood inhibit gullibility when evaluating nonverbal displays. Participants first received a false-feedback mood induction (being told that they have done well or badly on an anagram task), and then rated the genuineness of positive, neutral, and negative facial expressions by professional actors. Mood did influence nonverbal credulity, as judges in a positive mood were more likely to accept facial expressions as genuine and were more confident than those in the negative condition (see Figure 10.4).

Subsequently, using a similar procedure, we also looked at mood effects on believing highly specific emotional displays (Darwin, 1872; Ekman & Friesen, 1974). Happy and sad participants viewed six photographs showing

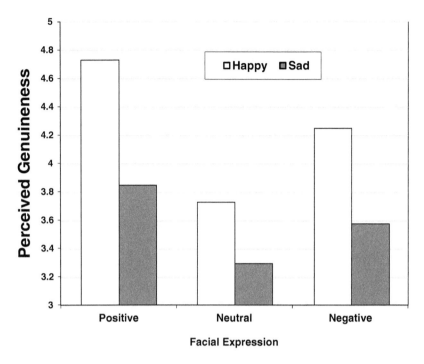

Figure 10.4 The effects of mood on the perceived genuineness of positive, neutral, and negative facial expressions: positive mood increases, and negative mood reduces credulity.

Source: Adapted from Forgas and East (2008b).

actors displaying the basic emotions of happiness, anger, sadness, disgust, surprise, and fear. Judges were asked to identify the emotion communicated and also assess its veracity. Mood again had a significant main effect on gullibility as negative mood reduced credulity across all emotional expressions. These results show that negative mood can significantly reduce nonverbal gullibility across all expressions studied, suggesting that this is robust effect that may occur in real-life situations where the identification of deceptive expressions is of considerable importance (Ciarrochi et al., 2006).

Mood Effects on Eyewitness Gullibility

Affect-induced differences in processing style may also have major implications for gullibility in eyewitness recall (see also Schwarz & Lee, Chapter 13 this volume). It is well established that eyewitness memories are easily contaminated by misleading information received after the target event, a form of fake memory gullibility (Loftus & Hoffman, 1989). A series of our studies (Forgas et al., 2005) investigated the effects of positive and negative mood on eyewitness gullibility, that is, the extent to which eyewitnesses incorporated later, misleading information into their recall of a target event. We did find that negative mood participants were less likely to incorporate later, misleading information into their recall of the details of complex scenes they witnessed (such as a car crash scene). In fact, negative mood almost completely eliminated the familiar "misinformation effect" (Loftus & Hoffman, 1989).

In another of this series of experiments, students in a lecture hall witnessed a staged incident between a lecturer and a female intruder. A week later, they received misleading information about the altercation embedded in questions about the encounter when in a negative or positive mood state (e.g., "Did you see the intruder in the brown coat?" – when in fact she was wearing a black coat). When the accuracy of their eyewitness memory was subsequently tested, negative mood almost completely eliminated eyewitness gullibility and the incorrect infusion of planted, misleading details into recall and recognition memory. A signal detection analysis confirmed that negative mood significantly improved eyewitnesses' ability to discriminate between correct and misleading, fake memory details (Figure 10.5).

It was surprising that eyewitnesses in such situations had no internal awareness of their mood-induced biases, and explicit instructions were ineffective to control them (Forgas et al., 2005). This pattern that is conceptually consistent with Dunning's (Chapter 12 this volume) work on self-gullibility.

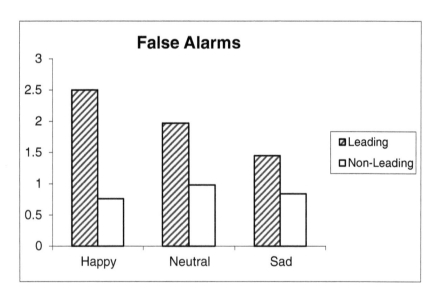

Figure 10.5 Mood effects on eyewitness gullibility: Experiencing negative mood when receiving misleading information reduces eyewitness distortions compared to neutral or positive mood participants.

Source: Adapted from Forgas et al. (2005).

On the Role of Affect in Gullibility   191

These experiments offer convergent evidence that negative moods can have significant adaptive effects on memory by reducing eyewitness gullibility and vulnerability to misleading information, consistent with negative moods promoting a more focused, accommodative processing style.

Discussion

Deciding what to believe and who to trust is one of the most difficult and cognitively demanding tasks we all face in everyday life. These results provide clear evidence that transient mood can influence the level of gullibility or skepticism in many social situations. These experiments show that negative mood reduces bullshit receptivity, decreases the truth bias when evaluating urban myths, improves the ability to detect deception, and reduces eyewitness gullibility. These findings broadly support our hypothesis that positive and negative moods trigger different information processing strategies (Bless & Fiedler, 2006). Mood also had a significant influence on people's accuracy at complex inferential tasks such as detecting deception. We found that people in a negative mood were better able than people in a positive or neutral mood to accurately identify lies. These results have some promising theoretical and practical implications for understanding the influence of mood on everyday social judgments in general, and gullibility in particular.

Theoretical Implications

The evidence reviewed here extends previous work on mood effects on social cognition in general, and impression formation in particular (Forgas & Bower, 1987; Forgas et al., 1984) to the new domain of gullibility versus skepticism. Veracity judgments represent a particularly demanding cognitive task that requires highly constructive processing (Forgas, 1995, 2002). It is just these kinds of open and indeterminate judgments that have been found to be particularly subject to mood-induced biases in the past (Fiedler, 2001; Forgas, 1994, 1995; Sedikides, 1995). Recent affect-cognition research suggests that negative affect functions like a mild, evolutionary warning signal, generally contributes to a more accommodative, cautious, and attentive processing style, and also promotes the selective priming and greater accessibility of negative information in memory. Positive moods, on the other hand, signal familiarity and safety and tend to produce a more benign, confident, and optimistic interpretation of complex social information, and reduced levels of suspiciousness (Forgas, 1999, 2002).

These results are also theoretically and empirically consistent with a growing body of literature highlighting the apparently beneficial and functional processing effects of negative mood in a variety of social cognitive tasks (Bless, 2001; Bless & Fiedler, 2006; Fiedler, 2001). In addition to priming negative information and increasing overall skepticism, negative affect also produced a specific advantage in sensitivity to detect fake, false, or misleading information

192   *Joseph P. Forgas*

and deception. These cognitive benefits confirm other evidence documenting the adaptive effects of negative affect in reducing some heuristic judgmental errors such as primacy and salience effects, and also improving the efficacy of strategic communications such as formulating persuasive messages (Forgas, 1998, 2007, 2011, 2013; Forgas et al., 2005).

Practical Implications

Given the human propensity to believe rather than disbelieve (see also Cooper & Avery, Chapter 16 this volume; Dunning, Chapter 12 this volume; Fiedler, Chapter 7 this volume; Myers, Chapter 5 this volume; Krueger et al., Chapter 6 this volume; Strack, Chapter 9 this volume), reducing gullibility in everyday social judgments is obviously highly desirable. Many professionals in the persuasion business, such as advertisers, salesmen, and politicians are implicitly aware that putting recipients into a positive mood is likely to promote credulity and the subsequent acceptance of misleading or manipulative claims. The present series of experiments provide clear empirical support for this intuitive belief. However, the empirical evidence also holds out some hope that more critical thinking, a greater focus on concrete details, and general skepticism can also be increased as a result of mild negative mood states. The ability to correctly discriminate between truths and lies and so avoid gullibility is of crucial importance in both of our personal and professional lives. The present demonstration of a mood effect on gullibility versus skepticism has some interesting practical implications for improving affective intelligence in everyday life, and could be incorporated in the training of applied professionals (Ciarrochi et al., 2006).

These findings may also help to focus attention on the beneficial but counterintuitive effects of negative mood and the possible undesirable consequences of positive mood in some real-life circumstances. There has been much emphasis on the various benefits of positive mood in the recent literature in clinical, organizational, counselling, and health psychology (Ciarrochi et al., 2006). Happy people are often thought to be more creative, flexible, motivated, and effective on a number of tasks (Forgas & George, 2001). Our findings, together with a growing number of recent experimental studies, suggest that positive affect may not be universally desirable. Several studies now show that people in a good mood are more likely to commit judgmental mistakes (Forgas, 1998, 2011, 2013), are more prone to eyewitness errors (Forgas et al., 2005), and are less effective persuaders (Forgas, 2007). To this list we may now add another important caveat: People in a positive mood may also be generally more gullible and less able to detect deception than are people in negative mood.

It is important to note that past evidence suggests that mood effects on cognition often depend on subtle contextual cues and the kind of processing strategy adopted by people in a given situation (Fiedler, 2001; Forgas, 1995, 2002; Forgas & Eich, 2013; Sedikides, 1995). For example, mood

On the Role of Affect in Gullibility 193

effects may be different or even absent when the deceptive communication is of direct personal relevance and people rely on more motivated processing strategies, or indeed, adopt a skeptical mindset (see Mayo, Chapter 8 this volume). Mood effects on gullibility versus skepticism may also be highly sensitive to a variety of other pragmatic and situational variables such as the motivations, personality, and affective intelligence of the individual. For example, Lane and DePaulo (1999) found that dispositionally dysphoric individuals were only better at detecting specific types of lies, namely false reassurances, perhaps because these are the type of deceptive communications they are most likely to be exposed to themselves.

Future research may well explore mood effects on skepticism and veracity judgments in more complex and realistic interactive situations. Even though considerable effort was made here to make the situations realistic, real-life instances of gullibility and deception may vary in a number of respects. Fortunately, to the extent that these results were consistent across a number of dependent measures and judgmental domains, and are also consistent with existing affect-cognition theories (Forgas, 2006, 2007), we can be reasonably confident that these findings are reliable.

In addition to exploring non-specific mood effects, future studies may also look at the consequences of specific emotions, such as fear, disgust, and anger on gullibility and skepticism (e.g., Lerner & Keltner, 2001). We know for example that fear and disgust are typically associated with avoidant behaviors (see also Schwarz & Lee, this volume), whereas anger tends to elicit aggression. It may well be that the specific behavioral tendencies associated with specific emotions also have a distinct influence on the tendency to trust or distrust communications from others, a promising topic for future investigations.

In summary, judging the veracity of social information in everyday situations can be a demanding cognitive task that requires highly constructive processing strategies (Bond & DePaulo, 2006; Forgas, 1995, 2002). Despite recent advances in affect research, we still do not know enough about how feelings impact on cognition in general, and the degree of skepticism or gullibility people bring to a particular task. These experiments extend recent research on affect and social cognition (Bower, 1981; Fiedler, 2001; Forgas, 1995, 2002) to the new domain of gullibility and skepticism, and show that negative mood can increase, and positive mood decrease gullibility and improve their accuracy in detecting deception. These results suggest that further research on affective influences on veracity judgments and the detection of deception should be of considerable theoretical as well as applied interest.

Acknowledgement

Support from the Australian Research Council, and the contribution of Diana Matovic, Alex Koch, Isabel Slater, and Rebekah East to this project is gratefully acknowledged.

194 *Joseph P. Forgas*

References

Albright, M. (2018). *Fascism: A warning*. New York, NY: HarperCollins.

Alter, A. L., & Oppenheimer, D. M. (2009). Uniting the tribes of fluency to form a metacognitive nation. *Personality and Social Psychology Review, 13*, 219–235.

Begg, I. M., Anas, A., & Farinacci, S. (1992). Dissociation of processes in belief: Source recollection, statement familiarity, and the illusion of truth. *Journal of Experimental Psychology, 121*, 446–458.

Bless, H. (2001). Mood and the use of general knowledge structures. In L. L. Martin (Ed.), *Theories of mood and cognition: A user's guidebook* (pp. 9–26). Mahwah, NJ: Lawrence Erlbaum.

Bless, H., & Fiedler, K. (2006). Mood and the regulation of information processing and behavior. In J. P. Forgas (Ed.), *Hearts and minds: Affective influences on social cognition and behavior* (pp. 65–84). New York, NY: Psychology Press.

Bond, C. F., Jr., & DePaulo, B. M. (2006). Accuracy of deception judgments. *Personality and Social Psychology Review, 10*, 214–234.

Bouhuys, A. L., Geerts, E., Mersch, P. P. A., & Jenner, J. A. (1996). Nonverbal interpersonal sensitivity and persistence of depression: Perception of emotions in schematic faces. *Psychiatry Research, 64*, 193–203.

Bower, G. H. (1981). Mood and memory. *American Psychologist, 36*, 129–148.

Carton, J. S., Kessler, E. A., & Pape, C. L. (1999). Nonverbal decoding skills and relationship well-being in adults. *Journal of Nonverbal Behavior, 23*, 91–100.

Ciarrochi, J. V., Forgas, J. P., & Mayer, J. D. (Eds.). (2006). *Emotional intelligence in everyday life* (2nd ed.). New York, NY: Psychology Press.

Clore, G. L., Schwarz, N., & Conway, M. (1994). Affective causes and consequences of social information processing. In R. S. Wyer & T. K. Srull (Eds.), *Handbook of social cognition* (pp. 323–417). Hillsdale, NJ: Lawrence Erlbaum.

Damasio, A. R. (1994). *Descartes error*. New York, NY: Grosset/Putnam.

Darwin, C. R. (1872). *The expression of the emotions in man and animals*. London: John Murray.

Dechêne, A., Stahl, C., Hansen, J., & Wänke, M. (2009). The truth about the truth: A meta-analytic review of the truth effect. *Personality and Social Psychology Review, 14*, 238–257.

DePaulo, B. M. (1992). Nonverbal behavior and self-presentation. *Psychological Bulletin, 111*, 203–243.

de Sousa, R. (1987). *The rationality of emotions*. Cambridge MA, MIT Press.

Ekman, P., & Friesen, W. V. (1974). Nonverbal behavior and psychopathology. In R. J. Friedman & M. Katz (Eds.), *The psychology of depression: Contemporary theory and research* (pp. 3–31). Washington, DC: Winston & Sons.

Ekman, P., Friesen, W. V., & Ellsworth, P. (1972). *Emotion in the human face: Guidelines for research and an integration of findings*. New York, NY: Pergamon Press.

Ekman, P., & O'Sullivan, M. (1991). Who can catch a liar? *American Psychologist, 46*, 913–920.

Elster, J. (1985). Sadder but wiser? Rationality and the emotions. *Social Science Information, 24*, 375–406.

Feshbach, S., & Singer, R. D. (1957). The effects of fear arousal and suppression of fear upon social perception. *Journal of Abnormal and Social Psychology, 55*, 283–288.

Fiedler, K. (1989). Suggestion and credibility: Lie detection based on content related cues. In V. Gheorghiu, P. Netter, H. J. Eysenck, & R. Rosenthal (Eds.), *Suggestibility, theory and research* (pp. 323–335). New York, NY: Springer.

Fiedler, K. (2001). Affective influences on social information processing. In J. P. Forgas (Ed.), *Handbook of affect and social cognition* (pp. 163–185). Hilssdale, NJ: Lawrence Erlbaum.

Fiedler, K., Fladung, U., & Hemmeter, U. (1987). A positivity bias in person memory. *Journal of Social Psychology, 17,* 243–246.

Fiedler, K., Lachnit, H., Fay, D., & Krug, C. (1992). Mobilization of cognitive resources and the generation effect. *Quarterly Journal of Experimental Psychology: Human Experimental Psychology, 45A,* 149–171.

Fiedler, K., & Walka, I. (1993). Training lie detectors to use nonverbal cues instead of global heuristics. *Human Communication Research, 20,* 199–223.

Fiedler, K., & Wänke, M. (2009). The cognitive-ecological approach to rationality in social psychology. *Social Cognition, 27,* 699–732.

Forgas, J. P. (1985). *Language and social situations* (Vol. 9). New York, NY: Springer.

Forgas, J. P. (1994). Sad and guilty? Affective influences on explanations of conflict episodes. *Journal of Personality and Social Psychology, 66,* 56–68.

Forgas, J. P. (1995). Mood and judgment: The affect infusion model (AIM). *Psychological Bulletin, 117,* 39–66.

Forgas, J. P. (1998). On being happy but mistaken: Mood effects on the fundamental attribution error. *Journal of Personality and Social Psychology, 75,* 318–331.

Forgas, J. P. (1999). On feeling good and being rude: Affective influences on language use and request formulations. *Journal of Personality & Social Psychology, 76,* 928–939.

Forgas, J. P. (2002). Feeling and doing: Affective influences on interpersonal behavior. *Psychological Inquiry, 13,* 1–28.

Forgas, J. P. (Ed.). (2006). *Affect in social thinking and behaviour.* New York, NY: Psychology Press.

Forgas, J. P. (2007). When sad is better than happy: Negative affect can improve the quality and effectiveness of persuasive messages and social influence strategies. *Journal of Experimental Social Psychology, 43,* 513–528.

Forgas, J. P. (2010). Don't worry, be sad! On the cognitive, motivational, and interpersonal benefits of negative mood. *Current Directions in Psychological Science, 22,* 225–232.

Forgas, J. P. (2011). Can negative affect eliminate the power of first impressions? Affective influences on primacy and recency effects in impression formation. *Journal of Experimental Social Psychology, 47,* 425–429.

Forgas, J. P. (2013). The upside of feeling down: The benefits of negative mood for social cognition and behaviour. In J. P. Forgas, K. Fiedler, & C. Sedikides (Eds.), *Social thinking and interpersonal behaviour* (pp. 221–238). New York, NY: Psychology Press.

Forgas, J. P., & Bower, G. H. (1987). Mood effects on person-perception judgments. *Journal of Personality & Social Psychology, 53,* 53–60.

Forgas, J. P., Bower, G. H., & Krantz, S. E. (1984). The influence of mood on perceptions of social interactions. *Journal of Experimental Social Psychology, 20(6),* 497–513.

Forgas, J. P., & Cromer, M. (2004). On being sad and evasive: Affective influences on verbal communication strategies in conflict situations. *Journal of Experimental Social Psychology, 40,* 511–518.

Forgas, J. P., & East, R. (2008a). On being happy and gullible: Mood effects on skepticism and the detection of deception. *Journal of Experimental Social Psychology, 44,* 1362–1367.

196 *Joseph P. Forgas*

Forgas, J. P., & East, R. (2008b). How real is that smile? Mood effects on accepting or rejecting the veracity of emotional facial expressions. *Journal of Nonverbal Behavior, 32,* 157–170.

Forgas, J. P., & Eich, E. (2013). Affective influences on cognition: mood congruence, mood dependence, and mood effects on processing strategies. In A. F. Healy & R. W. Proctor (Eds.), *Handbook of psychology: Experimental psychology* (Vol. 4, pp. 61–82). Hoboken, NJ: Wiley.

Forgas, J. P., & George, J. M. (2001). Affective influences on judgments and behavior in organizations: An information processing perspective. *Organizational Behavior and Human Decision Processes, 86,* 3–34.

Forgas, J. P., Kelemen, L., & László, J. (2015). Social cognition and democracy: An eastern European case study. In J. P. Forgas, K. Fiedler, & W. D. Crano (Eds.), *Social psychology and politics* (pp. 263–285). New York, NY: Routledge.

Forgas, J. P., Laham, S. M., & Vargas, P. T. (2005). Mood effects on eyewitness memory: Affective influences on susceptibility to misinformation. *Journal of Experimental Social Psychology, 41,* 574–588.

Forgas, J. P., Matovic, D., & Slater, I. (2018). Mood effects on bullshit receptivity: Positive affect increases, and negative affect reduces gullibility and the acceptance of meaningless statements as meaningful. Manuscript, UNSW, Sydney.

Harari, Y. N. (2014). *Sapiens: A brief history of humankind.* New York, NY: Vintage.

Hawkins, S. A., Hoch, S. J., & Meyers-Levy, J. (2001). Low-involvement learning: Repetition and coherence in familiarity and belief. *Journal of Consumer Psychology, 11,* 1–11.

Hilgard, E. R. (1980). The trilogy of mind: Cognition, affection, and conation. *Journal of the History of the Behavioral Sciences, 16,* 107–117.

Jones, E. E. (1964). *Ingratiation.* New York, NY: Appleton-Century-Crofts.

Koch, A. S., & Forgas, J. P. (2012). Feeling good and feeling truth: The interactive effects of mood and processing fluency on truth judgments. *Journal of Experimental Social Psychology, 48,* 481–485.

Koestler, A. (1978). *Janus: A summing up.* London: Hutchinson.

Kraut, R. (1980). Humans as lie detectors. *Journal of Communication, 30,* 209–216.

Lane, J. D., & DePaulo, B. M. (1999). Completing Coyne's cycle: Dysphorics' ability to detect deception. *Journal of Research in Personality, 33,* 311–329.

Lerner, J. S., & Keltner, D. (2001). Fear, anger, and risk. *Journal of Personality & Social Psychology, 81,* 146–159.

Levine, T. R., Park, H. S., & McCornack, S. A. (1999). Accuracy in detecting truths and lies: Documenting the veracity effect. *Communication Monographs, 66,* 125–144.

Loftus, E., & Hoffman, H. G. (1989). Misinformation and memory: The creation of new memories. *Journal of Experimental Psychology, 188*(1), 100–104.

Machiavelli, N. (1961). *The prince* (G. Bull, Trans.). London: Penguin.

McCornack, S. A., & Parks, M. R. (1986). Deception detection and relationship development: The other side of trust. In M. L. McLaughlin (Ed.), *Communication yearbook 9* (pp. 377–389). Beverly Hills, CA: Sage.

Niedenthal, P. M., Halberstadt, J. B., Margolin, J., & Innes-Ker, A. H. (2000). Emotional state and the detection of change in facial expression of emotion. *European Journal of Social Psychology, 30,* 211–222.

Oatley, K., & Jenkins, J. M. (1996). *Understanding emotions.* Malden, MA, and Oxford, UK: Blackwell.

O'Sullivan, M. (2003). The fundamental attribution error in detecting deception: The boy who cried wolf effect. *Personality and Social Psychology Bulletin, 29*, 1316–1327.

Pascal, B. (1643/1966). *Pensees*. Baltimore, MD: Penguin Books.

Pennycook, G., Cheyne, J. A., Barr, N., Koehler, D. J., & Fugelsang, J. A. (2015). On the reception and detection of pseudo-profound bullshit. *Judgment and Decision Making, 10*, 549–563.

Reber, R., & Schwarz, N. (1999). Effects of perceptual fluency on judgments of truth. *Consciousness and Cognition, 8*, 338–342.

Reber, R., Winkielman, P., & Schwarz, N. (1998). Effects of perceptual fluency on affective judgments. *Psychological Science, 9*, 45–48.

Schiffenbauer, A. (1974). When will people use facial information to attribute emotion? The effects of judge's emotional state and intensity of facial expression on attribution of emotions. *Representative Research in Social Psychology, 5*, 47–53.

Schwarz, N., & Clore, G. L. (1983). Mood, misattribution, and judgments of well-being: Informative and directive functions of affective states. *Journal of Personality and Social Psychology, 45*, 513–523.

Sedikides, C. (1995). Central and peripheral self-conceptions are differentially influenced by mood: Tests of the differential sensitivity hypothesis. *Journal of Personality & Social Psychology, 69*, 759–777.

Sokal, A. D. (1994). Transgressing the boundaries: Towards a transformative hermeneutics of quantum gravity. *Social Text, 46/47* (spring/summer), 217–252.

Sokal, A. D. (1996). A physicist experiments with cultural studies. *Lingua Franca, 6*(4), 62–64.

Toda, M. (1980). Emotion in decision-making. *Acta Psychologica, 45*, 133–155.

Unkelbach, C. (2006). The learned interpretation of cognitive fluency. *Psychological Science, 17*, 339–345.

Unkelbach, C., Bayer, M., Alves, H., Koch, A., & Stahl, C. (2011). Fluency and positivity as possible causes of the truth effect. *Consciousness and Cognition, 20*, 594–602.

Zajonc, R. B. (1980). Feeling and thinking: Preferences need no inferences. *American Psychologist, 35*, 151–175.

Zajonc, R. B. (2000). Feeling and thinking: Closing the debate over the independence of affect. In J. P. Forgas (Ed.), *Feeling and thinking: The role of affect in social cognition* (pp. 31–58). New York, NY: Cambridge University Press.

11 Gullible or Streetwise

How Does the Self Bias Information Processing?

C. Neil Macrae, Juliana L. Olivier, Johanna K. Falbén, and Marius Golubickis
UNIVERSITY OF ABERDEEN

What does it take for people to treat one coffee mug more positively than the next? Not much, it seems – one simply has to believe that it belongs to oneself. What is more, this special treatment appears to extend to everyday objects (such as pens, ties, and keychains) that one did not wish for, and neither needs, nor finds valuable. Considering something to be a personal belonging has been found to exert a powerful effect on cognition, influencing various aspects of how one engages with the object in question and, more broadly, the world around oneself. For example, in comparison to identical items owned by or associated with someone else, people are more attentive to their own items, remember their characteristics better, and price them higher when trying to sell them (e.g., Beggan, 1992; Morewedge & Giblin, 2015; Symons & Johnson, 1997; Truong & Todd, 2017).

Strikingly, it requires almost no persuasion for people to relate an object (or even an abstract shape) to themselves, and consequently to exhibit egocentric-like predispositions in their behavior towards it. That is, the wide-ranging effects that ownership has on human thinking and behavior are indicative of a host of self-serving tendencies that influence cognitive processing purely based on associations with the self. In other words, a proportion of people's choices, judgments, and appraisals in everyday social situations are guided by mostly unnoticeable egocentric biases (see also Fiedler, Chapter 7 this volume; Schwarz & Lee, Chapter 13 this volume). Of interest is whether these biases represent the operation of a gullible mind or a streetwise social perceiver. We suspect the latter.

Even though egocentrism is most pronounced in early childhood (Perner, 1991; Wimmer & Perner, 1983), adults continue to think and behave in a self-centered manner. It has been suggested that in comparison to children, adults have stronger and more efficient corrective processes that counteract the effects of egocentrism (e.g., thankfully adults rarely end game nights because they lost a hand of poker). In other words, adults and children are equally self-centered, but adults are better at correcting their initial (though potentially reasonable) egocentric reactions (Epley & Gilovich, 2004; Epley, Keysar, van Boven, & Gilovich, 2004). Nevertheless, the effects of such egocentric inclinations can be observed frequently in adult behavior (see Dunning, Chapter 12 this volume). In this chapter, we initially review how egocentrism impacts interpersonal communication, social interactions, and social perception. Interestingly, as the effects of self-centrism are already present much earlier in the processing stream, the influence of self-relevance on cognitive outcomes, such as memory and decision-making will also be discussed. Finally, we will present results from our laboratory suggesting that ownership yields a potent bias in decision-making across cultures, further indicating the apparently egocentric character of the human mind (see Oyserman, Chapter 14 this volume).

Interpersonal Communication

One instance in which people commonly give away their self-centered perspective is when they try to communicate with others. Put simply, individuals tend to assume others know what they know, and this assumption guides human interactions (Nickerson, 1999). Effective communication requires a certain level of shared knowledge (such as a common language), but it is further greatly facilitated by being able to rely on widely understood schemas, cultural references, and common experiences. In most social situations, our egocentric biases can aid communication, as the majority of people one interacts with indeed share most of the information one has, and people take that for granted (Tversky & Kahneman, 1974). For example, when suggesting to determine who has to take out the trash by playing rock–paper–scissors, one would typically assume that the person one is talking to knows that they are not expected to go find a rock, a sheet of paper, and a pair of scissors, and more often than not, one would be correct in assuming so. That being the case, relying on one's own knowledge to guide one's assumptions about how much information needs to be presented (or confirmed) usually simplifies everyday interactions – it makes people interpersonally streetwise.

Notwithstanding potential benefits, humans are somewhat gullible when it comes to estimating just how much shared knowledge they can refer to (Epley & Gilovich, 2006; Epley et al., 2004; Keysar, Lin, & Barr, 2003; Tversky & Kahneman, 1974). For example, in a communication game, Keysar et al. (2003) demonstrated that participants were guided by their egocentric view, acting in ignorance of the fact that their partner does not have the same information that they themselves do. Further complicating matters, even when people become aware of a knowledge discrepancy, they tend to make only minor corrections to their original account, thereby demonstrating their credulity with regard to generalizing knowledge and overestimating their communal understanding. To sum up, relying on one's own knowledge as a reference point for what others might know commonly aids interpersonal communication, serving as the basis for an educated guess that allows one to omit superfluous information.

200   *C. Neil Macrae et al.*

However, on occasion, this simplification can come at the cost of accuracy (e.g., Epley et al., 2004; Gilovich, Medvec, & Savitsky, 2000; Gilovich, Savitsky, & Medvec, 1998; Keysar et al., 2003), opening the door to potential misunderstandings and confusion.

Social Perception

Beyond verbal communication, the inflated importance people assign to all that affects them personally gives rise to many misperceptions in their interactions with others (see Dunning, Chapter 12 this volume). For example, they tend to overestimate the extent to which others notice their appearance and behavior, believing that everyone around them pays a great deal of attention to them (Gilovich & Savitsky, 1999). This conviction has been dubbed the "spotlight effect" (Gilovich et al., 2000). Consider, for a moment, what it would mean if the spotlight effect indeed accurately described people's everyday lives. It would imply that each individual experiencing this effect is either the only person in their surroundings deemed worthy of heightened attention by those around them, or that the individuals they believe are noticing them so much are also paying close attention to most others around them (which would be incredibly overwhelming). Clearly, neither interpretation withstands rational examination at a societal scale, yet the spotlight effect is well documented. Students wearing an embarrassing t-shirt have, for instance, been found to misjudge how many people notice them, and individuals taking part in a group project overestimated how much attention their colleagues were paying to them (Gilovich et al., 2000).

Similarly, people often overestimate how easily others detect their feelings and emotions (the so-called "illusion of transparency," Gilovich & Savitsky, 1999; Gilovich et al., 1998). For example, Gilovich et al. (1998) found participants to believe that they could not successfully cover up their distaste for an awful drink, and that others could easily detect their lies. Both the spotlight effect and the illusion of transparency have been attributed to insufficient internal adjustment of judgments – that is, people do not take their internal biases into account enough when making decisions (Gilovich et al., 2000; Gilovich & Savitsky, 1999; Gilovich et al., 1998). In other words, the powerful influence of egocentric predispositions comes from people's inability to escape their own particular perspective (Gilovich et al., 2000; Gilovich & Savitsky, 1999; Gilovich et al., 1998). This suggests that individuals may gullibly generalize their experience of being at the center of their own attention to other people, effectively leading them to adopt a self-centered world view. While such a mindset likely does not reflect the reality of most interpersonal encounters, there may, however, be benefits to this distortion, as will be suggested at relevant points throughout this chapter. Interestingly, similar biases have even been found to manifest via associations with the self as demonstrated by the effects of egocentrism on people's interactions with objects.

Ownership

Object ownership has been regarded as a psychological extension of the self (Beggan, 1992; James, 1890), such that individuals consider their personal belongings (e.g., car, house, and phone) to be part of their self-concept. This has often served to explain why people's appraisal of their own objects – compared to (otherwise equal) objects not owned by them – is distorted by a range of self-serving biases (Belk, 1988, 1991, 2014). For example, they become more attached to, and value their personal belongings more than identical items that are owned by somebody else. This is commonly referred to as the endowment effect (Kahneman, Knetsch, & Thaler, 1990; Knetsch & Sinden, 1984; Morewedge & Giblin, 2015). It suggests that the value of self-owned objects is inflated by the owner, compared to appraisals of identical items owned by anyone else (Maddux et al., 2010). For example, an individual may genuinely believe that their plain blue mug is worth more money than a stranger's, their least favorite colleague's, their best friend's, and even their mother's.

In everyday life, the endowment effect can give rise to complications when owners looking to sell their items ask for higher prices than potential buyers find justified (Beggan, 1992; Kahneman et al., 1990; Maddux et al., 2010; Morewedge & Giblin, 2015). This effect further appears to increase with time for consideration: the more time people have to decide how much they would be willing to buy or sell an item for, the larger the gap between the buyers' and sellers' prices (Ashby, Dickert, & Glöckner, 2012). Similarly, experiments have shown that participants buying or selling items for themselves overvalue these more than when they are making such decisions for another person (e.g., Morewedge, Shu, Gilbert, & Wilson, 2009). Notably, even owning a second item that is identical to the item to be sold does not prevent the endowment effect (Morewedge et al., 2009), thereby demonstrating that, rather than being grounded in considerations of practical value, the overvaluation of one's own belongings stems from biases in everyday thinking. These biases, however, may reflect the streetwise character of social perceivers. Feeling good about one's belongings can make one feel good about oneself (Beggan, 1992).

Even outside of economic exchanges, one can notice the effect of self-centered tendencies in everyday life. They can, for instance, become apparent when trying to clean out one's closet: one may be motivated to achieve such a goal, yet it can be difficult to give up one's personal belongings, even when they have not been used in years (Belk, 1988). Similarly, one can feel sad when an item breaks or is stolen, even when one considers its monetary value to be negligible (Belk, 1988). In experimental settings, the self-related biases associated with the endowment effect can be evoked simply by presenting participants with the owned object on a computer screen (e.g., Ashby et al., 2012) – people credulously adopt what they are shown only virtually, a real-life encounter is not required (Turk et al., 2011). The emergence of the endowment effect has also successfully been demonstrated by giving participants a small gift at the beginning of an experiment (e.g., a pen or a mug, Kahneman et al., 1990), and even by randomly assigning an object to the participant (the so-called "mere ownership effect," Beggan, 1992; Belk, 1988, 1991). From this line of research, it becomes apparent that people can be effortlessly persuaded to take ownership of an object, and immediately begin to display biases in their judgments.

The ease with which these egocentric tendencies are elicited further indicates that the human mind can very quickly adopt new objects as part of the self. While this ability may at first glance be mistaken for gullibility, it is more likely an adaptive strategy for looking after and maintaining one's possessions, which are not only representations of wealth, status, and social group memberships but have long played a crucial role in survival. From bows and arrows for hunter-gatherer societies to wallets and keys today, successfully attending to one's belongings can make the difference between a good and a bad day. Imagine, for instance, having to read every luggage tag rather than being able to instantly recognize one's own suitcase on an airport conveyer belt. To sum up, preferential treatment of self-owned objects makes us streetwise.

Memory

Beyond their immediate influence on judgments, egocentric biases have further been found to leave a lingering impression on human thinking. Their effects on memory perhaps constitute the most well-documented domain of self-related cognitive biases (Conway, 2005; Conway & Pleydell-Pearce, 2000; Heatherton et al., 2006; Symons & Johnson, 1997). They are characterized by better recognition and recall performance for stimuli associated with the self, compared to associations with others and no association at all, and are commonly referred to as "self-reference effects" (e.g., Conway, 2005; Macrae, Moran, Heatherton, Banfield, & Kelley, 2004; Symons & Johnson, 1997). Typically, this is demonstrated by asking participants to either process information by relating it to themselves (e.g., "Does 'honest' describe me?"), or to process it in relation to another person (e.g., "Does 'honest' describe Donald Trump?"). In an early demonstration of the self-reference effect, Rogers, Kuiper, and Kirker (1977) asked participants to judge trait adjectives structurally, phonemically, semantically, and self-referentially. The incidental encoding phase was followed by a surprise recall test. Comparing memory performance across the different word-processing conditions, Rogers and colleagues found a significant memory advantage for self-referentially processed words, suggesting that relating information to oneself constitutes an advantage during encoding that facilitates recall, and this holds true even when one did not expect to have to recall the information.

Beyond mere word recollections, more recent research has further found enhanced episodic memory for perceptual (e.g., images of objects) and other source information pertaining to self-referentially encoded items, indicating that the self-reference effect extends to non-critical, incidentally encoded information (e.g., Conway & Dewhurst, 1995; Cunningham, Turk, Macdonald, & Macrae, 2008; Leshikar, Dulas, & Duarte, 2015; Turk, Cunningham, & Macrae, 2008; van den Bos, Cunningham, Conway, & Turk, 2010). While this effect appears to not yet be reliably developed in children before the age of 5 (Sui & Zhu, 2005), some studies have found a source-memory advantage for information associated with the self in even younger children (e.g., Cunningham, Brebner, Quinn, & Turk, 2014; Ross, Anderson, & Campbell, 2011). The increased richness of episodic memory for self-relevant information has been attributed to increased integration, suggesting that self-representations bind together different types of information (Sui & Humphreys, 2015a). Again, enhanced memory for self-related material would indicate the operation of a streetwise mind.

A considerable number of studies exploring the influence the self exerts on memory takes advantage of the ownership effects described previously, comparing memory performance for self-owned to other-owned objects (e.g., Cunningham, Brady-van den Bos, & Turk, 2011; Cunningham et al., 2008; Cunningham, Vergunst, Macrae, & Turk, 2013; Englert & Wentura, 2016; Sparks, Cunningham, & Kritikos, 2016; van den Bos et al., 2010). By not directly asking participants to relate information (such as traits) to themselves, ownership experiments can arguably shed more light on how egocentric biases may affect people's memory in everyday contexts. Cunningham and colleagues (2008), for example, asked participants to sort items into baskets that belonged to themselves or somebody else in an ownership paradigm. Memory performance was greater for self-owned objects, compared to other-owned, suggesting that even for merely experimentally assigned objects, people's memory appears to favor their own over somebody else's (e.g., Cunningham et al., 2008; van den Bos et al., 2010). The observed memory advantages might be attributable to deeper processing of self-related information. Proponents of this view hold that the self serves as a potent schema, providing a rich set of knowledge structures associated with oneself (compared to others), which is readily available during information processing and encoding, thereby aiding memory performance (e.g., Rogers et al., 1977). Not only does this view fit nicely with findings of better episodic memory for self-referentially encoded information (e.g., van den Bos et al., 2010), but also with neuroimaging research that provides evidence for a distinct processing pathway for self-related information (e.g., trait adjectives, Heatherton et al., 2006). This suggests that self-referential processing offers a unique advantage over associations with other people (e.g., Bower & Gilligan, 1979), and that this advantage might occur very early in the processing stream (Dunning & Balcetis, 2013), thus setting the stage for subsequent biases in memory and even decision-making. And while memory seems to be exceedingly easily influenced by self-related information, again making it appear rather gullible, remembering what is directly relevant to the self especially well likely facilitates everyday life, as anyone who has ever misplaced their keys will know.

Decision-Making

Recent evidence shows that humans are faster and more accurate when making decisions that are relevant to themselves, compared to non-self-relevant decisions (Humphreys & Sui, 2015; Sui, He, & Humphreys, 2012; Sui & Humphreys, 2015a). This finding, called the "self-prioritization effect," has been investigated with a perceptual matching paradigm, in which participants learn pairings of shapes (e.g., triangle, circle, square) and labels (e.g., self, friend, stranger), and are subsequently asked to indicate whether the presented shape–label pairings match or mismatch the previously learned associations (Humphreys & Sui, 2015, 2016; Sui et al., 2012; Sui & Humphreys, 2015a). These experiments show that shapes associated with the self are processed more efficiently (i.e., faster response times and higher accuracy) than shapes associated with other labels (e.g., friend, stranger, Sui et al., 2012), indicating that people's impressionable minds readily accept such abstract associations. It has been suggested by proponents of the self-related integrative processing framework that self-relevance provides a form of associative "glue" for perception, memory, and decision-making, which, depending on the task context, can either facilitate or disrupt performance (Sui & Humphreys, 2015a). In other words, the self acts as a central mechanism in information processing. Notwithstanding the accumulated evidence in favor of self-prioritization, exactly *how* the self exerts its influence on decision-making is largely unknown.

Many decisions are driven by uncontrollable factors favoring one response over another. Consider, for example, trying to pick a sandwich to buy for lunch. It would take no time to choose one's regular option compared to a new one. Similarly, one might be quicker to pick a sandwich that is displayed at the counter (i.e., a more visually noticeable option), rather than choosing from the cafeteria's menu. In other words, people might have a predisposed preference for more familiar, frequent options, or they might be persuaded by the relative saliency and ease of one option compared to another (see Strack, Chapter 9 this volume). Similarly, on a daily basis individuals are unnoticeably swayed in expressing rapid judgments that are in fact underpinned by underlying biases in decision-making (White & Poldrack, 2014).

Bias is an essential component of decision-making and can provide useful information about cognition and its underlying processes (White &

Poldrack, 2014). Specifically, there are two different ways in which biased responding can occur. These refer to how a stimulus is processed and how a response is generated, respectively. Whereas variation in stimulus processing affects the evidence that is extracted from the item under consideration (i.e., stimulus bias), adjustments in response preparation influence how much evidence is required before a specific judgment is made (i.e., response bias). Having a priori knowledge allows one to make adjustments for the response one is going to make, such that, returning to the previous example, less evidence and time is required to order the more regular sandwich option. Contrastingly, in the absence of prior information, one might rely on the most salient information (e.g., sandwiches behind the counter), such that one's decision would be based on an evaluation of appearance. Each of these biases reflects a distinct underlying cognitive component and differentiating them has important theoretical implications for understanding decisional processing (White & Poldrack, 2014).

One way to differentiate stimulus and response biases in experimental settings is through application of the drift diffusion model of decision-making (Ratcliff, 1978). In the context of binary decision-making, this model describes decisions unfolding over time and assumes that information is continuously gathered until sufficient evidence has been acquired to initiate a response. In other words, individuals accumulate evidence over time until they reach one of the response thresholds. For example, one could continuously gather information about a pen presented to oneself until one either reaches the threshold for the decision that the pen belongs to oneself, or until one has sufficient evidence to decide that it belongs to someone else. Pertinent to the current enquiry, decisional processes can be biased in two different ways. Self could bias the speed and quality of information acquisition from the stimulus, such that one would, for example, be faster at processing the incoming sensory information from one's own personal belonging, compared to somebody else's. This would be interpreted as a measure of processing efficiency during decision-making (White & Poldrack, 2014). Alternatively, or additionally, response options related to the self could benefit from an a priori bias when making relevant decisions, such that self-biases could lead one to start the evidence accumulation process closer to the self-related (e.g., object is mine) than other-related response option (White & Poldrack, 2014). Put simply, it would take less information for one to identify and respond to one's own pen (compared to somebody else's pen), in the same way that one does not need much convincing to pick one's usual sandwich option.

Drift diffusion modeling can be informative of how exactly the self influences people's thinking and behavior (i.e., how the mind is gullible or streetwise with regards to the self), as it has the capacity to separate stimulus and response-related biases during decision-making (Voss, Rothermund, & Brandtstädter, 2008). In other words, this type of analysis

206 *C. Neil Macrae et al.*

offers an identification of the processes underpinning speeded self-related responses (e.g., self-prioritization effect), thereby providing valuable new insight into the existing literature on how self-relevance impacts thinking and doing. Specifically, if the mind is streetwise, what form does this streetwise processing take?

Self-Ownership Effect

To date, most demonstrations of the self-prioritization effect have relied on geometric shapes that serve as a proxy for the self (e.g., Sui et al., 2012; Sui, Liu, Mevorach, & Humphreys, 2013). Although this approach is experimentally expedient, it is notably removed from everyday social-cognitive functioning. This then raises the question of whether self-prioritization extends to more naturalistic processing conditions, such as objects associated with the self through ownership. On a daily basis, people interact with objects (e.g., mobile phones, clothes, pens) that belong to them or somebody else. Thus, interaction with a complex environment may benefit from enhanced item classification and recognition based on personal significance (e.g., owned by self vs. other). In other words, decision-making might be facilitated for personally owned objects, compared to identical items belonging to someone else (Ashby et al., 2012; Cunningham et al., 2008).

Evidence from our laboratory has illuminated the effects of self-ownership during decision-making (Golubickis, Falbén, Cunningham, & Macrae, 2018). Specifically, in a modified ownership task (Cunningham et al., 2008), participants were presented with items (pencils or pens) that were randomly assigned to – that is, owned by –either the self or a non-intimate other (a stranger). Their task was simply to classify the objects as either their own or owned by a stranger as quickly and accurately as possible. The experiment provided evidence that, in comparison to items owned by a stranger, objects belonging to the self were judged more rapidly. Submitting the data to a drift diffusion model analysis (HDDM package, see Wiecki, Sofer, & Frank, 2013) further revealed that task performance was underpinned by a prepotent response bias, such that participants required less evidence to respond to owned-by-self (vs. owned-by-stranger) objects. In other words, during the ownership task, participants made adjustments in response preparation, hence facilitating decision-making for self-relevant material.

In the previous experiment, decisions were made with respect to the self and a complete stranger, but what about judging objects that are owned by someone familiar, such as one's best friend? At least in the memory domain, there have been a number of demonstrations that the target of comparison to the self can influence the magnitude of the resultant effects. Specifically, when the self is compared to an intimate other (e.g., parent, best friend) rather than a non-intimate other (e.g., stranger), the benefits of self-referencing are sometimes reduced (Symons & Johnson, 1997). We explored this in a follow-up experiment, in which participants again performed an ownership task; however, this time, objects either belonged to the self or to the participant's best friend. Replicating the results from our previous study, the analysis revealed that the objects owned by the self were judged more rapidly than items owned by a friend. Similarly, drift diffusion analysis yielded evidence that these speeded self-ownership judgments originated from a predisposed response bias, such that less information was necessary to identify the object as self-owned.

These results not only demonstrate that self-ownership facilitates decision-making, regardless of whether the target of comparison is a stranger or one's best friend, but also reveal that task performance is underpinned by a pre-potent response bias for one's own (i.e., self-relevant) objects. The latter finding is particularly interesting as response preparation biases are often induced by some sort of pre-existing knowledge. For example, in binary decision-making tasks, this has been done by informing participants before each trial which response outcome is more probable (Mulder, Wagenmakers, Ratcliff, Boekel, & Forstmann, 2012), and by manipulating the frequency of the appropriate responses (i.e., unequal stimulus proportions; Ashby, 1983). Both of these manipulations have been found to result in a shift of the decision-process starting point (i.e., less evidence required) towards the more likely judgment. In the current experiments, no such information was provided, yet it appears that merely acquiring arbitrary ownership for the objects was sufficient for participants to make adjustments to their response preparation. As people more readily classified items as their own than someone else's based on a predisposition to selectively lower the respective evidence requirements, this arguably makes them more gullible for self-related false positives.

Reward might be a possible explanation for the displayed preference for self-relevant responses. It has been shown that response bias can be prompted by manipulating the pay-off of one judgment over another, such that participants are biased towards the rewarding (vs. unrewarding) outcome (Ashby, 1983; Bogacz, Brown, Moehlis, Holmes, & Cohen, 2006; Diederich & Busemeyer, 2006; Simen et al., 2009; van Ravenzwaaij, Mulder, Tuerlinckx, & Wagenmakers, 2012; White, Ratcliff, Vasey, & McKoon, 2010). It has been shown that self-relevance can activate brain regions associated with reward (Northoff & Hayes, 2011). For example, Krigolson, Hassall, Balcom, and Turk (2013) provided a gambling task in which participants could win or lose prizes for either themselves or someone else. The results revealed that self-relevant stimuli (i.e., items owned by self) as well as responses (i.e., trials on which a "self" response is made) were deemed more rewarding. Interestingly, this effect occurred regardless of whether participants won or lost. In other words, self-relevant responses were inherently rewarding, while responses unrelated to self were not, which might explain why humans tend to err on the side of self-owned rather than other-owned responses. Additionally, the brain areas associated with the self-prioritization effect have also been linked to processing reward-related information, as proposed by an integrative model of self, namely the self-attention network (Humphreys & Sui, 2016). Overall, self-relevant material is treated as more satisfying and rewarding than other kinds of information (Krigolson et al., 2013; Nayakankuppam & Mishra, 2005; Northoff & Hayes, 2011; Sui et al., 2012; Truong, Roberts, & Todd, 2017). Similarly, the response bias found in our experiments might be indicative of a pre-existing preference for the most rewarding option (i.e., objects are mine), suggesting that we lean towards the self-related option because of its potential payoff.

A recent study aimed to further examine the relative influence of self and reward, respectively, on responses in a perceptual-matching task (Sui & Humphreys, 2015b) by assigning rewards (high vs. low) to friend- and stranger-associated shapes, but not to self-associated shapes. The study found both self and high reward to independently influence response patterns. That is, despite receiving no reward, responses to self-related materials were advantaged relative to low-reward stimuli and did not differ from responses to high-reward items. It was proposed that self- and reward-based biases in decision-making emerge through different pathways. Notably, however, reward did not influence all participants equally. Specifically, participants who had indicated close personal distance to strangers showed weaker effects of self-bias and were more strongly affected by rewards, whereas the opposite pattern emerged for socially distant individuals (i.e., large self-advantage, non-significant reward effect). This finding suggests that individual differences may play an important role in determining how, and to what extent, egocentric biases impact our perception, thinking, and decision-making. It stands to reason that cultural differences might also exert a moderating influence on the products of self-referential processing (Markus & Kitayama, 2010) – but is this indeed the case?

Culture

It has been well documented that cultural factors exert a significant influence on the products of self-referential processing (see Oyserman, Chapter 14 this volume), including the ownership effect (Markus & Kitayama, 2010; Sparks et al., 2016). Western cultures are believed to promote independent self-construal (i.e., emphasis on the differences between self and others), whereas in Asian cultures, self-construal is deemed to be more interdependent. Here, self is thought to be interconnected with other people, especially family members, to a greater extent than in Western cultures (Markus & Kitayama, 1991). In memory, this results in an eliminated or even reversed self-referencing effect among East Asians, such that relating stimuli to one's mother leads to better memory performance than self-relevant encoding (Zhu & Zhang, 2002; Zhu, Zhang, Fan, &

Han, 2007). Similarly, this cultural variability has been shown to affect object ownership. Are people from interdependent cultures less gullible – or less likely – to preferentially respond to their own, newly acquired items? Cross-cultural research may offer answers to this question. In an ownership paradigm measuring memory performance, Sparks et al. (2016) randomly assigned objects (i.e., common shopping items) to the self, best friend, mother, or stranger. The Western sample displayed a typical self-reference benefit (Cunningham et al., 2008; van den Bos et al., 2010), such that items associated with the self were the most memorable, compared to other targets. In contrast, Asian participants showed no, or reversed, memorial advantages for self-relevant material, such that their mothers' items were equally or more likely to be remembered than their own. To sum up, at least in the context of memory, cultural socialization yields a potent influence on self-referential processing.

Decision-making, on the other hand, does not show such cultural variation of the self-prioritization effect (Humphreys & Sui, 2016; Sui & Humphreys, 2015a). Specifically, during a perceptual matching task, participants showed an advantage for self-relevant stimuli independently of their cultural backgrounds (Sui, Sun, Peng, & Humphreys, 2014). In other words, the self facilitated decision-making for both the Western and the Asian samples, even when the self was compared to the participant's mother. This once again raises the question of whether the cross-culturally observed effects of egocentrism also emerge when a more ecologically valid ownership task is employed. Specifically, would cultural differences in self-construal trigger different response-time effects between Western (i.e., self < mother) and Asian (i.e., mother < self) participants (Sparks et al., 2016), or would a standard self-prioritization effect emerge regardless of culture (Sui et al., 2012; Sui et al., 2014)?

To explore this, we conducted two experiments in which Asians were compared to Westerners in an ownership paradigm (Golubickis et al., in press). We acquired samples from Kuala Lumpur and Hong Kong (East Asia), both of which were contrasted with a separate set of participants living in Aberdeen (United Kingdom). The task was identical to our previous experiments; however, it had an important modification: Participants judged the ownership of the presented objects (i.e., pens and pencils) that supposedly belonged either to themselves or their mother. Across two experiments and cultures, a stable pattern of results emerged. Ownership facilitated decision-making, such that self-owned objects were judged faster than identical items owned by their mother for both the Western and Asian participants. As before, we submitted the data to drift diffusion modeling to explore the origins of this effect. Mirroring our previous experiments, the analysis revealed that decision-making was underpinned by a predisposed response bias, such that participants favored (i.e., required less evidence for) responses to self-owned items, compared to mother-owned, prior to the commencement of decisional processing.

210   *C. Neil Macrae et al.*

Importantly, this bias occurred for both the Asian and Western samples, indicating that both quickly adopted items as their own and were prepared to respond to them faster due to an a priori bias. This is in line with previous demonstrations that self-relevance facilitates decision-making among both cultural backgrounds alike (Sui et al., 2012; Sui et al., 2014), which suggests that humans across cultures may benefit from the effects of egocentric biases.

To sum up, the equivalence of stimulus-prioritization effects across cultures suggests that object identification is subject to egocentrism and resistant to cultural influence (Sui et al., 2012; Sui et al., 2014). The question of why cultural socialization impacts memorial benefits of self-relevant material therefore remains to be answered. Sparks et al. (2016) proposed that the explanation may lie in differential processing requirements posed by different tasks employed in investigations of the effects of egocentric biases. The memorial advantages associated with self-referencing are believed to originate from elaborative (i.e., post-perceptual) processing operations that enhance stimulus encoding and representation (Conway & Dewhurst, 1995; Johnson, Hashtroudi, & Lindsay, 1993; Keenan & Baillet, 1980; Klein & Loftus, 1988; Rogers et al., 1977; Symons & Johnson, 1997; Turk et al., 2013). Culture is stipulated to influence the degree to which self and other overlap in memory, resulting in differences in the representation of person knowledge (see Ng & Lai, 2009; Wuyun et al., 2014), which can account for divergent effects between Western and Asian participants (Sparks et al., 2016).

In contrast, decision-making tasks, such as the ones used in our experiments, require only low-level identification of self-owned (vs. other-owned) stimuli. At the basic level of analysis at which self and other are being differentiated, egocentric responses are likely the default product of perceptual processing (Northoff, 2016), leading our minds to prefer self-relevant stimuli. Operating in such a way, the streetwise mind is preferentially furnished with self-relevant (vs. other-relevant) material on which subsequent processing operations can be undertaken (Sui & Humphreys, 2017).

Conclusion

The present chapter examines evidence from various fields of research within psychology investigating how egocentrism affects cognition and behavior. Throughout, the effects of self-relevance on stimulus processing, judgments, and memories (among others) were found to occur in adults and children, and to be easily experimentally induced, suggesting that people's egocentric tendencies may influence their everyday lives in important and diverse ways. Given even minimal evidence to believe something is theirs, people will happily (i.e., gullibly) accept this proposition and act on it, such that additional processing resources are assigned towards their newly acquired personal belongings – they remember them better and make decisions regarding them faster (and more accurately) than for items they do not consider to be theirs. The self, therefore, appears to be acting as a central mechanism throughout people's interactions with the world (Sui & Humphreys, 2015a), guiding at least their initial reactions in an egocentric manner.

Despite the demonstrated scope and strength of egocentric biases, the question of why the human mind so readily accepts them has not yet been definitively answered (see Dunning, Chapter 12 this volume; Fiedler, Chapter 7 this volume; Oyserman, Chapter 14 this volume; Schwarz & Lee, Chapter 12 this volume). It has been suggested that the self plays a critical role in people's ability to communicate with, and relate to, their environment by serving as a stable reference point, thereby constituting an evolutionary advantage (see Oakley & Halligan, 2017). Extending this line of thinking, enhanced cognition (including decision-making and memory) for all that is relevant to the self may contribute to successful integration in this complex social world by continuously updating one's self-narrative and enabling important (i.e., self-relevant) decisions to be made very rapidly. In this view then, the self emerges as a highly efficient strategy for engaging with our environment, allowing individuals to prioritize what directly affects the basis of their social existence.

On a societal scale, an evolutionary advantage may further emerge from people's egocentric tendencies if these lead them to behave in a socially beneficial manner. The impression of being noticed substantially more than is actually the case (i.e., the spotlight effect) could, for example, make them behave in ways that others consider to be socially desirable, as has been suggested to occur when individuals believe they are being watched (although individual differences might moderate this phenomenon, e.g., Pfattheicher & Keller, 2015). Similarly, it stands to reason that assuming others cannot be fooled by one's attempts to hide one's feelings and emotions (i.e., the illusion of transparency) keeps one honest, which may also benefit society on the large scale. Taken together, this indicates that people's self-favoring strategies may make them streetwise.

While the cognitive processes that potentially underpin such a self-centered strategy have in the past largely been the subject of speculation, new analytical methods can provide tools that allow a peek into the cognitive "black box." The results from recent research by Golubickis and colleagues (Golubickis et al., 2018; Golubickis et al., in press), which took advantage of these analytic advances, lend support to the notion that, at least during the early stages of decision-making, people are inherently egocentric. Specifically, as evidenced in an a priori response bias toward self-relevant material, people require less evidence when responding to their own than other people's things. A cross-cultural investigation further revealed that such a self-bias is not only found in individualistic cultures, but is also exhibited by members of cultures in which the self is more strongly construed in relation to others, indicating that across cultures, individuals'

212　*C. Neil Macrae et al.*

decision-making benefits from their ability to respond faster to what is directly relevant to them. Put simply, the self seemingly matters most to everyone, and this may be adaptive.

References

Ashby, F. G. (1983). A biased random walk model for two choice reaction times. *Journal of Mathematical Psychology, 27*, 277–297.

Ashby, N. J. S., Dickert, S., & Glöckner, A. (2012). Focusing on what you own: Biased information uptake due to ownership. *Judgment and Decision Making, 3*, 254–267.

Beggan, J. K. (1992). On the social nature of nonsocial perception: The mere ownership effect. *Journal of Personality and Social Psychology, 62*, 229–237.

Belk, R. W. (1988). Possessions and the extended self. *Journal of Consumer Research, 15*, 139–168.

Belk, R. W. (1991). The ineluctable mysteries of possessions. *Journal of Social Behavior and Personality, 6*, 17–55.

Belk, R. W. (2014). The extended self unbound. *Journal of Marketing Theory and Practice, 22*, 133–134.

Bogacz, R., Brown, E., Moehlis, J., Holmes, P., & Cohen, J. D. (2006). The physics of optimal decision making: A formal analysis of models of performance in two-alternative forced-choice tasks. *Psychological Review, 113*, 700–765.

Bower, G. H., & Gilligan, S. G. (1979). Remembering information related to one's self. *Journal of Research and Personality, 13*, 420–432.

Conway, M. A. (2005). Memory and the self. *Journal of Memory and Language, 53*, 594–628.

Conway, M. A., & Dewhurst, S. A. (1995). The self and recollective experience. *Applied Cognitive Psychology, 9*, 1–19.

Conway, M. A., & Pleydell-Pearce, C. W. (2000). The construction of autobiographical memories in the self-memory system. *Psychological Review, 107*, 261–288.

Cunningham, S. J., Brady-van den Bos, M., & Turk, D. J. (2011). Exploring the effects of ownership and choice on self-memory biases. *Memory, 19*, 449–461.

Cunningham, S. J., Brebner, J. L., Quinn, F., & Turk, D. J. (2014). The self-reference effect on memory in early childhood. *Child Development, 85*, 808–823.

Cunningham, S. J., Turk, D. J., Macdonald, L. M., & Macrae, C. N. (2008). Yours or mine? Ownership and memory. *Consciousness and Cognition, 17*, 312–318.

Cunningham, S. J., Vergunst, F., Macrae, C. N., & Turk, D. J. (2013). Exploring early self-referential memory effects through ownership. *British Journal of Developmental Psychology, 31*, 289–301.

Diederich, A., & Busemeyer, J. R. (2006). Modeling the effects of payoff on response bias in a perceptual discrimination task: Bound-change, drift-rate-change, or two-stage-processing hypothesis. *Perception & Psychophysics, 68*, 194–207.

Dunning, D., & Balcetis, E. (2013). Wishful seeing: How preferences shape visual perception. *Current Directions in Psychological Science, 22*, 33–37.

Englert, J., & Wentura, D. (2016). How "mere" is the mere ownership effect in memory? Evidence for semantic organization processes. *Consciousness and Cognition, 46*, 71–88.

Epley, N., & Gilovich, T. (2004). Are adjustments insufficient? *Personality and Social Psychology Bulletin, 30*, 447–460.

Epley, N., & Gilovich, T. (2006). The anchoring-and-adjustment heuristic. *Psychological Science, 17*, 311–318.

Epley, N., Keysar, B., van Boven, L., & Gilovich, T. (2004). Perspective taking as egocentric anchoring and adjustment. *Journal of Personality and Social Psychology, 87*, 327–339.

Gilovich, T., Medvec, V. H., & Savitsky, K. (2000). The spotlight effect in social judgment: An egocentric bias in estimates of the salience of one's own actions and appearance. *Journal of Personality and Social Psychology, 78*, 211–222.

Gilovich, T., & Savitsky, K. (1999) The spotlight effect and the illusion of transparency: Egocentric assessments of how we are seen by others. *Current Directions in Psychological Science, 8*, 165–168.

Gilovich, T., Savitsky, K., & Medvec, V. H. (1998). The illusion of transparency: Biases assessments of others' ability to read one's emotional states. *Journal of Personality and Social Psychology, 75*, 332–346.

Golubickis, M., Falbén, J. K., Cunningham, W. A., & Macrae, C. N. (2018). Exploring the self-ownership effect: Separating stimulus and response biases. *Journal of Experimental Psychology: Learning, Memory and Cognition, 44*, 295–306.

Golubickis, M., Ho, N. S. P., Falbén, J. K., Mackenzie, K. M., Boschetti, A., Cunningham, W. A., & Macrae, C. N. (in press). Mine or yours? Exploring the self-ownership effect across cultures. *Culture and Brain.*

Heatherton, T. F., Wyland, C. L., Macrae, C. N., Demos, K. E., Denny, B. T., & Kelley, W. M. (2006). Medial prefrontal activity differentiates self from close others. *Social Cognitive and Affective Neuroscience, 1*, 18–25.

Humphreys, G. W., & Sui, J. (2015). The salient self: Social saliency effects based on self-bias. *Journal of Cognitive Psychology, 27*, 129–140.

Humphreys, G. W., & Sui, J. (2016). Attentional control and the self: The self-attention network (SAN). *Cognitive Neuroscience, 7*, 5–17.

James, W. (1890). *The principles of psychology.* New York, NY: Henry-Holt & Co.

Johnson, M. K., Hashtroudi, S., & Lindsay, D. S. (1993). Source monitoring. *Psychological Bulletin, 114*, 3–28.

Kahneman, D., Knetsch, J. L., & Thaler, R. H. (1990). Experimental tests of the endowment effect and the Coarse Theorem. *Journal of Political Economy, 98*, 1325–1348.

Keenan, J. M., & Baillet, S. D. (1980). Memory for personally and socially significant events. *Attention and Performance, 8*, 651–669.

Keysar, B., Lin, S., & Barr, D. J. (2003). Limits of theory of mind use in adults. *Cognition, 89*, 25–41.

Klein, S. B., & Loftus, J. (1988). The nature of self-referent encoding: The contributions of elaborative and organizational processes. *Journal of Personality and Social Psychology, 55*, 5–11.

Knetsch, J. L., & Sinden, J. A. (1984). Willingness to pay and compensation demanded: Experimental evidence of an unexpected disparity in measures of value. *Quarterly Journal of Economics, 99*, 507–521.

Krigolson, Q. E., Hassall, C. D., Balcom, L., & Turk, D. (2013). Perceived ownership impacts reward evaluation within medial-frontal cortex. *Cognitive, Affective & Behavioural Neuroscience, 13*, 262–269.

Leshikar, E., Dulas, M., & Duarte, A. (2015). Self-referencing enhances recollection in both young and older adults. *Aging, Neuropsychology, And Cognition*, *22*, 388–412.

Macrae, C. N., Moran, J. M., Heatherton, T. F., Banfield, J. F., & Kelley, W. M. (2004). Medial prefrontal activity predicts memory for self. *Cerebral Cortex*, *14*, 647–654.

Maddux, W. W., Yang, H., Falk, C., Adam, H., Adair, W., Endo, Y., . . . Heine, S. J. (2010). For whom is parting with possessions more painful? Cultural differences in the endowment effect. *Psychological Science*, *21*, 1910–1917.

Markus, H. R., & Kitayama, S. (1991). Culture and the self: Implications for cognition, emotion, and motivation. *Psychological Review*, *98*, 224.

Markus, H. R., & Kitayama, S. (2010). Cultures and selves: A cycle of mutual constitution. *Perspectives on Psychological Science*, *5*, 420–430.

Morewedge, C. K., & Giblin, C. E. (2015). Explanations of the endowment effect: An integrative review. *Trends in Cognitive Sciences*, *19*, 339–348.

Morewedge, C. K., Shu, L. L., Gilbert, D. T., & Wilson, T. D. (2009). Bad riddance or good rubbish? Ownership and not loss aversion causes the endowment effect. *Journal of Experimental Social Psychology*, *45*, 947–951.

Mulder, M. J., Wagenmakers, E. J., Ratcliff, R., Boekel, W., & Forstmann, B. U. (2012). Bias in the brain: A diffusion model analysis of prior probability and potential payoff. *Journal of Neuroscience*, *32*, 2335–2343.

Nayakankuppam, D., & Mishra, H. (2005). The endowment effect: Rose-tinted and dark-tinted glasses. *Journal of Consumer Research*, *32*, 390–395.

Ng, S. H., & Lai, J. C. L. (2009). Effects of culture priming on the social connectedness of the bicultural self: A self-reference effect approach. *Journal of Cross Cultural Psychology*, *40*, 170–186.

Nickerson, R. S. (1999). How we know – and sometimes misjudge – what others know: Imputing one's own knowledge to others. *Psychological Bulletin*, *125*, 737–759.

Northoff, G. (2016). Is the self a higher-order or fundamental function of the brain? The "basis model of self-specificity" and its encoding by the brain's spontaneous activity. *Cognitive Neuroscience*, *7*, 203–222.

Northoff, G., & Hayes, D. J. (2011). Is self nothing but a reward? *Biological Psychiatry*, *69*, 1019–1035.

Oakley, D. A., & Halligan, P. W. (2017). Chasing the rainbow: The non-conscious nature of being. *Frontiers in Psychology*, *8*, 1–16.

Perner, J. (1991). *Understanding the representational mind*. Cambridge, MA: Bradford Books/MIT Press.

Pfattheicher, S., & Keller, J. (2015). The watching eyes phenomenon: The role of a sense of being seen and public self-awareness. *European Journal of Social Psychology*, *45*, 560–566.

Ratcliff, R. (1978). A theory of memory retrieval. *Psychological Review*, *85*, 59–108.

Rogers, T. B., Kuiper, N. A., & Kirker, W. S. (1977). Self-reference and the encoding of personal information. *Journal of Personality and Social Psychology*, *35*, 677–688.

Ross, J., Anderson, J. R., & Campbell, R. N. (2011). Situational changes in self-awareness influence 3- and 4-year-olds' self-regulation. *Journal of Experimental Child Psychology*, *108*, 126–138.

Simen, P., Contreras, D., Buck, C., Hu, P., Holmes, P., & Cohen, J. D. (2009). Reward rate optimization in two-alternative decision making: Empirical tests of theoretical predictions. *Journal of Experimental Psychology: Human Perception and Performance*, *35*, 1865–1897.

Sparks, S., Cunningham, S. J., & Kritikos, A. (2016). Culture modulates implicit ownership-induced self-bias in memory. *Cognition, 153*, 89–98.

Sui, J., He, X., & Humphreys, G. W. (2012). Perceptual effects of social salience: Evidence from self-prioritisation effects on perceptual matching. *Journal of Experimental Psychology: Human Perception and Performance, 38*, 1105–1117.

Sui, J., & Humphreys, G. W. (2015a). The integrative self: How self-reference integrates perception and memory. *Trends in Cognitive Sciences, 19*, 719–728.

Sui, J., & Humphreys, G. W. (2015b). The interaction between self-bias and reward: Evidence for common and distinct processes. *Quarterly Journal of Experimental Psychology, 68*, 1952–1964.

Sui, J., & Humphreys, G. W. (2017). The self survives extinction: Self-association biases attention in patients with visual extinction. *Cortex, 95*, 248–256.

Sui, J., Liu, M., Mevorach, C., & Humphreys, G. W. (2013). The salient self: The left intra-parietal sulcus responds to social as well as perceptual salience after self-association. *Cerebral Cortex, 4*, 1060–1068.

Sui, J., Sun, Y., Peng, K., & Humphreys, G. W. (2014). The automatic and the expected self: Separating self-and familiarity biases effects by manipulating stimulus probability. *Attention, Perception, & Psychophysics, 76*, 1176–1184.

Sui, J., & Zhu, Y. (2005). Five-year-olds can show the self-reference advantage. *International Journal of Behavioural Development, 29*, 382–387.

Symons, C. S., & Johnson, B. T. (1997). The self-reference effect in memory: A meta-analysis. *Psychological Bulletin, 121*, 371–394.

Truong, G., Roberts, K. H., & Todd, R. M. (2017). I saw mine first: A prior-entry effect for newly acquired ownership. *Journal of Experimental Psychology: Human Perception and Performance, 43*, 192–205.

Truong, G., & Todd, R. M. (2017). SOAP Opera: Self as object and agent prioritizing attention. *Journal of Cognitive Neuroscience, 29*, 937–952.

Turk, D. J., Brady-van den Bos, M., Collard, P., Gillespie-Smith, K., Conway, M. A., & Cunningham, S. J. (2013). Divided attention selectively impairs memory for self-relevant information. *Memory & Cognition, 41*, 503–510.

Turk, D. J., Cunningham, S. J., & Macrae, C. N. (2008). Self-memory biases in explicit and incidental encoding of trait adjectives. *Consciousness and Cognition, 17*, 1040–1045.

Turk, D. J., van Bussel, K., Brebner, J. L., Toma, A. S., Krigolson, O., & Handy, T. C. (2011). When "it" becomes "mine": Attentional biases triggered by object ownership. *Journal of Cognitive Neuroscience, 23*, 3725–3733.

Tversky, A., & Kahneman, D. (1974). Judgment under uncertainty: Heuristics and biases. *Science, 185*, 1124–1131.

van den Bos, M., Cunningham, S. J., Conway, M. A., & Turk, D. J. (2010). Mine to remember: The impact of ownership on recollective experience. *Quarterly Journal of Experimental Psychology, 63*, 1065–1071.

van Ravenzwaaij, D., Mulder, M. J., Tuerlinckx, F., & Wagenmakers, E. J. (2012). Do the dynamics of prior information depend on task context? An analysis of optimal performance and an empirical test. *Frontiers in Psychology, 3*, 1–15.

Voss, A., Rothermund, K., & Brandtstädter, J. (2008). Interpreting ambiguous stimuli: Separating perceptual and judgmental biases. *Journal of Experimental Social Psychology, 44*, 1048–1056.

White, C. N., & Poldrack, R. A. (2014). Decomposing bias in different types of simple decisions. *Journal of Experimental Psychology: Learning, Memory, and Cognition, 40*, 385–398.

White, C. N., Ratcliff, R., Vasey, M. W., & McKoon, G. (2010). Using diffusion models to understand clinical disorders. *Journal of Mathematical Psychology*, *54*, 39–52.

Wiecki, T. V., Sofer, I., & Frank, M. J. (2013). HDDM: Hierarchical Bayesian estimation of the drift- diffusion model in python. *Frontiers in Neuroinformatics*, *7*, 1–10.

Wimmer, H., & Perner, J. (1983). Beliefs about beliefs: Representation and constraining function of wrong beliefs in young children's understanding of deception. *Cognition*, *13*, 103–128.

Wuyun, G., Shu, M., Cao., Z., Huang, W., Zou, X., Li, S., Zhang, X., Luo, H., & Wu, Y. (2014). Neural representations of the self and the mother for Chinese individuals. *PLoS ONE*, *9*, 1–6.

Zhu, Y., & Zhang, L. (2002). An experimental study on the self-reference effect. *Science in China Series C: Life Sciences*, *45*, 120–128.

Zhu, Y., Zhang, L., Fan, J., & Han, S. (2007). Neural basis of cultural influence on self-representation. *Neuroimage*, *34*, 1310–1316.

12 Gullible to Ourselves

David Dunning
UNIVERSITY OF MICHIGAN

The age of the Internet has produced a vast democratization of knowledge. Far more than in any past age, crucial information can be gained easily by anyone interested in seeking it – often with only a few flicks of their fingers on a computer's keyboard.

Therein, however, lies the problem. If far more people can gain information without any barriers, far more people can also provide it. Regrettably, among those providing it are the misinformed, bad actors, people with vested interests, and ideological zealots, all of whom may wish to distort or obscure the truth (see also Cooper & Avery, Chapter 16 this volume; Myers, Chapter 5 this volume). Information providers need not be even human. Thus, when all is said and done, we now have the technology to send information around the world in a nanosecond, but no way to insure that this information is worth paying attention to.

As such, as far as it comes to fact and expertise, the Internet has brought about a true age of uncertainty. As Kevin Kelley, of Wired magazine, put it, "Truth is no longer dictated by authorities, but is networked by peers. For every fact there is a counterfact" (Anderson & Rainie, 2017). In June 2017, a false story suggesting the founder of Ethereum had died in a car crash caused the company's market value to drop by $4 billion. The United States National Aeronautic and Space Administration (NASA) found that it had to publicly deny stories that it was running a child prostitution ring on Mars (Holley, 2017). The truth may be out there, but it is increasingly hidden behind curtains of deception, misdirection, and misinformation.

Thus, would it not be ironic in this new age of information, where it is uncertain which sources to trust, that the person we need to be wary of, the individual who might be most likely to deceive us, the one who is most likely to deflect us from truth, is ourselves?

In this chapter, I argue that the agent we are most gullible to – even in this brave new technological world – is ourselves, in that we often imbue too much faith in our own beliefs and opinions. If gullibility can be defined as "an unusual tendency toward being duped or taken advantage of" (Greenspan, 2008, p. 2), then that tendency rises to its most unusual levels

218 David Dunning

when we deal with our own beliefs and opinions. People are too quick to believe what the self has to say and to dismiss helpful information from others. In this chapter, I document this gullibility to self, and discuss why it is difficult for people to recognize who to seek advice from, namely, experts in their midst. Finally, I talk about first steps people must take to rid themselves of self-gullibility.

Overbelief in Self

Psychological research showing that people overbelieve themselves goes back many decades – indeed, back to the 1950s. Since that time, psychologists asked people to answer questions, make judgments, or render predictions, and have shown that people generally overestimate the likelihood that their conclusions will prove accurate (for classic reviews see Lichtenstein, Fischhoff, & Phillips, 1982; Moore & Healy, 2008).

Overconfidence

This literature, known as the overconfidence or overestimation literature, follows a typical format. Research participants first answer a question with a definable answer (e.g., such as *Did Shakespeare write more than 30 plays?*) or make a prediction (e.g., *Will you pay off your credit card by the end of the year?*) and then estimate the likelihood, up to 100%, that they will be right (Moore & Healy, 2008). The consistent finding is that people largely overestimate the chance that their conclusions will prove accurate. To be sure, if they are merely guessing, they seem to be aware of that fact. If they think the answer to a yes-or-no question is 50:50 to be right, they are, indeed, accurate roughly 50% of the time (see Lichtenstein et al., 1982; also Han & Dunning, 2018b). But on those occasions when they are certain of an answer, depending on the study and the topic, they are wrong on one out of every five answers they give (Fischhoff, Slovic, & Lichtenstein, 1977).

People often show their overbelief in other ways, offering answers that they endorse with too much exactitude, known as the overprecision effect (Moore & Healy, 2008). In this form of undue self-belief, research participants answer a question, such as *In what year did Thomas Edison invent the light bulb?*, and then are asked to provide a range around their answer that has the chance of capturing the true answer 80% of the time. For example, for *Thomas Edison*, they may suggest 1890 as their best guess, with the true answer 80% likely to be somewhere between the brackets of 1880 and 1900 (Dunning, 2018). Or, financial officers at mid-size to large companies might be asked to forecast the value of the S&P 500 stock index one to ten years in the future, and then give upper and lower bounds that have an 80% chance of capturing the index's true value at the end of the prediction period (Ben-David, Graham, & Harvey, 2013).

Work on the overprecision effect shows that people overestimate the exactness of their conclusions, in that the bounds they draw around their best guesses fail to contain the right answer as often as they think. In short, the truth has a habit of wandering much further away from where people's intuitions think it might be located. They may draw bounds that they think captures the true answer 80% or 90% of the time, but those bounds actually capture the truth only 35% to 40% of the time, depending on the study (Russo & Schoemaker, 1992). In the study of financial officers described above, for example, study participants drew boundaries that were too narrow, in that they captured the true value of the S&P in the future only 37% of the time, not 80% (Ben-David et al., 2013).

Importantly, this overbelief in one's answers is the most pronounced among those most likely to make the most mistakes. Namely, people largely fail to anticipate those topics and areas in life where they are likely to be incompetent and provide answers that are wrong. This has popularly come to be known as the Dunning–Kruger effect (Dunning, 2011; Dunning, Johnson, Ehrlinger, & Kruger, 2003; Ehrlinger, Johnson, Banner, Dunning, & Kruger, 2008; Kruger & Dunning, 1999), which formally suggests that people who lack expertise in an area suffer a double curse. First, their lack of expertise leads them to make many errors. Second, and more important, their lack of expertise prevents them from seeing their choices as errors. Put simply, they lack the very expertise they need to recognize just how much expertise they lack. As a consequence, they think they are doing just fine when, in fact, their performance suffers greatly.

A recent example in the realm of overprecision shows this pattern. Research participants were asked to estimate the approximate year in which 12 different historical events took place, like the end of the civil war, Hurricane Katrina hitting New Orleans, or the stock market crashing to begin the Great Depression. Participants were also asked to provide bounds around their best estimates that would contain the true year of the event about 80% of the time. The top 25% of performers in the study did quite well. They were off in their best guess estimates by roughly seven years on average, but their bounds captured the right answer about 63% of the time – not 80% as asked but close (Dunning, 2018).

Participants in the bottom 25% of performers, however, were off on average by 42 years on each and every estimate they made. To be sure, they had some insight into the problems of these answers, in that they provided bounds around those answers that were wider than those offered by the best performers, roughly 36 years apart rather than the confident 12 years apart offered by best performers. However, even these much wider bounds captured the true answer only 39% of the time. In short, this unknowledgeable group showed some insight into the fact that their answers were imprecise, but they largely failed to recognize just how imprecise and faulty their answers truly were (Dunning, 2018).

220   *David Dunning*

Belief in Wrong Answers

In a sense, this overbelief in self should not be a surprise. It is simply the product of having been asked to make a choice. Facing the request, people choose what they think to be the best choice. They select what they believe to be the optimal option given all the alternatives they can think of and all the information and reasoning they can bring to bear (Capen, Clapp, & Campbell, 1971; Dunning, in press; Han & Dunning, 2018a).

Often that choice is actually the best and all is well. However, often enough to cause problems, that choice can have the look and feel of a correct choice but still turn out to be wrong, or at least not as good as the individual believes it to be. In auctions, this is known as the "winner's curse," in that the person who bids the most for some object at an auction is usually the one who is the most likely to have overvalued it (Massey & Thaler, 2013; Thaler, 1988). This winner's curse similarly attaches itself to people's decisions. People often make the choice they overvalue.

We have seen evidence that wrong reasoning or knowledge often leaves people to be just as confident, and sometimes more, as does correct reasoning. For example, the day after the 2014 midterm elections in the United States, we surveyed roughly 350 respondents on their political views and beliefs about social and economic conditions in the country. Many of our questions were factual, in that true answers could be found by simple research over the Internet. We asked, for example, whether teenage pregnancy rates were at record highs, whether the stock market had gone up under the administration of Democratic President Barack Obama, and whether the poverty rate had gone down. Respondents showed only a modest awareness of the facts, getting on average only just over half of the questions right (Dunning & Roh, 2018; see also Myers, Chapter 5 this volume).

What was interesting, however, was how participants tended to get questions wrong. They had the option of saying "I don't know" to every question, but of the items they got wrong, they chose that option only about 35% of the time. More often than not, they gave an affirmative wrong answer – usually one congenial to their politics. For example, conservatives claimed that teenage pregnancies were at a record high (actually, no, they were at a 20-year low) and liberals would say that the poverty rate was down (at the time, it at nearly a 50-year high). As Figure 12.1 shows, on average, 35%–40% of what both groups claimed to be true was demonstrably false (Dunning & Roh, 2018).

This, however, was the key consequence of the finding. In the survey, we also asked respondents if they were a "well-informed citizen." We were pleased to find out positive ratings along this question were correlated with getting questions right. Ratings were also negatively correlated with the frequency with which respondents answered "I don't know."

What was troubling, however, was that respondents considered themselves well informed to the extent they gave affirmatively wrong answers to our

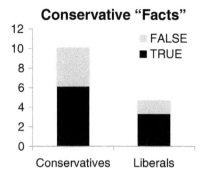 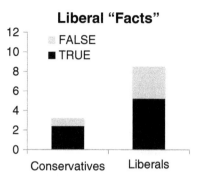

Figure 12.1 Number of true and false facts endorsed by conservatives and liberals as a function of the political "lean" of the fact.
Source: Adapted from Dunning and Roh (2018).

questions. In fact, wrong answers stoked overall self-impressions of being "well informed" almost as much as right answers. We have seen this pattern, as well, in surveys about financial literacy, civics, and world geography (Dunning & Roh, 2018). It is also linked to behavior. Respondents who provided more wrong answers to political questions also tend to be more active in politics, signing petitions, donating money, and organizing campaign events.

In essence, research has found that the problem with people is that they often have a difficult time distinguishing true knowledge from "what they know that isn't so." In computer programming terms, they often have a difficult time distinguishing *pattern* (correct and efficient approaches to programming challenges) from *anti-pattern* (misleading and mistaken responses to such challenges) (Laplante & Nelson, 2005). Both feed into higher confidence (Sanchez & Dunning, 2018; van Loon, de Bruin, van Gog, & van Merriënboer, 2013; Williams, Dunning, & Kruger, 2013).

Assuming Accuracy Without Feedback

People certainly often act as though their judgments are, if not the truth, pretty close to it. This assumption carries implications for tasks in which people receive little or incomplete feedback. On those decisions for which people receive no feedback, their subsequent behavior suggests that they simply take their unverified judgment as correct. Their decision stands as internally generated feedback, a process known as *constructive coding* (Elwin, Juslin, Olsson, & Enkvist, 2007).

Consider, for example, a human resource official at some company who has final authority in making hiring decisions. That official will receive feedback about some decisions – namely, about those applicants they ultimately hired, in that those applicants either succeed or fail at the job. But what about rejected applicants? About them, there will be no feedback. There will be no chance to see how many of them, as predicted, would have failed and how many, despite predictions, would have succeeded. People in the human resource official's position, however, will largely act as though those rejection decisions were all correct (Elwin, 2013; Henriksson, Elwin, & Juslin, 2010).

The social consequences of assuming accuracy without evidence or feedback can be profound. In one study, Fetchenhauer and Dunning (2010) asked college students to watch videotapes of 56 other students and to decide, for each, whether they would trust those people in a financial game. One group was given feedback about their judgments rather selectively – that is, only after they had decided to trust the person. Here, they could find out if their judgment was accurate or whether they had been too optimistic. However, they were not given any feedback about the other students they had decided were unworthy of trust.

Participants in this condition ended up too cynical about their peers, significantly underestimating how trustworthy their peers would prove to be in the game. This is not a surprise given the biased nature of the feedback they received plus their tendency to think of their judgments as right. Overly optimistic trust predictions were corrected by feedback. However, overly cynical predictions that led participants not to trust their peers produced no feedback, and thus no opportunities to learn about misplaced cynicism. Participants in another group, however, who were given feedback for each and every decision, regardless of whether they trusted or not, were much more accurate and optimistic about the behavior of their peers. They also earned more money when it came time to play the game.

Advice

One sees self-gullibility in what people make of the opinions and conclusions of others. People often discount or dismiss what other people have to say, usually to the detriment of the accuracy of their own self-views. People often tend to overbelieve in the value of their own intellect and rate their political and social beliefs as superior to other people (Hall & Raimi, 2018; Raimi & Leary, 2014; Toner, Leary, Asher, & Jongman-Sereno, 2013). Nearly two-thirds of Americans rate their overall intelligence as above average, a statistical impossibility (Heck, Simons, & Chabris, 2018). Finally, roughly a third of Americans view their expertise on vaccination to be at least as good as, if not better than, doctors and medical experts (Motta, Callaghan, & Sylvester, 2018).

Discounting Advice from Others

Although we give great weight to our own opinions and knowledge, suggestions from other people tend to be discounted or dismissed. The literature on advice-taking, found mostly in organizational psychology, provides the most direct demonstration of this tendency. In a typical advise-taking study, people are asked to estimate, for example, the current unemployment rate, or the population of some city, and then are presented the estimate (i.e., some advice) that another person has made. They are asked, in light of any disagreement, whether they would like to revise their original estimate. Often, they decide not to, sticking with their initial intuition. Or, instead, they may revise their original estimate somewhat, like a little less than a third of the way toward the other person's response.

However, in the main, they typically give their own original estimate more weight than they do the judgment of another person, a phenomenon known as *egocentric discounting* (Bonaccio & Dalal, 2006; Harvey & Fischer, 1997; Yaniv, 2004; Yaniv & Kleinberger, 2000). The issue with egocentric discounting is that people would achieve much greater accuracy if they gave the other person's estimate at least just as much weight as their own – if they had just split the difference between the two.

In sum, people, to their own disadvantage, often tend to give too much weight to their own supposed expertise than they do to the knowledge of others, doing so even if it makes sense to give the other person's conclusions more weight than their own.[1] Consider Soll and Larrick (2009), who paired research participants with an individual from another country. Each partner was asked to mull over their own countries and that of their partner, and then to make ten estimates about each country – such as the percentage who smoked, or lived in urban areas, or were under 15 years of age. They then showed each other their estimates and asked if they wanted to revise their estimates.

When considering their own country, respondents given the chance to revise their answers typically showed the usual pattern of egocentric discounting. They stuck to their original estimate nearly 40% of the time and split the difference with their partner only around 25% of the time. This pattern, however, is defensible, in that people presumably know more about their own country than their partner would.

What was telling was how respondents reacted when looking at their partner's estimates of that partner's own country. Participants did give weight to their partner's supposed expertise, but not as much as one might think, or as much as was warranted. Participants stuck with their original estimate only 10% of the time, but by far the most popular choice was to split the difference – that is, to give equal weight to one's own expertise as knowledge from a person obviously more familiar with the country in question.

Recent work on the Dunning–Kruger effect ratifies the observation that people fail to seek out expert advice as much as they should (Yan & Dunning, 2017). In three studies, participants took quizzes in which they could win small amounts of money for each question they got right. For each question, participants were given a chance to look at the answer of another person if they wanted. This would diminish the amount of money they could win for that question, but, of course, looking at another person's answer might

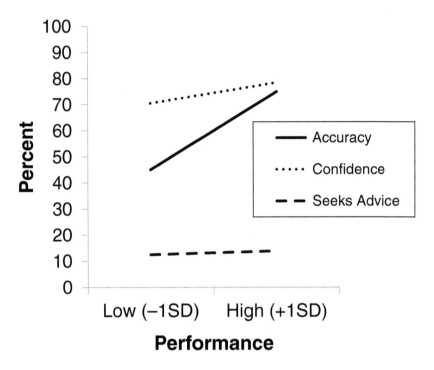

Figure 12.2 Confidence, accuracy, and advice-seeking rate of high and low performers taking a quiz on household safety issues.

Source: Adapted from Yan and Dunning (2017).

prevent the participant from making an error. In the first study, the topic was making a household safe for children. The respondents were people reporting having at least one child under the age of 6 at home, and were asked questions about preventing accidents and identifying household hazards.

Analyses showed that participants were not very enthusiastic about receiving advice, asking to see another person's response only 13% of the time, as shown in Figure 12.2. To be sure, participants overall asked for that advice on questions they were more likely to be wrong. However, respondents doing poorly on the quiz showed no more eagerness to receive advice, although they more clearly needed it, relative to participants doing well. As a consequence, they got many items wrong when they could have been alerted to their errors (Yan & Dunning, 2017).

Not Knowing Whom to Ask

People, however, often suffer a more fundamental problem when it comes to dealing with advice – left to their own devices, they do not necessarily know who to approach for the best advice. In short, needing advice presents something of a paradox. People need advice when their own expertise contains gaps (Caputo & Dunning, 2005; Wu & Dunning, 2018) and defects (Dunning & Roh, 2018; Marsh, Cantor, & Brashier, 2016; Williams et al., 2013). But, with those gaps and defects, how can they adequately judge the expertise of others to know the best one to approach? To recognize superior expertise would require people to already have some expertise themselves. However, those needing advice often simply do not have it.

In short, those seeking advice often suffer from what we term the *Cassandra Quandary*, in that they do not necessarily have adequate expertise to recognize superior expertise in others (Dunning & Cone, 2018). As Sir Arthur Conan Doyle (1915) once observed, through his immortal character Sherlock Holmes, "Mediocrity knows nothing above itself" (p. 25). The phenomenon is named after the princess Cassandra from Greek mythology and refers to what it means for the person to have superior expertise. Cassandra was given the gift of true prophecy, but was cursed by Apollo never to be believed by her peers. In essence, we suggest that in contemporary times, people with true knowledge often suffer the same fate, having their wise advice fall on deaf ears.

We have conducted several studies showing that people have much more difficulty identifying people with superior knowledge than they do those with inferior expertise. In one study on financial literacy, participants took a four-item financial literacy quiz and then were asked to grade the responses made by four other people to the quiz. Unbeknown to participants, the people they graded achieved scores on the quiz that ranged from zero to a perfect score of four. Their specific task was to rank order their peers' performances from worst to first, and asked to think explicitly about who they would be most likely to or least likely to approach for advice. A greater proportion of participants accurately identified the worst performer (43%) but they were far less competent in identifying the best one (29%) (Dunning & Cone, 2018). Of key note, shown in Figure 12.3, students doing badly on the quiz identified the top performer only 9% of the time. In short, those theoretically in most need of advice were by far the worst in identifying the best person to approach for advice.

This lopsided pattern arises, in part, because of people's gullibility to themselves. In short, people tend to assume their own opinions and conclusions are true. They then use those opinions to judge those of others. If another person agrees with them, they often assume that the other person is likely to be right. If the person disagrees, then the other person is likely to be misguided. This tactic works well if the other person is, indeed, an inferior performer. However, this strategy leads to calamity when the other person has superior expertise. Here, a difference of opinion is read as error on the part of the other person when it, in fact, is error on the part of the self. Thus, believing in one's own opinions often leads people to discount viewpoints that are superior to their own (Dunning & Cone, 2018).

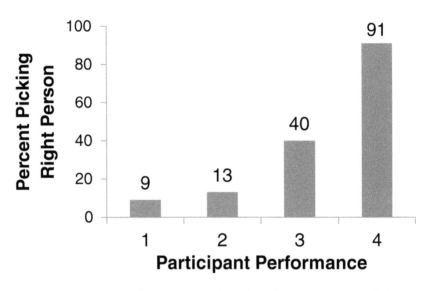

Figure 12.3 Percentage of participants picking the right person to approach for financial advice (i.e., the one with the perfect score) as a function of the participant's own score.

Source: Adapted from Dunning and Cone (2018).

One sees how this can lead to almost comical error in the domain of chess. In one study, we asked chess players of varying skill level to grade the moves made by six other chess players, whose performances ranged from terrible to near grand master level. Good chess players, near grand masters themselves, made sensible judgments about whether they could beat these other players after studying their moves. They were almost certain they could beat the player choosing terrible moves, but thought their chances were only 50:50 with the near grandmaster. Less skilled chess players reached a different, somewhat paradoxical, set of conclusions: They thought their chances with the terrible players were close to 50:50, but that they had a 70% chance of beating the near grand master. Apparently, after seeing near grand master moves, these less skilled players mistook these unfamiliar moves to be signs of flawed play (Dunning & Cone, 2018).

Differential Treatment of Self-Thought

Up to now, one can imagine that people's conclusions about their opinions and beliefs are somewhat sensible, or at least defensible, if inaccurate. People are given questions to answer and problems to solve, and they arrive at the best solution they can construct. Evolution has given humans much cognitive machinery to provide answers to puzzles posed to them and problems that must be solved. After all, we are the species that made it to the moon. However, it would be unreasonable to think that this human machinery is completely flawless. It may be designed to help people achieve answers to questions they must confront, but at times the machinery might be "too" helpful. At times, it must prompt people to be open to certain beliefs that should instead be shunned.

Thus, people tackle intellectual puzzles, and in the end they come up with the best solution or conclusion they can. No other solution seems more reasonable or superior (Dunning, in press). If any such other solution had emerged in their thinking, they would have chosen that other one. The problem people face is that their "best options" at times are products of faulty reasoning (see also Fiedler, Chapter 7 this volume; Krueger, Vogrincic-Haselbacher, & Evans, Chapter 6 this volume; Myers, Chapter 5 this volume; Strack, Chapter 9 this volume Unkelbach & Koch, Chapter 3 this volume) or mistaken premises (Mayo, Chapter 8 this volume; van Prooijen, Chapter 17 this volume). There is some glitch in their calculation or some crucial information is overlooked or unknown. But, in terms of effort and impartiality, people are trying honestly to achieve the best answer. Their only sin is assuming with too much certainty that their conclusions comprise, indeed, the best answers.

However, that is not always the case. At times, people do short-circuit their thinking to arrive at conclusions that they prefer. Or, they start out their thinking with the premise that they are intelligent and effective individuals – and no fact will be admitted that questions that self-view. In short, people conduct their thinking under the shadow of motivated reasoning, bending or directing their thinking in such a way to preserve favored pre-conceptions of the self and the world (Baumeister & Newman, 2004; Dunning, 2001; Kunda, 1990). Many contributors in this volume on gullibility reasonably assume that people commit gullibility out of some function or need. Gullible thinking might serve the purpose of cementing social relations (Baumeister, Maxwell, Thomas, & Vohs, Chapter 2 this volume), or assure people of their epistemological competence (Douglas, Sutton, & Cichocka, Chapter 4 this volume), or to manage potentially unpleasant emotions (Cooper & Avery, Chapter 16 this volume), or to confirm already decided-upon world views (van Prooijen, Chapter 17 this volume).

Thus, it would not be a surprise to find that people treat their own conclusions and reasoning differently than they do that of others. People are motivated to believe they are trustworthy intellects, but they are not so sure about other people (Dunning, in press; Kunda, 1990). Thus, they tend to place the reasoning of other people under closer scrutiny and skepticism than they do their own. For example, Gregg, Mahadevan, and Sedikides (2017) asked people to evaluate a novel theory about an alien planet. More specifically, they were asked to consider two species on that planet, the Niffites and the Luupites, and judge which was the predator and which was

228   *David Dunning*

the prey. Before they began, however, they were given a specific theory to test, and told that it had been assigned to them. It was their theory; they were to be identified with it. Other participants were told that the theory came from some other participant named "Alex."

The researchers found, as participants pored over information testing the theory, that people gave more lenient ratings to the information when it was supposedly consistent with their own theory than when it was with Alex's. As a consequence, at the end of the study, they believed in the theory they had been assigned to more. In a second study, they believed their own theory more than one that had been assigned to no one.

Other research suggests that this bias toward one's own theory may come from a superior sense that one is impartial and insightful. Namely, people tend to think of themselves as superior to other people along desirable traits, such as honesty, intelligence, and being a good driver (Dunning, 2005; Dunning, Heath, & Suls, 2004). Even prisoners locked up in British cells tend to describe themselves as more moral and ethical than the typical British citizens (Sedikides, Meek, Alicke, & Taylor, 2014). This sense of self-superiority also carries over to intellectual pursuits, with people often claiming better ability at reaching accurate and impartial judgments than their peers. In the ultimate irony, that is, people tend to have a bias toward claiming unusual abilities to reach unbiased conclusions (Pronin, Lin, & Ross, 2002).

Managing Our Opinions

What is one to do to avoid become a victim of gullibility? Take the case of Dr. Stephen Greenspan, who in 2008 at the age of 67 published his magnum opus on his life's work in psychiatry, *The Annals of Gullibility*, comprising decades of research and thought about what prompted people toward vulnerable gullibility, as well as how to avoid it.

It was only two days after the publication of his book that Dr. Greenspan got the phone call. The financial advisor managing part of his retirement investments in New York had just been arrested for fraud. The advisor was Bernie Madoff, who ultimately would be found to have fleeced a total of more than $65 billion from his clients. For Dr. Greenspan, a full third of his retirement investments had vanished into that total, gone forever (Griffin, 2009).

That the person who literally wrote the book on gullibility could be taken in himself is a cautionary tale for all of us. Beyond that, the overall lesson is that gullibility often requires two perpetrators. It requires not only someone with an alluring tale but also a recipient who makes a too confident judgment that the allurer can be trusted. We fall prey not only to the person with the tale, but to our own self-belief.

As such, we should be vigilant not only about other people but also our own judgment. For his own part, Dr. Greenspan (2009) admitted as much.

In subsequent writings, he admitted that there were warning signs that he had dismissed. He did not take the usual cautions he took when dealing with a topic – high finance, in this case – that he knew nothing about. He had suspended all the rules of caution and due diligence he knew full well he should live by.

In evaluations of evidence, it is customary to split the task into two assessments. One has to do with the strength of evidence; the other has to do with the weight the evidence should be given (Griffin & Tversky, 1992). Strength refers to the clarity or force with which evidence suggests one conclusion over all others. Weight refers to whether the evidence is sturdy, reliable, or credible. For example, a person on the witness stand may be adamant in his or her testimony (i.e., high in strength). But is it credible? The witness might have a reason to lie, and thus not to be given much weight.

The psychological literature suggests that judgments tend to overemphasize the strength of the evidence while underemphasizing weight (Griffin & Tversky, 1992; Jiang, Muhanna, & Pick, 1996; Nelson, Bloomfield, Hales, & Libby, 2001; see also Fiedler, Chapter 7 this volume, who makes similar arguments via the notion of "metacognitive myopia"). For instance, suppose you hold a coin in your hand that may be biased towards either heads or tails. To assess the bias, you flip it four times and it comes up heads each time. That is strong signal of bias, but should you give it much weight? After all the chance are 1 in 16 that all you have just seen is a random fluke of heads. Most people, however, will find the signal to be convincing. Certainly they will think the signal is stronger than if you, say, had flipped the coin 15 times and it came up heads on 11 of them. The strength of this new signal is not as strong as before (only 80%), but it turns out it should be given more weight, in that the chance of obtaining this result statistically is lower than the one before (2% vs. 7%, respectively) if the coin were really fair. What it gives up in strength it more than makes up for in weight, that is, how sturdy the result is.

Thus, one key to avoiding gullibility is to become more active in the assessment of weight. Not only should people pay attention to the stories being told, but should also be more adept at judging the credibility underlying those stories. Recent research has exactly focused on that: For example, researchers are actively working on media literacy classes to direct people to clues to help them weigh what stories they can believe on the Internet (Shellenbarger, 2016).

The discussion in this chapter suggests that any analysis of weight should go beyond an analysis of the evidence out there to also include the self within. People need to ask if they are in a position to credibly weigh any evidence in front of them, or whether they need help. They need to ask, for example, whether a story involves expertise beyond their ken. Are they considering a familiar or unfamiliar topic (Dunning et al., 2004)? They also need to ask whether they have considered all possible conclusions, or like Dr. Greenspan, just went with their intuition in hiring their financial advisor

230 *David Dunning*

(Williams et al., 2013). They have to ask whether they might harbor any ulterior motives that may distort their reasoning (Baumeister & Newman, 1994; Dunning, 2001; Kunda, 1990).

Concluding Remarks

The inevitable truth of modern life is that one must ultimately live under the shadow of potential vulnerability. As British novelist Graham Greene (1943) sagely noted, "It is impossible to go through life without trust," for to live without it would mean "to be imprisoned in the worst cell of all, oneself" (p. 43). As such, a central task for any individual is to learn how to trust without letting that trust slip into gullibility. What this chapter reinforces is the notion that mastering the art of trust necessarily includes learning when to trust – or to be wary of – one of the most important people in our lives, namely, ourselves.

Acknowledgements

Preparation of this chapter was supported by a grant from the University of Connecticut Institute for Humility and Conviction in Public Life, underwritten by the Templeton Foundation, entitled "Epistemic Trespassing in Public Discourse," awarded to David Dunning and Nathan Ballantyne.

Note

1 To be sure, people are influenced by others, as was shown in Sherif's original experiments on the auto-kinetic effect (Sherif, 1937). But here is an interesting question: What if Sherif had brought in two participants who had been exposed to differing norms about how much the light had moved in the darkness. Would they establish a new compromise norm or instead argue over how much the light had moved? After all, I always thought that dress was white and gold (BBC, 2015).

References

Anderson, J., & Rainie, L. (2017). *The future of truth and misinformation online.* Washington, DC: Pew Research Center.

Baumeister, R. F., & Newman, L. S. (1994). Self-regulation of cognitive inference and decision processes. *Personality and Social Psychology Bulletin, 20,* 3–19.

BBC. (2015, February 27). *Optical illusion: Dress colour debate goes global.* Retrieved from www.bbc.co.uk/news/uk-scotland-highlands-islands-31656935.

Ben-David, I., Graham, J. R., & Harvey, C. R. (2013). Managerial miscalibration. *Quarterly Journal of Economics, 128,* 1547–1584.

Bonaccio, S., & Dalal, R. S. (2006). Advice taking and decision-making: An integrative literature review, and implications for the organizational sciences. *Organizational Behavior and Human Decision Processes, 101,* 127–151.

Capen, E. C., Clapp, R. V., & Campbell, W. M. (1971). Competitive bidding in high-risk situations. *Journal of Petroleum Technology, 23,* 641–653.

Caputo, D. D., & Dunning, D. (2005). What you don't know: The role played by errors of omission in imperfect self-assessments. *Journal of Experimental Social Psychology, 41*, 488–505.

Conan Doyle, A. (1915). *The valley of fear*. New York, NY: George H. Doran.

Dunning, D. (2001). On the motives underlying social cognition. In N. Schwarz & A. Tesser (Eds.), *Blackwell handbook of social psychology: Volume 1: Intraindividual processes* (pp. 348–374). New York, NY: Blackwell.

Dunning, D. (2005). *Self-insight: Roadblocks and detours on the path to knowing thyself.* New York, NY: Psychology Press.

Dunning, D. (2011). The Dunning-Kruger effect: On being ignorant of one's own ignorance. In J. Olson & M. P. Zanna (Eds.), *Advances in experimental social psychology* (Vol. 44, pp. 247–296). New York, NY: Elsevier.

Dunning, D. (2018). *The Dunning-Kruger effect as assessed via the overprecision paradigm.* Unpublished manuscript, University of Michigan.

Dunning, D. (in press). The best option illusion in self and social assessment. *Self & Social Identity.*

Dunning, D., & Cone, J. (2018). *The Cassandra quandary: How flawed expertise prevents people from recognizing superior knowledge among their peers.* Unpublished manuscript. University of Michigan.

Dunning, D., Heath, C., & Suls, J. (2004). Flawed self-assessment: Implications for health, education, and the workplace. *Psychological Science in the Public Interest, 5,* 71–106.

Dunning, D., Johnson, K., Ehrlinger, J., & Kruger, J. (2003). Why people fail to recognize their own incompetence. *Current Directions in Psychological Science, 12,* 83–86.

Dunning, D., & Roh, S. (2018). *Everyday paralogia: How mistaken beliefs bolster a false sense of expertise.* Unpublished manuscript, University of Michigan.

Ehrlinger, J., Johnson, K., Banner, M., Dunning, D., & Kruger, J. (2008). Why the unskilled are unaware? Further explorations of (lack of) self-insight among the incompetent. *Organizational Behavior and Human Decision Processes, 105,* 98–121.

Elwin, E. (2013). Living and learning: Reproducing beliefs in selective experience. *Journal of Behavioral Decision Making, 26,* 327–337.

Elwin, E., Juslin, P., Olsson, H., & Enkvist, T. (2007). Constructivist coding: Learning from selective feedback. *Psychological Science, 18,* 105–110.

Fetchenhauer, D., & Dunning, D. (2010). Why so cynical? Asymmetric feedback underlies misguided skepticism in the trustworthiness of others. *Psychological Science, 21,* 189–193.

Fischhoff, B., Slovic, P., & Lichtenstein, S. (1977). Knowing with certainty: The appropriateness of extreme confidence. *Journal of Experimental Psychology: Human Perception and Performance, 3,* 552–564.

Greene, G. (1943). *The ministry of fear.* New York, NY: Penguin.

Greenspan, S. (2008). *Annals of gullibility: Why we get duped and how to avoid it.* Westport, CT: Praeger.

Greenspan, S. (2009, January 3). Why we keep falling for financial scams. *Wall Street Journal.*

Gregg, A. P., Mahadevan, N., & Sedikides, C. (2017). The SPOT effect: People spontaneously prefer their own theories. *Quarterly Journal of Experimental Psychology, 70,* 996–1010.

Griffin, D., & Tversky, A. (1992). The weighing of evidence and the determinants of confidence. *Cognitive Psychology, 24,* 411–435.

232 *David Dunning*

Griffin, G. (2009, December 2). Scam expert from CU expertly scammed. *Denver Post*.

Hall, M. P., & Raimi, K. T. (2018). Is belief superiority justified by superior knowledge? *Journal of Experimental Social Psychology*, *76*, 290–306.

Han, Y., & Dunning, D. (2018a). *Experts are more confident even when they are wrong.* Unpublished manuscript, University of Michigan.

Han, Y., & Dunning, D. (2018b). *The role of guessing in biased self-assessment: Implications for the Dunning-Kruger effect.* Unpublished manuscript, University of Michigan.

Harvey, N., & Fischer, I. (1997). Taking advice: Accepting help, improving judgment, and sharing responsibility. *Organizational Behavior and Human Decision Processes*, *70*, 117–133.

Heck, P. R., Simons, D. J., & Chabris, C. F. (2018). 65% of Americans believe they are above average in intelligence: Results of two nationally representative surveys. *PLoS ONE*, *13*, e0200103.

Henriksson, M. P., Elwin, E., & Juslin, P. (2010). What is coded into memory in the absence of outcome feedback? *Journal of Experimental Psychology: Learning, Memory, and Cognition*, *36*, 1–16.

Holley, P. (2017, July 1). No, NASA is not hiding kidnapped children on Mars. *Washington Post*.

Jiang, J. J., Muhanna, W. A., & Pick, R. A. (1996). The impact of model performance history information on users' confidence in decision models: An experimental examination. *Computers in Human Behavior*, *12*, 193–207.

Kruger, J., & Dunning, D. (1999). Unskilled and unaware of it: How difficulties in recognizing one's own incompetence lead to inflated self-assessments. *Journal of Personality and Social Psychology*, *77*, 1121–1134.

Kunda, Z. (1990). The case for motivated reasoning. *Psychological Bulletin*, *108*, 480–498.

Laplante, P. A., & Neill, C. J. (2005). *Antipatterns: Identification, refactoring and management.* Boca Raton, FL: Auerbach Publications.

Lichtenstein, S., Fischhoff, B., & Phillips, L. D. (1982). Calibration of probabilities: The state of the art to 1980. In D. Kahneman, P. Slovic, & A. Tversky (Eds.), *Judgment under uncertainty: Heuristics and biases.* Cambridge, UK: Cambridge University.

Marsh, E. J., Cantor, A. D., & Brashier, N. M. (2016). Believing that humans swallow spiders in their sleep: False beliefs as side effects of the processes that support accurate knowledge. *Psychology of Learning and Motivation*, *64*, 93–132.

Massey, C., & Thaler, R. H. (2013). The loser's curse: Decision making and market efficiency in the National Football League draft. *Management Science*, *59*, 1479–1495.

Moore, D. A., & Healy, P. J. (2008). The trouble with overconfidence. *Psychological Review*, *115*, 502.

Motta, M., Callaghan, T., & Sylvester, S. (2018). Knowing less but presuming more: Dunning-Kruger effects and the endorsement of anti-vaccine policy attitudes. *Social Science & Medicine*, *211*, 274–281.

Nelson, M. W., Bloomfield, R., Hales, J. W., & Libby, R. (2001). The effect of information strength and weight on behavior in financial markets. *Organizational Behavior and Human Decision Processes*, *86*, 168–196.

Pronin, E., Lin, D. Y., & Ross, L. (2002). The bias blind spot: Perceptions of bias in self and others. *Personality and Social Psychology Bulletin, 28,* 369–381.

Raimi, K. T., & Leary, M. R. (2014). Belief superiority in the environmental domain: Attitude extremity and reactions to fracking. *Journal of Environmental Psychology, 40,* 76–85.

Russo, J. E., & Schoemaker, P. J. H. (1992). Managing overconfidence. *Sloan Management Review, 33,* 7–17.

Sanchez, C., & Dunning, D. (2018). Overconfidence among beginners: Is a little learning a dangerous thing? *Journal of Personality and Social Psychology, 114,* 10–28.

Sedikides, C., Meek, R., Alicke, M. D., & Taylor, S. (2014). Behind bars but above the bar: Prisoners consider themselves more prosocial than non-prisoners. *British Journal of Social Psychology, 53,* 396–403.

Shellenbarger, S. (2016, November 21). Most students don't know when news is fake, Stanford study finds. *Wall Street Journal.*

Sherif, M. (1937). An experimental approach to the study of attitudes. *Sociometry, 1,* 90–98.

Soll, J. B., & Larrick, R. P. (2009). Strategies for revising judgment: How (and how well) people use others' opinions. *Journal of Experimental Psychology: Learning, Memory, and Cognition, 35,* 780–805.

Thaler, R. H. (1988). The winner's curse. *Journal of Economic Perspectives, 2,* 191–202.

Toner, K., Leary, M. R., Asher, M. W., & Jongman-Sereno, K. P. (2013). Feeling superior is a bipartisan issue: Extremity (not direction) of political views predicts perceived belief superiority. *Psychological Science, 24,* 2454–2462.

van Loon, M. H., de Bruin, A. B. H., van Gog, T., & van Merriënboer, J. J. G. (2013). Activation of inaccurate prior knowledge affects primary-school students' metacognitive judgments and calibration. *Learning and Instruction, 24,* 15–25.

Williams, E. F., Dunning, D., & Kruger, J. (2013). The hobgoblin of consistency: Algorithmic judgment strategies underlie inflated self-assessments of performance. *Journal of Personality and Social Psychology, 104,* 976–994.

Wu, K., & Dunning, D. (2018). Hypocognition: Making sense of the world beyond one's conceptual reach. *Review of General Psychology, 22,* 25–35.

Yan, H., & Dunning, D. (2017). *The paradox of advice: Behavioral implications self-misassessment.* Unpublished manuscript, University of Michigan.

Yaniv, I. (2004). Receiving other people's advice: Influence and benefit. *Organizational Behavior and Human Decision Processes, 93,* 1–13.

Yaniv, I., & Kleinberger, E. (2000). Advice taking in decision making: Egocentric discounting and reputation formation. *Organizational Behavior and Human Decision Processes, 83,* 260–281.

13 The Smell of Suspicion

How the Nose Curbs Gullibility

Norbert Schwarz
UNIVERSITY OF SOUTHERN CALIFORNIA

Spike W. S. Lee
UNIVERSITY OF TORONTO

Suspicion is a mental state of doubt, leading us to wonder whether things may not be what they seem to be. Is the pricey gadget really as good as the sales person suggests? Did that colleague really mean it when he complimented us, or did he merely want to make us more receptive for the request that followed a few minutes later? And what about the faint smell of perfume on the husband's jacket when he returned from that conference? Not surprisingly, many observers warned that suspicion can cloud the mind and undermine cooperation and social relationships (for a discussion from the seventeenth century, see Bacon, 1893). Others observed that suspicion motivates extensive information search (e.g., Fein, 1996) and (sometimes) sophisticated reasoning (e.g., Fein, McCloskey, & Tomlinson, 1997; Mayo, 2015) to reduce ambiguity. These analyses usually focused on attributes of specific acts or attributes of the actor, the perceiver, and the nature of their interdependence (e.g., Deutsch, 1958; Kee & Knox, 1970) to understand the antecedents of suspicion.

In contrast, everyday discourse often addresses suspicion in metaphorical terms that do not reference specific acts or attributes of the actor. Instead, perceivers may simply note that something "smells fishy" or does "not pass the smell test." While such metaphorical expressions have long been considered mere linguistic quirks, recent research showed that human thought about abstract concepts is grounded in more concrete sensory experience in the physical domain, as reviewed below. Building on this work, we tested whether incidental exposure to "smells of suspicion" is sufficient to influence people's behavior and trigger a "skeptical mindset" (see also Mayo, Chapter 8 this volume). This chapter summarizes what we learned.

We first identify metaphorical links between smell and suspicion and place them in the context of recent research into metaphors and grounded cognition. Next, we show that incidental exposure to fishy smells is sufficient to undermine cooperation in economic trust and public good games. Turning to suspicion's influence on reasoning, we further show that fishy smells increase the detection of misleading information and facilitate critical reasoning, including a more critical analysis of one's own beliefs (see also Dunning, Chapter 12 this volume). We highlight how other manipulations of distrust produce parallel effects, providing converging evidence for interpreting the influence of incidental smells as a case of suspicion. The observed relationship between suspicion and smell is bidirectional: exposure to a fishy smell induces social suspicion and the induction of suspicion through social means, conversely, increases people's sensitivity to metaphorically relevant odors. Taking a step back, we end the chapter by discussing the likely evolutionary basis of the smell–suspicion link and the role of incidental sensory experiences in the broader context of the situated, embodied, experiential, and pragmatic nature of human cognition.

Smell and Suspicion

A rapidly growing body of research highlights the role of sensory experience in cognition and emotion (for reviews, see Barsalou, 2008; Landau, 2017; Landau, Meier, & Keefer, 2010; S. W. S. Lee & Schwarz, 2014; Schwarz & Lee, 2019). The influences of interest are usually reflected in metaphors that link an abstract target concept with a more concrete source concept derived from sensory or bodily experience. For example, saying that a "warm" person discusses "weighty" matters with a "close" friend conveys social meanings through reference to the physical dimensions of temperature, weight, and spatial distance. More important, variations in perceivers' sensory experience have metaphor-consistent social effects: people perceive others as socially warmer after holding a warm rather than cold cup of coffee (Williams & Bargh, 2008a), consider the same book more important when its heft is increased through a concealed weight (Chandler, Reinhard, & Schwarz, 2012; Jostmann, Lakens, & Schubert, 2009), and experience more emotional distance after having marked spatially distant rather than close points on a Cartesian plane (Williams & Bargh, 2008b).

One of the sensory experiences metaphorically related to the psychological state of suspicion is smell. In languages around the world, saying that something does not "smell right," "has a smell," or fails to pass a "smell test" conveys that one doubts whether things are what seems to meet the eye. Linguistic analyses of 18 languages (Soriano & Valenzuela, 2008), including Arabic, Chinese, English, French, German, Hungarian, and Spanish, documented the smell–suspicion association in every language studied. However, languages differ in which odor they specify as the smell of suspicion. For example, in English, the smell of suspicion is "fishy," in German it is "foul," and Italians catch "a whiff" that remains unspecified. This suggests that the smell–suspicion link may be a universal conceptual metaphor with culture specific instantiations. When a smell is specified, it is the smell of decaying organic matter that may be used as food, suggesting that the smell–suspicion link is an evolved mechanism that protects against premature ingestion of "suspicious" material: When you bring it close to your mouth and it doesn't "smell right" you better check it out more carefully – it may be something that should be rejected rather than ingested.

236 *Norbert Schwarz and Spike W. S. Lee*

While this conjecture provides a plausible evolutionary account for why smell may be linked with suspicion, readers may wonder why this association should generalize beyond the assessment of smelly substances that one may eat? As observed for many subjective experiences – from bodily arousal (Zillman, 1978) to moods (Schwarz & Clore, 1983; see also Forgas, Chapter 10 this volume), emotions (Schwarz, Servay, & Kumpf, 1985) and meta-cognitive experiences of ease or difficulty (Schwarz et al., 1991) – people are more sensitive to their momentary experience than to its source (for reviews, see Schwarz, 2012; Schwarz & Clore, 2007). Hence, they misread their experience as bearing on whatever they currently focus on, even when the experience is elicited by an unrelated influence. We assume that the same is true for sensory experiences of metaphorical relevance and the subjective response they elicit – once a smell induces suspicion, it will be brought to bear on the task at hand. If so, a "suspicious" smell should influence one's response to a wide range of tasks to which suspicion may be relevant. Most importantly, it should reduce interpersonal trust and cooperation and influence judgment and reasoning in ways that parallel the influence of other manipulations of distrust and skepticism (see also Mayo, Chapter 8 this volume). Empirically, this is the case.

Fishy Smells Curb Social Cooperation

People are attuned to a wide variety of cues that signal whether to trust or suspect. These signals include attributes of the target person, such as reputation (Burt & Knez, 1996), facial features (Zebrowitz, 1997), and nonverbal behaviors (Bond et al., 1992); attributes of the perceiver, such as risk calculations (Dasgupta, 1988); and attributes of the context, such as social distance (Buchan & Croson, 2004), task structure (Sheppard & Sherman, 1998), and risk of betrayal (Bohnet & Zeckhauser, 2004). These cues reliably influence behavior in economic games designed to test different aspects of social cooperation (see also Krueger, Vogrincic-Haselbacher, & Evans, Chapter 6 this volume). Hence, these games are a suitable tool for testing the influence of incidental odors.

Trust Games: Will the Partner Reciprocate?

One type of economic game addresses issues of reciprocation: If I do something beneficial for you, will you reciprocate and do something good for me? In a typical game, decision-maker A receives an endowment from the researcher (say, $5 in quarters) and can freely decide how much of it, if any, he or she wants to send to decision-maker B. The researcher will increase any amount sent by some factor (say, a factor of 4), turning, for example, A's contribution of $2 into $8. Decision-maker B can then decide how much, if any, of this money he or she wants to send back to decision-maker A. If A suspects that B may walk off with the money, A should not share anything.

If A trusts B to reciprocate, A should send B as much money as possible, turning the initial $5 into $20 after the researcher quadruples it. Of that sum, a "fair" partner would supposedly return more than A's initial $5 – yet an unfair one may simply walk off with the full $20. Would A's decision be influenced by an incidental smell?

To test this possibility, we (S. W. S. Lee & Schwarz, 2012, study 1) had an experimenter spray fish oil, fart spray, or odorless water at a corner area in a campus building. Another experimenter, blind to the smell condition, approached students in the hallway and invited them to participate in a one-shot trust game with another "participant," who was a confederate. Both players were escorted to the sprayed area. Each player received 20 quarters ($5) and an investment form with instructions and response space. The true participant was always approached first and designated as the sender, who could decide how much money to send. Any amount sent would be quadrupled in value. As shown in Figure 13.1, participants in the odorless condition sent $3.34 of their $5 endowment to their partner. An incidental fishy smell significantly reduced this sum to $2.53, a drop of about 25%. This effect was specific to the fishy smell condition and not observed for a different aversive and disgusting smell, the smell of flatulence produced by an (aptly named) "fart spray." This negative influence of fishy smells on cooperation in one-shot trust games has been replicated by Sheaffer, Gal, and Pansky (2017, study 1).

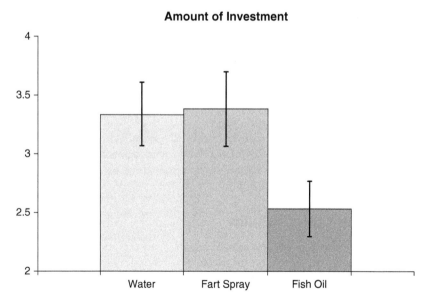

Figure 13.1 Amount of investment in a one-shot trust game as a function of incidental smell in study 1. Error bars represent standard errors.

Source: S. W. S. Lee and Schwarz (2012, study 1).

Public Good Games: Will the Partner Be a Free-Rider?

Another type of economic game addresses issues of free-riding: Will the partner contribute his or her share to a common good or take a free ride and enjoy the good without making a contribution? In this type of game, each participant receives an endowment (say, $5 in quarters) and decides how much he or she wants to contribute to a common pool. The researcher multiplies the money in the pool by some factor (say, 1.8). Finally, the amount in the pool is equally divided among all players, independent of what they contributed. If player A suspects that the other player(s) will not contribute, A should simply keep the endowment. If A can assume that the other(s) contribute as well, all are better off the larger the pool that will be equally divided among them.

Following the procedures described above, we (S. W. S. Lee & Schwarz, 2012, study 2) tested the influence of incidental smells on cooperation in this game. Exposure to a fishy smell again reduced cooperation: participants contributed $3.86 of their endowment under neutral smell conditions, but only $2.65 under fishy smell conditions. Incidental exposure to a fart smell did not significantly affect their contribution ($3.38).

Using a similar one-shot public good game, Sebastian, Kaufmann, and de la Piedad Garcia (2017) replicated the negative influence of incidental fishy smells, as well as the lack of influence of fart smell, in Australia. They also observed that a fishy smell was sufficient to overcome the influence of dispositional trust on cooperation. In their study, a measure of dispositional trust (taken from Yamagishi & Yamagishi, 1994) predicted participants' contributions under neutral smell conditions but not under fishy smell conditions.

Summary

In combination, these studies highlight that incidental exposure to a subtle smell with metaphorical meaning is sufficient to elicit suspicion about others' motives and trustworthiness, with adverse effects on cooperative behavior. The effect is not driven by the generic valence of the sensory experience but by its specific metaphorical associations, as the comparisons between fishy and farty smells indicate.

Fishy Smells Curb Gullibility

Suspicion is a mental state in which people "suspect" that something is wrong but are uncertain what it might be. They wonder how things may be different from what meets the eye and are likely to entertain alternative perspectives and interpretations to assess their plausibility. Indeed, experiences of suspicion and distrust are associated with increased generation of alternative interpretations (Fein, 1996; Schul, Burnstein, & Bardi, 1996), increased accessibility of opposing concepts (Schul, Mayo, & Burnstein, 2004), and more divergent reasoning (Mayer & Mussweiler, 2011). While the observation that fishy smells curb social cooperation is indicative of reduced trust, it is silent on whether incidental exposure to fishy smells also affects cognitive performance – after all, deciding not to part from one's money when something feels wrong does not require complex reasoning. We therefore turned to classic reasoning tasks to test whether incidental exposure to fishy smells curbs gullibility and increases critical thinking.

Identifying Misleading Information: There's Something Fishy About this Question

A key element of guarding against potential attempts to mislead us is the critical examination of what others have to say: Does their utterance make sense? May things be different from what was said? These concerns should prompt close attention to the details of a message to test whether something is wrong. Accordingly, people should be more likely to identify misleading information when they feel suspicious than when they do not. However, it is also conceivable that suspicion and the "skeptical mindset" it triggers foster the rejection of any information, independent of its veracity (see also Mayo, Chapter 8 this volume).

A task that allows researchers to assess people's sensitivity to misleading information that is subtly embedded in a seemingly innocuous question was developed by Erickson and Mattson (1981) and became known as the "Moses illusion." Participants are asked to answer trivia questions and informed that they may or may not encounter questions that lack a correct answer if taken literally. For example, the question "In which year did Obama fly to the moon?" presupposes something that did not happen, making it impossible to answer with a year. Participants are asked to mark those questions as ones that cannot be answered, while giving substantive answers to all questions that can be answered. In this paradigm, most people who are asked "How many animals of each kind did Moses take on the Ark?" answer "Two" despite being able to report that the biblical actor was Noah, not Moses, when directly asked (Erickson & Mattson, 1981). People fail to notice the distortion in the question because of the semantic overlap (Park & Reder, 2003) between Moses and Noah – both are old men associated with water in biblical stories. This gives the Moses question a feeling of familiarity or "fluency" (see also Unkelbach & Koch, Chapter 3 this volume) that reduces the likelihood that people notice that something is wrong – it feels like they heard this before.

Manipulations that make the question feel less familiar attenuate the Moses illusion. In general, familiar material is easier to process than novel material – it is easier to recognize, read, pronounce, and remember (Schwarz, 2004, 2015). But not everything that is easy to process is also familiar. Instead, the ease of processing may be due to other variables, such as a difficult to read print font, poor color contrast, or a hard to understand

240 *Norbert Schwarz and Spike W. S. Lee*

accent. Unfortunately, people are often more sensitive to their feelings than to where their feelings come from. They therefore misread ease of processing as bearing on what they are thinking about, even when it is merely due to an incidental variable, such as the print font (see also Forgas, Chapter 10 this volume). Hence, Song and Schwarz (2008) found that 88% of their participants failed to notice the distortion in the Moses question when it was presented in an easy to read print font (black Arial 12), whereas only 53% failed to notice when it was presented in a difficult to read print font (grey Brush script 12).

This experimental paradigm provides a test of the potential influence of fishy smells: Would an incidental fishy smell make it more likely that people notice something is wrong with Moses? To find out, we included the above Moses question and its likes in a questionnaire that participants completed in a booth that did or did not have a fishy odor (D. S. Lee, Kim, & Schwarz, 2015, study 1). Participants received instructions from an experimenter who was blind to conditions and were then assigned to an experimental booth in which another experimenter had attached a small piece of paper sprayed with fish oil (or water) under the table. As expected, an incidental fishy smell attenuated the Moses illusion. Whereas 83.3% of participants in the neutral smell condition failed to notice that something was wrong with Moses, only 58.1% failed to notice in the fishy smell condition. We also included an undistorted question, "Which country is famous for cuckoo clocks, chocolate, banks, and pocket knives?" The correct answer is "Switzerland" and participants' performance on this question was unaffected by the smell to which they were exposed, indicating that the smell of suspicion elicited critical analysis rather than a general tendency to reject statements as misleading.

In a different experimental paradigm, introduced by Loftus, Miller, and Burns (1978), misleading questions are used to implant false memories. In a typical study, participants see a series of slides that visually portray an event, for example, an accident involving a car and a pedestrian. Next, they answer questions about the event and some of these questions include a misleading proposition; for example, participants may be asked whether the car stopped at the stop sign, even though there was no stop sign in the scene they saw. After a delay, people who were asked a question that implied the presence of a stop sign erroneously "recognize" a stop sign as having been part of what they saw. This false memory effect is attenuated when participants are alerted that something may be wrong with the questions asked (Green, Flynn, & Loftus, 1982) or when a negative mood provides a more general problem signal (see Forgas, Chapter 10 this volume). Would a fishy smell similarly protect people against false memories? To find out, Sheaffer and her colleagues (2017, study 2) presented the misleading questions in a room that had been sprayed with a fishy or a pleasant smell. Next, they tested their participants' recognition memory 48 hours later, in a neutral smell context. Those who had thought about the questions in the presence of a fishy smell were now less likely to erroneously "recognize" objects that were mentioned in the questions, but absent in the original scene. Presumably, suspicion at the time of reading the questions resulted in closer scrutiny, which reduced the impact of the misleading information.

In combination, the Moses study (D. S. Lee et al., 2015, study 1) and false memory study (Sheaffer et al., 2017, study 2) converge on indicating that olfactory suspicion cues can curb gullibility. In the Moses study, an incidental fishy smell improved the identification of a misleading question without inducing a bias to falsely identify an undistorted question as problematic. In the false memory study, an incidental fishy smell decreased the likelihood that elements of the question were incorporated into the memory of the scene, presumably because participants noticed that something may be wrong with the question. Future research may fruitfully address whether fishy smells can also influence the impressions we form of other people, even when those people do not engage in any suspicious behavior. To date, research into suspicion effects in person perception has focused on conditions where suspicion is elicited by information about the target person (Fein, 1996; Hilton & Darley, 1991) and has largely neglected the potential influence of incidental suspicion.

Thinking Critically About One's Own Thoughts: May I Be Wrong?

Suspicion pertains to things others do or say. Hence, the influence of olfactory suspicion cues may be limited to how we think about information presented by others, as in the above experiments. However, incidental influences on how we feel and think usually generalize to unrelated tasks, as has been observed for moods and emotions (for a review, see Schwarz & Clore, 2007), distrust (for reviews, see Mayo, 2015; Mayo, Chapter 8 this volume), and a wide range of cognitive procedures (for a review, see Xu & Schwarz, 2018; see also Fiedler, Chapter 7 this volume; Krueger et al., Chapter 6 this volume; Strack, Chapter 9 this volume; Unkelbach & Koch, Chapter 3 this volume). Hence, the distrust elicited reasoning shifts observed in the preceding studies may carry over to how critically we examine our own thoughts.

Wason's (1960) classic rule discovery task lends itself to testing this possibility. In this task, participants are asked to discover the rule underlying the number series 2–4–6. Most assume that the rule is "+2." Next, they are instructed to test their assumption by generating a number series that the experimenter will mark as consistent or inconsistent with the correct rule. Following this feedback, participants can correct their hypothesis and state what they now think the correct rule is.

In all published studies, people overwhelmingly rely on a positive-testing strategy (Klayman & Ha, 1987) and generate number series that are consistent with their hypothesis (e.g., 6–8–10; for a review, see Oswald & Grosjean, 2004). The feedback they receive on these series always informs them that their series is compatible with the rule. Although correct, this affirmative feedback does not allow them to recognize that their hypothesis is false. The correct rule is, somewhat sneakily, "Any increasing series of numbers." Participants can only discover the correct rule when they generate at least some series that can falsify their own +2 hypothesis. Hence, discovery of the correct rule is facilitated by a negative testing strategy, aimed at disconfirmation, and impaired by a positive testing strategy, aimed at confirmation (for a review, see Oswald & Grosjean, 2004).

If distrust and suspicion make people consider how things may be otherwise, they may facilitate a negative testing strategy and hence improve detection of the correct rule. Indeed, Mayo, Alfasi, and Schwarz (2014, study 1) observed that people who are very low in dispositional trust perform better on this task than people high in dispositional trust. Moreover, experimentally inducing distrust through exposure to an untrustworthy face increases the prevalence of negative hypothesis testing, again resulting in improved rule discovery (Mayo et al., 2014, study 2; see also Mayo, Chapter 8 this volume). Would the presence of an incidental smell similarly induce people to be more critical in testing their own, self-generated hypotheses?

To find out, participants had to work on Wason's (1960) rule discovery task in a cubicle that had a fishy or neutral smell (D. S. Lee et al., 2015, study 2). They first received their instructions from an experimenter who was blind to conditions and were then assigned to a cubicle that another experimenter had prepared with the respective smell. After generating six test series, participants called the experimenter and received feedback on their series. Finally, they reported what they now thought the rule was, given the feedback they received.

The results parallel the findings of Mayo and colleagues (2014). Overall, all participants generated more confirmatory than disconfirmatory number series, independent of smell condition. Nevertheless, smell significantly influenced whether participants made *any* attempt to disconfirm. Specifically, 47.7% (21 out of 44) of the participants assigned to the fishy cubicle listed at least one negative hypothesis, whereas only 27.7% (13 out of 47) of those assigned to the neutral smelling cubicle did so. This difference in testing strategy is also reflected in the likelihood of discovering the correct rule. Whereas only 6.4% of the participants in the neutral smell condition discovered the correct rule, 20.5% in the fishy smell condition did so.

Sebastian and colleagues (2017) replicated this result in Australia, adding a fart spray condition as an additional control. In their study, participants exposed to an incidental fishy smell were twice as likely to generate at least one negative hypothesis test than participants exposed to an incidental fart smell. The latter condition did not significantly differ from a neutral smell condition, again indicating that the influence of fishy smells does not merely reflect their aversive or disgusting nature (S. W. S. Lee & Schwarz, 2012).

Summary

In combination, the reviewed studies indicate that incidental exposure to olfactory cues that are metaphorically related to suspicion can curb gullibility. They make people more likely to scrutinize information they receive from others, which increases the correct identification of misleading questions (D. S. Lee et al., 2015, study 1) and reduces the generation of false memories (Sheaffer et al., 2017, study 2). This more critical approach to information is not limited to the examination of material presented by others, but can carry over to assessments of one's own thoughts. When asked to test their own, self-generated hypotheses, people take a more critical approach to testing when exposed to a smell of suspicion (D. S. Lee et al., 2015, study 2; Sebastian et al., 2017). This influence of olfactory cues parallels the influence of other cues that something may be wrong, including chronic or temporary distrust (Mayo et al., 2014) and low processing fluency (Song & Schwarz, 2008).

Suspicion Increases Sensitivity to Fishy Smells

The reviewed findings are consistent with metaphors that associate suspicion with smell. The representational structure of these metaphors implies a unidirectional influence from smell to suspicion. However, such unidirectional metaphors can nevertheless produce bidirectional associations between their core concepts, as we discuss in detail elsewhere (S. W. S. Lee & Schwarz, 2012; S. W. S. Lee, 2016; see also, Ijzerman & Koole, 2011). Indeed, inducing social suspicion increases perceivers' sensitivity to fishy smells without affecting their sensitivity to other smells.

In several studies, we handed participants a set of test tubes containing fragrance oils or food substances, such as cinnamon, orange nectar, minced onion, and fish oil. Participants sniffed each tube and wrote down any smell that came to mind (S. W. S. Lee & Schwarz, 2012, studies 3a–3c). Prior to this task, the experimenter did or did not engage in behavior that suggested she may be hiding something, thus eliciting participants' suspicion. Three variants of this procedure, using different combinations and intensities of pleasant and unpleasant smells, converged on the same conclusion: a socially induced state of suspicion significantly enhances the correct identification of fishy smells. When the fishy smell was blatant and 50% of participants identified it correctly without suspicion, suspicion increased identification to 72.5%; when the smell was subtle and only 6.7% identified it without suspicion, suspicion increased correct identification to 33.3%. In contrast, suspicion did not significantly influence the identification of any of the other smells.

Additional research showed that suspicion selectively increases people's ability to detect subtle fishy smells presented at low levels of concentration (S. W. S. Lee & Schwarz, 2012, study 7). In this study, participants received 31 test flasks that contained either no odor or the target odor (fish oil or fart spray) at three different levels of concentration. They were asked to identify whether the target odor was present. As shown in Figure 13.2, compared with non-suspicious

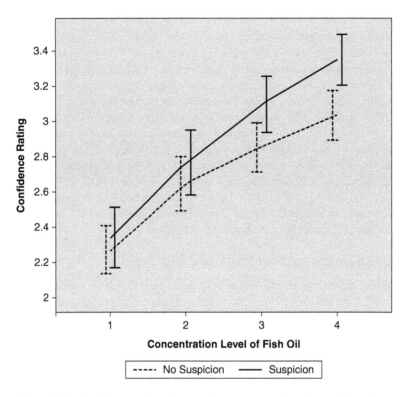

Figure 13.2 Confidence ratings for smell presence as a function of fish oil concentration with and without suspicion. Error bars represent 95% confidence intervals.

Source: S. W. S. Lee and Schwarz (2012, study 7).

participants, suspicious participants' confidence ratings increased more sharply with the concentration of fish oil, indicating that it increased their sensitivity to low levels of the odor. This was not observed for fart spray, indicating that the effect of suspicion is limited to metaphorically associated smells and does not generalize to other smells of an unpleasant nature. Equally important, suspicion did not increase participants' overall confidence ratings for fish oil or fart spray, indicating that it did not induce a response bias. Instead, the effect was limited to low levels of concentration of the metaphorically related smell, documenting increased odor specific sensory sensitivity.

Perspectives on Gullibility

The Situated, Experiential, Embodied, and Pragmatic Mind

The findings we reviewed in this chapter can be discussed from the perspective of evolutionary, cognitive, affective, and embodied theorizing.

The Smell of Suspicion   245

It is tempting to favor one or the other to identify the "real" process underlying the observed bidirectional relationships between olfactory cues, feeling, and thinking. However, the different theoretical perspectives are not mutually exclusive and we conclude this chapter with a discussion of their interplay.

Evolution

That smell and suspicion are associated in different cultures and languages around the globe (Soriano & Valenzuela, 2008) suggests a universal metaphorical association with culture-specific implementations. From an evolutionary perspective, it would be adaptive to step back and take the time for closer inspection when something that one may touch or ingest does not smell right. Indeed, a hesitant response to things that have the wrong smell is shared by many organisms (Herz, 2011). To be adaptive, this response should not be limited to the smell that is specified in the metaphors of one's culture but should also be elicited by other smells that pose the same adaptive problem. If so, a fishy smell should elicit suspicion even when one's culture that does not specify "fishy" as the smell of suspicion. The limited available evidence is compatible with this prediction. As noted earlier, Sheaffer and colleagues (2017) observed that fishy smells undermined cooperation in a public goods game (study 1) and attenuated the impact of misleading information (study 2). Importantly, they obtained these results with Israeli participants in studies administered in Hebrew, a language that does not specify "fishy" as the smell of suspicion. Future research may fruitfully explore the influence of a broader range of odors across a broader range of cultures and languages.

Metaphors

From an evolutionary perspective, smell-suspicion metaphors are themselves an expression of an evolved adaptive mechanism. But this does not preclude that the culture specific implementations of the general smell-suspicion metaphor can have a unique causal impact (see also Baumeister, Maxwell, Thomas, & Vohs, Chapter 2 this volume). Several aspects of this assumption are worth systematic testing. One pertains to the relative impact of different smells. Frequent exposure to the metaphors of one's culture should strengthen the link between suspicion and the culturally specified smell, which should make this particular smell more influential than other adaptively relevant smells. We would expect, for example, that "fishy" as well as "foul" smells can elicit suspicion in Americans as well as Germans but that both respond more strongly to the smell specified in their respective cultural metaphors. Unfortunately, any test of differences in the relative impact of different smells requires a calibration of smell intensity, which is a challenging task: how much of a fishy smell is equivalent to how much of a foul smell?

246 *Norbert Schwarz and Spike W. S. Lee*

More tractable is the influence of semantic representation. The smell specified by one's cultural metaphors becomes part of one's knowledge about suspicion. Hence, the general rules of *knowledge accessibility* apply. Indeed, priming English speakers with concepts of suspicion increases the accessibility of fish-related concepts (S. W. S. Lee & Schwarz, 2012, study 5). This makes them more likely, for example, to complete the letter string "FI__ING" with FISHING rather than FITTING, FILLING, or another applicable word. The increased accessibility of fish-related concepts, in turn, facilitates the correct identification of fishy smells (S. W. S. Lee & Schwarz, 2012, study 6). Theoretically, semantic representations provide a cognitive pathway for mutual influences between concepts related to suspicion and concepts related to smell that are independent of a concurrent online experience of suspicion. We assume that such knowledge effects are language based and culture specific, making it unlikely, for example, that concepts of suspicion would prime fish-related concepts for German participants.

Feelings

Smell is just one of many variables that can elicit suspicion (see Forgas, Chapter 10 this volume). Indeed, most research into suspicion and distrust has used other manipulations, ranging from memories of bad experiences to attributes of one's interaction partner (Burt & Knez, 1996) and incidental exposure to distrust worthy faces (Mayo et al., 2014). More important, such manipulations have produced results that parallel the impact of smells, as noted throughout this chapter (see Mayo, 2015; Mayo Chapter 8 this volume). These parallel effects highlight that the experience of suspicion is sufficient to reduce social cooperation and gullibility, independent of its specific induction.

As observed in many domains, people are more sensitive to their subjective experiences than to where these experiences come from. Hence, they misread their current feelings and fleeting thoughts as part of their response to whatever is in the focus of their attention. This influences the judgments they form and the processing strategy they choose, as conceptualized in feelings-as-information theory (for reviews, see Schwarz, 2012; Schwarz & Clore, 2007). From this perspective, incidental feelings of suspicion undermine cooperation because they are misperceived as part of one's response to the partner and the nature of the game. If participants became aware of the incidental nature of their feeling, its informational value would be undermined and its influence attenuated or eliminated as has been observed for moods (Schwarz & Clore, 1983), emotions (Schwarz et al., 1985), bodily arousal (Zillman, 1978) and metacognitive experiences of ease and difficulty (Sanna, Schwarz, & Small, 2002). Hence, subtle smells are likely to be more influential than intense smells, which attract more attention and carry a higher risk of awareness. Because feelings are associated with semantic and episodic information about circumstances in which they are experienced

(Bower, 1981; Bower & Forgas, 2001), they also bring to mind related declarative information that further feeds into judgment (for a review, see Forgas, 2001).

In addition to serving as input into a judgment, feelings inform people about the nature of the current situation. As assumed by many accounts of situated cognition (for a review, see Smith & Semin, 2004), thought processes are tuned to meet the requirements of the situation at hand. Feelings play a key role in this tuning process by providing rapidly available information about the current situation (Schwarz, 1990, 2002), usually preceding careful analysis (Zajonc, 1980). When distrust and suspicion signal that things may not be what they seem, processing is oriented towards potential alternative interpretations of reality (see Mayo, 2015; Mayo, Chapter 8 this volume). As reviewed above, this influence is sufficient to overcome one of the most robust biases in the psychology of reasoning, namely reliance on confirmatory hypothesis testing strategies (D. S. Lee et al., 2015; Mayo et al., 2014).

Importantly, suspicion is not the only feeling that can reliably influence people's reasoning strategies. As observed decades ago, people tend to pay less attention to the quality of an argument and are less likely to elaborate on its implications when they are in a happy rather than sad mood (Bless, Bohner, Schwarz, & Strack, 1990). Hence, weak arguments are more persuasive when the audience is in a positive mood, whereas strong arguments are more persuasive when the audience is in a negative mood. Both effects reflect that recipients tend to think less about the message when they feel good rather than bad, leading them to miss its weak as well as strong points (for a review, see Schwarz, Bless, & Bohner, 1991). Particularly relevant in the context of gullibility is the metacognitive experience of processing fluency, which figures prominently in intuitive assessments of truth (for reviews, see Schwarz, 2018; Schwarz, Newman, & Leach, 2016; see also Fiedler, Chapter 7 this volume; Strack, Chapter 9 this volume; Unkelbach & Koch, Chapter 3 this volume). In a nutshell, people's assessments of the veracity of a claim are dominated by five criteria: Is the claim compatible with other things I believe? Is it internally consistent? Does it come from a credible source? Are there many supporting arguments? Do others think so as well? Each of these criteria can be evaluated by drawing on relevant details (an effortful analytic strategy) or by attending to the ease with which the content can be processed (a less effortful intuitive strategy). As a large body of experimental research (reviewed in Schwarz, 2018) indicates, fluent processing provides an affirmative answer to each of these truth tests, even when more careful processing would identify the claim as faulty. Hence, any variable that increases processing fluency – from repetition (e.g., Hasher, Goldstein, & Toppino, 1977; Unkelbach & Koch, Chapter 3 this volume) and color contrast (e.g., Reber & Schwarz, 1999) to rhyme (e.g., McGlone & Tofighbakhsh, 2000), ease of pronunciation (e.g., Newman et al., 2014) and audio quality (e.g., Newman & Schwarz, 2018) – also increases acceptance of the fluently processed message, whereas disfluency curbs acceptance of the message.

Situated, Experiential, Embodied, and Pragmatic

While each of these perspectives sheds light on some aspect of the reviewed research, it is useful to consider their interplay in the overall picture of human feeling and thinking. As William James (1890) emphasized, thinking is for doing. We do things in specific contexts and our pragmatic pursuits benefit from close attention to the situation at hand. This renders the abundantly observed context sensitivity of human cognition beneficial, occasional errors and biases notwithstanding (Schwarz, 2007, 2010; Smith & Semin, 2004). Feelings play a key role in this process by providing fast information about the situation at hand, often before relevant sources can be identified (Zajonc, 1980). Moreover, we interact with the world through our bodies and experience it through our senses. This makes sensorimotor information important and, in evolutionary terms, ancient building blocks for knowledge representation and reasoning (Barsalou, 2008; Lakoff & Johnson, 1999). As the rapidly accumulating evidence for embodied cognition illustrates, higher mental processes are scaffolded onto phylogenetically and ontogenetically older sensorimotor processes, reflecting that evolution is largely a recycle and reuse enterprise (Anderson, 2010, 2014). Many of these linkages are reflected in conceptual metaphors (Lakoff & Johnson, 1999) that have stimulated extensive research into the role of sensorimotor inputs in human judgment and decision-making (for reviews, see Landau, 2017; S. W. S. Lee & Schwarz, 2014; Schwarz & Lee, 2019). The picture that emerges emphasizes the situated, experiential, embodied, and pragmatic nature of human cognition and these features "seep" into everything we do, allowing an incidental fishy smell to impair social cooperation and to curb our gullibility.

References

Anderson, M. L. (2010). Neural reuse: A fundamental organizational principle of the brain. *Behavioral and Brain Sciences, 33*, 245–266.

Anderson, M. L. (2014). *After phrenology: Neural reuse and the interactive brain.* Cambridge, MA: MIT Press.

Bacon, F. (1893). *Essays.* Baltimore, MD: Woodward.

Barsalou, L. W. (2008). Grounded cognition. *Annual Review of Psychology, 59*, 617–645.

Bless, H., Bohner, G., Schwarz, N., & Strack, F. (1990). Mood and persuasion: A cognitive response analysis. *Personality and Social Psychology Bulletin, 16*, 331–345.

Bohnet, I., & Zeckhauser, R. (2004). Trust, risk and betrayal. *Journal of Economic Behavior & Organization, 55*, 467–484.

Bond, C. F., Jr., Omar, A., Pitre, U., Lashley, B. R., Skaggs, L. M., & Kirk, C. T. (1992). Fishy-looking liars: Deception judgment from expectancy violation. *Journal of Personality and Social Psychology, 63*, 969–977.

Bower, G. H. (1981). Mood and memory. *American Psychologist, 36*(2), 129–148.

Bower, G. H., & Forgas, J. P. (2001). Mood and social memory. In J. P. Forgas (Ed.), *Handbook of affect and social cognition* (pp. 95–120). Mahwah, NJ: Lawrence Erlbaum Associates.

Buchan, N., & Croson, R. (2004). The boundaries of trust: Own and others' actions in the US and China. *Journal of Economic Behavior & Organization, 55*, 485–504.

Burt, R. S., & Knez, M. (1996). Trust and third-party gossip. In R. M. Kramer & T. R. Tyler (Eds.), *Trust in organizations: Frontiers of theory and research* (pp. 68–89). Thousand Oaks, CA: Sage.

Chandler, J., Reinhard, D., & Schwarz, N. (2012). To judge a book by its weight you need to know its content: Knowledge moderates the use of embodied cues. *Journal of Experimental Social Psychology, 48*, 948–952. doi:10.1016/j.jesp.2012.03.003

Dasgupta, P. (1988). Trust as a commodity. In D. Gambetta (Ed.), *Trust: Making and breaking cooperative relations* (pp. 49–72). New York, NY: Basil Blackwell.

Deutsch, M. (1958). Trust and suspicion. *Journal of Conflict Resolution, 2*, 265–279.

Erickson, T. A., & Mattson, M. E. (1981). From words to meaning: A semantic illusion. *Journal of Verbal Learning and Verbal Behavior, 20*, 540–552.

Fein, S. (1996). Effects of suspicion on attributional thinking and the correspondence bias. *Journal of Personality and Social Psychology, 70*, 1164–1184.

Fein, S., McCloskey, A. L., & Tomlinson, T. M. (1997). Can the jury disregard that information? The use of suspicion to reduce the prejudicial effects of pretrial publicity and inadmissible testimony. *Personality and Social Psychology Bulletin, 23*(11), 1215–1226.

Forgas, J. P. (2001). The affect infusion model (AIM): An integrative theory of mood effects on cognition and judgment. In L.L. Martin & G.L. Clore (Eds.), *Theories of mood and cognition: A user's guidebook* (pp. 99–134). Mahwah, NJ: Erlbaum.

Greene, E., Flynn, M. S., & Loftus, E. F. (1982). Inducing resistance to misleading information. *Journal of Verbal Learning and Verbal Behavior, 21*, 207–219.

Hasher, L., Goldstein, D., & Toppino, T. (1977). Frequency and the conference of referential validity. *Journal of Verbal Learning & Verbal Behavior, 16*, 107–112.

Herz, R. S. (2011). The emotional, cognitive, and biological basics of olfaction: implications and considerations for scent marketing. In A, Krishna (Ed.), *Sensory marketing* (pp. 117–138). London: Routledge.

Hilton, J. L., & Darley, J. M. (1991). The effects of interaction goals on person perception. *Advances in Experimental Social Psychology, 24*, 235–267.

IJzerman, H., & Koole, S. L. (2011). From perceptual rags to metaphoric riches – Bodily, social, and cultural constraints on sociocognitive metaphors: Comment on Landau, Meier, and Keefer (2010). *Psychological Bulletin, 137*, 355–361.

James, W. (1890). *Principles of psychology* (Vols. 1–2). New York, NY: Dover.

Jostmann, N. B., Lakens, D., & Schubert, T. W. (2009). Weight as an embodiment of importance. *Psychological Science, 20*, 1169–1174. doi:10.1111/j.1467-9280.2009.02426.x

Kee, H. W., & Knox, R. E. (1970). Conceptual and methodological considerations in the study of trust and suspicion. *Journal of Conflict Resolution, 14*, 357–366.

Klayman, J., & Ha, Y.-W. (1987). Confirmation, disconfirmation, and information in hypothesis testing. *Psychological Review, 94*, 211–228.

Lakoff, G., & Johnson, M. (1999). *Philosophy in the flesh: The embodied mind and its challenges to western thought.* New York, NY: Basic Books.

Landau, M. J. (2017). *Conceptual metaphor in social psychology: The poetics of everyday life*. New York, NY: Psychology Press.

Landau, M. J., Meier, B. P., & Keefer, L. A. (2010). A metaphor-enriched social cognition. *Psychological Bulletin, 136*, 1045–1067.

Lee, D. S., Kim, E., & Schwarz, N. (2015). Something smells fishy: Olfactory suspicion cues improve performance on the Moses illusion and Wason rule generation task. *Journal of Experimental Social Psychology, 59*, 47–50.

Lee, S. W. S. (2016). Multimodal priming of abstract constructs. *Current Opinion in Psychology, 12*, 37–44.

Lee, S. W. S., & Schwarz, N. (2012). Bidirectionality, mediation, and moderation of metaphorical effects: The embodiment of social suspicion and fishy smells. *Journal of Personality and Social Psychology, 103*, 737–749.

Lee, S. W. S., & Schwarz, N. (2014). Metaphors in judgment and decision making. In M. J. Landau, M. D. Robinson, & B. P. Meier (Eds.), *The power of metaphor: Examining its influence on social life* (pp. 85–108). Washington, DC: APA.

Loftus, E. F., Miller, D. G., & Burns, H. J. (1978). Semantic integration of verbal information into a visual memory. *Journal of Experimental Psychology: Human Learning and Memory, 4*, 19–31.

Mayer, J., & Mussweiler, T. (2011). Suspicious spirits, flexible minds: When distrust enhances creativity. *Journal of Personality and Social Psychology, 101*, 1262–1277.

Mayo, R. (2015). Cognition is a matter of trust: Distrust tunes cognitive processes. *European Review of Social Psychology, 26*(1), 283–327.

Mayo, R., Alfasi, D., & Schwarz, N. (2014). Distrust and the positive test heuristic: Dispositional and situated social distrust improves performance on the Wason rule discovery task. *Journal of Experimental Psychology: General, 143*(3), 985–990.

McGlone, M. S., & Tofighbakhsh, J. (2000). Birds of a feather flock conjointly (?): Rhyme as reason in aphorisms. *Psychological Science, 11*, 424–428.

Newman, E. J., Sanson, M., Miller, E. K., Quigley-McBride, A., Foster, J. L., Bernstein, D. M., & Garry, M. (2014). People with easier to pronounce names promote truthiness of claims. *PLOSone, 9*(2), 10.1371/journal.pone.0088671

Newman, E. J., & Schwarz, N. (2018). Good sound, good research: How audio quality influences perceptions of the researcher and research. *Science Communication, 40*(2), 246–257.

Oswald, M. E., & Grosjean, S. (2004). Confirmation bias. In R. F. Pohl (Ed.), *Cognitive illusions: A handbook on fallacies and biases in thinking, judgment, and memory* (pp. 79–96). New York, NY: Psychology Press.

Park, H., & Reder, L. M. (2003). Moses illusion. In R. F. Pohl (Ed.), *Cognitive illusions* (pp. 275–292). New York, NY: Psychology Press.

Reber, R., & Schwarz, N. (1999). Effects of perceptual fluency on judgments of truth. *Consciousness and Cognition, 8*, 338–342.

Sanna, L., Schwarz, N., & Small, E. (2002). Accessibility experiences and the hindsight bias: I-knew-it-all-along versus It-could-never-have-happened. *Memory & Cognition, 30*, 1288–1296.

Schul, Y., Burnstein, E., & Bardi, A. (1996). Dealing with deceptions that are difficult to detect: Encoding and judgment as a function of preparing to receive invalid information. *Journal of Experimental Social Psychology, 32*, 228–253.

Schul, Y., Mayo, R., & Burnstein, E. (2004). Encoding under trust and distrust: The spontaneous activation of incongruent cognitions. *Journal of Personality and Social Psychology, 86*, 668–679.

Schwarz, N. (1990). Feelings as information: Informational and motivational functions of affective states. In E. T. Higgins, & R. M. Sorrentino (Eds.), *Handbook of motivation and cognition: Foundations of social behavior* (Vol. 2, pp. 527–561). New York, NY: Guilford Press.

Schwarz, N. (2002). Situated cognition and the wisdom in feelings: Cognitive tuning. In L. F. Barrett & P. Salovey (Eds.), *The wisdom in feeling: Psychological processes in emotional intelligence* (pp. 144–166). New York, NY: Guilford.

Schwarz, N. (2004). Meta-cognitive experiences in consumer judgment and decision making. *Journal of Consumer Psychology, 14*, 332–348.

Schwarz, N. (2007). Attitude construction: Evaluation in context. *Social Cognition, 25*, 638–656.

Schwarz, N. (2010). Meaning in context: Metacognitive experiences. In B. Mesquita, L. F. Barrett, & E. R. Smith (Eds.), *The mind in context* (pp. 105–125). New York, NY: Guilford.

Schwarz, N. (2012). Feelings-as-information theory. In P. A. M. van Lange, A. Kruglanski, & E. T. Higgins (Eds.), *Handbook of theories of social psychology* (pp. 289–308). Thousand Oaks, CA: Sage.

Schwarz, N. (2015). Metacognition. In E. Borgida, & J. A. Bargh (Eds.), *APA handbook of personality and social psychology: Attitudes and social cognition* (Vol. 1, pp. 203–229). Washington, DC: APA.

Schwarz, N. (2018). Of fluency, beauty, and truth: Inferences from metacognitive experiences. In J. Proust & M. Fortier (Eds.), *Metacognitive diversity: An interdisciplinary approach* (pp. 25–46). New York, NY: Oxford University Press.

Schwarz, N., Bless, H., & Bohner, G. (1991). Mood and persuasion: Affective states influence the processing of persuasive communications. *Advances in Experimental Social Psychology, 24*, 161–199.

Schwarz, N., Bless, H., Strack, F., Klumpp, G., Rittenauer-Schatka, H., & Simons, A. (1991). Ease of retrieval as information: Another look at the availability heuristic. *Journal of Personality and Social Psychology, 61*, 195–202.

Schwarz, N., & Clore, G. L. (1983). Mood, misattribution, and judgments of well-being: Informative and directive functions of affective states. *Journal of Personality and Social Psychology, 45*, 513–523.

Schwarz, N., & Clore, G. L. (2007). Feelings and phenomenal experiences. In A. Kruglanski, & E. T. Higgins (Eds.), *Social psychology: Handbook of basic principles* (2nd ed., pp. 385–407). New York, NY: Guilford.

Schwarz, N., & Lee, S. W. S. (2019). Embodied cognition and the construction of attitudes. In D. Albarracín & B. T. Johnson (Eds.), *Handbook of attitudes* (2nd ed., Vol. 1, pp. 450–479). New York, NY: Taylor & Francis.

Schwarz, N., Newman, E., & Leach, W. (2016). Making the truth stick and the myths fade: Lessons from cognitive psychology. *Behavioral Science & Policy, 2*, 85–95.

Schwarz, N., Servay, W., & Kumpf, M. (1985). Attribution of arousal as a mediator of the effectiveness of fear-arousing communications. *Journal of Applied Social Psychology, 15*, 74–84.

Sebastian, P., Kaufmann, L., & de la Piedad Garcia, X. (2017, January). *In the nose, not in the beholder: Embodied cognition effects override individual differences.* Presented at the meetings of the Society for Personality and Social Psychology, San Antonio, TX. Retrieved from www.researchgate.net/publication/313997207_In_the_nose_not_in_the_beholder_Embodied_cognition_effects_override_individual_differences.

Sheaffer, R., Gal, R., & Pansky, A. (2017, September). I smell, therefore I recall accurately: The connection between fishy smells and resistance to misleading post-event information. In A. Pansky (Chair), *Memory retrieval and conditioning.* Presented at the meetings of the European Society for Cognitive Psychology, Potsdam, Germany.

Sheppard, B. H., & Sherman, D. M. (1998). The grammars of trust: A model and general implications. *Academy of Management Review, 23,* 422–437.

Smith, E. R., & Semin, G. R. (2004). Socially situated cognition: Cognition in its social context. *Advances in Experimental Social Psychology, 36,* 53–117.

Song, H., & Schwarz, N. (2008). *Fluency and the detection of distortions: Low processing fluency attenuates the Moses illusion. Social Cognition, 26,* 791–799.

Soriano, C., & Valenzuela, J. (2008, May 31). *Sensorial perception as a source domain: A cross-linguistic study.* Paper presented at the Seventh International Conference on Researching and Applying Metaphor (RaAM 7), Caceres, Spain.

Wason, P. C. (1960). On the failure to eliminate hypothesis in a conceptual task. *Quarterly Journal of Experimental Psychology, 12,* 129–140.

Williams, L. E., & Bargh, J. A. (2008a). Experiencing physical warmth influences interpersonal warmth. *Science, 322,* 606–607.

Williams, L. E., & Bargh, J. A. (2008b). Keeping one's distance: The influence of spatial distance cues on affect and evaluation. *Psychological Science, 19*(3), 302–308.

Xu, A.J., & Schwarz, N. (2018). How one thing leads to another: Spillover effects of cognitive mind-sets. *Current Directions in Psychological Science, 27*(1), 51–55.

Yamagishi, T., & Yamagishi, M. (1994). Trust and commitment in the United States and Japan. *Motivation and Emotion, 18,* 129–166.

Zajonc, R. B. (1980). Feeling and thinking: Preferences need no inferences. *American Psychologist, 35,* 151–175.

Zebrowitz, L. A. (1997). *Reading faces: Window to the soul?* Boulder, CO: Westview.

Zillman, D. (1978). Attribution and misattribution of excitatory reactions. In J. H. Harvey, W. I. Ickes, & R. F. Kidd (Eds.), *New directions in attribution research* (Vol. 2, pp. 335–368). Hillsdale, NJ: Erlbaum.

Part IV

Social and Cultural Aspects of Gullibility

14 Cultural Fluency, Mindlessness, and Gullibility

Daphna Oyserman
UNIVERSITY OF SOUTHERN CALIFORNIA

Introduction

People are typically not stymied by everyday life in their own culture – their culture provides an organizing lens so they have an implicit ("goes without saying") sense of what to expect in an array of everyday situations. In their own culture, people have a gut sense of the way details are woven together (Lin, Arieli, & Oyserman, 2018; Mourey, Lam, & Oyserman, 2015; Oyserman, 2011). They have a gut feel for the "right" food for breakfast, the "right" color for bridal dresses, the "right" colors and shapes for Valentine's cards; they know the "right" tone for obituaries. In ambiguous situations, they know which mental procedure to use – one that focuses on connecting and relating or one that focuses on separating and distinguishing, and whether to pursue action for personally "me"-framed or socially "us"-framed goals (Oyserman, 2017). These often-implicit culturally rooted predictions are automatically and rapidly tested against observation, yielding either an easy-to-process prediction-observation match or a more difficult-to-process prediction-observation mismatch (Oyserman, 2011, 2017). The terms *cultural fluency* and *cultural disfluency* were coined to highlight that the metacognitive experience of ease (difficulty) is a result of match (mismatch) with culturally rooted expectations (Oyserman, 2011). Cultural fluency serves three functions (Oyserman & Yan, 2018): Cognitively, it signals "all is well," conserving cognitive and attentional resources for the unexpected. Interpersonally, it reduces social friction among people sharing a cultural frame – all of whom experience a similar sense of fluency when situations unfold as expected. Intra-psychically, it provides a sense of purpose and meaning in life – a feeling of causal certainty.

However, as I outline in this chapter, cultural fluency also encourages the kinds of social intelligence failures that leave people credulous and gullible – willing to believe unlikely propositions and easily tricked into ill-advised actions. In this chapter, I use culture-as-situated cognition theory (e.g., Oyserman, 2011, 2015a, 2016, 2017; Oyserman & Yan, 2018) to explain these paradoxical consequences, laying out the theory and its implications in three sections. In the first section, I briefly outline culture-as-situated

256 *Daphna Oyserman*

cognition theory. In the longer second section, I summarize the research examining the downstream psychological consequences of cultural fluency and disfluency, which focuses on a number of markers of gullibility and credulity (inherence, depth of processing, and mindless consumption). In the third and final section, I briefly connect research findings back to questions of credulity and gullibility and highlight questions for future research.

Culture-as-Situated Cognition Theory

What Does "Situated" Cognition Mean?

Situated cognition or "thinking in the world" focuses on the impact of social contexts on thinking and action (Cesario, Grant, & Higgins, 2004; Fiske & Taylor, 2013; Meier, Schnall, Schwarz, & Bargh, 2012; Schwarz, 2007). Situated cognition approaches suggest that "thinking is for doing." The implication is that people are sensitive to their immediate environment, use the subset of all their knowledge that is accessible in the moment, and interpret what comes to mind in light of contextual demands (Fiske & Taylor, 2013; Schwarz, Bless, Wänke, & Winkielman, 2003).

What a situation implies depends on how one thinks about it – the accessible knowledge and metacognitive experience used to make sense of it. Accessible knowledge includes accessible semantic content (Srull & Wyer, 1979), goals (Förster, Liberman, & Friedman, 2007) and mental procedures (Oyserman & Lee, 2008; Wyer & Xu, 2010; Xu & Schwarz, 2017). Accessible metacognitive experiences of ease or difficulty while thinking about content, goals, and procedures matter as well (Bless & Schwarz, 2010; Fisher & Oyserman, 2017). What metacognitive experiences imply depends on the interpretive lens individuals use to make sense of these experiences (Alter & Oppenheimer, 2009; Briñol, Petty, & Tormala, 2006; Schwarz, 2004). Thus, a metacognitive experience of fluency or disfluency can imply something about the outside world or it can imply something about oneself (Alter & Oppenheimer, 2009; Fisher & Oyserman, 2017; Reber & Schwarz, 1999; Schwarz, 1994; Schwarz et al., 1991; Smith & Oyserman, 2015). Unless they have reason to exclude it, people tend to include accessible knowledge and metacognitive experience of ease (fluency) or difficulty (disfluency) in their judgments of the situation (Bless & Schwarz, 2010) and of themselves (Oyserman, Elmore, Novin, Fisher, & Smith, 2018).

While people are sensitive to what comes to mind and to their experience of thinking about what is on their mind, they are not sensitive to the specific source of their information or metacognitive experience (Schwarz, 2005, 2007; this can be termed metacognitive myopia, Fielder, Chapter 7 this volume). Hence, on-the-mind information or metacognitive experience likely carries over to a subsequent task. This is the case even if it is incidental to, rather than arising from, the task at hand (Bless & Schwarz, 2010; Schwarz & Clore, 1983).

How Does Culture Become a Form of Situated Cognition?

Culture-as-situated cognition theory (Oyserman, 2011, 2017; Oyserman & Lee, 2007) starts with the assumption that humans live in cultures, that cultures address universal demands of living with others, and that people make sense of what the immediate context seems to imply using a cultural lens. By emphasizing immediate context, culture-as-situated cognition theory de-emphasizes speculation about distal causation of current between-group differences and reconciles literature documenting what appear to be chronic cross-cultural differences with literature documenting situated flexibility (Oyserman, 2016).

The culture-as-situated cognition approach to cultural psychology highlights two largely overlooked points: First, culture can be represented as a set of associative knowledge networks. Second, these culturally rooted associative knowledge networks provide mental models, affording people the cultural expertise to predict how situations will likely unfold.

People have access to and can use multiple culturally rooted associative knowledge networks, which one they use depends on which is cued in context. These knowledge networks include both cultural mindsets (content, procedures, and goals related to overarching themes of individualism, collectivism, and honor) and specific culturally rooted (often implicit) knowledge about how things work (e.g., what brides wear, what breakfast entails). Immediate contexts make some subset of available cultural knowledge networks accessible in the moment. People use this subset to provide an organizing implicit frame and to make an automatic prediction about what will happen next. Thus, for example, people are better at quickly naming a distinct object in a visual array after an individualistic mindset is primed (Oyserman, Sorensen, Reber, & Chen, 2009). They are better at recalling where objects were in a visual array (Oyserman et al., 2009) and are willing to pay more to complete a set (Mourey, Oyserman, & Yoon, 2013) after a collectivistic mindset has been primed. The implication is that the cultural mindset accessible in the moment matters for meaning-making because accessible mindsets yield culturally rooted expectations. If expectations are not met, this requires attention to understand why observation mismatches with prediction.

Defining Culture Within Culture-as-Situated Cognition Theory

As a starting point, culture-as-situated cognition theory assumes that human culture developed from the survival necessity of connecting with others and adapting to group living (Boyd & Richerson, 1988; Cohen, 2001; Haidle et al., 2015; Oyserman, 2017; Schwartz, 1992). Living together requires that people coordinate and organize their relationships, clarify group boundaries, and notice and reward innovation so that they can imitate or exploit innovation as it occurs and otherwise fit in and know from whom and to whom they owe allegiance (Boyd & Richerson, 2005; Kurzban & Neuberg, 2005; Oyserman, 2011; Schwartz & Bardi, 2001). Though the basic problems of group living must be addressed, human-made cultural solutions can put more emphasis on one or another aspect of these depending on ecological niche. In each society, practices evolve to create "good enough" ways to regulate relationships, specify group boundaries and what to do about them, and spotlight when innovation is acceptable or valued (Boyd & Richerson, 2005; Cohen, 2001; Kurzban & Neuberg, 2005; Oyserman, 2011, 2017; Schwartz, 1992). Coordinating and organizing relationships and noticing and rewarding innovation requires "social tuning" –sensitivity to others' perspectives – and "self-regulation" – the ability to control the focus of one's attention (Chiu et al., 2015; Oyserman, 2017; Shteynberg, 2015). Indeed, people are sensitive to cues about when to imitate (fit in), when to innovate (Clegg & Legare, 2016; Legare & Nielsen, 2015), and when group boundaries matter (Boyd, Richerson, & Henrich, 2011; Haidle et al., 2015).

Solutions are "good enough," rather than optimal. However, once developed, they become "sticky" by virtue of being the ways "we" do things – "our" structures, practices, norms, and values (Cohen, 2001; Oyserman, 2015b). Taken together, this set of good enough solutions forms culture, the particular set of practices people in a particular society, time, and place share. Once developed, cultural solutions permeate all aspects of behavior, constrain and enable perception and reasoning, and provide a shared blueprint or outline for meaning-making across a variety of situations (Chiu, Gelfand, Yamagishi, Shteynberg, & Wan, 2010; Nisbett & Norenzayan, 2002; Oyserman, 2017; Shteynberg, Gelfand, & Kim, 2009; Shweder & LeVine, 1984; Triandis, 1972, 2007). In this way, culture is in part a set of associative knowledge networks, tacit operating codes, or meaning-making frameworks through which people make sense of their world (Geertz, 1973) and understand what they want, and how they go about getting it (Bond, 2002; Fiske, 2002; Kitayama & Markus, 1994; Sanchez-Burks, Nisbett, & Ybarra, 2000; Swidler, 1986). As a result, culturally appropriate situations seem intuitive, right, and obvious while culturally inappropriate situations seem odd, off-key, or even wrong.

Cultural Expertise and Culture-as-Situated Cognition

From a culture-as-situated cognition perspective, cultural expertise – knowing how things work in one's everyday life – is not reducible to whether a culture is comparatively more or less "individualistic," "collectivistic," or "honor" focused (Oyserman, 2017). Cultural expertise provides a way of knowing what to expect in everyday situations so the world feels sensible and orderly. Cultural expertise includes knowing which cultural mindset to use as the situation arises (e.g., an individualistic mindset when uniqueness is good and valued; a collectivistic mindset when connecting and relating matters; an honor mindset to know which aspects of reputation matter). Cultural expertise is not limited to sensitivity to cues as to which cultural mindset to use, it includes knowledge of how everyday life unfolds, knowledge of traditions and their sources. People gain cultural expertise by being socialized in a society; moving to or living in a society yields varying degrees of this expertise (Morris, Chiu, & Liu, 2015). Whatever way acquired, once culturally expert, people experience culture as the simple and obvious way things are. Imagine a beaming bride walking down the aisle toward her soon-to-be husband. What color is her dress? For Americans, responses to this question often take the form: "Well, I mean, the bride does not *have* to wear white." The implication is that the answer "white" is so obvious that being asked the question can feel like a trick or riddle in which the questioner must mean something other than the obvious answer that everyone knows. But note, knowing what to expect requires American cultural expertise, which Americans in America have without noticing it.

This experience of naturalness, obviousness, and ease is neither reserved for Americans nor only applicable to these answers. Answer content – what the easy, obvious, and natural answers are – may change across cultures as well as across time in a culture, but the feeling of obviousness does not. Knowing the culture – the values, norms, practices, and ways of being in a particular time and place – means that the answers spring to mind easily and feel obvious. Yet, despite this obviousness, variability exists. Consider again that bridal dress, brides can and sometimes do marry in dresses of all colors. Cultural fluency and disfluency, as detailed next, focuses on the implications drawn from this variability.

Cultural Fluency and Disfluency

What Is Cultural Fluency and Disfluency?

Cultural fluency and disfluency are the result of the interface between what observers' cultural expertise leads them to (implicitly) expect, what they actually observe, and the meaning they draw from their ensuing meta-cognitive experiences of ease or difficulty. What makes for a metacognitive experience of ease or difficulty is not the observation itself but the match or mismatch between observation and culturally rooted expectation. Experiencing match or mismatch requires having the cultural expertise to know (implicitly) what to expect. These expectations are rooted in one's culture – what one has learned explicitly or picked up implicitly through observation and socialization practices. In one's own culture, cultural fluency may be the norm –having cultural expertise means knowing what is likely to occur. Note that the experience of cultural fluency within one's own culture may also be bolstered by the tendency of expectations to guide perception of what is experienced (e.g., confirmation bias, Wason, 1960;

260 *Daphna Oyserman*

self-fulfilling prophecies; Merton, 1948; Snyder, 1984; stereotype confirmation, Hamilton & Trolier, 1986). In spite of this confirmatory tendency, observations sometimes violate expectations and as detailed below, cultural disfluency can arise from small differences from expectation.

What Makes Cultural Fluency and Disfluency Cultural?

The experience of cultural fluency and cultural disfluency is based in cultural knowledge. That is, as detailed below, without cultural knowledge, a cultural product cannot be experienced as disfluent or fluent – it simply is. Cultural knowledge sets up implicit expectations, which if met, yield easy to process information and if violated, yield more difficult to process information. To use a classic example, Bruner and Postman (1949) exposed American college students at Harvard and Radcliffe to playing cards and assessed latency to correctly identify the card. There were four groups of participants; one group saw playing cards in which suit and color fit cultural expectation. Another group saw playing cards in which suit and color misfit cultural expectations. The two other groups saw different proportions of matching and mismatching cards. Playing cards that mismatched cultural expectations took longer to correctly describe and the effect of mismatch was particularly pronounced in the context of matches or when presented as the first card. There is nothing inherent in the card's configuration that caused this – it is not that a heart or a diamond is easier to identify or that red is easier to process than black, it is that the participants came into the experiment with cultural knowledge of how playing cards look. Culture, of course, is dynamic. That experiment would only replicate with current American college students if playing cards were as common a pursuit as it seems to have been when that experiment was conducted.

In this way, cultural fluency and cultural disfluency differ from other sources of processing fluency, which are separate from cultural knowledge. For example, color contrast and type font used effect ease of processing through perceptual rather than cultural channels. It does not require cultural knowledge or cultural expectation for a message in black printed on white paper to be easier to process than a message in grey printed on grey paper. It does not require cultural knowledge for a message printed in 12-font to be easier to read than a message printed in 6-font.

To take another example, people often find giving a few examples easier than giving many examples but unless their attention is drawn to the source of their experience of ease or difficulty, they tend to draw on their experience of ease or difficulty to make inferences about truth (Schwarz & Lee, Chapter 13 this volume). The inferences people make after experiencing ease (or difficulty) when being asked to generate a few (or many) examples also do not appear to be culture-bound. That is, the lay theories of what ease of generation may imply for truth, expertise, and category size do not seem to be rooted in knowledge of a particular culture.

Cultural Fluency and Disfluency ≠ Positive and Negative Mood

Cultural disfluency is likely experienced as negative in the same way that other disfluency is – at a low level or "primitive" affective response as described by Gawronski and Bodenhausen (2007, 2011) as part of associative processing of propositions. Getting a measure of this kind of mood effect may require using either basic physiological measures or indirect measures such as liking or consumption (Winkielman, Berridge, & Wilbarger, 2005). While negative mood does influence cognitive processing (Forgas, Chapter 10 this volume), research to date has not found a connection between self-reported mood (obtained by the positive and negative affect scale; Thompson, 2007) and cultural fluency and disfluency. Thus, Mourey and colleagues (2015) found no effects of cultural fluency and disfluency on mood whether they focused on positive (e.g., weddings, holidays) or negative (e.g., funerals, obituaries) cultural events in three experiments in the United States and Hong Kong. Lin and colleagues (2018) replicated this pattern of null effects in two experiments with participants from the United States and Israel using different cultural events, Valentine's Day and breakfast. The implication is that cultural fluency and disfluency effects are not simply mood effects.

What Are the Consequences of Cultural Fluency and Disfluency?

When things unfold as expected (culturally rooted expectation matches observed reality) the metacognitive experience is of ease. Ease implies that there is no problem signal, no need to think more. In contrast, when things have not unfolded as implicitly expected (culturally rooted expectation mismatches observed reality) the metacognitive experience is of difficulty. Difficulty implies a possible problem, requiring consideration of why expectations were off the mark. Downstream consequences of cultural fluency and disfluency depend on whether people infer that the source of their experienced ease or difficulty is external to them (something is wrong in the situation) or due to something about themselves (something is wrong with me). As depicted graphically in Figure 14.1 and detailed in the next three sections, the meaning people draw from ease can be that "all's right with the world" or "no need to think" and the meaning people draw from difficulty can be "all might not be as it should be" or "something went awry here."

Cultural Fluency Matters for Gullibility: Inherence

Defining Inherence

Psychological inherence is the sense that existing patterns in the world are the natural order of things – the way things *ought to be* (Cimpian, 2015;

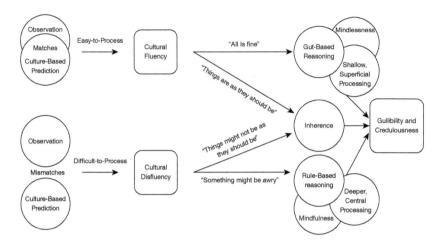

Figure 14.1 How cultural fluency and disfluency affects likely gullibility and credulousness via inherence, depth of processing, and cognitive style.

Salomon & Cimpian, 2014). It is an implicit process that leads people to explain observed patterns in terms of the inherent features of their constituents. So, for example, "girls wear pink, pink is a delicate color, so girls must wear pink because pink is a delicate color." Inherence is an important cognitive precursor of category learning via its connection to psychological essentialism, the belief that categories are stable, inevitable, and immutable facilitates category learning. Salomon and Cimpian (2014) developed a measure of inherence using items such as: "It seems right that pink is the color typically associated with girls," "It seems ideal that toothpaste is typically flavored with mint," "There are good reasons why dollar bills are green," "It seems natural to use red in a traffic light to mean 'stop,'" and "It seems ideal that weekends consist of Saturday and Sunday." Higher agreement implies that people assume that current social norms are natural and ideal rather than one possibility of many. Higher scores on inherence imply that the alternatives are not on the mind. People often fail to consider that the link between color and gender is arbitrary though culturally rooted. Though traditionally blue for boys and pink for girls may seem more obvious than the reverse, both were previously used interchangeably as "nursery" colors that symbolized youth rather than gender and when a color was to be chosen, blue was the one specified for girls (see Cimpian & Salomon, 2014 for a detailed review. The same is true for toothpaste, money, and weekends – that toothpaste can have various flavors or none at all, that currencies can be many colors, that weekend days are linked to societal customs and religions.

Cultural Fluency and Gullibility 263

Given the items used to assess inherence,[1] it may seem that psychological inherence is being operationalized as a cognitive limitation, a form of credulousness. It is. People who score higher in inherence are more likely to essentialize the world around them (Salomon & Cimpian, 2014). People who essentialize are more likely to experience differences as immutable. This undermines willingness to engage, trust, and cooperate with people from categories outside one's own (Bastian & Haslam, 2006; Chiu, Dweck, Tong, & Fu, 1997) and increases acceptance of stereotypes (Bastian & Haslam, 2006) and race-based inequality (Morton, Postmes, Haslam, & Hornsey, 2009; Williams & Eberhardt, 2008).

The Evidence

Lin et al. (2018) conducted five experiments to test the prediction that cultural fluency and cultural disfluency affect inherence. To trigger a cultural fluency or cultural disfluency experience, they showed cultural products to randomized participants separated into two groups. Each group saw versions of a cultural product. One group saw "right" (likely expected) versions and the other group saw "wrong" likely unexpected versions of the product. As a cover story, participants were told that their task was to rate the products for quality (or quality and attractiveness). After the product-rating task, participants read and rated their agreement or disagreement with the 15 inherence scale items and then rated the traditionality and similarity to expectation of the products that they had seen earlier. These ratings served as manipulation checks. Indeed, across studies, participants in the "right" condition rated the products as higher in quality, attractiveness, traditionality, and similarity to expectation than participants in the "wrong" condition. The specific product differed in each experiment to test the stability of the effect of cultural fluency and disfluency on inherence.

In the first experiment, Americans saw four Valentine's Day cards and were asked to rate the quality and attractiveness of each card. Half of participants saw versions of the "right" (likely expected) Valentine – cards that were decorated in hearts in pink and red and filled with warm sentiments. The other half of participants saw versions of the "wrong" (likely unexpected) Valentine – cards were neutral colored, not pink, were decorated with skulls, and the warm sentiments had a spooky undertone. The researchers conducted the experiment on Valentine's Day and again a month later. Inherence was lower for the group that had just seen the "wrong" Valentines compared to the "right" ones, whether on Valentine's Day or a month later. Results support the prediction that cultural fluency enhances and cultural disfluency undermines inherence. Participants made (implicit) predictions based on their Valentine's Day associative knowledge network, match and mismatch of observation to

264 *Daphna Oyserman*

prediction mattered for their momentary sense that the way things are is the way that they ought to be. Seeing the "right" rather than the "wrong" Valentine's Day card cued inherence. People rated the "wrong" cards as less attractive, lower in quality, and less traditional, but none of these ratings mattered, fitting the prediction that people are sensitive to their experiences of cultural fluency and disfluency but not to the source of these experiences.

In the second experiment, Israelis saw eight photographs of plated breakfasts and were asked to rate the quality and attractiveness of each. In Israel people typically eat some mix of raw vegetables – especially tomatoes and cucumber, olives, and some yogurt or fresh cheese along with bread or rolls. Cold or hot cereal, meat of any kind, and sweets of any kind are not typical. Eggs may be served but not gravy or sauce, waffles, French toast, or pancakes. Those randomized to the "right" (likely expected) breakfast group saw breakfast plates with raw vegetables, yogurt, and fresh rolls. In contrast, Israelis randomized to the "wrong" (likely unexpected) breakfast group saw breakfast plates with meats, cheeses, and pastries. Inherence was lower for the group that had just seen the "wrong" breakfasts compared to the "right" ones. As manipulation checks, people were asked to rate the photographs for quality and attractiveness and the breakfasts themselves for traditionality. As would be expected if they were disfluent, people rated the "wrong" breakfasts as less attractive, lower in quality, and less traditional. Fitting the prediction that people are sensitive to their experiences of cultural fluency and disfluency but not to the source of these experiences, people randomized to see the "wrong" breakfasts were lower in inherence than people randomized to see the "right" breakfasts – they were less likely to agree with the items on the Cimpian and Salomon (2015) inherence scale. This effect was not mediated by attractiveness, fluency, and quality ratings.

In the third experiment European Americans saw four photographs from a wedding of a European American bride and groom and were asked to rate the quality of each photograph. Those randomized to the "right" (likely expected) wedding group saw wedding photographs of a bride in a white gown, a groom in a black tuxedo, a white-fondant-iced tiered wedding cake, and a formal but homelike wedding setting. In contrast, those randomized to the wrong (likely unexpected) wedding group saw wedding photographs of a European American couple, the bride in a black gown and the groom in a white tuxedo, a black-fondant-iced tiered wedding cake, and a beautiful but industrial setting. Inherence was lower for the group that had just seen the "wrong" wedding scenes compared to the "right" ones. People rated the photographs with the "wrong" wedding scenes as lower in quality. They rated them as less traditional. These ratings did not affect inherence, fitting the prediction that people are sensitive to their experiences of cultural fluency and disfluency but not to the source of these experiences.

In the fourth experiment, Han Chinese saw five photographs from a wedding of a Han Chinese bride and groom and rated the quality of each photograph. Those randomized to the "right" (likely expected) wedding group saw wedding photographs of a Han Chinese couple, the bride in a white gown and the groom in a dark suit, guests in various outfits, and a car decorated with flowers. In contrast, those randomized to the "wrong" (likely unexpected) wedding group saw wedding photographs of a Han Chinese couple, the bride in a black gown and the groom in a dark suit, guests in various outfits, and a car decorated with fruits. Inherence was lower for the group that had just seen the "wrong" wedding scenes compared to the "right" ones; as before, quality and traditionality ratings did not affect the relationship between the kind of wedding viewed and inherence.

The fifth experiment involved American participants and took place just before Labor Day. Researchers randomized participants to one of three groups, adding a neutral control group, as detailed next. Each group saw four Labor Day shopping bags and was asked to rate the quality and attractiveness of the shopping bag designs. In the "right" (likely expected) group, the shopping bags had a "Happy Labor Day" logo with a red white and blue and patriotic-themed design of a flag or fireworks. In contrast, in the "wrong" (likely unexpected) group, the logo read "Shopping Bag" (no reference to Labor Day), with a vaguely environmentally friendly color scheme (brown and green) and environmental designs (animals, trees). The control group saw four photographs of shopping bags with a "Happy Labor Day" but with an environmentally friendly color scheme and animal or plant designs rather than a patriotic-themed color and design. Inherence was lower for the group that had just seen the "wrong" Labor Day designs compared to the "right" ones or the "control" ones. People rated the photographs with the "wrong" Labor Day bags as less attractive, lower in quality and less traditional. These ratings did not affect inherence, fitting the prediction that people are sensitive to their experiences of cultural fluency and disfluency but not to the source of these experiences.

A meta-analyses across the studies showed that the mean effect of viewing culturally fluent vs. disfluent products was small-to-moderate (d = .38). The 95% confidence interval (.24 to .53) suggested that the true effect of cultural fluency and disfluency on inherence ranges from small to moderate-to-large. Across studies, effects of condition were direct, not mediated or moderated by ratings of quality, attractiveness, or traditionality and the test of heterogeneity was not significant. Taken together, results fit the culture-as-situated cognition theory prediction that people are sensitive to their experiences of cultural fluency and disfluency but not to the source of these experiences. Experiences of cultural fluency or disfluency carry over to subsequent judgments even when the cultural experience is irrelevant to the judgment task.

266   *Daphna Oyserman*

In sum, across studies, the downstream consequence of experiencing a match with cultural expectations is preservation of a sense of inherence; this sense of inherence is disrupted by a mismatch with cultural expectations. If the world is as it should be, then there is no need to consider whether there is any reason for the current order of things. That implies that any message that can be packed in culturally fluent language and images will be processed as likely correct in its essence, the way things ought to be, without further processing. "As American as apple pie and baseball" is a saying that evokes this sense that once an element is included in the culturally fluent mix, it too will be tagged with acceptance without processing further.

Cultural Fluency Matters for Gullibility: Reasoning

Defining Reasoning

To form judgments, assess the quality of persuasive arguments, and make sense of their experiences, people can use gist-based, associative reasoning, and rule-based systematic reasoning. That is, they can process information in terms of their gut "feeling" using peripheral cues such as whether the information seems familiar. They can also process information in terms of rules, using central cues such as the quality of the arguments and whether the source of the information is credible.

The culture-as-situated cognition prediction is that in culturally fluent situations in which observation seems to match implicit expectations, processing can remain gist-based and shallow. In contrast, since experienced cultural disfluency is a problem signal, it should increase scrutiny of arguments, focusing attention on their quality and decreasing reliance on peripheral cues. The question relevant to gullibility and credulousness is whether cultural fluency results in sticking with gist-based reasoning in contexts requiring systematic reasoning and whether it bolsters shallow processing of persuasive arguments. In this section, I focus on evidence related to systematic reasoning. In the next section, on mindlessness, I focus on evidence related to reliance on peripheral cues.

The Evidence

Mourey et al. (2015) addressed the question of whether the predicted effect of cultural fluency and cultural disfluency on reasoning styles is found by testing participants on a task specifically devised to have a gut-based and a rule-based answer (a version of the three-item cognitive reflection task (CRT), Frederick, 2005). Here is an example from the original CRT task: "A fishing rod and fishing bait cost $11 in total. The fishing rod costs $10 more than the bait. How much does the bait cost?" The gut-based ("wrong") response is $1 based on the gist focus on the "$10" piece of information resulting in simply subtracting $10 from $11 ($11–$10 = $1). The rule-based ("correct") response is $.50 based on the rule-based focus on the "$10 more" as a piece of information resulting in the equation: $11= n + (n + $10). People give the gut-based or the rule-based response – with only a few people giving un-codeable answers (in the above example, answers other than $1.00 or $.50).

As detailed next, Mourey and colleagues (2015) conducted four relevant experiments. One experiment involved having or not having the color pink as a border on Valentine's Day or after Valentine's Day. Two experiments involved photographs of weddings. A final experiment involved reading obituaries. In each experiment the researchers randomized participants into two groups. One group saw versions of a cultural product that met likely expectation (they looked "right"). In contrast, the other group saw versions of the same product that likely mismatched with their culture-based expectations (they looked somehow "wrong") or were irrelevant to their culture-based expectations (control groups). After the rating task, all participants were asked to "Click the arrow to proceed to the next task" (the cognitive task).

The first experiment took place in Ann Arbor, Michigan (United States) and in Hong Kong, S.A.R. China. In each country, participants were randomized to see either a pink border or not while working on the cognitive task. In each country, participants were either given the task on Valentine's Day or a week after Valentine's Day. The four-condition between subject design included one cultural fluency group – in this condition, participants saw pink on Valentine's Day.[2] Pink is the "right" color for Valentine's Day but only on Valentine's Day, otherwise it is just a color. The other three groups were control groups, testing the prediction that the group experiencing cultural fluency would reason less systematically than the group that participated on Valentine's Day without the pink border, the group that experienced a pink border but not on Valentine's Day, and the group that experienced neither a pink border nor Valentine's Day. The pink alone and Valentine's Day alone cues were assumed not to be sufficient to activate the Valentine's Day associative knowledge network. Fitting the prediction that people are sensitive to their experiences of cultural fluency and disfluency, systematic-reasoning was lower for the group that had just seen the "right" color at the "right" time (pink on Valentine's Day). They were more likely to give the wrong $10 answer than participants in the three other conditions – and people in these latter three groups did not differ from each other.

The second and third experiments took place in the U.S. American group, where participants rated the quality of a wedding photographer's photographs. American participants randomized to the "right" condition saw eight photographs of a bride in white, a groom in black, their white-fondant-iced tiered wedding cake, and their wedding party with

268   *Daphna Oyserman*

bridesmaids and groomsmen. The eight photographs American participants randomized to the "wrong" condition saw were from the same wedding photographer's website but showed a bride in a dress with some green and purple and a groom whose tuxedo also had some purple. Their tiered wedding cake was decorated with colorful cogs, and there was no wedding party. Participants rated the quality of each photograph. Then they were given the cognitive task and rated the traditionality of the photographs that they had seen overall. Systematic reasoning was lower for the group that had just seen the "right" wedding photographs compared to the "wrong" ones. Effects were not due to photograph quality ratings or wedding traditionality, fitting the prediction that people are sensitive to their experiences of cultural fluency and disfluency but not to the source of these experiences.

In a fourth experiment, American participants read two versions of the same obituary and made a choice as to which version the family should use.[3] American participants randomized to the "right" condition read two versions of an obituary in which the deceased was praised and her loss mourned by her children. Americans randomized to the "wrong" condition read two versions of an obituary in which the deceased was not praised and her loss not mourned by her children. After making their choice, participants were given the cognitive task and rated the traditionality of the obituaries that they had seen overall. Systematic reasoning was lower for the group that had just seen the "right" obituaries compared to the "wrong" ones. Effects were not due to traditionality, fitting the prediction that people are sensitive to their experiences of cultural fluency and disfluency but not to the source of these experiences.

In sum, all four experiments supported the prediction that culture-based metacognitive experience of ease (fluency) and difficulty (disfluency) influences cognitive style. Each study showed that fluent and disfluent conditions differed. The pink on Valentine's Day study suggested that the difference was due to the undermining effect of cultural fluency – systematic reasoning was less likely in the cultural fluency condition than in control conditions. Cultural fluency preserved gut-based associative processing. Cultural disfluency shifts processing to rule-based systematic processing. These studies document that processing ease when likely expectations matched observation and processing difficulty when likely expectations mismatched observation carried over to the next judgment task. A single study meta-analyses across the experiments yielded a moderate-to-large effect size ($d = .46$) and 95% confidence interval (.26 to .65) and the test of heterogeneity was not significant. The implication is that the true effect of cultural fluency and disfluency on processing style is in the moderate-to-large range and that results are not dependent on the particular samples or cultural situations used. Across studies, cultural fluency effects were direct, not mediated or moderated by ratings of quality or traditionality. Taken together, results fit the culture-as-situated cognition theory prediction that people are sensitive to their experiences of cultural fluency and disfluency but not to the source of these experiences. Experiences of cultural fluency or disfluency carry over to subsequent judgments even when the cultural experience is irrelevant to the judgment task.

Cultural Fluency Matters for Gullibility: Mindless Consumption

Defining Mindless Consumption

Mindless consumption occurs when people choose, buy, consume, or take, as if without thinking, on impulse. I use the term mindless consumption whether what is being consumed is a food, a consumer good, or a persuasive argument. I do so to highlight that the underlying process of "mindlessness" entails shallow processing based on superficial cues and reliance on gut-based rather than rule-based processing. The literature on the relationship between cultural fluency and disfluency and mindless consumption whether of food, consumer goods, or persuasive arguments is just emerging.

Culture-as-situated cognition theory predicts that culturally fluent situations, ones that unfold as likely expected, will increase propensity toward mindless consumption and credulity – easy persuasion with superficial cues that fit culture-based associative knowledge networks. People should be more likely to go with the flow – approach when contexts cue approach and avoid when contexts cue avoidance – and to be persuaded by peripheral cues under conditions of cultural fluency. Note that this effect should be limited to situations in which experienced fluency (ease) and disfluency (difficulty) are interpreted as being about the context itself rather than as being about the self. If experienced cultural fluency and disfluency are taken to imply something about the self, then cultural disfluency is depleting, yielding a sense of "Perhaps I am not competent." In this section, I provide the emerging evidence on mindless consumption.

The Evidence

Mourey and colleagues (2015) addressed the question of mindless consumption in four experiments. In one experiment, the dependent variable was the weight of food American participants put on their plates, in a second experiment it was the size of the portion American and Hong Kong Chinese participants chose in a virtual buffet, in the third and fourth experiments, the dependent variable was the likelihood of buying a consumer product.

In one naturalistic field experiment, American participants attending actual 4th of July or Labor Day picnics were randomized to receive one

270   *Daphna Oyserman*

of two different plates as they waited to choose their picnic. After putting their food on their plates, plate weight was unobtrusively obtained. On the 4th of July, participants were given either a patriotic themed plate or a non-decorated control plate. On Labor Day, participants were given either a non-decorated control plate or a plate with animals and plants. Participants provided a culturally fluent plate put significantly more (by weight) food on their plates than those provided a control plate (25% more). Participants provided a culturally disfluency plate put significantly less food on their plate (18% less) than those provided a control plate. The field study method only allowed for a simple debrief. Participants reported not noticing the plate decorations.

In a second more controlled experiment, college student participants in Ann Arbor, Michigan (United States) and Hong Kong S.A.R. China were asked to go online to rate the quality of a local Chinese buffet. Half of participants were invited to participate during Chinese New Year and half a month after Chinese New Year. When students went online, they were given a plate, shown prepared dishes, and asked what size portion they would like to try. The plates were randomly assigned to have either a red or black border. This two (during Chinese New Year or not) by two (red or not) by two (American, Chinese) design yielded a cultural fluency group (Chinese New Year and red and Chinese) and seven control conditions. Participants in the cultural fluency group chose more food than other participants. Red is a color associated with Chinese New Year for Chinese, after Chinese New Year it is just a color. Mindless consumption was higher in the cultural fluency group than in the Chinese comparison groups and the American groups. Indeed, our American participants were unaware of the timing of Chinese New Year and did not associate red with this holiday.

In a third experiment, participants were exposed to the wedding photographs described in the prior section. They were asked to rate the quality of the photographs and then offered a wedding-irrelevant consumer product (a shovel) and asked about their likelihood of purchasing it. Likelihood to purchase was higher in the cultural fluency condition in which participants saw the "right" wedding compared to the "wrong" wedding and effects were not mediated by participant-reported quality or traditionality ratings.

In a fourth experiment, participants were exposed to the obituaries described in the prior section and then offered a funeral-irrelevant consumer product (a key fob charger, a key fob phone finder) and asked about their likelihood of purchasing it. Likelihood to purchase was higher in the cultural fluency condition in which participants saw the "right" obituary compared to the "wrong" obituary and effects were not mediated by participant-reported traditionality ratings.

All four experiments supported the prediction that culture-based metacognitive experience of ease (fluency) and difficulty (disfluency)

Cultural Fluency and Gullibility 271

influences mindless consumption. Each study showed that fluent and disfluent conditions differed. The results of the patriotic holiday picnic study suggested that the difference was due both to the mindlessness boosting effect of cultural fluency and to the mindfulness boosting effect of cultural disfluency. More food was put on the plate when the plate had patriotic theme decorations rather than being plain and less food was put on the plate when the decorations of plants and animals did not fit the patriotic theme. The cues were cultural – people who did not know the culture were unaware of and not influenced by what would have been a match to expectation – they had nothing to expect. Mindlessness did not require that the cultural event be positive, mindless choice was higher for culturally fluent funeral and wedding cues. Cultural fluency preserves or even boosts mindless "go with the flow" use of superficial cues. Cultural disfluency shifts to mindful processing and use of more central cues. These studies document that processing ease when likely expectations matched observation and processing difficulty when likely expectations mismatched observation carried over to the next judgment task.

A single study meta-analyses across the experiments yielded a small-to-moderate effect size ($d = .28$) and 95% confidence interval (.12 to .44) and the test of heterogeneity was not significant. The implication is that the true effect of cultural fluency and disfluency on mindlessness is in the small-to-moderate range and that results are not dependent on the particular samples or cultural situations used. Across studies, cultural fluency effects were direct, not mediated or moderated by ratings of quality or traditionality. Taken together, results fit the culture-as-situated cognition theory prediction that people are sensitive to their experiences of cultural fluency and disfluency but not to the source of these experiences. Experiences of cultural fluency or disfluency carry over to subsequent judgments even when the cultural experience is irrelevant to the judgment task.

Future Directions: Cultural Fluency, Gullibility, and Credulity

Taking a culture-as-situated cognition approach to culture spotlights an underappreciated aspect of culture, which is that it allows people to get through their days without much thought while also alerting them when attention might be warranted. In their own culture, people mostly experience situations that match their (implicit) expectations. The ensuing metacognitive experience of ease implies that not much thought is needed; however, situations vary, and sometimes these (implicit) expectations are violated. When that happens, the ensuing metacognitive experience is one of difficulty. Something feels awry, and closer consideration is warranted. The terms "cultural fluency" and "cultural disfluency" capture both

272 *Daphna Oyserman*

the cultural and the metacognitive (thinking about thinking) aspects of this process. Cultural fluency and disfluency are the result of the interface between what observers' cultural expertise leads them to (implicitly) expect, what they actually observe, and the meaning they draw from their ensuing metacognitive experience of ease when observation and expectation match or difficulty when observations violate expectations. Interpretation is the result of drawing meaning from the metacognitive experience of *ease* when culturally rooted implicit expectations match observations and from the metacognitive experience of *difficulty* when culturally rooted implicit expectations are violated (or do not match observations). Downstream consequences for thinking, feeling, and doing depend on whether people infer that the source of experienced ease or difficulty is external (in the situation) or internal (themselves). Interpretation does not require explicit self-reportable thoughts or emotions such as "This is not traditional!" or "This is not similar to what I do!" or "I don't feel happy!" or "I feel anxious!" or "I feel angry!"

Culture-as-situated cognition theory predicts that accessible culturally rooted associative knowledge networks focus attention on some cues and not on others. People automatically make predictions as to what will happen next and experience cultural fluency when observation matches expectation. As summarized in this chapter, an emerging body of evidence supports the culture-as-situated cognition theory prediction that one function of cultural expertise is to provide predictions as to how life will unfold. When these predictions seem to be supported, yielding a good enough match with unfolding reality, people experience cultural fluency. Cultural fluency is associated with higher inherence – the feeling that the way things are now is the way they ideally ought to be, more gut-based – associative reasoning, and more mindlessness. In contrast, when observation does not support prediction, people experience cultural disfluency. Cultural disfluency is associated with lower inherence, more systematic reasoning, and more mindfulness. The average size of this cultural disfluency effect is moderate-to-large for shift to systematic, top-down, date-driven processing, and drop in experienced inherence, while the average size of the effect on mindless consumption is small. The implication of these results is that cultural fluency should be associated with higher willingness to accept and even act on claims or persuasive arguments that provide poor quality arguments but do not disrupt or even themselves trigger cultural fluency – they are framed to fit culturally rooted expectations. Making a small choice, decision, or commitment within a culturally fluent context that one would otherwise not make can trigger a spiral of congruent choices particularly if the culturally fluent context remains accessible. Cooper and Avery (Chapter 16 this volume) describe how this course of action can be difficult to undo for people who are sensitive to the possibility that they were duped or overly credulous.

Culture-as-situated cognition theory also predicts that culturally relevant cues require attention and care; hence, the quality of persuasive argument matters in culturally disfluent situations. There are two as yet not fully explored implications of this formulation: First, effects on willingness to accept shallow arguments. Second, effects on willingness to justify the current state of affairs.

Consider first shallow arguments. A cultural fluency perspective implies that culturally irrelevant cues are either unnoticed or are noticed but processed shallowly. In order for people to be motivated to centrally process an argument in the first place, the topic must feel relevant to them (see Macrae, Olivier, Falbén, & Golubickis, Chapter 11 this volume). Once an argument is experienced as relevant, it will be processed differently in a culturally fluent vs. a culturally disfluent context. Cultural disfluency is predicted to reduce certainty in the links in an associative knowledge network. Of course if the same culturally disfluent experience is repeated, then, over time, this should result in the network accommodating new knowledge (see Unkelbach & Koch, Chapter 3 this volume). How long this process takes is as yet unstudied but once it occurs, the formerly disfluent will become fluent.

Consider next the link between a cultural fluency perspective and system justification. Through affecting inherence, cultural fluency and disfluency are likely to have implications for people's perception of whether social system is fair and just with culturally fluency carrying over to a more general sense that the current state of affairs is ideal (Hussak & Cimpian, 2015; Jost & Hunyady, 2005; Kay et al., 2009). Because the link between gullibility, credulousness, and cultural fluency is just beginning to be explored, future research is needed to test the prediction that people are more willing to act on information provided in a culturally fluent context. Research to date has shown willingness to consume but has not directly tested acceptance of persuasive arguments. Future research testing responsivity to weak arguments, and truth judgments given culturally fluent vs. disfluent cues is sorely needed.

People do not want to be gullible (Cooper & Avery, Chapter 16 this volume) but at the same time, they are less likely to use top-down systematic processing in settings that feel culturally fluent, which match their expectations. Cultural fluency bolsters a feeling of inherence, that things are as they should be and might reduce people's likelihood of processing for an alternative to a presented argument or claim (Mayo, Chapter 8 this volume). While experiencing cultural fluency may be a subtle mood enhancer (Forgas, Chapter 10 this volume), future research is needed to consider ways in which cultural disfluent experiences might help reduce people's willingness to suspend disbelief in processing potentially dubious claims. Cultural fluency may support gullibility and credulousness simply because getting through the day typically does not involve processing information through a lens of suspicion, but quite the opposite, processing through a lens that facilitates experience of inherence – that all is right with the world.

Notes

1 Items such as: "It seems right that pink is the color typically associated with girls," "It seems ideal that toothpaste is typically flavored with mint," "There are good reasons why dollar bills are green," "It seems natural to use red in a traffic light to mean 'stop,'" and "It seems ideal that weekends consist of Saturday and Sunday."
2 Note that pink is part of the associative knowledge network for Valentine's Day but unlike the Valentine's Day card itself, the color pink is not exclusive to Valentine's Day.
3 To create the two versions, the researchers rearranged the order of the sentences but kept the content exactly the same. The "wrong" obituary was found in an online edition of a local newspaper and was lightly edited to create the "right" version. For example "had no hobbies ... will not be missed" in the original was edited to "had numerous hobbies ... will be missed."

References

Alter, A. L., & Oppenheimer, D. M. (2009). Uniting the tribes of fluency to form a metacognitive nation. *Personality and Social Psychology Review, 13*(3), 219–235.

Bastian, B., & Haslam, N. (2006). Psychological essentialism and stereotype endorsement. *Journal of Experimental Social Psychology, 42*(2), 228–235.

Bless, H., & Schwarz, N. (2010). Mental construal and the emergence of assimilation and contrast effects: The inclusion/exclusion model. *Advances in Experimental Social Psychology, 42*, 319–373.

Bond, M. H. (2002). Reclaiming the individual from Hofstede's ecological analysis: A 20-year odyssey: Comment on Oyserman et al. (2002). *Journal of Personality and Social Psychology, 128*(1), 73–77.

Boyd, R., & Richerson, P. J. (1988). *Culture and the evolutionary process.* Chicago, IL: University of Chicago Press.

Boyd, R., & Richerson, P. J. (2005). *The origin and evolution of cultures.* Oxford: Oxford University Press.

Boyd, R., Richerson, P. J., & Henrich, J. (2011). The cultural niche: Why social learning is essential for human adaptation. *Proceedings of the National Academy of Sciences, 108*(Suppl. 2), 10918–10925.

Briñol, P., Petty, R. E., & Tormala, Z. L. (2006). The malleable meaning of subjective ease. *Psychological Science, 17*(3), 200–206.

Bruner, J. S., & Postman, L. (1949). On the perception of incongruity: A paradigm. *Journal of Personality, 18*(2), 206–223.

Cesario, J., Grant, H., & Higgins, E. T. (2004). Regulatory fit and persuasion: Transfer from "feeling right." *Journal of Personality and Social Psychology, 86*(3), 388–404.

Chiu, C. Y., Dweck, C. S., Tong, J. Y. Y., & Fu, J. H. Y. (1997). Implicit theories and conceptions of morality. *Journal of Personality and Social Psychology, 73*(5), 923–940.

Chiu, C. Y., Gelfand, M. J., Harrington, J. R., Leung, A. K. Y., Liu, Z., Morris, M. W., . . . Zou, X. (2015). A conclusion, yet an opening to enriching the normative approach of culture. *Journal of Cross-Cultural Psychology, 46*(10), 1361–1371.

Chiu, C. Y., Gelfand, M. J., Yamagishi, T., Shteynberg, G., & Wan, C. (2010). Intersubjective culture: The role of intersubjective perceptions in cross-cultural research. *Perspectives on Psychological Science, 5*(4), 482–493.

Cimpian, A., & Salomon, E. (2014). The inherence heuristic: An intuitive means of making sense of the world, and a potential precursor to psychological essentialism. *Behavioral and Brain Sciences, 37*(5), 461–480.

Cimpian, A. (2015). The inherence heuristic: generating everyday explanations. In R. Scott and S. Kosslyn (Eds.), *Emerging trends in the social and behavioral sciences: an interdisciplinary, searchable, and linkable resource* (pp. 1–15). Hoboken, NJ: John Wiley & Sons.

Clegg, J. M., & Legare, C. H. (2016). Instrumental and conventional interpretations of behavior are associated with distinct outcomes in early childhood. *Child Development, 87*(2), 527–542.

Cohen, D. (2001). Cultural variation: considerations and implications. *Psychological Bulletin, 127*, 451–471.

Fisher, O., & Oyserman, D. (2017). Assessing interpretations of experienced ease and difficulty as motivational constructs. *Motivation Science, 3*(2), 133–163.

Fiske, A. P. (2002). Using individualism and collectivism to compare cultures – a critique of the validity and measurement of the constructs: Comment on Oyserman et al. (2002). *Psychological Bulletin, 128*, 78–88.

Fiske, S. T., & Taylor, S. E. (2013). *Social cognition: From brains to culture.* New York, NY: Sage.

Förster, J., Liberman, N., & Friedman, R. S. (2007). Seven principles of goal activation: A systematic approach to distinguishing goal priming from priming of non-goal constructs. *Personality and Social Psychology Review, 11*, 211–233.

Frederick, S. (2005). Cognitive reflection and decision making. *Journal of Economic Perspectives, 19*(4), 25–42.

Gawronski, B., & Bodenhausen, G. V. (2007). Unraveling the processes underlying evaluation: Attitudes from the perspective of the APE model. *Social Cognition, 25*(5), 687–717.

Gawronski, B., & Bodenhausen, G. V. (2011). The associative–propositional evaluation model: Theory, evidence, and open questions. *Advances in Experimental Social Psychology, 44*, 59–127.

Geertz, C. (1973). *The interpretation of cultures* (Vol. 5019). New York, NY: Basic Books.

Haidle, M. N., Bolus, M., Collard, M., Conard, N. J., Garofoli, D., Lombard, M., . . . Whiten, A. (2015). The nature of culture: An eight-grade model for the evolution and expansion of cultural capacities in hominins and other animals. *Journal of Anthropological Sciences, 93*, 43–70.

Hamilton, D. L., & Trolier, T. K. (1986). Stereotypes and stereotyping: An overview of the cognitive approach. In J. F. Dovidio & S. L. Gaertner (Eds.), *Prejudice, discrimination, and racism* (pp. 127–163). San Diego, CA: Academic Press.

Hussak, L. J., & Cimpian, A. (2015). An early-emerging explanatory heuristic promotes support for the status quo. *Journal of Personality and Social Psychology, 109*(5), 739–752.

Jost, J. T., & Hunyady, O. (2005). Antecedents and consequences of system-justifying ideologies. *Current Directions in Psychological Science, 14*(5), 260–265.

Kay, A. C., Gaucher, D., Peach, J. M., Laurin, K., Friesen, J., Zanna, M. P., & Spencer, S. J. (2009). Inequality, discrimination, and the power of the status quo:

276 *Daphna Oyserman*

Direct evidence for a motivation to see the way things are as the way they should be. *Journal of Personality and Social Psychology, 97*(3), 421–434.

Kitayama, S., & Markus, H. R. (Eds.). (1994). *Emotion and culture: Empirical studies of mutual influence.* Washington, DC: American Psychological Association.

Kurzban, R., & Neuberg, S. (2005) Managing ingroup and outgroup relationships. In D. M. Buss (Ed.), *The handbook of evolutionary psychology* (pp. 653–675). Hoboken, NJ: John Wiley & Sons.

Legare, C. H., & Nielsen, M. (2015). Imitation and innovation: The dual engines of cultural learning. *Trends in Cognitive Sciences, 19*(11), 688–699.

Lin, Y., Arieli, S., & Oyserman, D. (2018). Cultural fluency means all is right with the world. Manuscript under review.

Meier, B. P., Schnall, S., Schwarz, N., & Bargh, J. A. (2012). Embodiment in social psychology. *Topics in Cognitive Science, 4*(4), 705–716.

Merton, R. K. (1948). The self-fulfilling prophecy. *The Antioch Review, 8*(2), 193–210.

Morris, M. W., Chiu, C. Y., & Liu, Z. (2015). Polycultural psychology. *Annual Review of Psychology, 66*, 631–659.

Morton, T. A., Postmes, T., Haslam, S. A., & Hornsey, M. J. (2009). Theorizing gender in the face of social change: Is there anything essential about essentialism? *Journal of Personality and Social Psychology, 96*(3), 653–664.

Mourey, J. A., Lam, B. C., & Oyserman, D. (2015). Consequences of cultural fluency. *Social Cognition, 33*(4), 308–344.

Mourey, J. A., Oyserman, D., & Yoon, C. (2013). One without the other: Seeing relationships in everyday objects. *Psychological Science, 24*(9), 1615–1622.

Nisbett, R. E., & Norenzayan, A. (2002). Culture and cognition. In D. L. Medin (Ed.), *Stevens' handbook of experimental psychology* (3rd ed., pp. 561–597). New York, NY: Wiley.

Oyserman, D. (2011). Culture as situated cognition: Cultural mindsets, cultural fluency, and meaning making. *European Review of Social Psychology, 22*(1), 164–214.

Oyserman, D. (2015a). Culture as situated cognition. In R. Scott and S. Kosslyn (Eds.), *Emerging trends in the social and behavioral sciences: An interdisciplinary, searchable, and linkable resource* (pp. 1–11). Hoboken, NJ: John Wiley & Sons.

Oyserman, D. (2015b). Values: psychology of. In J. D. Wright (Ed.), *International encyclopedia of the social and behavioral sciences* (Vol. 25, 2nd ed., pp. 36–40). New York, NY: Oxford Elsevier Science.

Oyserman, D. (2016). What does a priming perspective reveal about culture: Culture-as-situated cognition. *Current Opinion in Psychology, 12*, 94–99.

Oyserman, D. (2017). Culture three ways: Culture and subcultures within countries. *Annual Review of Psychology, 68*, 435–463.

Oyserman, D., Elmore, K., Novin, S., Fisher, O., & Smith, G. C. (2018). Guiding people to interpret their experienced difficulty as importance highlights their academic possibilities and improves their academic performance. *Frontiers in Psychology, 9*(781).

Oyserman, D., & Lee, S. W. S. (2007). Priming "culture." In S. Kitayama & D. Cohen (Eds.), *Handbook of cultural psychology* (pp. 255–279). New York, NY: Guilford Press.

Oyserman, D., & Lee, S. W. (2008). Does culture influence what and how we think? Effects of priming individualism and collectivism. *Psychological Bulletin, 134*(2), 311–342.

Oyserman, D., Sorensen, N., Reber, R., & Chen, S. X. (2009). Connecting and separating mind-sets: Culture as situated cognition. *Journal of Personality and Social Psychology, 97*(2), 217–235.

Oyserman, D., & Yan. V. X. (2018). Making meaning: A culture-as-situated cognition approach to the consequences of cultural fluency and disfluency. In S. Kitayama and D. Cohen (Eds.), *Handbook of cultural psychology* (pp. 536–565). New York, NY: Guilford Press.

Reber, R., & Schwarz, N. (1999). Effects of perceptual fluency on judgments of truth. *Consciousness and Cognition, 8*(3), 338–342.

Salomon, E., & Cimpian, A. (2014). The inherence heuristic as a source of essentialist thought. *Personality and Social Psychology Bulletin, 40*(10), 1297–1315.

Sanchez-Burks, J., Nisbett, R. E., & Ybarra, O. (2000). Cultural styles, relationship schemas, and prejudice against out-groups. *Journal of Personality and Social Psychology, 79*(2), 174–189.

Schwartz, S. H. (1992). Universals in the content and structure of values: Theoretical advances and empirical tests in 20 countries. *Advances in Experimental Social Psychology, 25*, 1–65.

Schwartz, S. H., & Bardi, A. (2001). Value hierarchies across cultures: Taking a similarities perspective. *Journal of Cross-Cultural Psychology, 32*(3), 268–290.

Schwarz, N. (1994). Judgment in a social context: Biases, shortcomings, and the logic of conversation. *Advances in Experimental Social Psychology, 26*, 123–162.

Schwarz, N. (2004). Metacognitive experiences in consumer judgment and decision making. *Journal of Consumer Psychology, 14*(4), 332–348.

Schwarz, N. (2005). When thinking feels difficult: Meta-cognitive experiences in judgment and decision making. *Medical Decision Making, 25*(1), 105–112.

Schwarz, N. (2007). Attitude construction: Evaluation in context. *Social cognition, 25*(5), 638–656.

Schwarz, N., Bless, H., Strack, F., Klumpp, G., Rittenauer-Schatka, H., & Simons, A. (1991). Ease of retrieval as information: Another look at the availability heuristic. *Journal of Personality and Social psychology, 61*(2), 195–202.

Schwarz, N., Bless, H., Wänke, M., & Winkielman, P. (2003). Accessibility revisited. In Bodenhausen & A. J. Lambert (Eds.), *Foundations of social cognition: A Festschrift in honor of Robert S. Wyer, Jr.* (pp. 51–77). Mahwah, NJ: Erlbaum.

Schwarz, N., & Clore, G. L. (1983). Mood, misattribution, and judgments of well-being: Informative and directive functions of affective states. *Journal of Personality and Social Psychology, 45*(3), 513–523.

Shteynberg, G. (2015). Shared attention. *Perspectives on Psychological Science, 10*(5), 579–590.

Shteynberg, G., Gelfand, M. J., & Kim, K. (2009). Peering into the "magnum mysterium" of culture: The explanatory power of descriptive norms. *Journal of Cross-Cultural Psychology, 40*(1), 46–69.

Shweder, R. A., & LeVine, R. A. (Eds.). (1984). *Culture theory: Essays on mind, self and emotion.* Cambridge: Cambridge University Press.

Smith, G. C., & Oyserman, D. (2015). Just not worth my time? Experienced difficulty and time investment. *Social Cognition, 33*(2), 85–103.

Snyder, M. (1984). When belief creates reality. *Advances in Experimental Social Psychology, 18*, 247–305.

Srull, T. K., & Wyer, R. S. (1979). The role of category accessibility in the interpretation of information about persons: Some determinants and implications. *Journal of Personality and Social Psychology, 37*(10), 1660–1672.

Swidler, A. (1986). Culture in action: Symbols and strategies. *American Sociological Review, 51*(2), 273–286.

Thompson, E. R. (2007). Development and validation of an internationally reliable short-form of the positive and negative affect schedule (PANAS). *Journal of Cross-Cultural psychology, 38*(2), 227–242.

Triandis, H. C. (1972). *The analysis of subjective culture.* Oxford: Wiley-Interscience.

Triandis, H. C. (2007). Culture and psychology: A history of the study of their relationship. In S. Kitayama & D. Cohen (Eds.), *Handbook of cultural psychology* (pp. 59–76). New York, NY: Guilford Press.

Wason, P. C. (1960). On the failure to eliminate hypotheses in a conceptual task. *Quarterly Journal of Experimental Psychology, 12*(3), 129–140.

Williams, M. J., & Eberhardt, J. L. (2008). Biological conceptions of race and the motivation to cross racial boundaries. *Journal of Personality and Social Psychology, 94*(6), 1033–1047.

Winkielman, P., Berridge, K. C., & Wilbarger, J. L. (2005). Unconscious affective reactions to masked happy versus angry faces influence consumption behavior and judgments of value. *Personality and Social Psychology Bulletin, 31*(1), 121–135.

Wyer, R. S., & Xu, A. J. (2010). The role of behavioral mind-sets in goal-directed activity: Conceptual underpinnings and empirical evidence. *Journal of Consumer Psychology, 20*(2), 107–125.

Xu, A. J., & Schwarz, N. (2017). How one thing leads to another: Spillover effects of behavioral mind-sets. *Current Directions in Psychological Science, 27*(1), 51–55.

15 Scientific Gullibility

Lee Jussim
RUTGERS UNIVERSITY

Sean T. Stevens
NYU, STERN SCHOOL OF BUSINESS

Nathan Honeycutt
RUTGERS UNIVERSITY

Stephanie M. Anglin
CARNEGIE MELLON UNIVERSITY

Nicholas Fox
RUTGERS UNIVERSITY

"Gullible" means easily deceived or cheated. In this chapter, we focus on the deception aspect of gullibility. What does gullibility have to do with social psychology? Scientific gullibility occurs when individuals, including scientists, are "too easily persuaded that some claim or conclusion is true, when, in fact, the evidence is inadequate to support that claim or conclusion." In this chapter, we review evidence of the sources and manifestations of scientific gullibility in (mostly) social psychology, and also identify some potential preventatives.

Before continuing, some clarifications are necessary. We have no insight into, and make no claims about, what any scientist "thinks" or "believes." What we can address, however, are statements that have appeared in scholarship. In this chapter, when a paper is written as if some claim is true, we take that to mean that it is "accepted," "believed," "assumed to be valid," and/or "that the scientist was persuaded that the claim was valid and justified." When we do this, we refer exclusively to written statements in the text, rather than to someone's "beliefs," about which we have no direct information. Issues of whether and why scientists might make claims in scientific scholarship that they do not truly believe are beyond the scope of this chapter, though they have been addressed elsewhere (e.g., Anomaly, 2017).

Furthermore, we distinguish scientific gullibility from being wrong. Scientists are human, and make mistakes. Even fundamental scientific methods and statistics incorporate uncertainty, so that, sometimes, a well-conducted study could produce a false result – evidence for a phenomenon, even though the phenomenon does not exist, or evidence against the existence of some phenomenon that does. Thus, scientific gullibility is more than being wrong; error is baked into the nature of scientific exploration.

280 *Lee Jussim et al.*

We define *scientific gullibility* as being wrong, in regards to the strength and/ or veracity of a scientific finding, when the reasons and/or evidence for knowing better were readily available. Thus, demonstrating scientific gullibility means showing that (1) scientists have often believed something that was untrue, and (2) there was ample basis for them to have known it was untrue.

Overview

Why should scientists be interested in better understanding their own gullibility? We think it is because most of us do not want to be gullible (see Cooper & Avery, Chapter 16 this volume). Although there may be a small number who care more about personal success, they are likely rare exceptions. Most researchers genuinely want to know the truth and want to produce true findings. They want to be able to critically understand the existing literature, rather than believe that false claims are true. A better understanding of scientific gullibility then, can (1) reduce the propensity to believe scientific claims that are not true; and (2) increase awareness of the logical, evidentiary, methodological, and statistical issues that can call attention to claims that warrant increased skeptical scrutiny. In this context, then, we suggest the following five flags of gullibility as a starting point, we also welcome suggestions for additional symptoms of gullibility:

> *Criteria 1.* Generalization of claims that are based on data obtained from small, potentially unrepresentative samples.
>
> *Criteria 2.* Causal inference(s) drawn from correlational data.
>
> *Criteria 3.* Scholarship offering opposing evidence, an opposing argument, or a critical evaluation of the claim being presented as fact is overlooked (e.g., not cited).
>
> *Criteria 4.* Claims, and possibly generalized conclusions, are made without citing empirical evidence supporting them.
>
> *Criteria 5.* Overlooking (e.g., not citing and/or engaging with) obvious and well-established (in the existing scientific literature) alternative explanations.

We first review basic methodological and interpretive standards involved in scientific inference. Next, we review evidence regarding the psychology of gullibility. In general, and in science, why do people often believe things that are untrue when they should have known better? A series of cases are then reviewed, where there was, and may still be, belief in erroneous conclusions, and where the evidence revealing how and why those conclusions are erroneous is sufficiently apparent. We conclude the chapter with recommendations for reducing scientific gullibility, including possible reforms to the academic incentive structure.

Methods, Statistics, and Their Interpretation

It may seem obvious to state that, in science, claims and conclusions require evidence. But, as we shall show below, even this most basic standard has been violated by some social psychological scholarship, as some canonical claims rest on almost no evidence at all. Assuming some sort of empirical evidence does exist, its mere existence does not automatically support any particular conclusion, even if the article reporting the conclusion says it does. Basic and widely accepted methodological standards in social psychology include obtaining representative samples of people, preferably from many places all over the world, if one wishes to generalize findings; that large samples are needed to minimize uncertainty in parameter estimates; and that causal inference requires experimentation.

Standards for Data Collection

High power can usually be obtained with a large sample or through use of within subject designs. Although high-powered designs do not guarantee high quality, low-powered designs typically produce results with such high levels of uncertainty (as indicated by wide confidence intervals surrounding point estimates) that it is difficult to conclude the findings mean very much (Fraley & Vazire, 2014). Causal inferences are least problematic when hypotheses are tested with experiments, though experimentation alone does not guarantee correct causal inferences. Statistical uncertainties, methodological imperfections, and the potential that untested alternative explanations remain all constitute threats to the validity of experimentally based causal inferences. Additionally, researchers can sometimes influence the behavior of their subjects (Jussim, 2012; Jussim, Crawford, Anglin, Stevens, & Duarte, 2016), and random assignment to condition and experimenter blindness are two well-established ways of reducing this potential influence.

Standards for Data Interpretation

We use the term "fact" as elucidated by Stephen Jay Gould (1981): "In science, 'fact' can only mean 'confirmed to such a degree that it would be perverse to withhold provisional assent.'" We agree and add this corollary: Anything *not* so well established that it would *not* be perverse to withhold provisional assent is *not* an established scientific fact. When there are conflicting findings and perspectives in a literature, it is not perverse to believe otherwise, rendering it premature for scientists to present some claim as an established fact.

The presentation of confirmatory evidence is not sufficient to establish the veracity of a claim, even if the confirmatory evidence cited is relevant and sound (Roberts & Pashler, 2000). In other words, the conclusion may still not be justified, as evidence inconsistent with the conclusion that is on

282   *Lee Jussim et al.*

at least as sound a footing may exist. The presence of such evidence should prevent the conclusion from being presented as an established fact. Even in the absence of conflicting evidence, claims based on a limited body of research (e.g., a small number of studies with small samples; a single study) require further investigation before they can be considered established. Furthermore, the validity of some conclusion hinges not merely on the consistency of the data with that conclusion, but with the ability to eliminate alternative explanations for the same data (Roberts & Pashler, 2000).

Finally, it behooves social psychologists (and social scientists in general) to acknowledge there is a multiverse of potential ways to construct each unique data set for analysis (Steegen, Tuerlinckx, Gelman, & Vanpaemel, 2016). Within this multiverse, researchers may have to make many decisions about how to proceed, and thus the published findings typically represent one of many ways to analyze the data. Acknowledging this may limit social psychologists' vulnerability to drawing conclusions of questionable veracity (see Miller & Chapman, 2001; Nunes et al., 2017; Roberts & Pashler, 2000).

The Psychology of Scientific Gullibility

What are the sources of scientific gullibility? Although there may be many, in this chapter, we focus on four: motivated reasoning, excess scientism, status biases, and status quo biases.

Motivated Reasoning

A number of factors sometimes lead scientists to reach conclusions that have questionable validity. How can individuals who are trained to be objective, methodical, and precise make such errors? One way is through motivated reasoning (MacCoun, 1998), which occurs when the desire to reach a particular conclusion, rather than an accurate conclusion, influences the processing of evidence (Kahan, Jenkins-Smith, & Braman, 2011). People may be motivated to reach conclusions they would like to be true (*desirability bias*; Tappin, van der Leer, & McKay, 2017), conclusions they believe are true based on prior evidence and experience (*confirmation bias*; Nickerson, 1998), or a combination of the two.

Many theorists argue that motivated reasoning is driven by "hot," affective processes: information produces an intuitive response, which then guides cognitive processing of the information. When information supports preferred conclusions, people experience positive affect and easily accept the evidence (Klaczynski, 2000; Munro & Ditto, 1997). When information supports an undesired (or belief-inconsistent) conclusion, however, people experience negative affect and critique, ignore, or reject the evidence on irrelevant grounds (Klaczynski, 2000; Munro & Ditto, 1997). These processes – particularly confirmation biases – can also be driven by "cold," logical cognitive strategies (Fischhoff & Beyth-Marom, 1983; Koehler, 1993). Beliefs form from prior evidence and experience, and thus it may be rational to subject new evidence that deviates from prior knowledge to greater scrutiny.

Moreover, although the desire to reach a particular conclusion can bias information processing, when accuracy motivations are strong, people may process evidence systematically in order to draw accurate conclusions based on the quality of the evidence, regardless of their prior or desired beliefs (Anglin, 2016; Klaczynski, 2000). People are motivated to reach conclusions that are compatible with their beliefs and preferences, but they are also motivated to be accurate (Hart et al., 2009), and can only arrive at desired conclusions if they are justifiable (Haidt, 2001).

What strategies allow people to justify their desired conclusions? They seek out evidence supporting a favored conclusion while ignoring evidence challenging that view (*positive* or *confirmatory information seeking and hypothesis testing*; Klayman & Ha, 1987), evaluate evidence more favorably (e.g., as more accurate, reliable, and convincing) when it supports versus challenges a desired conclusion (*biased evaluation*), deduce the relevance or meaning of evidence based on its consistency with desired conclusions (*biased interpretation*), assign greater weight to evidence supporting desired conclusions (*selective weighting*), and selectively retrieve supportive (but not conflicting) evidence from memory (*biased recall*).

Scientists are not immune to these biases (Jussim, Crawford, Anglin, Stevens et al., 2016; Lilienfeld, 2010). In fact, research suggests that individuals with greater knowledge and expertise on a topic may be susceptible to motivated reasoning (Ditto et al., in press). At each stage of the research process, researchers' beliefs and motives can influence their research decisions. Collectively, the beliefs and motives of researchers – particularly political beliefs – may form significant blind spots or vulnerabilities, increasing the risk that certain questions aren't asked or investigated, that data are misinterpreted, or that conclusions of a convenient, exaggerated, or distorted nature are generated (Duarte et al., 2015; Jussim, 2012; Tetlock, 1994).

We have previously elaborated on political confirmation biases and how they may influence each stage of the research process (Stevens, Jussim, Anglin, & Honeycutt, 2018). Whether explicitly realized by researchers or not, these biases can exert their influence in a variety of ways. For instance, when generating hypotheses, researchers may, unintentionally, selectively expose themselves to research supporting a desired narrative or conclusion, neglecting to account for alternative perspectives or conflicting evidence. During data collection researchers can fall prey to experimenter or expectancy effects (Jussim, 2012; Jussim, Crawford, Anglin, Stevens et al., 2016), and when analyzing and interpreting results there are a number of researcher degrees of freedom available that can produce inaccurate, but desired conclusions (Simonsohn, Nelson, & Simmons, 2014; Wicherts et al., 2016).

284 *Lee Jussim et al.*

Glorification of p < .05: "It Was Published, Therefore It Is a Fact"

Scientism refers to exaggerated faith in the products of science (Haack, 2012; Pigliucci, 2018). One particular manifestation of scientism is reification of a conclusion based on its having been published in a peer-reviewed journal. These arguments are plausibly interpretable as drawing an equivalence between "peer-reviewed publication" and "so well established that it would be perverse to believe otherwise" (for examples, see, e.g., Fiske, 2016; Jost et al., 2009). They are sometimes accompanied with suggestions that those who criticize such work are either malicious or incompetent (Fiske, 2016; Jost et al., 2009; Sabeti, 2018), and thus reflect this sort of scientism. Especially because ability to cite even several peer-reviewed publications in support of some conclusion does not make the conclusion true, this is particularly problematic (see, e.g., Flore & Wicherts, 2015; Jussim, 2012; Jussim, Crawford, Anglin, Stevens et al., 2016; Simonsohn et al., 2014).

One of the most important gatekeepers for an article entering a peer-reviewed journal is a statistically significant result, or $p < .05$ (Simmons, Nelson, & Simonsohn, 2011). The undue reification of "peer reviewed" as "fact" itself implies a reification of $p < .05$, to the extent that $p < .05$ is a necessary finding to get some empirical work published (Nuijten, Hartgerink, van Assen, Epskamp, & Wicherts, 2016). Here is a list of conclusions that are *not* justified by $p < .05$:

1   The researcher's conclusion is an established fact.
2   The main findings are reliable or reproducible.
3   The difference or relationship observed is real, valid, or bona fide.
4   The difference or relationship observed cannot be attributed to chance.

In fact, the only thing $p < .05$ *might* establish, as typically used, is that the observed result, or one more extreme, has less than a 5% chance of occurring, if the null is true. Even that conclusion is contingent on both the underlying assumptions not being too severely violated, and on the researcher not employing questionable research practices to reach $p < .05$ (Simmons et al., 2011).

It gets worse from there. P-values between .01 and .05 are improbable if the effect under study is truly nonzero (Simonsohn et al., 2014). When a series of studies produces a predominance of p-values testing the key hypotheses in this range, it is possible that the pattern of results obtained (despite reaching $p < .05$) is more improbable than are the obtained results under the null for each study. Consider a three-experiment sequence where one degree of freedom F-tests of the main hypothesis, with error degrees of freedom of 52, 50, and 63, have values of 5.34, 4.18, and 4.78, respectively, and correspond to effect sizes ranging from d = .55 to .64. The corresponding p-values are .025, .046, and .033, respectively. If we assume an average underlying effect size of d = .60, the probability of getting three values between .01 and .05 is itself .014 (this probability can be easily obtained from the website http://rpsychologist.com/d3/pdist).

In other words, the likelihood of getting this pattern of results, with a true effect size of d = .60, is even more improbable than are obtaining those results under the null. This is not some concocted hypothetical. It is exactly the results reported in one of the most influential papers in all of social psychology, the first paper to produce evidence that stereotype threat undermines women's math performance; a paper that, according to Google Scholar, has been cited over 3,000 times (Spencer, Steele, & Quinn, 1999).

There are two bottom lines here. Treating conclusions as facts because they appear in peer-reviewed journals is not justified. Treating findings as "real" or "credible" simply because they obtained $p < .05$ is not justified. Some claims in some peer-reviewed articles are justified and some statistical findings do provide strong evidence in support of some claim. Excess scientism occurs, however, when the quality of the evidence, and the strength of the conclusions reached on the basis of that evidence, are not critically evaluated, and, instead, the mere fact of publication and $p < .05$ are presented as or presumed to be a basis for believing some claim is true.

Status Quo and Status Biases

Status Quo Biases

Laypeople are prone to metacognitive myopia (see Fielder, Chapter 7 this volume), and are often biased toward maintaining the current scientific consensus on a topic (Samuelson & Zeckhauser, 1988). Moreover, people often hold a false belief in small numbers, erroneously believing that a sample is representative of the population and that a study is more likely to replicate than the laws of chance would predict (Tversky & Kahneman, 1971). Seminal studies may thus be perceived as holding an exaggerated level of truth.

Does metacognitive myopia impact social psychologists? There are good reasons to think it does. When a paper, or finding, achieves canonical status it may be widely accepted by social psychologists as "truth." It can be quite difficult to change the canon once some finding has been published and integrated into common discourse in the field (Jussim, Crawford, Anglin, Stevens et al., 2016). This is so even when stronger contradictory evidence emerges (Jussim, 2012). Papers that challenge accepted or preferred conclusions in the literature may be held to a higher threshold for publication. For example, replication studies regularly report samples much larger than the original study (see Table 15.1), suggesting they have been held to a higher methodological and evidentiary standard.

Table 15.1 Social psychology bias for the status quo?

Publication	Narrative	Key Aspects of Methods	Citations	
			Total	*Since 1996*
Darley and Gross (1983)	Stereotypes lead to their own confirmation; stereotype bias in the presence but not absence of individuating information	People judge targets with vs. without relevant individuating information. Single experiment. N = 59–68, depending on analysis	1,355	1,154
Baron, Albright, and Malloy (1995)	Failed replication of Darley and Gross (1983). Positive results in opposite direction: stereotype bias in the absence of individuating information; individuating information eliminated stereotype bias	Close replication (and extension) of Darley and Gross (1983). Two experiments. Total N = 161.	75	72
			Total	*Since 2017*
Spencer et al. (1999)	Stereotype threat for women and math; apprehension of being judged by the negative stereotype leads to poorer math performance	Three experiments. Total N = 177.	3,023	294
Finnigan and Corker (2016)	Failed replication of the stereotype threat effect in Chalabaev, Major, Sarrazin, and Cury (2012), modeled closely on Spencer et al. (1999). No significant main effect or interaction effect for threat or performance avoidance goals	Pre-registered. Close replication of Chalabaev et al. (2012), and extension from Spencer et al. (1999). Single experiment. Total N = 590	9	9
			Total	*Since 2013*
Bargh, Chen, and Burrows (1996)	Automatic effects of stereotypes on behavior	Two experiments. Total N = 60	4,387	1,570
Doyen, Klein, Pichon, and Cleeremans (2012)	Failed replication of Bargh et al. (1996). No effects of stereotypes on behavior except when experimenters were not blind to condition	Two close replication and extension experiments. Total N = 170	404	386
			Total	*Since 1984*
Snyder and Swan (1978)	People seek to confirm their interpersonal expectations	Four experiments. Total N = 198. People chose among confirmatory or disconfirmatory leading questions (no option was provided for asking diagnostic questions)	1,152	1,060
Trope and Bassok (1983)	People rarely seek to confirm their interpersonal expectations. Instead, they seek diagnostic information	Three experiments. Conceptual replication. Total N = 342. People could seek information varying in the extent to which it was diagnostic vs. confirmatory	166	161

Note: Citation counts were obtained from Google Scholar (January 28, 2017).

This may, in part, result from repeated citations of the "canonical" finding, as mere repetition can increase the subjective truth of a message (see e.g., Myers, Chapter 5 this volume; Unkelbach & Koch, Chapter 3 this volume). This repetition-truth could be particularly potent in cases where the "canonical" finding is consistent with a preferred narrative in the field. Indeed, there may be a number of zombie theories remaining in psychology despite substantial and sustained criticism (e.g., Meehl, 1990), as even when an article is retracted, scientists continue to cite it (Greitemeyer, 2014). When the original authors acknowledge that new evidence invalidates their previous conclusions, people are less likely to continue to believe the overturned findings (Eriksson & Simpson, 2013). However, researchers do not always declare they were wrong, even in the face of evidence to the contrary.

Status Biases

One of the great arguments for the privileged status of science is universalism (Merton, 1942/1973); scientific claims are supposed to be evaluated on the basis of the quality of the evidence rather than the status of the person making the claim. The latter can be referred to as a status bias and it may play a role in influencing scientists' perceptions and interpretations of research. Sometimes referred to as an eminence obsession (Vazire, 2017), or the "Matthew Effect" (Merton, 1968), the principle underlying status bias is that the "rich get richer." Having a PhD from a prestigious university, currently being employed by a prestigious university, and/or having an abundance of grant money, awards, publications, and citations, are used as a heuristic for evaluating work. That is, the work of scientists fitting into one or more of these categories frequently may get a pass, and be evaluated less critically (Vazire, 2017).

Empirically, status biases have been demonstrated in a variety of academic contexts. Peer reviewers for a prominent clinical orthopedic journal were more likely to accept, and evaluated more positively, papers from prestigious authors in their field than identical papers evaluated under double-blind conditions (Okike, Hug, Kocher, & Leopold, 2016). In the field of computer science research, conference paper submissions from famous authors, top universities, and top companies were accepted at a significantly greater rate by single-blind reviewers than those who were double-blind (Tomkins, Zhang, & Heavlin, 2017). Peters and Ceci (1982) demonstrated a similar effect on publishing in psychology journals, reinforcing the self-fulfilling nature of institutional-level stereotypes.

Evidence of Scientific Gullibility

Thus far we have defined scientific gullibility, articulated standards for distinguishing scientific gullibility from simply being wrong, reviewed basic

288 *Lee Jussim et al.*

standards of evidence, and reviewed the evidence regarding potential social psychological factors that lead judgments to depart from evidence. But is there any evidence of actual scientific gullibility in social psychology? One might assume that scientific gullibility occurs rarely among social psychologists. We are in no position to reach conclusions about how often any of these forms of gullibility manifest, because that would require performing some sort of systematic and representative sampling of claims in social psychology, which we have not done. Instead, in the next section, we take a different approach. We identify examples of prominent social psychological claims that not only turned out be wrong, but that were wrong because scientists made one or more of the mistakes we have identified. In each case, we identify the original claim, show why it is likely erroneous, and discuss the reasons this should have been known and acknowledged.

Conclusions Without Data: The Curious Case of Stereotype "Inaccuracy"

Scientific articles routinely declare stereotypes to be inaccurate either *without a single citation*, or by citing an article that declares stereotype inaccuracy without citing empirical evidence. We call this "the black hole at the bottom of declarations of stereotype inaccuracy" (Jussim, Crawford, Anglin, Chambers et al., 2016), and give some examples: "[S]tereotypes are maladaptive forms of categories because their content does not correspond to what is going on in the environment" (Bargh & Chartrand, 1999, p. 467). "To stereotype is to allow those pictures to dominate our thinking, leading us to assign identical characteristics to any person in a group, regardless of the actual variation among members of that group" (Aronson, 2008, p. 309). No evidence was provided to support either claim.

Even the American Psychological Association (APA), in its official pronouncements, has not avoided the inexorable pull of this conceptual black hole. APA first declares: "Stereotypes 'are not necessarily any more or less inaccurate, biased, or logically faulty than are any other kinds of cognitive generalizations,' and they need not inevitably lead to discriminatory conduct" (APA, 1991, p. 1064). They go on to declare: "The problem is that stereotypes about groups of people often are *overgeneralizations and are either inaccurate or do not apply to the individual group member in question* ([Heilman, 1983], note 11, at 271)" (emphasis in original).

The APA referenced Heilman (1983), which does *declare* stereotypes to be inaccurate. It also reviews evidence of bias and discrimination. But it neither provides nor reviews empirical evidence of stereotype inaccuracy. A similar pattern occurs when Ellemers (2018, p. 278) declares, "Thus, if there is a kernel of truth underlying gender stereotypes, it is a tiny kernel" without citing scholarship that assessed the accuracy of gender stereotypes.

These cases of claims without evidence regarding inaccuracy pervade the stereotype literature (see Jussim, 2012; Jussim, Crawford, Anglin,

Chambers et al., 2016, for reviews). It may be that the claim is so common that most scientists simply presume there is evidence behind it – after all, why would so many scientists make such a claim, without evidence? (see Duarte et al., 2015; Jussim, 2012; Jussim, Crawford, Anglin, Chambers et al., 2016; Jussim, Crawford, Anglin, Stevens et al., 2016, for some possible answers). Given this state of affairs, it seems likely that when the next publication declares stereotypes to be inaccurate without citing any evidence, it, too, will be accepted.

Large Claims, Small Samples

Studies with very small samples rarely produce clear evidence for any conclusion; and, yet, some of the most famous and influential social psychological findings are based on such studies. Social priming is one example of this. One of the most influential findings in all of social psychology, priming elderly stereotypes causing people to walk more slowly (Bargh, Chen, & Burrows, 1996, with over 4,000 citations as of this writing), was based on two studies with sample sizes of 30 each. It should not be surprising that forensic analyses show that the findings of this and similar studies are extraordinarily unlikely to replicate (Schimmack, Heene, & Kesavan, 2017), and that this particular study has been subject to actual failures to replicate (Doyen, Klein, Pichon, & Cleeremans, 2012).

A more recent example involves power posing, the idea that expansive poses can improve one's life (Carney, Cuddy, & Yap, 2010). That is an extraordinarily confident claim for a study based on 42 people. It should not be surprising, therefore, that most of its claims simply do not hold up under scrutiny (Simmons & Simonsohn, 2017) or attempts at replication (Ranehill et al., 2015).

Failure to Eliminate Experimenter Effects

Experimenter effects occur when researchers evoke hypothesis-confirming behavior from their research participants, something that has been well known for over 50 years (e.g., Rosenthal & Fode, 1963). Nonetheless, research suggests that only about one-quarter of the articles in *Journal of Personality and Social Psychology* and *Psychological Science* that involved live interactions between experimenters and participants explicitly reported blinding those experimenters to the hypotheses or experimental conditions (Jussim, Crawford, Anglin, Stevens et al., 2016; Klein et al., 2012).

Although it is impossible to know the extent to which this has created illusory support for psychological hypotheses, it is not impossible for this state of affairs to lead to a high level of skepticism about findings in any published report that has not explicitly reported experimenter blindness. This analysis is not purely hypothetical. In a rare case of researchers correcting their own research, Lane et al. (2015) reported failures to replicate their earlier findings (Mikolajczak et al., 2010, same team). They noted that experimenters had not previously been blind to condition, which may have caused a phantom effect. Research has also demonstrated that some priming "effects" occurred *only* when experimenters were not blind to condition (Gilder & Heerey, 2018). Much, if not all, social psychological experimentation that involves interactions between experimenters and participants, and that fails to blind experimenters, warrants high levels of skepticism, pending successful (preferably pre-registered) replications that do blind experimenters to hypothesis and conditions. Based on content analysis of the social psychological literature (Jussim, Crawford, Anglin, Stevens et al., 2016; Klein et al., 2012), this may constitute a large portion of the social psychological experimental literature.

Inferring Causation from Correlation

Inferring causality from correlation happens with regularity in psychology (e.g., Nunes et al., 2017), and, as we show here, in work on intergroup relations. Gaps between demographic groups are routinely presumed to reflect discrimination, which, like any correlation (in this case, between group membership and some outcome, such as distribution into occupations, graduate admissions, income, etc.), might but does not necessarily explain the gap. For example, when men receive greater shares of some desirable outcome, sexism is often the go-to explanation (e.g., Ledgerwood, Haines, & Ratliff, 2015; van der Lee & Ellemers, 2015), even when alternative explanations are not even considered (Jussim, 2017b). Sometimes, it is the go-to explanation even when an alternative explanation (such as Simpson's paradox) better explains the discrepancy (e.g., Albers, 2015; Bickel, Hammel, & O'Connell, 1975).

Similarly, measures of implicit prejudice were once presented as powerful sources of discrimination (e.g., Banaji & Greenwald, 2013) based on "compelling narratives." The logic seemed to be something like (1) implicit prejudice is pervasive, (2) inequality is pervasive, (3) therefore, implicit prejudice probably explains much inequality. We call this a "phantom" correlation because the argument could be and was made in the absence of any direct empirical link between any measure of implicit prejudice and any real-world gap. Indeed, even the more modest goal of linking implicit prejudice to discrimination has proven difficult (Mitchell, 2018). It should not be surprising, therefore, to discover that evidence indicates that implicit measures predict discrimination weakly at best (e.g., Forscher et al., 2016).

Furthermore, evidence has been vindicating the view proposed by Arkes and Tetlock (2004) that implicit "bias" measures seem to reflect social realities more than they cause them (Payne, Vuletich, & Lundberg, 2017; Rubinstein, Jussim, & Stevens, 2018). Thus, although it may well be true that there is implicit bias, and it is clearly true that there is considerable inequality of all sorts between various demographic groups, whether the main causal direction is from bias to inequality, or from inequality to "bias" remains unclear. This seems like an example of scientific gullibility, not because the implicit bias causes inequality link is known to be "wrong," but because dubious and controversial evidence has been treated as the type of well-established "fact" appropriate for influencing policy and law (Mitchell, 2018).

Overlooking Contrary Scholarship

The "power of the situation" is one of those canonical, bedrock "findings" emblematic of social psychology. It is true that there is good evidence that, *sometimes* situations are quite powerful (Milgram, 1974). But the stronger claim that also appears to have widespread acceptance is that personality and individual differences have little to no effect once the impact of the situation is accounted for (see e.g., Jost & Kruglanski, 2002; Ross & Nisbett, 1991). The persistence of an emphasis on the power of the situation in a good deal of social psychological scholarship provides one example of overlooking scholarship that has produced contrary evidence (Funder, 2006, 2009).

There are many problems with this claim, but with respect to scientific gullibility the key one is that it is usually without actually comparing the "power of the situation" to evidence that bears on the "the power of individual differences." The typical effect size for a situational effect on behavior is about the same as the typical effect size for a personality characteristic – and both are rather large relative to other social psychological effects (Fleeson, 2004; Fleeson & Noftle, 2008; Funder, 2006, 2009). It is not "gullibility" for those to believe in the "power of the situation" simply based on ignorance of the individual differences data. It is gullibility to make such claims without identifying and reviewing such evidence.

The Fundamental Publication Error: Correctives do not Necessarily Produce Correction

The fundamental publication error refers to the belief that just because some corrective to some scientific error has been published, that there has been scientific self-correction (Jussim, 2017a). A failure to self-correct can occur, even if a corrective has been published, by ignoring the correction, especially in outlets that are intended to reflect the canon. With most of the examples presented here, not only are the original claims maintained by violation of fundamental norms of scientific evidence, but ample corrections have been published. Nonetheless, the erroneous claims persist. Despite the fact that dozens of studies have empirically demonstrated the

292 *Lee Jussim et al.*

accuracy of gender and race stereotypes, claims that such stereotypes are inaccurate still appear in "authoritative" sources (e.g., Ellemers, 2018; see Jussim, Crawford, & Rubinstein, 2015 for a review). Similarly, the assumption that inequality reflects discrimination, without consideration of alternatives, is widespread (see, e.g., reviews by Hermanson, 2017; Stern, 2018; Winegard, Clark, & Hasty, 2018).

Table 15.1 shows how studies that have been subject to critiques and failed pre-registered replications continue to be cited far more frequently than either the critiques or the failed replications, even after those critiques and failures have appeared. Although blunt declarations that situations are more powerful than individual differences are no longer common in the social psychological literature, the emphasis on the power of the situation manifests as blank slatism and as a belief in "cosmic egalitarianism" – the idea that, but for situations, there would be no mean differences between any demographic groups on any socially important or valued characteristics (Pinker, 2002; Winegard et al., 2018). Thus, the examples presented here are not historical oddities; they reflect a state of scientific gullibility in social psychology.

Reducing Scientific Gullibility

Changing Methods and Practices

Some researchers are actively working on ways to reduce gullibility and increase valid interpretations of published findings, many of which are aimed at reforming the academic incentive structure. Simply put, within academia, publications represent credibility and currency. The more a researcher publishes, and the more those publications are cited by others in the field, the more their credibility as a researcher increases. This can then lead to more publications, promotions, and funding opportunities. Thus, publishing one's findings is essential, and one of the most prominent gatekeepers of publication is the p<.05 threshold. Yet, such a metric can promote questionable research practices (Simmons et al., 2011; Simonsohn et al., 2014). These findings may constitute an example of Goodhart's Law – that when a measure becomes a desirable target it ceases to become a good measure (Koehrsen, 2018) – at work among researchers.

One intervention aimed at reducing behaviors that artificially increase the prevalence of p-values just below 0.05 is preregistration. Preregistration requires a researcher to detail a study's hypotheses, methods, and proposed statistical analyses prior to collecting data (Nosek & Lakens, 2014). By pre-registering a study, researchers are not prevented from performing exploratory data analysis, but they are prevented from reporting exploratory findings as confirmatory (Gelman, 2013).

Because of growing recognition of the power of pre-registration to produce valid science, some journals have even begun embracing the registered report. A registered report is a proposal to conduct a study with clearly defined methods and statistical tests that is peer reviewed before data collection. Because a decision to publish is made not on the nature or statistical significance of the findings, but on the importance of the question and the quality of the methods, publication biases are reduced. Additionally, researchers and journals have started data-sharing repositories to encourage the sharing of non-published supporting material and raw data. Openly sharing methods and collected data allows increased oversight by the entire research community and promotes collaboration. Together, open research materials, preregistration, and registered reports all discourage scientific gullibility by shedding daylight on the research practices and findings, opening studies to skeptical evaluation by other scientists, and therefore, increasing clarity of findings and decreasing the influence of the types status and status quo biases discussed earlier.

Benefits of Intense Skepticism

Extraordinary claims should require extraordinary evidence. Thus, subjecting scientific claims to intense, organized skepticism and scrutiny is necessary to sift unsubstantiated claims from ones justified and well supported. Such organized skepticism is one of the core norms of science (Merton, 1942/1973). Indeed, people are better at identifying flaws in other people's evidence-gathering than their own (Mercier & Sperber, 2011), and a dissenting minority within a group can reduce conformity pressures on decision-making (Crano, 2012), producing deeper thought that can lead to higher-quality group decisions (Nemeth, Brown, & Rogers, 2001). Science is a collective enterprise, where the independent operations of many accumulate into a bigger picture. Making high-quality group decisions (e.g., regarding what constitutes the canonical findings) is therefore important, and one way to do so is to subject scientific research to intense skepticism and scrutiny by other members of the scientific community.

The Evolutionary Psychology of Gender Differences: A Case Study in the Benefits of Intense Skepticism

One area of research that has received an intense amount of skepticism, scrutiny, and criticism from social psychologists, is the idea of evolved gender differences in the psychological and behavioral characteristics of human males and females (Geher & Gambacorta, 2010; Pinker, 2002; von Hippel & Buss, 2018). One common criticism often leveled against evolutionary psychology is that it is a political effort led by conservatives, emphasizing biological determinism, to advance a political agenda that defends current social arrangements and inequalities (for a more elaborate discussion of these criticisms, see Pinker, 2002; Tybur & Navarrete, 2018).

294 *Lee Jussim et al.*

The premise on which this is based – that evolutionary psychologists are primarily conservative – has been disconfirmed. Surveys of evolutionary psychologists reveal they are as liberal, if not more, than their colleagues (Tybur, Miller, & Gangestad, 2007; see von Hippel & Buss, 2018 for a review).

More importantly for our discussion of scientific gullibility is that evolutionary psychologists have been clear for decades that their approach emphasizes an interaction between genes and the sociocultural environment. For instance, in his landmark study on mate preferences, Buss (1989, p. 13, emphasis added) noted the following: "Currently unknown are the *cultural and ecological* causes of variation from country to country in (1) the magnitudes of obtained sex differences, and (2) the absolute levels of valuing reproductively relevant mate characteristics." It is quite difficult to detect even a whiff of biological determinism in that statement, as it implies a need to research the *cultural and ecological* causes of variation. This study has been cited over 4,000 times and was a featured paper in *Behavioral and Brain Sciences* that was accompanied by a number of responses. To continue to imply that evolutionary psychology emphasizes biological determinism suggests that the critics are either (a) unaware of one of the most important papers in evolutionary psychology; (b) are aware of it, but have not read it; or, (c) are aware of it, have read it, and have decided to still insist the approach emphasizes biological determinism.

Nevertheless, despite the (ongoing) controversy (see, e.g., Galinsky, 2017), the level of controversy and mutual skepticism (between advocates and opponents of evolutionary psychology explanations for gender differences) has helped advance social psychology's understanding of gender. Meta-analyses and large sample studies (N >10,000) from different theoretical perspectives have investigated gender differences within and across cultures (see Stevens & Haidt, 2017). A collaborative effort by researchers with different research backgrounds, and in some cases adversarial perspectives, concluded that there are important gender differences between males and females that influence cognition and behavior, *which result from a complex interaction of innate (i.e., biological) factors and the sociocultural environment* (Halpern et al., 2007).

Intense skepticism – of purely cultural explanations for sex differences and of purely biological ones – has been a boon to the scientific research seeking to understand those differences. A similar skepticism directed especially to the canonical claims in social psychology could be most productive – are they based on any evidence? Are they based on a handful of small N studies? Have there been any successful pre-registered replications? Have they explicitly considered, and ruled out, alternative explanations? All research, but especially foundational research, should be subject to this sort of skepticism, at least if we want to reduce scientific gullibility and increase scientific support for our field's major claims.

Strong Inference

Strong inference involves two main strategies that are synergistic, and that, when used together, offer considerable promise to limit scientific gullibility and produce rapid scientific advances (Platt, 1964; Washburn & Skitka, in press). The two strategies involve (1) seeking conditions that might disconfirm one's predictions and (2) comparing theories or hypotheses that make alternative or opposing predictions in some research context. Platt (1964, p. 350) also speculated on obstacles to the use of strong inference:

> The difficulty is that disproof is a hard doctrine. If you have a hypothesis and I have another hypothesis, evidently one of them must be eliminated. The scientist seems to have no choice but to be either soft-headed or disputatious. Perhaps this is why so many tend to resist the strong analytical approach – and why some great scientists are so disputatious.

Nonetheless, strong inference can reduce gullibility by making use of one of the few known antidotes to all sorts of biases: consider the opposite (Lord, Lepper, & Preston, 1984). If, for example, a field has a theoretical bias (see e.g., Funder, 1987; Jussim, 2012) or political biases (Duarte et al., 2015), then scientific literature may become filled with lots of evidence providing weak and biased tests seeming to confirm certain notions. Combine this with excessive scientism, and one has a recipe for gullibility on a grand scale, because few scientists will dive into the individual studies in sufficient depth to debunk them.

However, adoption of strong inference can and has limited such biases. Washburn and Skitka (in press) review several cases where strong inference was used to minimize political biases. For example, one can adopt what they call a "negative test strategy": hypothesize *the opposite* of what one prefers. If liberals generally prefer evidence of liberal superiority, a liberal social scientist could add in hypotheses about conservative superiority. Interestingly, when this was done with respect to prejudice, the long-standing claim that liberals were generally less prejudiced than conservatives was disconfirmed, replaced by the understanding that overall levels of prejudice are similar, but directed towards different groups (Brandt, Reyna, Chambers, Crawford, & Wetherell, 2014). Similarly, for example, Rubinstein et al. (2018) used strong inference to compare perspectives emphasizing the power of stereotypes versus individuating information to bias implicit and explicit person perception. Perspectives emphasizing the power of individuating information were supported, thereby limiting bias in favor of bias.

Credibility Categories

Recently, Pashler and De Ruiter (2017) proposed three credibility classes of research. Class 1, the most credible, is based on work that has been published, successfully replicated by several pre-registered studies, and in which publication biases, HARKing (Kerr, 1998), and p-hacking can all be ruled out as explanations for the effect. Work that meets this standard can be considered a scientific fact, in the Gouldian sense of being well established. Class 2 research is strongly suggestive but falls short of being a well-established "fact." It might include many published studies, but there are few, if any, pre-registered successful replications, and HARKing and p-hacking have not been ruled out. Class 3 evidence is that yielded by a small number of small sample studies, without pre-registered replications, and without checks against HARKing and p-hacking. Such studies are preliminary and should not be taken as providing strong evidence of anything, pending stronger tests and pre-registered successful replications.

Pashler and De Ruiter's (2017) system could have prevented social psychology from taking findings such as stereotype threat (Steele & Aronson, 1995), social priming (Bargh et al., 1996), and power posing (Carney et al., 2010) as "well established." Had the field not had a norm of excessive scientism, and, instead, treated these findings as suggestive, and warranting large-scale pre-registered replication attempts, much of the current "replication crisis" may have been avoided. To be fair, the value of pre-registration was not widely recognized until relatively recently, which may help explain why it was not used. But our main point remains intact; absent pre-registration, or large, high-powered replications, such work should have been considered preliminary and suggestive at best, especially considering the small sample sizes on which it was based.

Pashler and De Ruiter's (2017) system is an important contribution to understanding when past literature in social psychology provides a strong versus weak evidentiary basis for or against some theory, hypothesis, or phenomenon. Nonetheless, we also think it is less important that researchers use this exact system, than it is that they develop some *systematic* way of assigning credibility to research based on factors such as sample size, consideration of alternative explanations, pre-registration, open data, and materials, etc. In fact, the field's view of how to evaluate research credibility is still evolving, and Pashler and De Ruiter's system is not the final word; in fact, it is more like an initial attempt to systematize strength of past evidence. Whatever system one uses, we predict that a closer attention to the credibility of research, rather than a simple acceptance of something as fact just because it was published, will go a long way to reducing scientific gullibility.

Conclusion

Scientific gullibility is a major problem because it has contributed to the development of a dubious scientific "canon" – findings that are taken as so well established that they are part of the social psychological fundament, as evidenced by their endorsement by the American Psychological

Association, and their appearance in outlets that are supposed to reflect only the most well-established phenomena, such as handbook and annual review chapters. Gullibility begins with treating results from small sample size studies as well established "facts," a lack of transparency surrounding data analysis, failure to understand limitations of statistical analyses, underestimation of the power of publication biases, or an over-reliance on $p<.05$. Researchers also sometimes give undue credibility to papers that oversell findings, tell compelling narratives that aren't substantiated by the data, or report data that support desired conclusions with insufficient skepticism. Findings that have been roundly refuted or called into question in the empirical literature are often not extirpated from the canon.

In this chapter, we articulated and provided evidence for six scientific gullibility red flags that can and do appear in the research literature: (1) large claims being made from small and/or potentially unrepresentative samples, (2) many published reports of experiments do not state that experimenters were blind to hypotheses and conditions, (3) correlational data being used as evidence of causality, (4) ignoring scholarship articulating clear opposing evidence or arguments, (5) putting forth strong claims or conclusions that lack a foundation in empirical evidence, and (6) neglecting to consider plausible alternative explanations for findings. Although we are not claiming that the whole social psychological literature reflects gullibility, it is also true that little is currently of sufficient quality to fall into Pashler and de Ruiter's (2017) class 1 of "established fact." On the other hand, we see no evidence of consensus in the field to use their system. Absent some such system, however, it remains unclear which areas of social psychology have produced sound science and established facts, and which have been suggestive at best and entirely false at worst. Our hope is that by revealing these influences on, standards for recognizing, and ways to limit scientific gullibility, we have contributed something towards social psychology producing a canon that is based on valid and well-justified claims.

References

Albers, C. J. (2015). Dutch research funding, gender bias, and Simpson's paradox. *Proceedings of the National Academy of Sciences, 112*(50), E6828–E6829.

American Psychological Association (APA). (1991). In the supreme court of the United States: *Price Waterhouse v. Ann B. Hopkins* (amicus curiae brief). *American Psychologist, 46,* 1061–1070.

Anglin, S. (2016). The psychology of science. Unpublished doctoral dissertation.

Anomaly, J. (November 29, 2017). The politics of science: Why scientists might not say what the evidence supports. *Quillette.com.* Retrieved from http://quillette. com/2017/11/29/politics-science-scientists-might-not-say-evidence-supports.

Arkes, H., & Tetlock, P. E. (2004). Attributions of implicit prejudice, or would Jesse Jackson fail the Implicit Association Test? *Psychological Inquiry, 15*(4), 257–278.

Aronson, E. (2008). *The social animal* (10th ed.). New York, NY: Worth.

Banaji, M. R., & Greenwald, A. G. (2013). *Blindspot: Hidden biases of good people.* New York, NY: Delacorte Press.

Bargh, J. A., & Chartrand, T. L. (1999). The unbearable automaticity of being. *American Psychologist, 54,* 462–479.

Bargh, J. A., Chen, M., & Burrows, L. (1996). Automaticity of social behavior: Direct effects of trait construct and stereotype activation on action. *Journal of Personality and Social Psychology, 71,* 239–244.

Baron, R. M., Albright, L., & Malloy, T. E. (1995). The effects of behavioral and social class information on social judgment. *Personality and Social Psychology Bulletin, 21,* 308–315.

Bickel, P. J., Hammel, E. A., & O'Connell, J. W. (1975). Sex bias in graduate admissions: Data from Berkeley. *Science, 187,* 396–404.

Brandt, M. J., Reyna, C., Chambers, J. R., Crawford, J. T., & Wetherell, G. (2014). The ideological-conflict hypothesis: Intolerance among both liberals and conservatives. *Current Directions in Psychological Science, 23,* 27–34.

Buss, D. M. (1989). Sex differences in human mate preferences: Evolutionary hypotheses tested in 37 cultures. *Behavioral and Brain Sciences, 12*(1), 1–14.

Carney, D. R., Cuddy, A. J., & Yap, A. J. (2010). Power posing: Brief nonverbal displays affect neuroendocrine levels and risk tolerance. *Psychological Science, 21*(10), 1363–1368.

Chalabaev, A., Major, B., Sarrazin, P., & Cury, F. (2012). When avoiding failure improves performance: Stereotype threat and the impact of performance goals. *Motivation and Emotion, 36*(2), 130–142.

Crano, W. D. (2012). *The rules of influence: Winning when you're in the minority.* New York, NY: St. Martin's Press.

Darley, J. M., & Gross, P. H. (1983). A hypothesis-confirming bias in labeling effects. *Journal of Personality and Social Psychology, 44,* 20–33.

Ditto, P. H., Liu, B. S., Clark, C. J., Wojcik, S. P., Chen, E. E., Grady, R. H., & Zinger, J. F. (in press). At least bias is bipartisan: A meta-analytic comparison of partisan bias in liberals and conservatives. *Perspectives on Psychological Science.*

Doyen, S., Klein, O., Pichon, C., & Cleeremans, A. (2012). Behavioral priming: It's all in the mind, but whose mind? *PLoS One, 7,* e29081.

Duarte, J. L., Crawford, J. T., Stern, C., Haidt, J., Jussim, L., & Tetlock, P. E. (2015). Political diversity will improve social psychological science. *Behavioral and Brain Sciences, 38.* https://doi.org/10.1017/S0140525X14000430

Ellemers, N. (2018). Gender stereotypes. *Annual Review of Psychology, 69,* 275–298.

Eriksson, K., & Simpson, B. (2013). Editorial decisions may perpetuate belief in invalid research findings. *PloS One, 8*(9), e73364.

Finnigan, K. M., & Corker, K. S. (2016). Do performance avoidance goals moderate the effect of different types of stereotype threat on women's math performance? *Journal of Research in Personality, 63,* 36–43.

Fischhoff, B., & Beyth-Marom, R. (1983). Hypothesis evaluation from a Bayesian perspective. *Psychological Review, 90*(3), 239.

Fiske, S. T. (2016). A call to change science's culture of shaming. *APS Observer, 29*(9).

Fleeson, W. (2004). Moving personality beyond the person-situation debate: The challenge and opportunity of within-person variability. *Current Directions in Psychological Science, 13,* 83–87.

Fleeson, W., & Noftle, E. (2008). The end of the person-situation debate: An emerging synthesis in the answer to the consistency question. *Social and Personality Psychology Compass, 2,* 1667–1684.

Flore, P. C., & Wicherts, J. M. (2015). Does stereotype threat influence performance of girls in stereotyped domains? A meta-analysis. *Journal of School Psychology, 53*(1), 25–44.

Forscher, P. S., Lai, C. K., Axt, J. R., Ebersole, C. R., Herman, M., Devine, P. G., & Nosek, B. A. (2016). A meta-analysis of change in implicit bias. Unpublished manuscript.

Fraley, R. C., & Vazire, S. (2014). The N-pact factor: Evaluating the quality of empirical journals with respect to sample size and statistical power. *PloS One, 9*(10), e109019.

Funder, D. C. (1987). Errors and mistakes: Evaluating the accuracy of social judgment. *Psychological Bulletin, 101,* 75–90.

Funder, D. C. (2006). Towards a resolution of the personality triad: Persons, situations, and behaviors. *Journal of Research in Personality, 40,* 21–34.

Funder, D. C. (2009). Persons, behaviors, and situations: An agenda for personality psychology in the postwar era. *Journal of Research in Personality, 43,* 120–126.

Galinsky, A. (August 9, 2017). Google's anti-diversity crisis is a classic example of right vs. right. *Fortune.* Retrieved from http://fortune.com/2017/08/09/google-james-damore-diversity.

Geher, G., & Gambacorta, D. (2010). Evolution is not relevant to sex differences in humans because I want it that way! Evidence for the politicization of human evolutionary psychology. *EvoS Journal: The Journal of the Evolutionary Studies Consortium, 2*(1), 32–47.

Gelman, A. (2013). Preregistration of studies and mock reports. *Political Analysis, 21*(1), 40–41.

Gilder, T. S. E., & Heerey, E. A. (2018). The role of experimenter belief in social priming. *Psychological Science,* 1–15. doi: 10.1177/0956797617737128

Gould, S. J. (1981). *Evolution as fact and theory.* Retrieved from www.stephenjaygould.org/ctrl/gould_fact-and-theory.html.

Greitemeyer, T. (2014). Article retracted, but the message lives on. *Psychonomic Bulletin & Review, 21*(2), 557–561.

Haack, S. (2012). Six signs of scientism. *Logos and Episteme, 3,* 75–95.

Haidt, J. (2001). The emotional dog and its rational tail: A social intuitionist approach to moral judgment. *Psychological Review, 108*(4), 814.

Halpern, D. F., Benbow, C. P., Geary, D. C., Gur, R. C., Hyde, J. S., & Gernsbacher, M. A. (2007). The science of sex differences in science and mathematics. *Psychological Science in the Public Interest, 8,* 1–51.

Hart, W., Albarracín, D., Eagly, A. H., Brechan, I., Lindberg, M. J., & Merrill, L. (2009). Feeling validated versus being correct: a meta-analysis of selective exposure to information. *Psychological Bulletin, 135*(4), 555.

Heilman, M. E. (1983). Sex bias in work settings. *Research in Organizational Behavior, 5,* 269–298.

Hermanson, S. (2017). Implicit bias, stereotype threat, and political correctness in philosophy. *Philosophies, 2,* 1–17. doi:10.3390/philosophies2020012.

Jost, J. T., & Kruglanski, A. W. (2002). The estrangement of social constructionism and experimental social psychology: History of the rift and prospects for reconciliation. *Personality and Social Psychology Review, 6,* 168–187.

Jost, J. T., Rudman, L. A., Blair, I. V., Carney, D. R., Dasgupta, N., Glaser, J., & Hardin, C. D. (2009). The existence of implicit bias is beyond reasonable doubt: A refutation of ideological and methodological objections and executive summary of ten studies that no manager should ignore. *Research in Organizational Behavior, 29*, 39–69. doi: 10.1016/j.riob.2009.10.001

Jussim, L. (2012). *Social perception and social reality: Why accuracy dominates bias and self-fulfilling prophecy.* New York, NY: Oxford University Press.

Jussim, L. (2017a). Accuracy, bias, self-fulfilling prophecies, and scientific self-correction. *Behavioral and Brain Sciences, 40*, 44–65. doi:10.1017/S0140525X16 000339, e18.

Jussim, L. (2017b). Gender bias in science or biased claims of gender bias? [Blog post]. Retrieved from www.psychologytoday.com/blog/rabble-rouser/201707/gender-bias-in-science-or-biased-claims-gender-bias.

Jussim, L., Crawford, J. T., Anglin, S. M., Chambers, J. R., Stevens, S. T., & Cohen, F. (2016). Stereotype accuracy: One of the largest and most replicable effects in all of social psychology. In T. Nelson (Ed.), *The handbook of prejudice, stereotyping, and discrimination* (pp. 31–63). Hove, UK: Psychology Press.

Jussim, L., Crawford, J. T., Anglin, S. M., Stevens, S. M., & Duarte, J. L. (2016). Interpretations and methods: Towards a more effectively self-correcting social psychology. *Journal of Experimental Social Psychology, 66*, 116–133.

Jussim, L., Crawford, J. T., & Rubinstein, R. S. (2015). Stereotype (in) accuracy in perceptions of groups and individuals. *Current Directions in Psychological Science, 24*(6), 490–497.

Kahan, D. M., Jenkins-Smith, H., & Braman, D. (2011). Cultural cognition of scientific consensus. *Journal of Risk Research, 14*, 147–174.

Kerr, N. I. (1998). HARKing: Hypothesizing after results are known. *Personality and Social Psychology Review, 2*, 196–217.

Klaczynski, P. A. (2000). Motivated scientific reasoning biases, epistemological beliefs, and theory polarization: A two-process approach to adolescent cognition. *Child Development, 71*, 1347–1366.

Klayman, J., & Ha, Y. W. (1987). Confirmation, disconfirmation, and information in hypothesis testing. *Psychological Review, 94*(2), 211.

Klein, O., Doyen, S., Leys, C., Magalhães de Saldanha da Gama, P. A., Miller, S., Questienne, L. & Cleeremans, A. (2012). Low hopes, high expectations: Expectancy effects and the replicability of behavioral experiments. *Perspectives on Psychological Science, 7*, 572–584.

Koehler, J. J. (1993). The influence of prior beliefs on scientific judgments of evidence quality. *Organizational Behavior and Human Decision Processes, 56*(1), 28–55.

Koehrsen, W. (2018). Unintended consequences and Goodhart's Law [Blog Post]. Retrieved from https://towardsdatascience.com/unintended-conse quences-and-goodharts-law-68d60a94705c.

Lane, A., Mikolajczak, M., Treinen, E., Samson, D., Corneille, O., de Timary, P., & Luminet, O. (2015). Failed replication of oxytocin effects on trust: The envelope T ask case. *PloS One,10*(9), e0137000. http://dx.doi.org/10.1371/journal.pone.0137000

Ledgerwood, A., Haines, E., & Ratliff, K. (2015). Not nutting up or shutting up: Notes on the demographic disconnect in our field's best practices conversation [Blog post]. Retrieved from http://sometimesimwrong.typepad.com/wrong/2015/03/guest-post-not-nutting-up-or-shutting-up.html.

Lilienfeld, S. O. (2010). Can psychology become a science? *Personality and Individual Differences, 49*, 281–288.

Lord, C. G., Lepper, M. R., & Preston, E. (1984). Considering the opposite: A corrective strategy for social judgment. *Journal of Personality and Social Psychology*, 47, 1231–1243.

MacCoun, R. J. (1998). Biases in the interpretation and use of research results. *Annual Review of Psychology*, 49, 259–287.

Meehl, P. E. (1990). Appraising and amending theories: The strategy of Lakatosian defense and two principles that warrant using it. *Psychological Inquiry*, 1, 108–141, 173–180.

Mercier, H., & Sperber, D. (2011). Why do humans reason? Arguments for an argumentative theory. *Behavioral and Brain Sciences*, 34(2), 57–74.

Merton, R. K. (1942/1973). The normative structure of science. In N. W. Storer (Ed.), *The sociology of science* (pp. 267–278). Chicago, IL: University of Chicago Press.

Merton, R. K. (1968). The Matthew effect in science. *Science*, 159(3810), 56–63.

Mikolajczak, M., Gross, J. J., Lane, A., Corneille, O., de Timary, P., & Luminet, O. (2010). Oxytocin makes people trusting, not gullible. Psychological *Science*, 21(8), 1072–1074.

Milgram, S. (1974). *Obedience to authority: An experimental view*. New York, NY: Harper & Row.

Miller, G. A., & Chapman, J. P. (2001). Misunderstanding analysis of covariance. *Journal of Abnormal Psychology*, 110(1), 40.

Mitchell, G. (2018). Jumping to conclusions: Advocacy and application of psychological research. In J. T. Crawford and L. Jussim (Eds.), *The politics of social psychology*. New York, NY: Psychology Press.

Munro, G. D., & Ditto, P. H. (1997). Biased assimilation, attitude polarization, and affect in reactions to stereotype-relevant scientific information. *Personality and Social Psychology Bulletin*, 23(6), 636–653.

Nemeth, C., Brown, K., & Rogers, J. (2001). Devil's advocate versus authentic dissent: Stimulating quantity and quality. *European Journal of Social Psychology*, 31(6), 707–720.

Nickerson, R. S. (1998). Confirmation bias: A ubiquitous phenomenon in many guises. *Review of General Psychology*, 2(2), 175.

Nosek, B. A., & Lakens, D. (2014). Registered reports: A method to increase the credibility of published results. *Social Psychology*, 45, 137–141.

Nuijten, M. B., Hartgerink, C. H., van Assen, M. A., Epskamp, S., & Wicherts, J. M. (2016). The prevalence of statistical reporting errors in psychology (1985–2013). *Behavior research methods*, 48(4), 1205–1226.

Nunes, K. L., Pedneault, C. I., Filleter, W. E., Maimone, S., Blank, C., & Atlas, M. (2017). "I know correlation doesn't prove causation, but ...": Are we jumping to unfounded conclusions about the causes of sexual offending?. *Sexual Abuse*. doi: 1079063217729156

Okike, K., Hug, K. T., Kocher, M. S., & Leopold, S. S. (2016). Single-blind vs. double-blind peer review in the setting of author prestige. *JAMA*, 316(12), 1315–1316.

Pashler, H. & De Ruiter, J. P. (October, 2017). Taking responsibility for our field's reputation. *Observer*. Association for Psychological Science. Retrieved from www.psychologicalscience.org/observer/taking-responsibility-for-our-fields-reputation.

Payne, B. K., Vuletich, H. A., & Lundberg, K. B. (2017). The bias of crowds: How implicit bias bridges personal and systemic prejudice. *Psychological Inquiry, 28*(4), 233–248.

Peters, D. P., & Ceci, S. J. (1982). Peer review practices of psychological journals: The fate of published articles, submitted again. *Behavioral and Brain Sciences*, 5, 187–255.

Pigliucci, M. (2018). The problem with scientism. *Blog of the APA*. Retrieved from https://blog.apaonline.org/2018/01/25/the-problem-with-scientism.

Pinker, S. (2002). *The blank slate: The modern denial of human nature*. New York, NY: Viking.

Platt, J. R. (1964). Strong inference. *Science, 146*, 347–353.

Ranehill, E., Dreber, A., Johannesson, M., Leiberg, S., Sul, S., & Weber, R. A. (2015). Assessing the robustness of power posing: No effect on hormones and risk tolerance in a large sample of men and women. *Psychological Science, 26*, 653–656.

Roberts, S., & Pashler, H. (2000). How persuasive is a good fit? A comment on theory testing. *Psychological Review, 107*(2), 358.

Rosenthal, R., & Fode, K. L. (1963). The effect of experimenter bias on the performance of the albino rat. *Behavioral Science, 83*, 183–189.

Ross, L., & Nisbett, R. E. (1991). *The person and the situation: Perspectives of Social Psychology*. New York, NY: McGraw-Hill.

Rubinstein, R.S., Jussim L., & Stevens, S. T. (2018). Reliance on individuating information and stereotypes in implicit and explicit person perception. *Journal of Experimental Social Psychology, 75*, 54–70.

Sabeti, P. (2018). For better science, call off the revolutionaries. *Boston Globe: Ideas*. Retrieved from www.bostonglobe.com/ideas/2018/01/21/for-better-science-call-off-revolutionaries/8FFEmBAPCDW3IWYJwKF31L/story.html.

Samuelson, W., & Zeckhauser, R. (1988). Status quo bias in decision making. *Journal of Risk and Uncertainty, 1*(1), 7–59.

Schimmack, U., Heene, M., & Kesavan, K. (2017). Reconstruction of a train wreck: How priming research went off the rails [Blog post]. Retrieved from https://replicationindex.wordpress.com/2017/02/02/reconstruction-of-a-train-wreck-how-priming-research-went-of-the-rails.

Simmons, J. P., Nelson, L. D., & Simonsohn, U. (2011). False-positive psychology: Undisclosed flexibility in data collection and analysis allows presenting anything as significant. *Psychological Science, 22*, 1359–1366. https://doi.org/10.1177/0956797611417632

Simmons, J. P., & Simonsohn, U. (2017). Power posing: P-curving the evidence. *Psychological Science, 28*(5), 687–693.

Simonsohn, U., Nelson, L. D., & Simmons, J. P. (2014). P-curve: A key to the file drawer. *Journal of Experimental Psychology: General, 143*(2), 534–547. http://doi.org/10.1037/a0033242

Snyder, M., & Swann, W. B., Jr. (1978). Hypothesis-testing processes in social interaction. *Journal of Personality and Social Psychology, 36*, 1202–1212.

Spencer, S. J., Steele, C. M., & Quinn, D. M. (1999). Stereotype threat and women's math performance. *Journal of Experimental Social Psychology, 35*(1), 4–28.

Steegen, S., Tuerlinckx, F., Gelman, A., & Vanpaemel, W. (2016). Increasing transparency through a multiverse analysis. *Perspectives on Psychological Science, 11*(5), 702–712.

Steele, C. M., & Aronson, J. (1995). Stereotype threat and the intellectual performance of African Americans. *Journal of Personality and Social Psychology, 69*, 797–811.

Stern, C. (2018). Does political ideology hinder insights on gender and labor markets? In J. T. Crawford & L. Jussim (Eds.), *The politics of social psychology* (pp. 44–61). New York, NY: Psychology Press.

Stevens, S. T., & Haidt, J. (2017). The Google memo: What does the research say about gender differences? Retrieved from https://heterodoxacademy.org/2017/08/10/the-google-memo-what-does-the-research-say-about-gender-differences.

Stevens, S. T., Jussim, L., Anglin, S. M., & Honeycutt, N. (2018). Direct and indirect influences of political ideology on perceptions of scientific findings. In B. Rutjens & M. Brandt (Eds.), *Belief systems and the perception of reality* (pp. 115–133). Oxford: Routledge.

Tappin, B. M., van der Leer, L., & McKay, R. T. (2017). The heart trumps the head: Desirability bias in political belief revision. *Journal of Experimental Psychology: General, 146*(8), 1143.

Tetlock, P. E. (1994). Political psychology or politicized psychology: Is the road to scientific hell paved with good intentions? *Political Psychology, 15*, 509–529.

Tomkins, A., Zhang, M., & Heavlin, W. D. (2017). Reviewer bias in single-versus double-blind peer review. *Proceedings of the National Academy of Sciences, 114*(48), 12708–12713.

Trope, Y., & Bassok, M. (1983). Information-gathering strategies in hypothesis-testing. *Journal of Experimental Social Psychology, 19*(6), 560–576.

Tversky, A., & Kahneman, D. (1971). Belief in the law of small numbers. *Psychological Bulletin, 76*(2), 105.

Tybur, J. M., Miller, G. F., & Gangestad, S. W. (2007). Testing the controversy: An empirical examination of adaptationists' attitudes towards politics and science. *Human Nature, 18*, 313–328.

Tybur, J. M., & Navarrete, C. D. (2018). Interrupting bias in psychological science: Evolutionary psychology as a guide. In J. T. Crawford and L. Jussim (Eds.), *The politics of social psychology*. New York, NY: Psychology Press.

van der Lee, R., & Ellemers, N. (2015). Gender contributes to personal research funding success in the Netherlands. *Proceedings of the National Academy of Sciences, 112*(40), 12349–12353.

Vazire, S. (2017). Our obsession with eminence warps research. *Nature News, 574*(7661), 7.

von Hippel, W., & Buss, D. M. (2018). Do ideologically driven scientific agendas impede understanding and acceptance of evolutionary principles in social psychology? In J. T. Crawford & L. Jussim (Eds.), *The politics of social psychology* (pp. 7–25). New York, NY: Psychology Press.

Washburn, A. N., & Skitka, L. J. (in press). Strategies for promoting strong inferences in political psychology research. In B. T. Rutjens and M. J. Brandt (Eds.), *Belief systems and the perception of reality*.

Wicherts, J. M., Veldkamp, C. L., Augusteijn, H. E., Bakker, M., van Aert, R., & van Assen, M. A. (2016). Degrees of freedom in planning, running, analyzing, and reporting psychological studies: A checklist to avoid p-hacking. *Frontiers in Psychology, 7*, 1832.

Winegard, B. M., Clark, C. J., & Hasty, C. R. (2018). Equalitarianism: A source of liberal bias. Unpublished manuscript. Retrieved from https://osf.io/hmn8v.

16 Gullibility and the Envelope of Legitimacy

Joel Cooper and Joseph J. Avery
PRINCETON UNIVERSITY

Gullibility and the Envelope of Legitimacy

We consider gullibility to be an uncomfortable feeling state precipitated by the perception that one has been persuaded to believe something that is not true. The experience is not only uncomfortable, it is threatening to one's sense of self-worth. Accordingly, people will undergo considerable effort to avoid and reduce it. A viable method of avoidance is to believe that something false is true rather than believe that we have been duped. In the vernacular, we may "double down" on our belief, becoming even more certain that the position held is true.

We do not expect every communicative act to be entirely truthful, but we do expect that communication will lie within a reasonable distance of the truth. This reasonable distance is what we call the "envelope of legitimacy." It is our contention that, if one is persuaded to believe a position that lies outside the envelope of legitimacy and subsequently learns that the communication was untrue, this is when one is likely to feel the unpleasant tension state of gullibility and to double down on one's false belief. In short, people would rather believe that a lie is true than believe that they were duped – if that lie falls outside the envelope of legitimacy. In the succeeding sections, we will develop the conceptual underpinnings for this idea. Then we will discuss our recent empirical work concerning factors affecting the current political beliefs of individuals who voted in the 2016 U.S. presidential election.

An Infamous Case of Gullibility

On the evening before Halloween, 1938, Orson Welles began his weekly radio broadcast with the disclaimer that the Mercury Theater would present a dramatization of H. G. Wells' *War of the Worlds*. By the time his broadcast had ended, hundreds of thousands of American listeners were seized with panic as they tried to flee monsters from the planet Mars. In the dramatization, listeners heard what was portrayed as a series of news bulletins. One of the bulletins described unusual explosions on Mars while another indicated that there had been a disturbance in a field in the small town of Grover's Mill, New Jersey, where a "huge flaming object" had landed. A CBS news reporter and a Princeton University astronomy professor allegedly raced to the scene to describe that monsters too hideous to describe were emerging from the object. Within the next few minutes, the monsters had decimated the state police and were in full control of the area. The National Guard was called and it, too, proved no match for the objects.

The consequences of the great deception were brief but spectacular. It was estimated that 6 million listeners heard the broadcast and that at least 1 million believed that Martians had invaded the United States (Cantril, 1940). They believed that Martians had been sighted in many major cities across the country and that New York City itself had been wiped from the Earth. People cried, screamed, and prepared for the end. Mr. William Dock was famously photographed with his shotgun, ready to do battle with any Martian that dared attack his farm. Others got into their cars to drive as far away as they possibly could, while still others huddled with loved ones to await their ends. "We all kissed one another and felt we would all die," admitted one respondent. The reaction was not confined to any educational, geographic or racial group. The *New York Times* reported that that in several communities, physicians showed up at hospitals to help care for the injured, and college students sped along highways to spend their last moments with their families.

Orson Welles' broadcast underscored the plausibility of the implausible. Not only was the program's premise a fantasy, but Welles had clearly stated that the Mercury Theater was a drama. The program itself was rife with internal inconsistencies of time and space. Nonetheless, it caused more than a million people to become frightened, many of whom took action to flee from the Martian menace. During the ensuing decades, commentators have speculated on the gullibility of the audience with a concern for whether such gullibility could lead to a future bout of mass hysteria.

Toward an Operational Definition of Gullibility

The Oxford Dictionary defines gullibility as the tendency to be easily persuaded. Jussim, Stevens, Honeycutt, Anglia, and Fox (Chapter 15 this volume) add, "easily deceived or cheated." These definitions imply that extreme persuasibility is the property of the individual. It is sometimes seen as synonymous with naïveté or foolishness (Rotter, 1980). Viewed as an element of personality, it should transcend time and situation. The implication of this perspective is that people who are gullible are generally easy to persuade or deceive. They are the kinds of people who believe what they are told not only about creatures invading from other planets but about most anything conveyed to them by authority. They believe in séances and believe political rhetoric that emanates from the pens or mouths of populist leaders. However, the search for personality variables in persuasion

306 Joel Cooper and Joseph J. Avery

has proved elusive (Cooper, Blackman, & Keller, 2016), and the search for reliable individual differences in the degree of gullibility has been no exception (Mercier, 2017). Rotter (1980), for example, examined the relationship between gullibility and interpersonal trust and could find no systematic evidence that reliable individual differences in trust were related to people's tendency to believe statements that most people would see as untrue

Mercier (2017) views gullibility as source-based rather than a characteristic of certain impressionable people. He maintains that gullibility emanates from the undue influence of "focal sources, often authority figures, be they religious leaders, demagogues, TV anchors or celebrities" (Mercier, 2017, p. 104). Such focal sources may be gifted orators, as in the case of Adolf Hitler, or they may make use of seemingly simple communicative techniques, such as repetition, a hallmark of Donald Trump's oratory style (see Myers, Chapter 5 this volume; Unkelbach & Koch, Chapter 3 this volume, for discussions of repetition and its relation to gullibility). Certainly, history is replete with communicators who had the ability to convince masses to believe propaganda that, in retrospect, facilitates our using the term gullible to describe their falling prey to the communicators' messages. From Huey Long to Adolf Hitler, communicators have had the special charisma, power, and the ability to persuade.

Another conceptualization considers gullibility to be a faulty response to a persuasive communication (see also Fiedler's discussion of metacognitive myopia, Chapter 7 this volume). In this view, gullibility is conceptualized as believing someone's communication despite good evidence that the person should not be believed (Rotter, 1980). The gullible audience simply fails to consider reasons for disbelief. This might be conceptualized as the difference between inhabiting a gullible mindset versus inhabiting a skeptical one, especially as a primary, default process (Mayo, Chapter 8 this volume). It is the basis of the phenomenon known as the Barnum effect (Meehl, 1956), whereby individuals give high accuracy ratings to descriptions of their personalities that supposedly are tailored specifically to them but that are, in fact, vague and general enough to apply to a wide range of people. People fail to notice that the statements are at a level of abstraction that makes them applicable to almost anyone.

Even when people do check the trustworthiness of the source and the information, persuasion that we can call gullibility occurs. In the response to the *War of the Worlds* broadcast, almost everyone who Cantril (1940) interviewed and those who were quoted in newspapers around the country made an attempt to check the veracity of the information. One person reported looking out of her window and seeing traffic on the street. "They all must be fleeing the invasion," she reported. Another person looked out of his window and saw no traffic at all on his street. "The roads must be clogged on account of the Martians," he concluded. Another person quickly tuned to another of his favorite stations. He heard static. He concluded that the Martians had knocked the station off the air. Another

Gullibility and the Envelope of Legitimacy 307

listener turned his dial to find corroboration. He heard church music. "They all must be praying," he thought.

We may be better able to identify gullibility than define it. When large numbers of people fall for an implausible assertion, we have little trouble identifying it as an instance of gullibility. Almost all newspapers on the morning of October 31, 1938, used terms like duped and gullible to describe the hysteria and the widespread belief that creatures from the planet Mars had landed. Why? Because the untruthful premise was so outrageous that people found it difficult to identify disconfirming evidence. Although people may have checked for corroborating evidence, many ultimately accepted the premise that the Martians had landed. The only question left was what to do about it. As some of the reactions to the *War of the Worlds* broadcast attest, it is difficult to be certain of how to disconfirm the assertion (see van Prooijen, Chapter 17 this volume). And disconfirmation may be more difficult as the assertion becomes more outrageous. As Adolf Hitler mused in *Mein Kampf*,

> People will believe a big lie sooner than a little one; and if you repeat it frequently enough people will sooner or later believe it . . . In the big lie, there is always a certain force of credibility . . . they fall victim to the big lie since they themselves often tell small lies but would be ashamed to resort to large-scale falsehoods. It would never come into their heads to fabricate colossal untruths and they would not believe that others could have the impudence to distort the truth so infamously.
>
> (Hitler, 1935, vol. 1, ch. X)

Gullibility as an Internal State

We view gullibility as a specific response to a persuasive communication. We view it as an internal state – *an uncomfortable feeling state that is prompted by the perception that one has been persuaded to believe something that is not true.* Not all persuasion results in the feeling of gullibility, even when people realize they have been misled. The feeling of gullibility is associated with the magnitude of the untruth but is not isomorphic with it. It is also associated with source and communication characteristics but is not identical to those variables either. Let us consider a more mundane circumstance than being persuaded that the Earth was invaded by Martians. Consider a person persuaded to believe the veracity of a television commercial that promised that a new vitamin supplement would produce 15 pounds of weight loss in a single week. Convinced of the extraordinary impact the supplement could have on his life, a consumer purchases the tablet, only to find that it has no effect whatsoever. Our consumer may or may not feel gullible as a result of his being persuaded to believe the unlikely proposition of 15 pounds of weight loss in a week. Under some circumstances, the consumer may feel disappointed in the outcome but nonetheless conclude that the purchase was a reasonable one, even if it was unlikely to further his weight-loss goal. He might vow not to believe a similar communication in the future, become annoyed with the radio station that aired the commercial or vow never to believe a person wearing a white lab coat in an infomercial.

On the other hand, being persuaded to purchase the unlikely pill may cause the individual to experience the unpleasant tension state of gullibility. This person believes that his own sense of self-esteem has been implicated. His experience is self-directed. Good and worthy people do not fall for schemes. Good and worthy people do due diligence. They check the credibility of the source, the reasonableness of the claims, and/or the evidence that the claim is valid. This person may use terms like, "I fell for it," to describe his belief in the advertiser's claims. The experience is unpleasant, aversive, and motivates him to reduce it.

People who listened to the *War of the Worlds* broadcast responded in many different ways. Some disbelieved in the first instance, realizing they had been listening to a drama. Some were angry. Still others viewed their being persuaded as their own fault. It is this reaction that we term gullibility. Mr. T. Owen Miller of Washington, DC, captured this view of gullibility when he said, "I admit that I am one of the many thousands who showed incredible stupidity, lack of nerve and ignorance while listening to Mr. Welles' broadcast."

Gullibility and Dissonance

The claim that gullibility is an aversive, unpleasant reaction to having been persuaded is akin to the feeling of cognitive dissonance that occurs in the presence of inconsistent cognitions. Like dissonance, gullibility is a condition that people seek to reduce. At the operational core of gullibility is one's having been persuaded to believe something, or to do something, only to find that what one was led to believe is false. One way to reduce felt gullibility is to accept the improbable belief as true. In the vernacular, you "double down" on your belief, becoming even more certain that it is a true and valid position (see Dunning, Chapter 12 this volume). The person who bought his miracle diet cure, and who feels gullible as a result of its not working, comes to believe that it is actually working. He may even take action to lose weight in other ways in order to avoid the unpleasant feeling of gullibility. The person who believed that Martians had landed will have a difficult time doubling down on that belief . . . but he still may try. One woman from Newark, New Jersey, reported running from her apartment, hoping to drive to her mother's house before the Martians destroyed the city. When she arrived at the street, a man told her that he had heard an announcement that it was all a hoax. She refused to believe him and told him to "start praying."

Among the most well-known examples of gullibility in the psychological literature is the reaction of the group of people who believed that the world would end in a cataclysmic flood. It was arguably the first research specifically designed to test the implications of cognitive dissonance theory (Festinger, Riecken, & Schachter, 1956). Members of the group were persuaded by its founder that the end of the world was imminent and that beings from the planet Clarion would descend to Earth on a rocket ship to whisk the true believers to safety while the rest of the planet was destroyed by the flood. This preposterous communication from Clarion was allegedly delivered to the group by automatic writing, using the founder as a medium. The true believers – known as the Seekers – included people from all walks of life, including educated professionals. They had been persuaded by what they thought was automatic writing from Clarion to believe that the world would end. In dramatic fashion, they prepared for the world's end and awaited the arrival of the spaceship from Clarion that would save them from destruction.

The evidence that they had been wrong was obvious. The morning following the expected cataclysm dawned with no destruction and no spaceship. The feeling of tension must have been palpable. How could they live with the shame of believing the preposterous story? How could they deal with their feelings of gullibility? We believe that people take steps to reduce their experience of gullibility. They convince themselves that they had not been duped after all. Just as our weight supplement consumer tried to convince himself that the supplement he took really was working, the group of cataclysm believers found a way to convince themselves that they had not been wrong after all. In their well-known response to the disconfirmation, the group received a new message from planet Clarion: "That this little group sitting so long shined so much light upon the world, that God has decided to save the Earth from destruction." And they "doubled down." They did not shrink back to their homes with the knowledge that they had been deceived. To the contrary, they shouted their "success" for all to hear. They sent out press releases, wrote flyers, and talked to whoever would listen to make sure that the entire world would learn that they had been correct in their beliefs.

The Envelope of Legitimacy

We do not always feel gullible when we are persuaded to believe. An editorial may extol the virtues of a particular piece of legislation or a particular candidate. A celebrity may tell us that he eats a "breakfast cereal of champions" and an economist from the conservative Freedom Foundation may present convincing arguments for a reduction in corporate tax rates. The arguments in these persuasive messages may convince us, may fail to convince us, or may convince us temporarily. We may be persuaded in the short term, but return to our original beliefs over time. Despite being persuaded to believe something that we ultimately feel is not correct, we do not ordinarily feel gullible. We do not experience the unpleasant state of gullibility.

310   *Joel Cooper and Joseph J. Avery*

In broad terms, people are aware of two seemingly incompatible principles. On the one hand, in social discourse, we presume that people are telling us the truth (Grice, 1975). The social world would be difficult to navigate if people's utterances were independent of their truth value. In evolutionary social psychology, scholars have argued that the tendency to believe and trust what others assert appears to be an evolutionary universal, a highly adaptive feature of humans in ancestral societies, where (1) the world was relatively stable and slow-changing and (2) most communications came from intimately known others within a primary group whose trustworthiness was known (see Acedo-Carmona & Gomila, 2015). Trusting others seems to be a powerful evolutionary inclination.

Paul Grice (1975) laid out a number of principles or maxims that people use in civil discourse with each other. In his "maxim of quality," Grice pointed out that a speaker is presumed to be speaking the truth and not knowingly communicating information that the speaker knows to be false. At the same time, most of us do tolerate a degree of dishonesty and dissimulation under certain circumstances. A person might compliment a colleague on his new tie, without fully meaning it. The athlete with his picture on the "breakfast of champions" cereal box might not actually enjoy or eat it. Candidates for public office may describe their virtuous deeds, but we would not be surprised to find that it is exaggeration or hyperbole. We hold a degree of healthy skepticism (see Mayo, Chapter 8 this volume) that allows us to recognize that not all statements are completely true.

Grice's maxim of quality and the principle of healthy skepticism circumscribe an *envelope of legitimacy*. It is our contention that people feel gullible when they are persuaded to believe something that lies outside the envelope of legitimacy. Inside the envelope are positions that are true or that do not stray too far from the truth. A student's statement that she maintained an A average in college when, in fact, she had only earned an A– is more likely to lie inside the envelope of legitimacy than if she had only maintained a C average. In addition to the magnitude of distance from the truth, the social circumstances also contribute to what is inside or outside the envelope of legitimacy. A person who expresses an opinion about his wife's new suit is expected to be truthful if she is going for a job interview but may have greater flexibility if she is deciding what to wear for a casual engagement.

As another example, consider communicative acts in the realm of politics. Newspaper reporters are expected to be veridical in their articles, and thus they have a small envelope of legitimacy. News "commentators," given the context of their reporting and the expectations for commentary and opinion pieces, have a wider envelope of legitimacy. It may further be the case that political candidates have even wider envelopes when they are engaged in political campaigning. Thus, the same statement may be within the envelope of legitimacy when made by a political candidate, on the border of the envelope when made by a news commentator, and outside the envelope when made by a newspaper reporter. In short, the envelope of legitimacy will vary as a function of the context, which includes at least the platform from which the statement is made and the type of communicator. While we do not expect every communicative act to be entirely truthful, we do expect that communication will lie within a reasonable distance of the truth given the communicative context. If we are persuaded to believe a position that lies outside the envelope of legitimacy for a particular communicator in a particular circumstance, and subsequently learn that the communication was untrue, this is when we are likely to feel the unpleasant tension state of gullibility.

Approximating the Size of the Envelope of Legitimacy

In the original conceptualization of cognitive dissonance, Festinger (1957) held that two cognitions were in a dissonant relationship if one cognition followed from the obverse of the other. A perplexing aspect of that conceptualization was how to determine when two cognitions were truly dissonant. Was there a way to determine how discrepant one cognition needed to be from another cognition in order for it to arouse dissonance? If a U.S. citizen believed in the right to bear arms but made a statement advocating a ban on assault rifles, are the two cognitions discrepant? If so, are they sufficiently discrepant to arouse dissonance?

Fazio, Zanna, and Cooper (1977) proposed a resolution to determine the degree of discrepancy that is needed for two cognitions to be psychologically inconsistent. Based on prior classic work by Sherif, Sherif, and Nebergall (1965) on latitudes of acceptance and rejection, Fazio and colleagues (1977) proposed that people have their own latitudes when it comes to discrepancy. Participants were asked to identify positions on a variety of issues that they believed were acceptable (latitude of acceptance) or not acceptable (latitude of rejection) in light of their own position on the issues. As predicted, the unpleasant feeling of cognitive dissonance occurred only when participants advocated for positions that were outside of their own latitudes of acceptance, regardless of whether they were on the same side of the midpoint of the issue.

We believe that the envelope of gullibility is a conceptually similar construct. People have their own conceptions of the degree to which a communicator can violate the maxim of quality. Some amount of dissimulation is acceptable, even if not desirable. Beyond that latitude fall utterances whose degree of falsehood lies in an unacceptable range. A person *feels* gullible when he or she believes the communication that lies in the latitude of rejection. A person who claims on his resume to have been a university graduate when in fact he dropped out after freshman year would most likely be perceived to have made a statement outside of the envelope of legitimacy. The perceiver experiences gullibility when he or she believes the statement and ultimately realizes that it is not true.

The Motivation to Protect Against Gullibility

We are proposing that gullibility is an unpleasant feeling and that people will undergo considerable effort to avoid and reduce it. We are proposing that people would rather believe that a lie is true than believe that they were duped, if that lie falls outside the envelope of legitimacy. Why should this be so? Elliot Aronson wrestled with this question when he commented on the motivational roots of cognitive dissonance. Why should people be upset when they act inconsistently with their beliefs? Rather than maintaining that people are hardwired to reject inconsistency, Aronson (1968) believed that cognitive dissonance is an experience that implicates the self as unworthy. People generally think that they are good and decent people and have a reasonably positive self-concept. Good and decent people should say what they believe and believe what they say. Only a "schnook" would engage in dissonant behavior. And most people do not think of themselves as schnooks (Aronson, 1999). According to Aronson, at the very heart of dissonance theory are people trying to maintain a sense of self-worth that had been brought into question by dissonant behavior.

Stone and Cooper (2003) amplified this view especially in conditions in which personal self-standards are made salient. They found that when the self was made salient, people responded to inconsistency by protecting their sense of self-esteem. The more their self-esteem was compromised by their inconsistent behavior, the more dissonance they experienced – that is, they changed their attitudes to protect their self-worth. As Dunning (Chapter 12 this volume) and Myers (Chapter 5 this volume) imply, the ultimate source of our gullibility is often ourselves.

In summary, the experience of gullibility occurs when people discover that they have believed a statement that lies outside the envelope of legitimacy and that the statement was not true. The limits of the envelope of legitimacy will depend on the circumstances of the untruth, including an assessment of the communicator, the communication, and the importance of the act. Because gullibility is threatening to people's sense of self-worth, it is experienced as an unpleasant state of tension that people try to avoid or reduce. Rather than diminishing its importance, one way people reduce the aversive experience of gullibility is by convincing themselves that the lie is true.

Empirical Research

Gullibility in the Era of Donald Trump

Donald Trump surprised the pundits when he squeaked to an Electoral College victory in the 2016 U.S. presidential election. He survived as a candidate despite publicity that would have ended the campaigns of most candidates. Allegations of sexual assault rolled off his back, his own Planet

Gullibility and the Envelope of Legitimacy   313

Hollywood admissions of his crude sexual attitudes and behavior did not derail his candidacy nor did the coarse and demeaning language with which he castigated his opponents.

Although he entered the presidency on January 21, 2017 with the lowest popularity rating of any president in modern times, his behavior continued to spiral downward in ways that would sink the electoral careers of most politicians. Anyone who voted for Trump expecting him to "pivot" and become more "presidential" had to be disappointed by the President's first year in office. But Trump's popularity has not shown much change, despite his unpopular stances on immigration, his partial embrace of white nationalists in Charlottesville, Virginia, or his reference to the countries of Latin America and Africa as "s***holes."

"I could stand in the middle of Fifth Avenue and shoot somebody and I wouldn't lose any voters," said candidate Trump during the 2016 primaries. It appears he may be right.[1] A Quinnipiac poll taken in February 2018 showed that people had the same impression of Trump's leadership and personal characteristics after his tumultuous first year in office as they had before the presidential election. Despite his inflammatory public statements, people did not see him as any less moral than they had prior to the election. Republican voters in particular saw the President as highly moral, giving him the same 65% approval on that dimension that they had given him prior to the election.

Many voters cast their ballots for Donald Trump because they believed he was an effective deal maker. He could get things done. His failure to pass health care legislation, his inability to secure funding for his infamous wall (especially from Mexico) – neither stopped people from reporting (in the same poll) that they saw him as an equally strong leader now as they did when he told the public of his extraordinary deal-making skills.

We suspect that many of the people who supported Donald Trump in the election felt gullible after a year of inconsistency between what he had promised and what he had accomplished. People who voted for Trump knew of his history of being a showman, a TV personality, a businessman whose casinos struggled financially, and whose "university" failed to educate students. Nonetheless, they made their choice, hoping that his deeds as president would match his rhetoric. When his deeds did not match the rhetoric, Trump voters risked feeling as gullible as Orson Welles' radio audience.

One of the specific promises that characterized nearly every one of candidate Trump's campaign rallies was his pledge to build a 2,000-mile wall along the U.S. border with Mexico – paid by Mexico. There is ample reason to be skeptical that this promise will ever come to fruition, including the consistent and not surprising reaction of the Mexican government. We suggest that the Mexican wall promise is a statement that lies outside most people's envelope of legitimacy. Our analysis suggests that, precisely because the promise of the wall lies outside the envelope of legitimacy, many Trump voters will continue to believe it will be built. They will attempt to avoid the unpleasant feeling of gullibility by denying all evidence. They may double down and become even more convinced that the United States will build, and Mexico will pay for, the wall across the border.

In the current research, we predict that citizens in the United States who voted for Donald Trump are more likely to believe the campaign promises that have very little likelihood of coming true. The more outlandish the promises, the less likely they are to come true, but the more likely they are to be believed by people who made the decision to vote for Trump.

We also believe that people differ in how concerned they are about gullibility. Although most people are sensitive to feeling gullible, we believe that there is a dimension such that some people are extremely concerned while others are less so. Accordingly, we predict that people who voted for Trump will steadfastly believe in his campaign promises, including the least likely ones. Importantly for our theory, this effect will be greatest in those who are most sensitive to the aversive feeling of gullibility.

To test this, we asked participants to answer a series of questions, including two questions designed to assess gullibility sensitivity: "I get upset when I find out that something I was led to believe is not true," and "It's an uncomfortable feeling to learn that someone I trusted deceived me." Both were scored on a five-point Likert scale. Participants then were asked to indicate, again on five-point Likert scales, the extent of their current belief in four campaign promises made by Donald Trump during 2016, when was he was then–Candidate Trump. The promises included: (1) "A wall between the United States and Mexico will be built," (2) "Obamacare will be repealed," (3) "China will be declared a currency manipulator," and (4) "The carried interest tax loophole will be eliminated." Participants also were asked to indicate, on a five-point Likert scale, the extent of their current belief in a promise that had been made neither by Donald Trump nor Hillary Clinton ("Marijuana will be made 100% legal"). Lastly, participants were asked to indicate, on a −7 to 7 scale, their approval of Trump prior to the 2016 election and their approval of Trump at the time of the survey (May 2018).

Our population included 425 participants from Amazon's Mechanical Turk. Of these, 225 had voted for Hillary Clinton in the 2016 U.S. Presidential Election, and 200 had voted for Donald Trump. The mean age (± SD) of the participants was 37.3 ± 13.3 years. The population was 45% male and 55% female. Most participants (greater than 78%) were white.

Absolute means accorded with commonsense expectations: 2016 approval of Trump was 4.18 for Trump voters and −5.22 for Clinton voters (Welch two-tailed t-test, $p < .001$). The 2018 approval of Trump was 3.65 for Trump voters and −5.33 for Clinton voters (Welch two-tailed t-test, $p < .001$). Belief in the four policy positions was 3.51 for Trump voters and 2.49 for Clinton voters (Welch two-tailed t-test, $p < .001$). Across all participants, Cronbach's alpha for the four policy items was .74. For the gullibility sensitivity measure, which was comprised of the two gullibility items, Cronbach's alpha was .60.

As predicted, there was a significant two-way interaction of voter type (Trump vs. Clinton) and gullibility sensitivity on belief in the four policy items ($p = .03$). For Trump voters, belief in the four policies showed a marginally significant positive correlation with gullibility sensitivity ($p = .07$, $\beta = .12$, R-squared = .02) (Figure 16.1). Those Trump voters who found feelings of gullibility to be upsetting were also more likely to believe that Trump's campaign promises were still going to come true. For Clinton voters, there was not a statistically significant relationship between gullibility sensitivity and belief in the four Trump policy promises ($p = .20$, $\beta = -.11$, R-squared = .007), with the trend even being negative (Figure 16.1).

It is important to show that people who are sensitive to gullibility are not merely predisposed to believe *any* proposal. Their increased belief is restricted to policies that they were led to believe by the candidate for whom they voted. Accordingly, we asked people for their support for a policy to legalize marijuana, which had not been endorsed by either candidate. As expected, for this item, the interaction effect entirely disappeared, with both Trump and Clinton voters showing the same trend. The two-way interaction of voter type and gullibility sensitivity on belief in the policy item was not significant ($p = .87$). For Trump voters, belief in the item was negatively correlated with gullibility sensitivity and the effect was not significant ($p = .33$, $\beta = -.12$, R-squared = .005), and the same was the case for Clinton voters ($p = .25$, $\beta = -.15$, R-squared = .006) (Figure 16.2).

Our results also were as predicted when we considered the approval ratings for Trump as a function of gullibility sensitivity. There was a

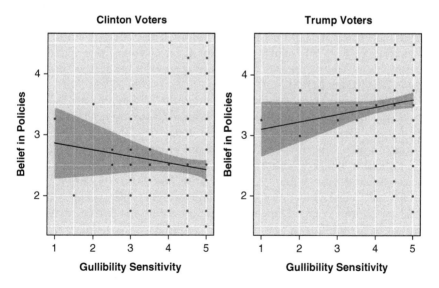

Figure 16.1 Plots of models of beliefs that President Trump's campaign promises will come true and sensitivity to the aversive feeling of gullibility (N = 425). The shaded regions are the 95% confidence intervals.

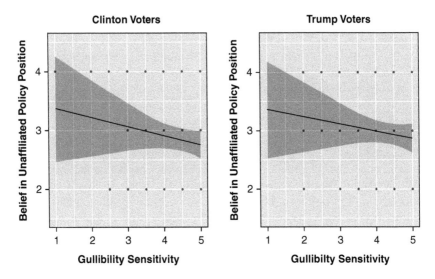

Figure 16.2 Plots of models of belief in a policy position that was not endorsed by either Donald Trump or Hillary Clinton (N = 425). The shaded regions are the 95% confidence intervals.

significant two-way interaction of voter type and gullibility sensitivity on both pre-election and post-election approval ratings. Beginning with pre-election approval ratings, the two-way interaction of voter type and gullibility sensitivity to 2016 approval ratings was significant ($p < .001$). Trump voters who showed greater sensitivity to gullibility also showed greater approval of Trump ($\beta = .25$), although the effect failed to reach significance ($p = .26$) (Figure 16.3). For Clinton voters, the relationship between gullibility sensitivity and Trump approval was negative ($p < .001$, $\beta = -1.42$) (Figure 16.3).

As with the pre-election approval ratings, for 2018 approval ratings, the two-way interaction of gullibility sensitivity and vote cast to 2018 approval ratings was significant ($p = .02$). Trump voters who showed greater sensitivity to gullibility showed no meaningful change in approval of Trump ($p = .95$, $\beta = .02$). For Clinton voters, the relationship between gullibility sensitivity and Trump approval was negative ($p < .001$, $\beta = -1.01$).

Overall, our results provide consistent evidence that, compared with Hillary Clinton voters, Donald Trump voters who exhibited greater sensitivity to the unpleasant tension state of gullibility were significantly more likely to believe that Trump's campaign promises, including ones that seemed increasingly unlikely, would come true. A similar pattern held for approval ratings, thus supporting the proposition that voters who are more sensitive to the aversive feeling of gullibility are also more likely to double down on their belief in and support for the candidate for whom they voted.

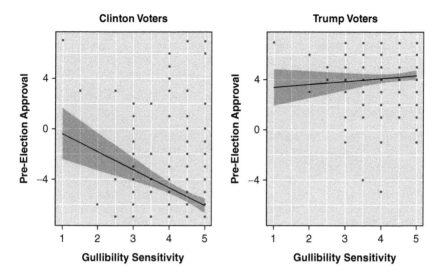

Figure 16.3 Plots of models of approval of Donald Trump in 2016 (pre-election) and sensitivity to the aversive feeling of gullibility (N = 425). The shaded regions are the 95% confidence intervals.

Conclusion

We believe that gullibility is a feeling state akin to the affective state of cognitive dissonance. It is negative, unpleasant, and needs to be reduced. People experience gullibility when they realize that they have believed a proposition that was untrue and that the belief fell outside the envelope of legitimacy. On some occasions, people have no choice but to accept their gullibility. The listeners who believed Orson Welles' *War of the Worlds* broadcast eventually had to face the incontrovertible realization that Martians had not invaded our planet. However, many instances of false belief in a persuasive message leave room for ambiguity (see Strack, Chapter 9 this volume). Reduction of gullibility results in the ironic increase in a version of the original belief with an accompanying belief in the veracity of the communicator. The continued belief in the conspiracy of fake news may be an illustration of this phenomenon as those who seek to avoid gullibility deny evidence that potentially contradicts their beliefs. It is possible, further, that such behavior is adaptive, necessary for the flourishing of long-term relationships, including political ones (Baumeister, Maxwell, Thomas, & Fox, Chapter 2 this volume).

We conclude by wondering if there is a window of time after which people will face their own gullibility. Can we continue to believe that a proposition is true even if the passage of time produces no evidence of its truth value? If the Mexican wall is never built, will people who sought to avoid gullibility eventually decide that dealing with truth is better than avoiding gullibility? This is a proposition for future testing.

Note

1 And that he may be aware of some of the underlying psychological forces at work. As Krueger, Vogrincic-Haselbacher, and Evans (Chapter 6 this volume) point out, "[T]he term fake news has been popularized by politicians who themselves hold dubious records of truthfulness."

References

Acedo-Carmona, C., & Gomila, A. (2015). Deciding to cooperate in northern Ghana: Trust as an evolutionary constraint across cultural diversity. *Spanish Journal of Psychology, 18*, e91.

Aronson, E. (1968). Dissonance theory: Progress and problems. In R. P. Abelson, E. Aronson, W. J. McGuire, T. M. Newcomb, M. J. Rosenberg, & P. H. Tannenbaum (Eds.), *Theories of cognitive consistency: A sourcebook*. Chicago, IL: Rand McNally.

Aronson, E. (1999). Dissonance, hypocrisy and the self-concept. In J. Mills & E. Harmon-Jones (Eds.), *Cognitive dissonance: Progress on a pivotal theory in social psychology*. Washington, DC: APA.

Cantril, H. (1940). *The invasion from Mars*. Princeton, NJ: Princeton University Press.

Cooper, J., Blackman, S. F., & Keller, K. K. (2016). *The science of attitudes*. New York, NY: Routledge.

Fazio, R. H., Zanna, M. P., & Cooper, J. (1977). Dissonance and self-perception: An integrative view of each theory's proper domain of application. *Journal of Experimental Social Psychology, 13*, 464–479.

Festinger, L. (1957). *A theory of cognitive dissonance*. Redwood City, CA: Stanford University Press.

Festinger, L, Riecken, H. W., & Schachter, S. (1956). *When prophecy fails*. Minneapolis, MN: University of Minnesota Press.

Grice, H. P. (1975). *The logic of conversation*. In P. Cole and J. L. Morgan (Eds), *Syntax and semantics* (Vol. 3, pp. 41–58.) New York, NY: Academic.

Hitler, A. (1935). *Mein Kampf*. Munich: NSDAP.

Meehl, P. E. (1956). Wanted – A good cookbook. *American Psychologist, 11*, 262–272.

Mercier. (2017). How gullible are we? A review of the evidence from psychology and social science. *Review of General Psychology, 21*(2), 103–122.

Rotter, J. B. (1980). Interpersonal trust, trustworthiness, and gullibility. *American Psychologist, 35*, 1–7.

Sherif, C. W., Sherif, M., & Nebergall, R. E. (1965). *Attitude and attitude change: The social judgment-involvement approach*. Philadelphia, PA: Saunders.

Stone, J., & Cooper, J. (2003). The effect of self-attribute relevance on how self-esteem moderates attitude change in the dissonance process. *Journal of Experimental Social Psychology, 39*, 508–515.

17 Belief in Conspiracy Theories
Gullibility or Rational Skepticism?

Jan-Willem van Prooijen
VU AMSTERDAM

Conspiracy theories are widespread in our society. Surprisingly large numbers of citizens believe allegations that the Moon landings were filmed in a TV studio, that humans created the HIV virus in the lab, and that the 9/11 terrorist strikes were an inside job of the U.S. government (e.g., Douglas, Sutton, & Cichocka, Chapter 4 this volume; Sunstein & Vermeule, 2009; van Prooijen, 2018). Conspiracy theories are commonly defined as assumptions about a group of actors that colludes in secret agreement to reach goals widely seen as evil (Bale, 2007). While conspiracy theories sometimes turn out to be true (e.g., the Iran–Contra scandal), quite often conspiracy theories are implausible in light of logic or scientific evidence, and therefore deviate from mainstream narratives. People who strongly believe conspiracy theories hence are highly skeptical of regular news sources and official readings of events, and often proclaim to be rational human beings who "just ask questions." A qualitative analysis of interviews with citizens active in the Dutch conspiracy milieu reveals that believers actively reject the qualification "conspiracy theorist," and prefer to see themselves as "critical freethinkers" that positively distinguish themselves from "the sheeple,"[1] who are gullible and easily manipulated by powerholders (Harambam & Aupers, 2017). This self-perception as a critical and rational thinker is underscored by the following quote, which is drawn from a conspiracist website (www.sheep killers.com) explicitly focused on protecting, and opening the eyes of, "the sheep" who supposedly are led astray by the powerful and immoral leaders that rule our nations: "If you think 9/11 was the result of cave-dwelling terrorists attacking our country, bringing down airplanes with box-cutters and collapsing entire buildings into their footprints, you really are a sheep."

How rational is the tendency to believe conspiracy theories? Looking at the specific contents of a range of conspiracy theories, one needs to acknowledge how well crafted, complex, and creative many conspiracy theories are. For instance, conspiracy theories about the 9/11 terrorist strikes often assume that not the impact of the planes but controlled demolition made the Twin Towers collapse. These theories are based on scientifically

320   *Jan-Willem van Prooijen*

grounded arguments about the steel construction of the Twin Towers, the temperatures at which steel melts (about 2,750 °F) and the maximum temperatures reached by burning kerosene (about 1,500 °F).[2] Even extremely far-fetched conspiracy theories are remarkably well designed. For instance, the flat-earth movement endorses the theory that our planet Earth is in fact flat, and that the public has been deceived for over 400 years by scientists and world governments to believe that the earth is round (or, to be more precise, somewhat oval). Their arguments include detailed accounts of how NASA routinely manipulates or fabricates satellite pictures, testimonies of airplane pilots who confirm to not see the Earth's curvature at high altitude, and technical descriptions of how airplane windows are designed to provide a perceptual illusion of a curving Earth.

While in the present contribution I will not seriously examine the contents of these conspiracy theories (I am comfortable asserting here that the impact of the planes and the fires that subsequently erupted caused the collapse of the Twin Towers on 9/11, and that the Earth is round albeit not perfectly so), I will seriously consider two opposing hypotheses about the social psychology of conspiracy theories. The first hypothesis is that, as suggested above, belief in conspiracy theories is grounded in a mindset characterized by rational skepticism. According to this view, people who believe conspiracy theories are indeed "critical freethinkers" who do not take official readings of events for granted, but instead carefully and independently collect and examine evidence to form their own objective judgments. Their conclusions may sometimes be wrong (just like scientists sometimes make honest mistakes when interpreting research data), but the epistemic process through which believers construct or accept conspiracy theories is deliberative, analytic, and utilizes the approach of a "lay scientist." I refer to this idea as the *rational conspiracist hypothesis*.

The second and alternative hypothesis, however, is that belief in conspiracy theories is grounded in a mindset characterized by gullibility. According to this view, people construct or accept conspiracy theories through System 1 processes including heuristics, emotions, and intuitive thinking (see also Myers, Chapter 8 this volume; Unkelbach & Koch, Chapter 3 this volume). A deep-rooted distrust in power holders or other groups leads believers to reflexively reject official accounts of impactful events, and to uncritically accept implausible conspiracy theories. Through motivated reasoning and the confirmation bias, believers subsequently justify their suspicious sentiments by selectively embracing evidence that supports their theory and rejecting evidence inconsistent with it, providing the illusion of a well-elaborated and irrefutable argument. I refer to this idea as the *gullible conspiracism hypothesis*. In the following, I review the psychological literature on conspiracy theories to test these two competing hypotheses. I will specifically examine the empirical relationships of belief in conspiracy theories with (1) a range of implausible beliefs that do not involve conspiracies, (2) cognitive biases, (3) stereotyping, and (4) cognitive style.

Belief in Conspiracy Theories

Although conspiracy theories vary widely in content, the tendency to believe them is grounded in similar underlying psychological processes. This insight is consistent with the finding that the single best predictor of belief in one conspiracy theory is belief in a different conspiracy theory (Abalakina-Paap, Stephan, Craig, & Gregory, 1999; Goertzel, 1994; Swami et al., 2011; Wood, Douglas, & Sutton, 2012). These findings are often interpreted as evidence that people differ in the extent to which they have a conspiratorial mindset that predisposes them to attribute impactful societal events to the deliberate actions of hostile conspiracies (e.g., van Prooijen & van Dijk, 2014). Relatedly, people differ structurally in their "conspiracy mentality," that is, an individual difference variable designed to assesses people's tendency to perceive a world full of conspiracies (Imhoff & Bruder, 2014). Furthermore, belief in conspiracy theories is highly susceptible to contextual factors. For instance, conspiracy theories gain momentum particularly following impactful societal crisis events (van Prooijen & Douglas, 2017). These insights have contributed to the study of belief in conspiracy theories as a growing research field in the social sciences (for overviews, see Douglas et al., Chapter 4 this volume; van Prooijen, 2018; van Prooijen & van Vugt, 2018).

To assess the two competing hypotheses put forward in this chapter, here I propose more specific predictions that can be tested through a review of the empirical research literature. If the rational conspiracist hypothesis is true, it stands to reason that people who believe conspiracy theories are rational, or at least not irrational, in many other perceptual or cognitive domains. In particular, based on the rational conspiracist hypothesis one would expect that belief in conspiracy theories is either unrelated or negatively related with (a) implausible beliefs that do not involve conspiracies, such as beliefs in the paranormal, superstition, and pseudoscience; (b) cognitive biases that are well known to produce irrational judgments and decision-making; and (c) stereotyping, which involves mental simplifications and overgeneralizations of social categories. As to cognitive style (d), conspiracy beliefs should be positively related with a tendency to recognize the complexity of difficult problems. Furthermore, analytic thinking, and not intuitive thinking, should stimulate belief in conspiracy theories.

If the gullible conspiracist hypothesis is true, however, one would expect that to the extent people believe conspiracy theories more strongly, they are more likely to (a) also believe implausible beliefs that do not involve conspiracies, (b) display cognitive biases, and (c) engage in stereotyping. In their cognitive style (d), conspiracy beliefs should predict a tendency to perceive difficult problems in an oversimplified fashion; moreover, analytic thinking should predict *skepticism* of conspiracy theories instead of belief in them. I will now assess the empirical evidence for these two competing hypotheses.

Conspiracy Theories and Implausible Beliefs

How is belief in conspiracy theories related with a range of implausible beliefs that are common, that do not involve conspiracies, and that are not supported by any evidence? Various studies examined the relationships between conspiracy beliefs and supernatural beliefs, such as superstition and belief in paranormal phenomena. These studies typically find a reliable positive correlation: The more strongly people believe conspiracy theories, the more likely it is that they also hold a range of supernatural beliefs. For instance, Darwin, Neave, and Holmes (2011) found positive correlations of conspiracy beliefs with beliefs in psi, witchcraft, spiritualism, extraordinary life forms, and precognition. Other studies confirm these positive relationships. For instance, Lobato, Mendoza, Sims, and Chin (2014) found positive correlations between conspiracy beliefs and beliefs in the paranormal and pseudoscience. The positive relationships between conspiracy beliefs and belief in various supernatural beliefs have been frequently replicated, and are now well established in this research domain (e.g., Barron, Morgan, Towell, Altemeyer, & Swami, 2014; Newheiser, Farias, & Tausch, 2011; Swami et al., 2011; van Prooijen, Douglas, & De Inocencio, 2018).

An interesting illustration of how conspiracy beliefs are related with other implausible beliefs can be found in a seminal paper that introduced "pseudo-profound bullshit" and "bullshit receptivity" as viable academic terms (Pennycook, Cheyne, Barr, Koehler, & Fugelsang, 2015). Pseudo-profound bullshit refers to statements that appear to have a deeper meaning but actually are empty. Bullshit receptivity refers to people's tendency to perceive such statements as profound, that is, as containing some deeper truth. To measure this construct, Pennycook and colleagues (2015) designed a scale consisting of statements that are grammatically correct, yet contain randomly chosen buzzwords (example items include "Hidden meaning transforms unparalleled abstract beauty" and "Good health imparts reality to subtle creativity"). Results revealed that participants' ratings of such statements as profound significantly predicted a range of variables indicative of gullibility, including reduced analytic thinking, reduced verbal intelligence, increased paranormal belief, and increased faith in intuition (see also Forgas, Chapter 10 this volume). Of importance for the present purposes, bullshit receptivity also predicted an increased tendency to believe conspiracy theories (Pennycook et al., 2015, study 4).

The empirical relationships between conspiracy beliefs and such implausible beliefs are not necessarily harmless: Conspiracy theories can lead to irrational and harmful behavior. For instance, the link between conspiracy theories and belief in pseudoscience has real consequences for people's health. One study reveals that belief in conspiracy theories predicts a preference for alternative medicine over regular, evidence-based medical approaches (Lamberty & Imhoff, 2018). Furthermore, in South Africa AIDS conspiracy theories are common, which for instance stipulate that AIDS

Belief in Conspiracy Theories

was created by pharmaceutical companies in the lab to sell antiretroviral drugs, and that not the HIV virus but these drugs are dangerous to people's health. A study conducted in Cape Town revealed that belief in such AIDS conspiracy theories is a major predictor of reduced condom use among both men and women (Grebe & Nattrass, 2012). In sum, belief in conspiracy theories reliably and consistently predicts a range of implausible beliefs and irrational behaviors, which supports the gullible conspiracist hypothesis and contradicts the rational conspiracist hypothesis.

Conspiracy Theories and Cognitive Biases

The second test of the competing hypotheses put forward here pertains to cognitive biases. It is reasonable to assume that people with a truly rational, critical mindset less likely fall prey to cognitive biases that deteriorate decision-making as compared to people with an irrational, uncritical mindset (Myers, Chapter 8 this volume). One cognitive bias of interest is the conjunction fallacy. This is an error in probabilistic reasoning characterized by overestimating the likelihood that two events co-occur (Tversky & Kahneman, 1983). A well-known example of the conjunction fallacy is that after a stereotypical description of a woman being a feminist, many people rate the probability that she is a feminist *and* a bank teller as higher than the probability that she is a bank teller. In fact, the statistical probability of a combination of two constituents co-occurring (feminist and bank teller) can never be higher than the probability of one of the individual constituents occurring (bank teller).

One study investigated the relationships between conspiracy beliefs, paranormal beliefs, and conjunction fallacies in a range of judgment domains (Brotherton & French, 2014). Specifically, some of the conjunction statements were neutral; some of the conjunction statements were in the context of paranormal phenomena (e.g., about a person dreaming her sister's house is on fire, and the sister's house actually being on fire); and some of the conjunction statements involved possible conspiracies (e.g., about CEOs of petrol companies discussing the implications of a new device that increases fuel efficiency in cars, and the inventor of the device being found dead in his home). Results revealed that belief in conspiracy theories predicted an increased proportion of conjunction fallacies across judgment domains (i.e., neutral, paranormal, and conspiratorial). In fact, although paranormal beliefs also predicted increased conjunction fallacies, the effects were stronger for conspiracy beliefs across all three types of conjunction contexts.

A related yet distinct cognitive bias that has been examined in the context of conspiracy beliefs is illusory pattern perception. Specifically, the human mind automatically and functionally looks for patterns, that is, meaningful and causal relationships between stimuli. Detecting the actual causal relationships between stimuli is important for any organism to adapt to their environment, for instance to distinguish friends from foes, edible foods from poisons, safe from dangerous situations, and so on. These functional qualities of pattern perception notwithstanding, one consequence of this cognitive mechanism is that people often detect non-existing patterns by perceiving causal and meaningful relationships between stimuli that are in fact unrelated. Such illusory pattern perception for instance predicts habitual gambling (Wilke, Scheibehenne, Gaissmaier, McCanney, & Barrett, 2014).

Of importance to the present purposes, illusory pattern perception positively predicts belief in conspiracy theories. In a series of studies, participants' tendency to perceive patterns in randomly generated strings of coin toss outcomes was associated with increased belief in conspiracy theories; similar findings were obtained for perceiving patterns in the chaotic modern art paintings by Jackson Pollock (van Prooijen et al., 2018). Moreover, a recent study examined participants' perception of a range of existing, yet most likely spurious correlations that occur in everyday life (e.g., an increase in chocolate consumption is correlated with an increase in Nobel Prize winners in a country). The researchers found that the more strongly participants believed that these correlations in fact represented a direct causal relationship, the more strongly they believed conspiracy theories (van der Wal, Sutton, Lange, & Braga, 2018).

Pattern perception is generally considered to be one out of two key cognitive components of conspiracy beliefs (Shermer, 2011; van Prooijen & van Vugt, 2018). The second cognitive component is agency detection: The human mind automatically makes a judgment of the intentionality behind the actions of others. Were certain outcomes caused by an intentional agent? Like pattern perception, also agency detection is, in principle, a functional cognitive mechanism to effectively navigate one's social world. For instance, agency detection smoothes social interaction through increased mutual understanding of others' actions, and helps to make valid judgments of accountability when an actor caused harm (van Prooijen, 2018). But people also make mistakes in agency detection by perceiving agency where none exists. One study assessed to what extent participants detected agency in the inanimate geometric figures from the classic Heider and Simmel (1944) footage, and found that such hyperactive agency detection predicted increased conspiracy beliefs (Douglas, Sutton, Callan, Dawtry, & Harvey, 2016). Likewise, the related construct of anthropomorphism – that is, the tendency to ascribe human qualities to nonhuman stimuli – is positively correlated with belief in conspiracy theories (Brotherton & French, 2015; Imhoff & Bruder, 2014). In sum, belief in conspiracy theories is reliably associated with a range of cognitive biases, specifically the conjunction fallacy, illusory pattern perception, and errors in agency detection.

Conspiracy Theories and Stereotyping

By definition, stereotyping is an oversimplification of groups of people, and it therefore seems reasonable to assume that a rationally skeptic mindset is associated with decreased stereotyping, and that gullibility is

Belief in Conspiracy Theories 325

associated with increased stereotyping. How does stereotyping relate to conspiracy beliefs? One line of evidences comes from research on individual differences commonly known to reflect increased stereotyping, notably authoritarianism and social dominance orientation. Research found qualified support for the idea that these individual difference variables positively predict conspiracy beliefs. Specifically, various studies found a positive relationship of these individual difference variables with belief in specific conspiracy theories (e.g., the belief that President Kennedy was killed by a conspiracy), but no relationship with a generalized tendency to perceive a world full of conspiracies (e.g., Abalakina-Paap et al., 1999; Swami, 2012). At first blush, the evidence for authoritarianism and social dominance orientation as predictors of conspiracy beliefs seems inconsistent. How can this apparent discrepancy between specific versus generic conspiracy beliefs be reconciled?

An important piece of this puzzle is offered in a study by Imhoff and Bruder (2014) who investigated conspiracy mentality (i.e., a generic tendency to perceive conspiracies in the world) in relation to authoritarianism, social dominance orientation, and stereotyping of a range of specific societal groups. These researchers replicated the finding that conspiracy mentality is unrelated to these two individual difference variables, but also, offered an explanation for this: Authoritarianism and social dominance orientation mainly predicts stereotyping of low-power or low-status societal groups, such as Muslims, asylum seekers, and gypsies. Conspiracy mentality, in contrast, mainly predicts stereotyping of *high*-power groups, including politicians, managers, big companies, and so on. A series of studies supported these ideas, by testing how stereotypes of a range of high-power versus low-power groups are related with conspiracy mentality, authoritarianism, and social dominance orientation. Furthermore, conspiracy mentality positively predicted anti-Americanist and anti-capitalist sentiments in a sample of German participants. It thus appears that besides specific conspiracy beliefs also a more general conspiracy mentality positively predicts stereotyping, but of high-power groups instead of low-power groups.

One exceptional category in Imhoff and Bruder's (2014) study was stereotyping of Jewish people (i.e., anti-Semitism), as this variable was positively correlated with all constructs of interest, that is, conspiracy mentality, authoritarianism, and social dominance orientation (see also Swami, 2012). Indeed, Jewish conspiracy theories are widespread in the world (e.g., allegations that there is a Jewish plot to attain world domination) and are common among extremist groups of varying ideological signatures (Bartlett & Miller, 2010). Such belief in Jewish conspiracy theories is a major predict of anti-Semitism (Golec de Zavala & Cichocka, 2012; Kofta & Sedek, 2005). In fact, historians have noted that Jewish conspiracy theories played a major role in fueling anti-Semitic sentiments in Nazi-Germany during the 1930s and 1940s (e.g., beliefs that a Jewish conspiracy caused the German defeat in the First World War; Moreover, Hitler believed that both capitalism and

326 *Jan-Willem van Prooijen*

communism were the result of Jewish conspiracies for world domination. For details, see Pipes, 1997).

More generally, it has been noted that believing conspiracy theories requires perceivers to ascribe hostile and evil qualities to an out-group – the conspiracy – which is facilitated by negative stereotypes of the out-group in question (van Prooijen & van Vugt, 2018). It thus seems that conspiracy theories go hand in hand with stereotyping of the alleged group of conspirators. General conspiracy mentality predicts stereotyping of the powerful groups frequently implicated in conspiracy theories; likewise, conspiracy theories about minority groups predicts stereotyping of the minority group in question. Both specific and more general conspiracy beliefs hence positively predict stereotyping, particularly of groups that are suspected to be part of the conspiracy.

Conspiracy Theories and Cognitive Style

Presumably the most direct test of the rational versus gullible conspiracist hypotheses pertains to how conspiracy believers versus disbelievers differ in their cognitive style. I will examine how conspiracy beliefs are related with mental simplicity, and more generally how conspiracy beliefs are related with System 1 thinking (i.e., intuitive and emotional) versus System 2 thinking (i.e., deliberative and analytic). As to mental simplicity, one series of studies found evidence that political extremism – at both sides of the spectrum – predict conspiracy theories (van Prooijen, Krouwel, & Pollet, 2015). Of interest for the present purposes, two Dutch nationally representative samples revealed that these findings were mediated by increased beliefs among extremists that there are simple solutions to the complex problems that society faces. Consistently, various studies found that higher education predicts a decreased likelihood to believe conspiracy theories (Douglas et al., 2016) and this relationship is partly mediated by a tendency to perceive simple solutions for complex problems among the lower educated (van Prooijen, 2017). Furthermore, conspiracy beliefs are related with an illusion of explanatory depth for political issues, that is, people's tendency to overestimate the depth and knowledge of their understanding of complex political events (Vitriol & Marsh, 2018). Conspiracy theories hence are rooted in a belief that complex societal and political problems actually have simple causes and simple solutions.

A study by Swami, Voracek, Stieger, Tran, and Furnham (2014) experimentally investigated the relationship between analytic thinking and conspiracy beliefs. These authors first measured base-rate levels of conspiracy thinking, and invited participants back into the lab at a later time. Then, in several studies the authors induced manipulations that varied whether or not participants were stimulated to think analytically. Results revealed that analytic thinking reduced belief in conspiracy theories. Furthermore, intuitive thinking predicted increased belief in conspiracy theories.

Correlational findings are consistent with these results. For instance, van Prooijen (2017) found that the previously mentioned relationship between lower education and increased belief in simple solutions (which in turn predicted increased conspiracy beliefs) was mediated by reduced analytic thinking. Furthermore, Ståhl and van Prooijen (2018) found that a capacity to think analytically in and of itself is insufficient to reduce conspiracy beliefs; one also needs to be motivated to be rational and rely on evidence to come to informed judgments. These studies all consistently suggest that System 2 thinking stimulates skepticism of conspiracy theories instead of belief in them.

If System 2 thinking reduces belief in conspiracy theories, does emotional System 1 thinking increase belief in them? Evidence indeed suggests that particularly negative emotions increase conspiracy theories. Experimental manipulations of lacking control (van Prooijen & Acker, 2015; Whitson & Galinsky, 2008), and subjective uncertainty (van Prooijen & Jostmann, 2013; Whitson, Galinsky, & Kay, 2015) have been found to increase conspiracy beliefs. Correlational evidence supports these experimental findings by revealing that conspiracy theories are related with feelings of powerlessness (Abalakina-Paap et al., 1999), trait anxiety (Grzesiak-Feldman, 2013), and feelings of relative deprivation (van Prooijen, Staman, & Krouwel, 2018). Such findings on the role of negative emotions are consistent with historical observations that conspiracy theories gain momentum among the public particularly in the wake of anxiety-provoking societal crisis events, such as terrorist attacks, wars, earthquakes, fires, and floods (Brotherton, 2015; Pipes, 1997; van Prooijen & Douglas, 2017). In sum, the evidence indicates that System 1 thinking – emotional, intuitive, and heuristic – promotes belief in conspiracy theories. System 2 thinking – analytic, deliberative, and rational – promotes skepticism of conspiracy theories.

Discussion and Conclusion

The evidence overwhelmingly supports the gullible conspiracist hypothesis and contradicts the rational conspiracist hypothesis. The more strongly people believe conspiracy theories, the more likely it is that they also endorse implausible non-conspiratorial beliefs including paranormal phenomena, superstition, pseudo-science, and pseudo-profound bullshit. Furthermore, conspiracy beliefs predict an increased susceptibility to a range of common cognitive biases, including the conjunction fallacy, illusory pattern perception, and hyperactive agency detection. Belief in conspiracy theories also predict increased stereotyping, particularly of stigmatized minority groups that often are accused of conspiracy formation (e.g., Jewish people) as well as of powerful groups that are common actors in conspiracy theories (politicians, managers, capitalists, and so on). Finally, conspiracy beliefs are rooted in System 1 thinking, not in System 2 thinking. In particular, belief in conspiracy theories is associated with lower education levels, a tendency to perceive complex societal issues as simple, an increased illusion of explanatory depth in one's understanding of political issues, and reduced analytic thinking. Instead, intuitive thinking and negative emotions increase belief in conspiracy theories.

The findings reviewed here are hence consistent with a model suggesting that the decision to reject official readings of impactful events, and to subsequently embrace conspiracy theories, is often made reflexively instead of reflectively. Once accepted, a conspiracy theory is highly resilient to change as believers engage in epistemic processes that are tainted by motivated reasoning and the confirmation bias: Believers selectively embrace evidence and expert testimonies that support their suspicions, and reject evidence and expert testimonies that disconfirms them (Brotherton, 2015). The net result is an extensive theory that appears well elaborated, and supported by a lot of evidence. But while such theories may seem articulate, the decision to accept far-fetched conspiracy theories as true is actually rooted in gullibility.

Two important observations need to be clarified in light of this conclusion. First, one might reason that people who believe conspiracy theories *are* critical and skeptic, but specifically about official readings of events and legitimate powerholders. Second, one might note that conspiracy theories can be quite rational from time to time. Corruption does occur in politics, business, and science, and there are many examples of conspiracy theories that turned out true eventually (e.g., Watergate; see Wright & Arbuthnot, 1974). I do not dispute either of these observations, and would like to clarify here that true skepticism is different from gullibly accepting whatever policy-makers propose. A "healthy" critical mindset includes constructively scrutinizing the actions of power holders, and expressing concern whenever one suspects malpractice or bad policy. But true skepticism also implies critically assessing the evidence for accusations of conspiracy formation, and recognizing when such accusations are implausible (see also Fiedler, Chapter 7 this volume). Put differently, what true skepticism does *not* entail is uncritically accepting bizarre conspiracy theories such as that the Earth is flat, that human beings never landed on the Moon, or that on 9/11 the impact of two passenger airplanes – flying at high speed and full of kerosene – had absolutely nothing to do with the Twin Towers collapsing shortly thereafter.

While conspiracy beliefs are rooted in gullibility, this does not mean that conspiracy beliefs necessarily originate from closed-mindedness. In fact, studies found positive correlations between belief in conspiracy theories and the personality variable openness to experience (Swami et al., 2011; Swami et al., 2013). An interesting distinction here is between reflexive versus reflective open-mindedness (Pennycook et al., 2015). Reflexive open-mindedness refers to an intuitive mindset that is open to any new experience or information. Reflective open-mindedness, in contrast, refers to a critical mindset that is open to, yet also critically analyzes, new opportunities or ideas. Integrating these insights with the evidence presented in this chapter, it is possible that people who believe conspiracy theories are much like skeptics and scientists in their curiosity of, and openness to, novel ideas; but unlike skeptics and scientists, these novel ideas are evaluated through an intuitive, reflexive mindset instead of through a reflective mindset.

One limitation of the current analysis, and a challenge for future research, pertains to sampling. I started out this chapter with the notion that people who are active on conspiracist websites perceive themselves as "critical freethinkers" (Harambam & Aupers, 2017). But while people who actively propagate conspiracy theories in online focus groups can be included in qualitative analyses, it is unclear at best if, and in what numbers, they took part in the quantitative studies that formed the basis of the current analysis. Put differently, there may be structural differences between the presumably small group of citizens that actively comes up with, and publishes online, novel conspiracy theories, as opposed to the large group of citizens that passively reads, believes, and spreads them. Based on the present analysis it is impossible to exclude the possibility that coming up with novel conspiracy theories, and successfully disseminating them among a large audience, is a creative process that requires analytic skills. Future research might therefore focus on differences in rationality versus gullibility between people who actively and successfully create new conspiracy theories versus people who passively accept them.

To conclude, in the present chapter I compared the two opposing ideas that (a) belief in conspiracy theories originates from rational skepticism versus (b) belief in conspiracy theories originates from gullibility. The studies reviewed here unequivocally support the second idea. The mental processes that characterize rational skepticism fuels *dis*belief in most conspiracy theories. While conspiracy theorists appear to have much faith in their beliefs, on average one may question the accuracy of their self-perception as "critical freethinkers" (see also Dunning, Chapter 12 this volume). To return to the observations that motivated the current contribution: While some conspiracist websites are keen on persuading citizens who disbelieve conspiracy theories to think more critically, the present chapter suggests that these "sheep" in the end may not be the gullible ones.

Notes

1 A common term among conspiracy theorists, combining "the people" with "sheep."
2 Note that while these arguments are correct in principle, the 9/11 "Melted Steel Theory" is flawed as it does not take into account the fact that the steel construction of the Twin Towers did not have to melt for the buildings to collapse. The temperatures reached by burning kerosene that day were more than sufficient to weaken the steel construction up to the point that it could not carry the weight of the higher floors anymore (for details, see Dunbar & Reagan, 2011).

References

Abalakina-Paap, M., Stephan, W., Craig, T., & Gregory, W. L. (1999). Beliefs in conspiracies. *Political Psychology, 20*, 637–647.

Bale, J. M. (2007). Political paranoia v. political realism: On distinguishing between bogus conspiracy theories and genuine conspiratorial politics. *Patterns of Prejudice, 41*, 45–60.

Barron, D., Morgan, K., Towell, T., Altemeyer, B., & Swami, V. (2014). Associations between schizotypy and belief in conspiracist ideation. *Personality and Individual Differences, 70*, 156–159.

Bartlett, J., & Miller, C. (2010). *The power of unreason: Conspiracy theories, extremism and counter-terrorism.* London: Demos.

Brotherton, R. (2015). *Suspicious minds: Why we believe conspiracy theories.* New York, NY: Bloomsbury Sigma.

Brotherton, R., & French, C. C. (2014). Belief in conspiracy theories and susceptibility to the conjunction fallacy. *Applied Cognitive Psychology, 28*, 238–248.

Brotherton, R., & French, C. C. (2015). Intention seekers: Conspiracist ideation and biased attributions of intentionality. *PLoS ONE, 10*, e0124125.

Darwin, H., Neave, N., & Holmes, J. (2011). Belief in conspiracy theories: The role of paranormal belief, paranoid ideation and schizotypy. *Personality and Individual Differences, 50*, 1289–1293.

Douglas, K. M., Sutton, R. M., Callan, M. J., Dawtry, R. J., & Harvey, A. J. (2016). Someone is pulling the strings: Hypersensitive agency detection and belief in conspiracy theories. *Thinking and Reasoning, 22*, 57–77.

Dunbar, D., & Reagan, B. (2011). *Debunking 9/11 myths: Why conspiracy theories can't stand up to the facts.* New York, NY: Hearst Books.

Goertzel, T. (1994). Belief in conspiracy theories. *Political Psychology, 15*, 733–744.

Golec de Zavala, A., & Cichocka, A. (2012). Collective narcissism and anti-Semitism in Poland. *Group Processes and Intergroup Relations, 15*, 213–229.

Grebe, E., & Nattrass, N. (2012). AIDS conspiracy beliefs and unsafe sex in Cape Town. *AIDS and Behavior, 16*, 761–773.

Grzesiak-Feldman, M. (2013). The effect of high-anxiety situations on conspiracy thinking. *Current Psychology, 32*, 100–118.

Harambam, J., & Aupers, S. (2017). "I am not a conspiracy theorist": Relational identifications in the Dutch conspiracy milieu. *Cultural Sociology, 11*, 113–129.

Heider, F., & Simmel, M. (1944). An experimental study of apparent behavior. *American Journal of Psychology, 57*, 243–259.

Imhoff, R., & Bruder, M. (2014). Speaking (un-)truth to power: Conspiracy mentality as a generalized political attitude. *European Journal of Personality, 28*, 25–43.

Kofta, M., & Sedek, G. (2005). Conspiracy stereotypes of Jews during systemic transformation in Poland. *International Journal of Sociology, 35*, 40–64.

Lamberty, P., & Imhoff, R. (2018). Powerful pharma and its marginalized alternatives? Effects of individual differences in conspiracy mentality on attitudes towards medical approaches. *Social Psychology, 49*, 255–270.

Lobato, E., Mendoza, J., Sims, V., & Chin, M. (2014). Examining the relationship between conspiracy theories, paranormal beliefs, and pseudoscience acceptance among a university population. *Applied Cognitive Psychology, 28*, 617–625.

Newheiser, A.-K., Farias, M., & Tausch, N. (2011). The functional nature of conspiracy beliefs: Examining the underpinnings of belief in the *Da Vinci Code* conspiracy. *Personality and Individual Differences, 51*, 1007–1011.

Pennycook, G., Cheyne, J. A., Barr, N., Koehler, D., & Fugelsang, J. A. (2015). On the reception and detection of pseudo-profound bullshit. *Judgment and Decision Making, 10*, 549–563.

Pipes, D. (1997). *Conspiracy: How the paranoid style flourishes and where it comes from.* New York, NY: Simon & Schuster.

Shermer, M. (2011). *The believing brain: From ghosts and gods to politics and conspiracies – How we construct beliefs and reinforce them as truths.* New York, NY: Henry Holt.

Ståhl, T., & van Prooijen, J.-W. (2018). Epistemic rationality: Skepticism toward unfounded beliefs requires sufficient cognitive ability and motivation to be rational. *Personality and Individual Differences, 122*, 155–163.

Sunstein, C. R., & Vermeule, A. (2009). Conspiracy theories: Causes and cures. *Journal of Political Philosophy, 17*, 202–227.

Swami, V. (2012). Social psychological origins of conspiracy theories: The case of the Jewish conspiracy theory in Malaysia. *Frontiers in Psychology, 3*, 1–9.

Swami, V., Coles, R., Stieger, S., Pietschnig, J., Furnham, A., Rehim, S., & Voracek, M. (2011). Conspiracist ideation in Britain and Austria: Evidence of a monological belief system and associations between individual psychological differences and real-world and fictitious conspiracy theories. *British Journal of Psychology, 102*, 443–463.

Swami, V., Pietschnig, J., Tran, U. S., Nader, I. W., Stieger, S., & Voracek, M. (2013). Lunar lies: The impact of informational framing and individual differences in shaping conspiracist beliefs about the moon landings. *Applied Cognitive Psychology, 27*, 71–80.

Swami, V., Voracek, M., Stieger, S., Tran, U. S., & Furnham, A. (2014). Analytic thinking reduces belief in conspiracy theories. *Cognition, 133*, 572–585.

Tversky, A., & Kahneman, D. (1983). Extensional versus intuitive reasoning: The conjunction fallacy in probability judgement. *Psychological Review, 91*, 293–315.

van der Wal, R., Sutton, R. M., Lange, J., & Braga, J. (2018). Suspicious binds: Conspiracy thinking and tenuous perceptions of causal connections between co-occurring and spuriously correlated events. *European Journal of Social Psychology, 48*, 970–989.

van Prooijen, J.-W. (2017). Why education predicts decreased belief in conspiracy theories. *Applied Cognitive Psychology, 31*, 50–58.

van Prooijen, J.-W. (2018). *The psychology of conspiracy theories.* Oxford: Routledge.

van Prooijen, J.-W., & Acker, M. (2015). The influence of control on belief in conspiracy theories: Conceptual and applied extensions. *Applied Cognitive Psychology, 29*, 753–761.

van Prooijen, J.-W., & Douglas, K. M. (2017). Conspiracy theories as part of history: The role of societal crisis situations. *Memory Studies, 10*, 323–333.

van Prooijen, J.-W., Douglas, K., & De Inocencio, C. (2018). Connecting the dots: Illusory pattern perception predicts beliefs in conspiracies and the supernatural. *European Journal of Social Psychology, 48*, 320–335.

van Prooijen, J.-W., & Jostmann, N. B. (2013). Belief in conspiracy theories: The influence of uncertainty and perceived morality. *European Journal of Social Psychology, 43*, 109–115.

van Prooijen, J.-W., Krouwel, A. P. M., & Pollet, T. (2015). Political extremism predicts belief in conspiracy theories. *Social Psychological and Personality Science, 6,* 570–578.

van Prooijen, J.-W., Staman, J., & Krouwel, A. P. M. (2018). Increased conspiracy beliefs among ethnic and Muslim minorities. *Applied Cognitive Psychology, 32,* 661–667.

van Prooijen, J.-W., & van Dijk, E. (2014). When consequence size predicts belief in conspiracy theories: The moderating role of perspective taking. *Journal of Experimental Social Psychology, 55,* 63–73.

van Prooijen, J.-W., & van Vugt, M. (2018). Conspiracy theories: Evolved functions and psychological mechanisms. *Perspectives on Psychological Science, 13,* 770–788.

Vitriol, J. A., & Marsh, J. K. (2018). The illusion of explanatory depth and endorsement of conspiracy beliefs. *European Journal of Social Psychology, 48,* 955–969.

Whitson, J. A., & Galinsky, A. D. (2008). Lacking control increases illusory pattern perception. *Science, 322,* 115–117.

Whitson, J. A., Galinsky, A. D., & Kay, A. (2015). The emotional roots of conspiratorial perceptions, system justification, and belief in the paranormal. *Journal of Experimental Social Psychology, 56,* 89–95.

Wilke, A., Scheibehenne, B., Gaissmaier, W., McCanney, P., & Barrett, H. C. (2014). Illusory pattern detection in habitual gamblers. *Evolution and Human Behavior, 35,* 291–297.

Wood, M. J., Douglas, K. M., & Sutton, R. M. (2012). Dead and alive: Beliefs in contradictory conspiracy theories. *Social Psychological and Personality Science, 3,* 767–773.

Wright, T. L., & Arbuthnot, J. (1974). Interpersonal trust, political preference, and perceptions of the Watergate affair. *Personality and Social Psychology Bulletin, 1,* 168–170.

Index

Acceptance bias, 9
Accuracy, 8, 61, 65, 88, 106, 107, 124, 188, 190, 193, 200, 204, 221–222, 288, 292, 306, 329
Advertising, 8, 14, 83, 125, 152
Affect, 15, 179–193, 261–263, 317; and gullibility, 180–182, 246–247
Affect infusion model, AIM, 181
Alchemy, 3, 78
Anchoring, 12, 93, 107, 108, 127, 165–167
Anti-semitism, 325
Anxiety, 8, 23, 66, 83, 327
Assimilation vs contrast effects, 64, 112, 162, 165, 168–169
Attachment, 21–36, 66
Attribution of responsibility, 23, 24, 46, 93, 123–125

Bait-and-switch in relationships, 33
Bayes rule, 11, 13, 14, 103, 105–107, 110, 112, 115, 124, 132
Behavioral economics, 14
Bounded rationality, 7, 124, 135, 136
Bullshit receptivity, 182–186, 322–323

Cassandra quandary, 225
Causal explanations, 9, 56, 62, 63, 65, 67, 89, 108, 133–135, 245, 256, 280, 281, 290–291, 297, 323
Climate change hypothesis, 2, 14, 62, 69, 83, 86, 110
Clustering illusion, 7
Cognitive dissonance, 112, 308, 309, 311, 312, 317
Cognitive fluency, 46–48, 49, 53–54, 185–186
Cognitive processes and gullibility, 103–115, 323–324

Cognitive style, 262, 268, 320, 321, 326–327
Collective gullibility, 6
Communication, 5, 16, 30, 53, 54–56, 114, 182, 192, 193, 199–200, 304–312
Communism, 325–326
Conditional reasoning, 132–133
Confirmation bias, 14, 87–88, 142, 149, 186, 259, 282, 283, 320, 328
Conformity, 11, 67, 111, 161, 293
Conjunction fallacy, 64, 124, 160, 323, 324, 327
Consensual reality, 2, 3, 10–11
Conservatism, 294
Conspiracy theories, 2, 5, 13, 16, 61–72, 112, 319–329
Consumerism, 152, 163, 269–271
Correlation vs causation, 280, 290–291, 297
Correspondence bias, 126–127, 186, 187, 188
Credibility categories, 295–296
Cultural fluency, 15–16, 255–276
Culture, 3, 6, 15, 22, 23, 104, 208–211, 235, 245, 246, 255–267, 294; and expertise, 258–260; and situated cognition, 256–259

Deception, 15, 21, 22, 35, 110, 111, 115, 182, 186–188, 191, 192, 193, 217, 279, 305
Definition of gullibility, 305–307
Depression, 23, 25, 133, 188, 219
Discounting, 29, 84, 222–224
Dual-process approach, 106–107, 115
Dunning-Kruger effect, 92, 219, 223

Economics, 4, 62, 170–173, 201–202
Egocentric bias, 198, 199–212, 223–224
Embodied cognition, 151–152, 244, 248
Emotion *see* affect

334 *Index*

Enlightenment, 5, 6, 12, 105, 106, 112
Envelope of legitimacy, 16, 304, 305, 307, 308–317
Epistemic motives, 13, 73, 61–65, 106, 230, 320, 328
Epistemology, 2, 11–12, 14, 61–65, 105–107
Equality, 6–7, 263, 290–292
Etymology, 1
European Union, 1, 4, 63
Evolutionary theory, 5, 7, 8, 11–12, 16, 21–36, 211, 245, 293
Existential motives, 13, 61, 65–67, 69, 72, 131
Experimenter effects, 289–290
Eyewitness memory, 45, 88, 182, 189–191, 192

Fake news, 5, 43, 52, 54, 77–94, 113, 317, 318
False beliefs, 43, 53, 56, 77–94, 108, 112, 113
False memories, 14, 141, 144, 240–242
Falsification, 3, 4, 62
Familiarity effect, 12, 45–46, 52, 84, 163, 182, 185, 239
Fascism, 1, 4, 77, 325–326
Female gullibility, 26–27, 33
Female orgasm, 30–31
Female sex drive, 29–30
Feminism, 3–4, 5
Flat earth, 2, 3, 320
French revolution, 13
Functions of gullibility, 3, 4, 54, 55, 61–65
Fundamental publication error, 291–292

Gender, 5, 28, 29, 30, 135, 262, 288, 292, 293, 294
Gender relations, 21–36
Grice's maxims, 310
Grievance studies, 3–4
Group polarization, 11, 14, 90–92
Gullibility: and affect, 15, 23–24, 25–27;criteria for, 2–3, 280; and culture, 15, 208–210, 255–273; definition of, 1–2, 159, 279–280, 305–307; and the envelope of legitimacy, 304–318; functions of, 3–4, 5–6, 21–36, 54–55; gullible mindset, 143–153; history of, 3–4; and information repetition, 42–57, 83–84;

and metacognitive myopia, 123–136; and public affairs, 4–5, 7–8, 13–14, 16, 77–94; in relationships, 21–36; and science, 16, 279–297; and self-bias, 199–212; theories of, 103–115

Heuristics, 7, 9–10, 12, 14, 64, 108, 110, 123, 159–162, 165–167
History, 3–4, 5–6, 12–13
Homeopathy, 6, 109
Hot vs cold cognition, 7, 282
Humanism, 6
Hungary, 1, 4, 45

Identity politics, 5
Illusory correlation, 89–90, 93, 110
Implicit prejudice, 290–291
Individualism, 6, 257
Inductive reasoning, 14, 115; *see also* epistemology
Information repetition, 13, 42–57
Intentionality, 22, 64, 108, 165, 186, 324
Internet, 5, 12, 43, 55, 56, 91, 113, 184, 217, 220, 229
Interpersonal communication, 53, 188, 199–200

Judgmental errors, 12, 23, 182, 182

Latitude of acceptance vs rejection, 311
Left-wing ideology, 3, 4, 68
Legitimacy, 314–318
Liberty, 6–7
Love and irrationality, 23–24, 26–27

Male gullibility, 27–29, 33
Marriage, 21–36
Marxism, 4–5
Mate preferences, 293–294
Meaning, 7–9, 62, 182–186
Mein Kampf, 307
Memes, 5, 12
Metacognitive experience, 266–269
Metacognitive myopia, 11–12, 14, 123–136
Middle ages, 3–4
Mindless consumption, 269–271
Mood *see* affect
Motivated reasoning, 282–284

Narcissism and conspiracy theories, 67, 68
Need to belong, 67, 68

Index

Need for cognitive closure, 63–64
Nonverbal credulity, 186–189

Object ownership, 201–202
Olfactory information, 15, 234–253
Over-belief in the self, 10, 92–93, 217–230

Personality, 14, 24, 25, 65, 147, 150, 153, 159, 193, 291, 305, 313, 328
Persuasion, 21, 43, 57, 115, 159, 192, 198, 269, 305, 306, 307
Philosophy, 9, 41, 105–107, 180
Political propaganda, 1, 4, 8, 77–94
Politics, 1, 4–5, 7–8, 13–14, 16, 52, 68, 77–94, 103, 283, 310, 315
Populism, 4, 5
Post-modernism, 3–4
Preregistration of research, 292–293
Primates, 5, 22, 26, 27–28, 29
Priming paradigm, 148, 150–151, 165, 166, 168, 171, 181, 191, 246, 289, 290, 296
Public affairs, 7, 8, 13–14, 16, 68, 77–94, 103

Randomness, 7–9, 89–90
Rational conspiracist hypothesis, 320–321
Rationality, 7, 13, 14, 23, 106, 108, 109, 111, 123, 124, 125, 127, 135, 136, 170, 171, 180, 329
Reducing scientific gullibility, 292–293
Reflective impulsive model, 164–165
Relationships, 22, 24, 27, 29, 31, 234, 257, 293–294, 317
Religion, 3–4, 9, 13, 63, 93, 262
Repetition and gullibility, 42–57, 306
Romantic relationships, 21–36

Sample-size insensitivity, 130–133
Sampling, 289, 329
Schema-plus-tag model, 143–146
Scientific gullibility, 16, 279–303
Self-bias, 199–212
Self-esteem, 14, 16, 67, 308, 312
Self-gullibility, 15, 217–230
Self-justification, 14, 87–88, 90
Self-ownership effect, 206–208
Self-relevance, 15, 199–212

Self-serving bias, 10, 15, 198–212
Sexual economics, 33, 34
Sexuality, 21–36
Situated cognition, 256–257
Skeptical mindset, 14, 141–153, 193, 234
Skepticism, 2–3, 9, 14, 65, 93, 103, 140–153, 179–180, 234, 293, 294, 306, 319–329
Slavery, 6, 84
Smell and suspicion, 234–248
Social comparison, 14, 159–174
Social epistemology, 10–11
Social influence, 161–162
Social media, 5, 43, 53, 91, 103, 113, 125, 126, 136
Social perception, 200–201
Sokal's hoax, 3–4, 182–183
Spinozan model, 141–146
Standards for data collection, 281
Statistical illiteracy, 88–89
Statistics, 281–282, 284, 289, 290–291
Status quo biases, 285–287
Stereotype accuracy, 288–289
Stereotyping and gullibility, 324–326
Stigma, 327
Subjective familiarity, 45–46
Superstition, 8, 89, 90, 93, 109, 179, 321, 322, 327
Suspicion and smell, 234–248
System 1 – System 2 processing, 320, 326, 327

The mask of love, 24–26
Thought suppression, 145–146
Trump, 1, 4–5, 16, 78, 80, 83, 85, 87, 165, 202, 306, 312, 313–317
Trust, 5, 104–105, 113–115, 151, 236–238, 306
Truth, 46–49, 50–51, 52–53
Truth bias, 83, 182, 184–186, 191

Ultimatum game, 170–173
Urban myths, 182, 184–186, 191
US, 77–94
Utopia, 7

War of the Worlds, 304–305, 306, 308
Wason task, 87, 123, 142, 149, 150, 241–242
Witches, 3, 8, 33, 78, 179, 322

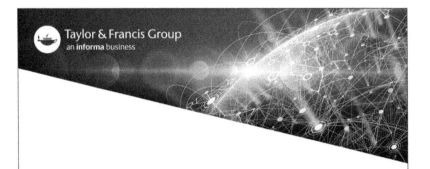

CPSIA information can be obtained
at www.ICGtesting.com
Printed in the USA
LVHW052300010420
651908LV00008B/64